Mary,
Music,
and
Meditation

MUSIC AND THE EARLY MODERN IMAGINATION
Massimo Ossi, *editor*

Mary, Music, and Meditation

Sacred Conversations in Post-Tridentine Milan

Christine Getz

INDIANA UNIVERSITY PRESS
Bloomington and Indianapolis

This book is a publication of

Indiana University Press
Office of Scholarly Publishing
Herman B Wells Library 350
1320 East 10th Street
Bloomington, Indiana 47405 USA

iupress.indiana.edu

Telephone orders   800-842-6796
Fax orders   812-855-7931

Manufactured in the
United States of America

Library of Congress
Cataloging-in-Publication Data

Getz, Christine Suzanne, [date].
    Mary, music, and meditation :
sacred conversations in post-
Tridentine Milan / Christine Getz.
        p. cm. — (Music and
        the early modern imagination)
    Includes bibliographical references
and index.
    978-0-253-00787-2 (cloth :
alk. paper)
    978-0-253-00796-4 (ebook)
    1. Mary, Blessed Virgin, Saint—
Devotion to—Italy—Milan.
2. Mary, Blessed Virgin, Saint—
Songs and music—History and
criticism. 3. Church music—
Catholic Church—16th century.
4. Church music—Italy—Milan—
16th century. I. Title.
ML3033.8.M54 G48 2013
781.71/20094521109031
                        2012036072

1 2 3 4 5 18 17 16 15 14 13

TO MY PARENTS

Contents

Acknowledgments   ix

INTRODUCTION

Marian Devotion and Meditation
in Post-Tridentine Milan   1

CHAPTER 1

Venerating the Veil: The Madonna of Miracles
at Santa Maria presso San Celso   17

CHAPTER 2

The Art of Lamenting: The Cult of the
Madonna Addolorata at Santa Maria dei Servi   46

CHAPTER 3

Singing Before a Madonna on the Pilaster:
The Society of the Ave Maria in Duomo   69

CHAPTER 4

Invoking the Mulier Fortis:
The Confraternity of the Rosary   82

CHAPTER 5

Clothed in the Sun and Standing on the Moon:
Meditating Motherhood in the Cult of the
Madonna del Parto   108

EPILOGUE

The Case of Santa Maria Segreta   143

Appendix A: Documents 149

Appendix B: Pay Records for the Singers
of the Ave Maria in Duomo 165

Appendix C: Contents of Selected Collections
by Milanese Composers 172

Appendix D: Musical Examples 186

Notes 297

Bibliography 333

Index 345

Acknowledgments

This project is the result of a long-standing love affair with the city of Milan that began in 1989 when I spent the year there as a Rotary Foundation Scholar, and was partially driven by the opportunity to participate in the biennial international conference *La musica e il sacro* sponsored by the A.M.I.S.-Como and the Società Italiana di Musicologia between the years 2001 and 2009. The feedback I received from my fellow conference participants, and especially conference organizer Maurizio Padoan, was invaluable in shaping this project. The archival work for this project was graciously supported by a fellowship that accompanied my University of Iowa Dean's Scholar Award, a 2007 Career Development Award from the University of Iowa, a 2009 University of Iowa International Programs Summer Fellowship, and Iowa Arts and Humanities Grants for the years 2005, 2007, and 2009.

I am especially indebted to Padre Silvano Danieli of the Pontificia Facoltà Teologica "Marianum" in Rome, Roberto Fighetti of the Archivio della Veneranda Fabbrica del Duomo in Milan, Lucia Aiello of the Archivio dei Luoghi Pii Elemosinieri (A.S.P. "Golgi-Redaelli) in Milan, Giordano Monzio-Copagnoni of the Pontificio Istituto Ambrosiano di Musica Sacra in Milan, and Monsignor Bruno Bosatra and Fabrizio Pagani of the Archivio Storico Diocesano in Milan, as well as the archivists and staff of the Biblioteca Ambrosiana, the Biblioteca dei Servi di Maria, the Archivio di Stato, the Biblioteca Nazionale Braidense, the Archivio Storico Civico e Biblioteca Trivulziana, the Biblioteca Communale Sormani, the Biblioteca del Conservatorio "Giuseppe Verdi," the Civica Raccolta delle Stampe "Achille Bertarelli," and the Biblioteca d'Arte-Castello Sforzesco in Milan, the Biblioteca Provinciale dei Frati Minori Cappuccini del Piemonte in Torino, the Biblioteca Capitolare in Vercelli, the Biblioteca Nazionale Centrale in Florence, and the Biblioteca Nazionale Centrale Vittorio Emmanuele and Biblioteca Casanatense in Rome for their assistance in gaining access to the rare sources necessary for this project, as well as for their advice on various matters along the way. I wish to thank the Sibley

Library of the Eastman School of Music, the Biblioteca Nacional in Madrid, the Biblioteca Malatestiana in Cesena, and the Civico Museo Bibliografico Musicale in Bologna for providing microfilms or photocopies of rare musical sources used for this project, as well as Robert Kendrick for sharing his copy of the *Pratum musicum* (1634) with me. I further wish to thank the editorial staff and readers at Indiana University Press, and especially Massimo Ossi, whose insightful suggestions and careful attention to detail were instrumental in bringing this project to completion, as well as the University of Iowa and the Lloyd Hibberd Endowment of the American Musicological Society for their generous support in defraying certain costs of publication. Finally, these acknowledgements would not be complete without mentioning the graduate students, faculty, and staff of the School of Music at the University of Iowa. They are a constant source of inspiration and it is a privilege to work with them.

Mary, Music, and Meditation

Introduction

❦

Marian Devotion and Meditation in Post-Tridentine Milan

> And while you are working to recover from the blows of
> Divine Wrath, do not allow the arms to rust which you have
> to this point employed, exercising them continually in the
> frequency of the holy sacraments, in prayers, in heavenly
> [thoughts], in alms, in processions, in visiting the churches and
> altars, and, finally, persevere in many other Christian activities
> which, thanks to the Lord, you already have started well, in
> order that you are able with these arms to fight valiantly.
>
> —*Nicolo Sfondrato Milanese,*
> *Bishop of Cremona to the City of Milan, 1578*[1]

The coincidence of the famine of 1570 and the plague of 1576 with
a sharp economic inflation that peaked in 1581 left the citizens of
Post-Tridentine Milan feeling uneasy and prepared to engage with the
mysteries of life after death in much the same way that many in the
post-9/11 world were compelled to reengage with concepts of spirituality.[2] The notion that God had sent the plague of 1576 as punishment
for the city's wantonness and worldliness and that he would stay it as
a reward for appropriate demonstrations of spirituality had become
strongly entrenched in the Milanese psyche by 1578. The confidence
Milanese citizens of the era invested in devotional demonstrations
as protection against divinely wrought iniquities is perhaps no more
clearly seen than in Carlo Borromeo's four civic processions with the
reliquary containing the sacred nail, public displays of faith intended to

infuse the collective consciousness with remorse for its past frivolities and spiritual malaise by inviting citizens to identify with the suffering of Christ. The processions reportedly attracted participants from all walks of Milanese society and were regarded as almost singlehandedly responsible for eradicating the city of disease. Nearly every manuscript and printed history of Milan surviving from the era recounts how a barefoot Carlo Borromeo humbly bore the crucifix containing the sacred nail at the head of the procession as it wound its way from the Duomo to one of the city's principal churches like a modern Christ winding his way up Mount Calvary.[3]

Carlo Borromeo is, of course, best known today for his participation in the final sessions of the Council of Trent and his subsequent application of Tridentine reforms in the Diocese of Milan, effectively transforming the city into a model of ecclesiastical efficiency and spiritual fervor second only to Rome.[4] Yet as many scholars have noted, Borromeo did not entirely reinvent the wheel. Rather, he introduced order to preexisting institutions by demanding proper record-keeping with regard to the sacraments, closely supervising the activities of the clergy and religious, and subordinating lay confraternities and oratories to the parishes in which they were housed. His ecclesiastical reforms were accomplished largely through convening provincial and diocesan councils and by making regular pastoral visits to the churches of the diocese, but his efforts at evangelization of the faithful were channeled through frequent appearances before the public in connection with specific devotional activities. Carlo Borromeo promoted the Schools of Christian Doctrine, the Confraternity of the Most Blessed Sacrament, the Company of the Cross, the Society of the Ave Maria, and, ultimately, the Confraternity of the Rosary by participating in their functions in a visible way, and it fell to his successors Gaspare Visconti and Federico Borromeo to maintain the status quo. Under Carlo Borromeo, devotional activities crowded the social arena and achieved a level of importance equal to, if not surpassing, carnival and theatrical entertainments. This phenomenon is evidenced in the diaries kept by two gentlemen resident in Milan at the close of the century— Urbano Monte and Giambattista Casale.

Monte and Casale hailed from different social strata, but together they represent the mainstream of literate Milan at the close of the sixteenth century. Urbano Monte (1544–1613) was born into a noble Milanese family that traced its roots back at least two centuries to both the Milanese patriarch Angelo Monte and a branch of the Hapsburg dynasty. Most of Urbano's ancestors, including his father, Giovanni Battista, were buried in the family chapel at Santa Maria dei Servi, where the family seemed to enjoy a close relationship with the Servite fathers. Like that of much of the Milanese nobility, Urbano's wealth was concentrated in properties, although additional family income was accrued through civil service. His only living brother, Cesare, was somewhat estranged from the family and served in the imperial forces until his death in 1584, thereby leaving Urbano to play the role of dutiful son to his father, Giovanni Battista. Urbano and his father spent the years following the plague embroiled in a bitter financial squabble with their in-laws, the Dardanova, which they eventually won legally, but never quite resolved financially.[5] In 1579, at the age of thirty-five, Urbano married Margarita Niguarda in an effort to enlarge the family's financial holdings and sphere of influence.[6] He appears to have been a member of the Company of the Cross at San Babila, an organization dedicated to the care and redemption of the incarcerated, for his diary includes copies of several notarial instruments pertaining to the society and he recounts a few of its activities in great detail.[7] His perspective on civic life was, in large part, shaped by the neighborhood now marked by the Corso Vittorio Emmanuele, namely the parishes of San Babila, Santa Maria dei Servi, and the Duomo.

Whereas Monte was a member of the Milanese nobility, Giambattista Casale (d. 1629?) was a Milanese merchant and tradesman. The son of one Bernadino Casale Milanese, Giambattista Casale made his living, at least initially, as a carpenter or cabinet-maker. Through his friendship with his confessor, P. Castellino de Castello, he became heavily involved in the schools of Christian Doctrine in Milan, serving as a teacher, assistant prior, prior, and deputy in the Congregatione di SS. Giacomo e Filippo in Porta Nova, as well as a visitor to the Schools of Christian Doctrine in the Porta Nova. Casale was the executor of the estate left by Castellino to the Congregatione di SS. Giacomo e Filippo, a job that he reportedly performed without remuneration for twelve years while supplementing his income as a baler. In 1582 the Congregatione rewarded him for this service by providing him a house and shop near the church of San Dalmazio.[8] Casale married twice, the first time on 4 October 1552 to Angela della Riva, the daughter of Francesco della Riva. She died in January 1561 after bearing him several children in close succession, the majority of whom did not survive infancy.[9] A mere three months after her death, Giambattista took a second wife in Catelina dell'Aqua.[10] Like Casale, Catelina was active in the Christian Doctrine schools, teaching and serving as the "silencer" (one who maintained order) in the girls' Scuola di SS. Cosmo e Damiano.[11] Although both Giambattista and Catelina survived the plague, the records show that they were profoundly affected by it, losing a number of sisters, brothers, nieces, nephews, and other relatives in October 1576 alone.[12] In addition to participating avidly in the Schools of Christian Doctrine, they and their children were members of the Confraternity of the Rosary at Santa Maria della Rosa and the Duomo.[13]

Despite their differing social and economic situations, Monte and Casale often reported on the same seminal local events, and their accountings of them are remarkably similar in content. Both record the entries of new governors, archbishops, and other royal dignitaries, the famous assassination attempt on Carlo Borromeo in 1569, the annual processions of the sacred nail, the celebrations associated with the various provincial councils and jubilees, the esequie for Anne of Austria in the Duomo in 1581, the introduction of the Gregorian calendar in October 1582, the death of Carlo Borromeo in 1584, and the visit of a Japanese delegation to Milan in 1585. Monte was obsessed, however, with family financial squabbles and took a greater interest in local politics, often copying pertinent decrees and notarial instruments into his text, while Casale seems to have been especially preoccupied with renovations and devotions taking place in the local churches, especially the Duomo, Santa Maria della Rosa, Santa Maria presso San Celso, and San Fedele. Monte also was a modestly gifted artist, and included in his volumes elaborate drawings, several of which are in color, of his family's coat of arms, the epitaphs on the catafalque of Anne of Austria, and the Japanese ambassadors who visited in 1585. Aside from a pair of carnival jousts that were a source of tension between the local government and Carlo Borromeo, however, descriptions of secular entertainments are notably absent from both diaries. Yet accounts of religious festivals, processions, and devotions abound, thus suggesting that these had largely replaced secular pursuits in the writers' civic consciousness.[14]

For Milan, a city historically devoted to the Virgin, the city's reengagement with its sacred traditions served only to strengthen an already firmly ensconced affection for the Virgin. In 1594, for example, the Milanese historian Paolo Morigia observed that the city of Milan boasted forty-two churches devoted to the Virgin within the city walls alone, and as many as three hundred in the diocese.[15] In addition to the more formal Marian institutions to which Morigia refers, moreover, cultic images attributed with miraculous powers could be found on the streets, and the population attended several of these with great devotion, leaving mementos in supplication and gifts of gratitude.[16] Urbano Monte's family, for example, worshiped an image known as the Madonna of San Lorenzo, popular among residents living in his quarter. The Madonna reportedly stood across the Piazza of the Largo di San Lorenzo and was the source of several miracles recorded in 1585:

> The first one she performed was that of a hunchbacked young man who was there every Saturday to put a candle at the feet of the aforementioned figure, and needed [because of his infirmity] to stand up with a little force. The aforementioned hunchback, wishing to arrive at the place where he usually placed the aforementioned candle with both personal discomfort and labor, while kneeling simply asked of Our Lady that she would be good enough to give him grace so that he would not feel the desire to place said candle until he carried out his devotion with a better heart as she desired. And thus carrying out his prayer every time that he put a candle there, behold, little by little in a period of a few days he was upright and well as if he never had been hunchback, which was a thing to see. The neighbors asked how he was thus healed. Given the whole wave [of gossip about] the miracle, many began to visit the aforementioned image with their prayers.
>
> The second miracle was one in which an individual on a troublesome horse passing the shrine at random was thrown to the ground near there, and just having touched the ground, he was grasped by a pair of casts on the chest of the aforementioned horse, and, therefore, he turned toward the aforementioned image at the same time that he had the casts and, demanding her help, he immediately jumped from the horse well, without any ill effects from the casts.
>
> The third miracle was that when many people were visiting the aforementioned image, behold, a carriage driver was sleeping on top of the carriage which the patrons had dismounted a little earlier, and a deafening noise was made near there for which cause the horses were surprised, and, therefore, fled, having also thrown to the ground there the carriage driver, and run near the image where there was a large crowd of persons. They were turning there among them with such great fury that all, not having any other refuge, took recourse to Our Lady in

a whisper. The aforementioned horses and the carriage were taken and held safe at hand without any injury of the persons passing until the carriage driver arrived and climbed up and controlled them.[17]

The Milanese public placed great confidence in the healing powers of the Madonna of San Lorenzo. Monte reports, in fact, that when his son Giovanni Battista was healed of a bloody flux that lasted ten days and left him very weak, his wife presented the Madonna of San Lorenzo with a silver image of the child in gratitude for her intervention.[18]

The miracles of these street-corner Madonnas often were so widely retold and the images themselves so faithfully venerated that the authorities were forced to either move them into an indoor church or to construct a church in their honor in order to accommodate the influx of devotees. Such was the case with the Madonna of the Passione, a street-corner image of the deploration of Christ that was transported into Santa Maria della Passione in 1590 after it reportedly transferred blood onto the hand of a devotee who had kissed the image. Casale recorded the miracle and its aftermath enthusiastically in his diary:

> Memorial how in the year 1590 on the day of 25 August that Madonna that was at the end of the retaining wall of the garden of the fathers of the Passione in Milan on the street by Santo Pietro Chiesato performed a miracle. It was on the wall that looks towards the Porta Ticinese. And the first miracle was on Saturday the day after the feast of San Bartholomew, which miracle was that [when] one wishing for the purpose of devotion to kiss the chest of the Lord, who was in the lap of the Madonna as when he was taken down from the cross, the hand of the aforementioned man remained colored with blood that flowed from the chest of the Lord, or so it was said . . . and on the 30th of the same month it was taken down carefully and carried into the church of the Passione to the third chapel on the right hand of the entrance into the church. And the procession was one only with the reverend fathers of the Passione and a large number of people in great devotion.[19]

Perhaps the most successful formalization of a Marian cult surrounding a "street image" was that of the Madonna of Miracles at Santa Maria presso San Celso. Housed in a crude chapel rather than in a niche on the street, the Madonna of Miracles was a painting of the Madonna and Child on a pilaster in a small chapel constructed over

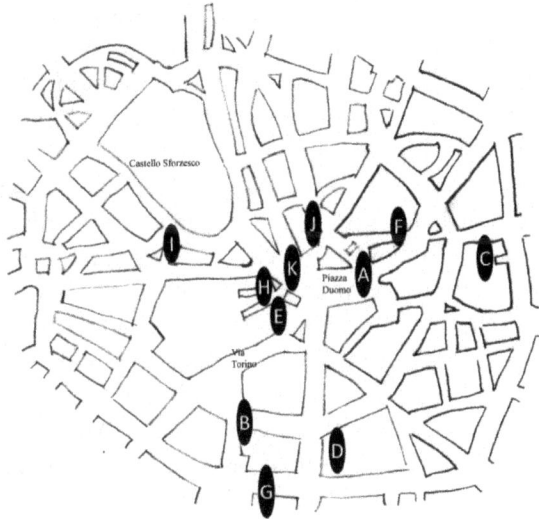

Legend

A Duomo
B S. Lorenzo
C S. Maria della Passione
D S. Maria presso S. Celso
E S. Maria Beltrade
F S. Maria dei Servi
G S. Eustorgio
H S. Maria della Rosa
I S. Protasio al Porto Giovio
J S. Maria della Scala
K S. Maria Segreta

FIGURE I.I. Location of the Churches.

the spot where St. Ambrose had recovered the body of the martyred St. Nazarenus in 395. It achieved notoriety in 1485 when the Madonna in the painting came alive and appeared to a group of worshippers during Mass, eradicating the city of a breakout of the plague and leaving her veil behind in the process. As word of the miracle spread abroad, pilgrims from all over Europe began to flock to the site. In an effort to control the influx of pilgrims into the city and maintain a semblance of order to the devotional activities associated with the image, Duke Ludovico Maria Sforza arranged for a church to be built on the site (keeping the painting, of course, intact), provided additional benefices in order to staff the site with adequate clergy, and constructed a special access point for those arriving from outside the city walls.[20] The cult at that point achieved a level of ducal sponsorship that definitely helped to sustain it over the long term, but it had originated around a neighborhood icon and its continued popularity was grounded in the devotion with which it was attended by both the locals and foreign visitors.

Although the cult of the Madonna of Miracles was supervised by a confraternity of eighteen deputies selected from among the nobility, its devotions, unlike most of the exercises associated with Milanese confraternities of the era, were intended for the general public of both sexes, and the surviving evidence reveals that the noble and merchant classes of Milan were especially attracted to the Vespers services held there on the first Sunday of the month during the latter half of the sixteenth century and on Saturday evenings during the early seventeenth century.[21] In these, music played a major role in the exegesis of the liturgy, and both the documentation and the accounts of onlookers suggest that every effort was made to provide a sumptuous musical tapestry.[22] Laywomen were encouraged to participate in devotions to the Madonna of Miracles, but were prohibited, of course, from taking roles in governance or performing the liturgy. According to Morigia, Milanese gentlewomen were especially fond of saying the Little Office of the Virgin in her honor, and, like their male counterparts, also attended the services; recited the Ave Maria, Salve Regina, and the Rosary; and gave gifts of bread, wine, and money to the poor every Saturday.[23] The only other Marian devotion known to engage such a large and socially diverse segment of the Milanese public prior to 1580 was the singing of the Ave Maria at the altar of Santa Maria del Pilone in the Duomo at the Vespers hour, a grassroots devotion which emerged around 1485 in response to the preaching of a mendicant friar in the piazza of the Duomo.[24]

When, during the last fifteen years of his career, Carlo Borromeo sought to exhort the Milanese populace to greater contemplation of things divine, one of the principal devotions to which he turned was the singing of the Ave Maria at the Vespers hour in the Duomo, transferring the popular practice from Santa Maria del Pilone to the newly constructed Marian altar of the Madonna dell'Arbore.[25] He intended that the altar of the Madonna dell'Arbore become a focal point of Marian worship in the Duomo, and, to this end, he took the bold step, to the chagrin of Dominicans in the city who had traditionally controlled such societies, of also instituting a Confraternity of the Rosary there.[26] These initiatives seem to have opened the proverbial flood gates with regard to Marian devotion by underscoring avenues by which individuals of varied social classes and both sexes might participate in organized devotions to the Virgin of a confraternal or pseudo-confraternal nature. If the account of Giambattista Casale of the founding of the Confraternity of the Rosary in the Duomo is any indication, it was met with tremendous enthusiasm, such great enthusiasm in Casale's case, in fact, that he enrolled his family despite the fact that they already belonged to a Confraternity of the Rosary elsewhere:

Memorial how in 1584 on the 25th of March the Illustrious
Cardinal Borromeo erected the Company of the Most Holy
Rosary in the Duomo and ordered that the Madonna del
Arbore be called the Madonna of the Most Holy Rosary. And
he wished that on that day the aforementioned Madonna be
carried in procession in which there was His Most Reverend
Lord, all the clergy of the Duomo, so many people that it was
a wonder to erect this blessed and holy devotion of the Most
Holy Rosary. . . . On the first of April 1584, that is eight days
after the aforementioned procession, I inscribed myself and my
son David in the aforementioned Company of the Most Holy
Rosary in the Duomo because of my devotion, even though
many years ago I inscribed in the aforementioned company of
la Rosa together with my wife Catelina, and David and Angela
my children. I also inscribed Catelina and Angela in the Rosary
of the Duomo on the 2nd of April 1584.[27]

The archival documentation reveals, as will be shown in the succeeding chapters, that existing Confraternities of the Rosary, such as
that at Santa Maria della Rosa, were spurred to new heights in terms of
the quality of their services with the introduction of the Confraternity
of the Rosary in the Duomo. Moreover, new chapters of Confraternities
of the Rosary were founded in the diocese, and other groups, such as
the Servites at Santa Maria dei Servi, also erected lay confraternities
open to the general public. In addition, worship at non-confraternal
Marian altars, such as those for the Madonna del Parto, took on a
liturgical dimension that was transferred through literature and music
to devotions in the private sphere.

Several Marian cults and lay confraternities in Milan that served
a large cross-section of the local population, the female one included,
sponsored devotions that featured special liturgies with a strong musical dimension, among them the Madonna of Miracles at Santa Maria
presso San Celso, the Madonna Addolorata at Santa Maria dei Servi,
the Society of the Ave Maria in Duomo, and the Confraternity of the
Rosary in the Duomo and at Santa Maria della Rosa. Within their
exercises music was a principal means by which the liturgy and other
devotional texts were delivered. Music, of course, did not work alone,
but rather in tandem with images and meditational literature specific to
the cult, and consideration of the latter, in particular, helps us to understand how music functioned in evangelizing and educating the laity.

Other less formally organized cults, such as that observed at the altars of the Madonna del Parto at the Duomo, Santa Maria della Scala, and Santa Maria presso San Celso, inspired liturgical compositions for the feasts with which they were most closely associated, as well as didactic polyphony intended for domestic use.

Aside from the Society of the Ave Maria in Duomo, all of the aforementioned cults were partially dependent upon meditation books in the vernacular as a means of elucidating the spiritual concepts on which they were founded and assisting their lay devotees in achieving an elevated sense of identification with the Virgin in meditating those concepts. Some books were rather prescriptive, leading the reader by the hand via a narrative that instructed him how to visualize a specific event in the life of the Virgin or a particular aspect of her character, meditate upon it, and then pray for intercession. Such an approach can be seen in Alberto da Castello's *Rosario della Gloriosa Vergine Maria. Con le stationi & Indulgetie delle Chiese di Roma per tutto l'anno,* a Rosary meditation book that enjoyed several reprintings in Venice during the last quarter of the sixteenth century. In meditating, for example, on the Presentation in the Temple, the reader is instructed to contemplate the moment by mentally constructing a picture of it. To this end, the meditation contains extensive graphic detail, and is interlaced with a prophetic quote from chapter six of the Song of Songs, a text that Medieval writers frequently appropriated to scripturally validate the historical event, which is itself omitted from the Biblical accounts involving the Virgin:

> Hail Mary. Contemplate here devoted soul, how at the age of three years, the glorious Virgin was presented to God in the temple before the High Priest by her relatives, according to the vow made by them. And reaching the steps of the temple, which were fifteen, ascended them with much agility for her age to the great admirations of the onlookers, who marveled at her most knowledgeable and eloquent manner of speech, and at the deep bows that she made to the temple, at the altar and to the High Priest, which seemed that they had been practiced by her for a long time. Where is well verified that said in Chapter 6 of the Song of Songs: *Quae est ista, quae progreditur quasi aurora consurgens, pulchra et luna, electa ut Sol, terribilis ut castrorum acies ordinata?* Who is this who walks like the light of dawn, when she rises in the morning, is beautiful as the moon, elect as the sun for the splendor of the virtues

and graces, and terrifying as a regular squadron of soldiers, because of the repugnance of every vice and diabolical suggestion? Whence this ascent of fifteen stairs signifies that she had to climb over the nine legions of angels and the six levels of saints. It is not surprising that our Lord gave the Virgin Mary so much vigorousness in climbing those steps, because he wished to show how admirably she must ascend to the perfection of all the virtues and of every good. And that she was given every virtue and similarly appears manifestly to all as the mirror of every holiness.[28]

Other volumes featured meditations in the form of a colloquy between the reader and the Virgin, with the writer functioning as a sort of mediator between the two, sometimes narrating and sometimes directing the conversation. This approach can be seen in Bartolomeo Scalvo's *Le Meditationi del Rosario della Gloriosissima Maria Vergine,* a series of Rosary meditations issued in Latin and Italian by the diocesan printer Pacifico Pontio in 1569, and thereafter reprinted in the vernacular with numerous illustrations by the Venetian printers Domenico and Giovanni Battista della Guerra in 1583. Its meditation on the Presentation in the Temple quotes the same scriptural passage from the Song of Songs as does the *Rosario della Gloriosa Maria Vergine,* but here the reader addresses the Virgin directly through the voice of the writer:

> HAIL MARY, et cetera. Pray for us sinners. Most benign Virgin, pray for us sinners. Most benign Virgin, so called because three years after your glorious birth according to the ancient custom and rite of the law, you were presented in the temple with solemn ceremony before a large crowd, which with admiring glances admired in you a most rare resplendent light of honesty, a singular simulacrum of innate virtue and divine grace, a virginal modesty, and a seriousness of purpose in explaining your ideas, in the divine praises, a pious ardent and most devoted manner of praying, and, finally, an admirable humility and religiosity in offering true adoration and principal honor to the supreme Father, so that great reason seemed heard in resounding voices: (Cant. 6) *Quae est ista, quae progreditur, quasi Aurora consurgens, pulchra ut Luna, electa ut sol, terribilis ut Castrorum acies ornata?* So that we, who celebrate the day of this holy [feast of the] Presentation, meditating your intercession and prayers, are made worthy of being presented in the temple which is Christ in celestial Glory. Amen.[29]

Still other books, such as that prepared by Morigia for Santa Maria presso San Celso,[30] were catechistic and prescriptive, outlining the general doctrine of the cult and merely pointing the reader to the specific prayers and offices to be meditated.

The process of affective meditation, or meditation which relied upon empathetic identification as a means of evoking love toward and acquiring knowledge of God, is foundational to many of the books. Affective meditation had already begun gaining currency in Post-Tridentine Italy through the dissemination of the *Spiritual Exercises* of Ignatius of Loyola.[31] The *Exercizes,* which received multiple printings in Latin during the second half of the sixteenth century and were routinely issued in Italian by the first quarter of the seventeenth century, detailed a four-week retreat in which the exercitant meditated his sins during the first week, the early life and ministry of Christ during the second, the Passion during the third, and the Resurrection during the final week. The *Exercizes* relied collectively upon the techniques of imagination, visualization, structural segmentation, and repetition as the means of drawing progressively nearer to God.[32] This highly organized yet personalized method of spiritual reform had its roots in the popular late Medieval *Meditationes Vitae Christi* of the Carthusian Ludolf of Saxony (d. 1378),[33] which originally circulated primarily in Latin, but were translated and disseminated in a variety of European vernacular languages during the fourteenth and fifteenth centuries.[34] It has been suggested that the *Exercizes* were originally intended primarily for use by the members of the Society of Jesus, but by 1550 Ignatius was arguing in the Society's Constitutions that dissemination of the *Exercises,* at least in spirit, largely comprised the Society's ministry.[35] The documentation has shown, moreover, that following the public sanction of the *Exercizes* in 1548 via the breve "Pastoralis officii" of Paul III, they were adopted into the instruction of many religious orders, either in their original individualized format or adapted to groups that completed them in either the proscribed month or protracted periods of eight to ten days.[36] Although most lay segments of the Italian population did not likely encounter the *Exercizes* in their original context, they did experience the meditational techniques espoused in them through the evangelical preaching of the Jesuits, which relied heavily upon imagination, visualization, segmentation, and repetition in the teaching of doctrine and its supportive laude.[37] The *Exercizes* were foundational, moreover, to the education of a number of post-Tridentine ecclesiastics and monastics who were instrumental in reshaping public piety, including Carlo Borromeo.[38] Thus, it is not surprising that the affective meditation taught by Ignatius served as a model for many Marian meditation books of the period.

Although the style of Post-Tridentine meditation books devoted to the Virgin differs from cult to cult and writer to writer, the Marian books seem to share several general principles, the most striking of which is the insertion of quotes, often in the original Latin, from the Latin vulgate, the apocrypha, the liturgy, and sermons of Medieval theologians. Latin quotes from the vulgate, well-known antiphons, and frequently sung hymns are especially plentiful, and seem to suggest either that the readers had at least a passing familiarity with them or that assisting the reader in building a Biblical and liturgical lexicon was among the primary goals of the writers. These two possibilities are not mutually exclusive, as the level of religious education of one reader obviously differed from that of another, and the motivation for the practice likely lies somewhere between. Yet the widespread application of quotation suggests that readers were at least somewhat acquainted with the liturgy, much of which was derived from Biblical texts, and this familiarity was a touchstone for the motets and sacred concerti that were sung in connection with the cults. Even if the listener did not understand the Latin text of the polyphony itself, he could tap into its hermeneutic significance through the loose association of a key phrase or two with both a particular meditation and the feast or feasts on which the text was performed every year. While it is probable that composers, celebrants, performers, ecclesiastics, and others proficient in Latin received the polyphony in a more nuanced way, the ubiquitous use of quotation in the meditation books reveals that the laity of the Post-Tridentine era understood much more of the liturgy and, therefore, the music than we sometimes acknowledge.

The application of standard rhetorical devices, the most prominent of which is repetition, to meditational practices is another feature that many of the books share, and this technique is readily seen at play in the two aforementioned meditations on the Presentation in the Temple. In the former, the symbol of the fifteen steps, no doubt an allusion to the fifteen mysteries of the Rosary, appears several times in differing guises throughout the brief meditation. In the latter, the phrase "Most benign Virgin" is repeated at the outset and then subsequently amplified by enumerating the various virtues that would justify such an acclamation. Other writers are even more systematic in their use of repetition. The third meditation of Archangelo Ballotino's *Pietosi affetti di compassione sopra li dolori della B.V. Maria,* for example, contemplates the pain suffered by the Virgin during the ascent on Calvary and the subsequent crucifixion of Christ. It is divided into three large sections, each of which considers a successive word or words of the phrase *Stabat iuxta Crucem Iesu Mater eius* from John 19: 25.[39] In the first of these, the word "Stabat" is isolated and repeated at the outset of each of five successive paragraphs. Thus, the resulting structure is one in which anaphora controls the large-scale form, while the device enumeratio, or expansion through detail, provides the content. The entire meditation is presented in the style of a colloquy between the Virgin and the reader interlaced with quotes from the liturgy, the scriptures, and selected sermons.[40] Although various forms of repetition such as those enumerated above are among the most frequently used rhetorical devices, the meditation books also employ others, such as hypophora (the raising and answering of successive questions), erotesis (the raising of questions left unanswered because of the obvious nature of the answers), gradatio (the arranging of ideas or concepts in the order of their importance), and apostrophe (the interruption of a discourse to directly address someone, most typically, in the case of Marian meditation books, the Virgin). Study of the *Spiritual Exercizes* of Ignatius of Loyola shows that many of these devices were transferred quite naturally to the formal process of meditation, just as they were adapted to musical composition.[41]

Finally, many of the books rely on decorative woodcuts as a means of illustrating the content of individual meditations. Castello's *Rosario della Gloriosa Vergine Maria* and the later editions of Scalvo's *Le Meditationi del Rosario* include a woodcut to accompany each of the one hundred and fifty meditations. These appear to assist the meditation process by providing visual clarification of the theological concepts associated with the meditation in question. Meditation 34 from part three of Scalvo's *Le Meditationi del Rosario,* for example, is dedicated to a Contemplation of the Virgin that focuses upon her elect status as the vessel for the incarnate word made flesh, and highlights the humility and sacrifice required of her in facilitating the redemption. The accompanying woodcut depicts her standing on the moon and dressed in the sun, a direct reference to the phrase "Electa ut sol" that theologians commonly employed in describing the Virgin as the instrument for the word made flesh (figure 1.2).[42] The meditation books devoted to the Madonna del Parto tend to feature fewer illustrations, but nearly all of them include, at the very least, woodcuts of the three primary events upon which the meditations focus, namely the Annunciation, the Visitation, and the Birth of Christ. The woodcuts are often encased in elaborate floral or Rosary-like borders, thus underscoring the relationship of the Madonna del Parto to the cult of the Rosary.[43] Several of them even include other ornate woodcuts glorifying the Rosary itself. In any case, Castello goes so far as to suggest in his foreword to the readers that the woodcuts in his Rosary meditations were included so that even the illiterate might make ample use of the book. While reaching the illiterate may have been of importance to those preparing meditations for the Rosary and the Madonna del Parto, it seems not to have been a primary concern of Ballotino and Angelo Francesco Tinosi, two of the most prolific writers of meditations for the Madonna Addolorata. Their meditations contain very few visual accoutrements, instead relying more heavily upon quotation and rhetorical devices to construct their arguments. Yet Ballotino does acknowledge the utility of art in meditating the Virgin,[44] and Tinosi used physical attributes extending from the head to the feet as a means of organizing Marian meditations.[45]

Neither of our Milanese diarists, Urbano Monte and Giambattista Casale, appears to have been trained in music, although Casale in particular showed great interest in the organs installed in the city during his lifetime. Yet when these gentlemen attended a liturgical function, they stepped into an already familiar world shaped as a Marian meditation book in which music became the vehicle for rhetorical delivery of well-known texts, and the decoration of the edifice in which it was performed provided the visual amplification of the theological concepts it espoused. Using archival and early printed sources, the surviving music and decoration, and the extant meditation books, the subsequent chapters, therefore, reconstruct, as accurately as is possible without the convenience of a time machine, the lay experience of music as meditation in five Marian cults of Post-Tridentine Milan that welcomed the participation of both sexes and all social classes and made extensive use of polyphonic music in their services: the Madonna of Miracles at Santa Maria presso San Celso, the Madonna Addolorata at Santa Maria dei Servi, the Society of the Ave Maria in Duomo, the Confraternity of the Rosary, and the Madonna del Parto.

FIGURE 1.2. Bartolomeo Scalvo, *Le Meditationi del Rosario della Gloriosissima Maria Vergine* (Venezia: Domenico e Giovanni Battista della Guerra, 1583), 355, Milano, Biblioteca Nazionale Braidense Gerli 2313, by permission of the Ministero per i Beni e le Attività Culturale.

Chapter 1

❧❋❧

Venerating the Veil

The Madonna of Miracles
at Santa Maria presso San Celso

"This most sacred virgin, as the tabernacle of God,
was the idea of perpetual virginity, the form of everlasting
honesty, the school of every virtue."

—*Paolo Morigia*[1]

HISTORY OF THE CULT OF THE MADONNA OF MIRACLES

Directly south of the Duomo of Milan on the Corso Italia stands the imposing church of Santa Maria presso San Celso. One of the most popular pilgrimage sites in early modern Milan, Santa Maria presso San Celso is the home of the Madonna of Miracles, an image credited with healing numerous devotees of their infirmities and relieving the city of the devastating plagues of 1485 and 1576.[2] The edifice originated as a small chapel that marked the location where St. Nazarenus, who, along with St. Celsus, was martyred around 395. According to the surviving accounts, the construction of the original chapel was initiated by St. Ambrose, who recovered both bodies and transferred that of St. Nazarenus to the Chiesa degli Apostoli in the Porta Romana (now San Nazaro), but left that of St. Celsus in its original grave on the site of the martyrdom and ordered it marked by a small chapel. Another second small chapel thereafter was erected over the adjacent spot where the body of St. Nazarenus reportedly had been found, and there an image of the Madonna and Child was painted on a pilaster.[3] During the tenth century, Archbishop Landolfo razed the chapel dedicated to St. Celsus and built a larger church, campanile, and monastery for the Benedictines in its place, but left the other chapel housing the painting of the Madonna and Child intact. Because the painting was one of the city's most prized objects of devotion, the chapel in which it was contained soon achieved regional status as a pilgrimage destination. In the 1430s Filippo Maria Visconti, then duke of Milan, decided to streamline the devotions there by refurbishing the interior and providing the clerical support for daily masses on the site. He initiated the construction of a central altar in the chapel and appointed five ducal chaplains, each of which was funded through benefices carrying remunerations of one hundred lire annually, to say daily masses there.[4]

On 30 December 1585 the chaplain Giovanni Pietro Porra was saying his daily mass in the chapel when two angels purportedly raised the veil on the painted figure of the Virgin and revealed an apparition of the Virgin to those congregants present.[5] Serviliano Latuada, quoting the testimony made by Giacopina Lattuada before Cardinal Archbishop Giovanni Arcimboldo and Vicar General Dottore Giambattista de' Ferri, reports that "at the Post Communion of the Mass she saw the live image of the blessed Virgin with shining countenance and great splendor, with arms open and with her little baby son on her arm."[6] This apparition supposedly hovered for the time required to pray the Ave Maria twice, after which the crowd began shouting "misericordia." The Virgin thereafter disappeared and left her veil behind.[7] The veil and the signed testimony of eighteen congregants who witnessed the event were subsequently submitted to diocesan and Vatican authorities, and the Virgin was immediately credited with eradicating the plague of 1485. Thus was born the Milanese cult of the Madonna of Miracles.[8]

Word of the Madonna's healing powers quickly spread, and both local and foreign visitors flocked to the site. In his history the cult, which was first published in 1594 and reprinted as late as 1713, Paolo Morigia observed that by the end of the sixteenth century as many one thousand persons visited the shrine daily. Even if Morigia's figures are more figurative than accurate, they give a clear impression of the significance of the cult for the local populace:

> There are many days in which the number of visitors exceeds
> two hundred thousand, and very many others one hundred

thousand, including all the first Sundays of the month and the feasts of the glorious Mother. The large multitude of people that converges there seems a large river in its flowing of the waters; there is as well not a day in which a thousand visitors do not pass this most praiseworthy devotion.[9]

During the years immediately following the miracle of the veil, one of the most pressing practical problems faced by Ludovico Maria Sforza, then regent to the duke of Milan, was the control of crowds in the area surrounding the chapel. His first response to the unexpected influx of pilgrims was to further stabilize the religious activity at the chapel by appointing a confraternity of eighteen Milanese noblemen, one in recognition of each of the official witnesses to the miracle, to oversee Marian devotions on the site. The devotions supervised by this body of noblemen were to be sustained by the five ducal chaplaincies founded by Filippo Maria Visconti along with thirteen additional ones supported by Ludovico Maria Sforza himself. As might have been expected, the activities provided by Ludovico Maria's new confraternity only served to augment interest in the cult, and by 1493 the chapel was literally unable to contain the massive crowds that arrived on a daily basis. As a result, Ludovico Maria ordered the construction of a larger church, Santa Maria presso San Celso, to house the daily devotions there, and a special gate, the Porta Ludovico, through which the many foreign pilgrims might be admitted to the city in an orderly manner.[10] The church's first architects included Giacomo Dolcebuono, Cristoforo Solari, Giovanni Antonio Amadeo, Cristoforo Lombardo, and Cesare Caesarino,[11] all of whom made major contributions to other important Milanese projects such as the Duomo and the Certosa di Pavia.

Decoration of the interior, which was largely under the supervision of Giovan Battista Crespi (il Cerano) and Giulio Cesare Procaccini, was begun in earnest around 1550 and continued apace into the first decade of the seventeenth century alongside the decoration of the façade.[12]

THEOLOGY OF THE MADONNA OF MIRACLES

Exactly how the cult of the Madonna of Miracles defined itself is not entirely clear from the extant documentation. According to the local calendar compiled by Paolo Morigia and published by Giovanni Battista Bidelli in 1603, the four celebrations for which Santa Maria presso San Celso served as the central civic location included the translation of San Nazaro on 10 May, the Assumption on 15 August, the Presentation of the Virgin on 21 November, and the exhibition of the miraculous veil on 30 December.[13] The archival documentation from the latter half of the sixteenth century and the early seventeenth century, however, shows extensive outlays only for the feast of the Assumption[14] and much less impressive ones for the feast of the veil.[15] It further mentions the funding of a fifth feast, the Espettatione della Madonna, which appears to have been celebrated in connection with the Annunciation on 25 March.[16] Annibale Fontana's relief of the Assumption on the façade of the church and his sculpture of the same posted on the main altar (figure 1.1) further point toward the importance attached to this particular feast.[17] Although the Gospels are silent on the translation of Mary, the belief that the Virgin's body was immediately taken to heaven in glory upon her death was widely accepted by the sixteenth century. The theology had its roots in early eastern stories about her death or translation and Medieval sermons on the same, and was considered confirmed by Revelation 12:1 ("And there appeared a great wonder in heaven; a woman clothed in the sun, and the moon under her feet, and upon her head a crown of twelve stars"), as well as by selected passages from the Song of Songs. With her Assumption and its attendant triumph over the grave, Mary was vested with supernatural powers that transcended time and space, thus rendering her the ideal advocate for man.[18]

Much of the archival and iconographical evidence seems to indicate a cult oriented around the theology of the Assumption, but the façade (figure 1.2) combines a number of related Marian images and, when taken as a whole, adheres to a Marian program that emphasizes Mary's role as the second Eve—a Virgin free of original sin who crushed the serpent by bringing forth the Christ child. Such a Marian program is, of course, in keeping with the general ideology of the Assumption. Yet the design of the façade, the construction of which was begun by Galeazzo Alessi in 1565, was reconceived several times by different designers, including Dolcebuono, Caesarino, Lombardo, and Alessi, and its final program, captured on four tiers capped by a tympanum, seems equally strongly focused upon the Annunciation. The ground tier features three symmetrically arranged doors flanked by statues of Adam and Eve. Directly above the large central door is an Annunciation. This Annunciation is the centerpiece of the second and third tiers, which also feature large window spaces and bas-reliefs of the four prophets (Jeremiah, Ezekiel, Isaiah, and Zacchariah), and scenes from the lives of

Interno di S.ta Maria presso S. Celso

Eretta nel 1491 dalla Scuola de Fabbricieri

L'Architettura e di Messer Perugino

Deposto nell' I.R. Bibblioteca

FIGURE 1.1. Ferdinando Arrigoni, Chiesa di Santa Maria presso San Celso (interno), acquatinta, from Ranieri Fanfani editore Milanese, *Raccolta di vedute interne delle principali chiese di Milano,* 1826, by permission of the Civica Raccolta delle Stampe Achille Bertarelli, Castello Sforzesco-Milano.

Christ and the Virgin, including the Nativity, Adoration of the Magi, and Presentation, all symmetrically arranged. The latter motif is continued in bas-reliefs of the Nativity, Marriage at Cana, Visitation, and Flight into Egypt on the fourth tier, and the façade is crowned with a bass relief of the Resurrection and an Assumption flanked by four angels. Although the programmatic content is fairly coherent, the contributors were various and included not only the aforementioned designers but also artists of the next generation. Stoldo Lorenzi contributed the statues of Adam and Eve, the Annunciation, the prophets, and the smaller reliefs on the second and third levels, while the other bass reliefs and the figures on the tympanum were executed by Annibale Fontana.[19]

With its combination of imagery referencing the Annunciation and Assumption through the lens of the Virgin's victory over the serpent, then, the program at least hints at the Immaculate Conception, a Roman doctrine widely disputed since the twelfth century which held that the Virgin was conceived without the spot of original sin. Although the miracle stories of Anselm and the account of the birth of the Virgin in the apocryphal book of James contributed greatly to the promulgation of the doctrine and the institution of local feasts commemorating the event, Biblical scholars of the Renaissance looked to Jerome's translation of Genesis 3:15 for confirmation of the doctrine: "I will put enmities between thee and the woman, and thy seed and her seed: she shall crush thy head, and thou shalt lie in wait for her heel (Douay)."[20]

Thus, this theme of a second Eve who triumphs over the devil is illustrated by the strategic placement of the Annunciation and Assumption, not to mention other events in which the Virgin figured prominently, at successive levels above Lorenzi's statues of Adam and Eve. Such an interpretation of the program is further suggested by Paolo Morigia in his volume dedicated to the church and its cult:

> It is impossible to firmly believe that in the human species there is found at any time a man or woman able to murder that mystical serpent of carnal temptation only with a glance . . . lo the Virgin, who changed minds, and the souls under her care in chaste and blessed love.[21]

How consciously or even vigorously either the architects or Morigia intended to communicate support of the doctrine, however, remains unclear, for while Morigia argues vigorously for the Virgin's spotless nature and makes reference to certain symbols associated with the cult of the Immaculate Conception, such as the mirror, he also calls

FIGURE 1.2. Ferdinando Cassina, *Le fabbriche più cospicue a Milano* (Milano: Ferdinando Cassina e Domenico Pedrinelli, 1840), San Celso XX, Facciata della chiesa della Beata Vergine presso S. Celso, Milano, courtesy of Milano, Biblioteca d'Arte. Copyright © Commune di Milano.

forth the writings of Bernard of Clairvaux, one of the doctrine's strongest opponents. Moreover, Morigia seems more concerned with promoting a cult that prizes the Virgin as an intercessor, a spotless vessel, and model of feminine virtue than he does with proving that the Virgin was conceived without original sin rather than purified in the womb as the Dominicans, the most vigorous sixteenth-century opponents of the Immaculate Conception, would have it. A similar observation might be made about the program of the façade, which, while it clearly suggests the doctrine, is equally concerned with the miraculous power, both accessory and intercessory, of the Virgin.

Morigia's aforementioned *Historia,* the only instruction book dedicated to the cult of the Madonna of Miracles, is somewhat wide ranging in content, as it spends considerable time discussing the virtue of the Virgin and explaining the symbolism behind her many odors. In many writings of the period, however, the Virgin's sweet scent and spotless virtue were the very powers she wielded against the devil on behalf of mankind, and this seems to be why Morigia is so strongly focused upon them here. He also argues vigorously, however, for the Virgin's intercessory power, calling her the medicine of the infirmed, the secure harbor of those who navigate, the advocate of kings, the guide of the errant, the liberator of prisoners, the defender of the abandoned, the hope of the desperate, the solace of those in tribulation, and an aid of the oppressed,[22] and claims that the veil itself had become an instrument by which to access the Virgin's mercy:

> And Our Lady has demonstrated many miracles because of it, and has rendered diverse graces to pregnant women who, not being able to bring forth and in pain of death, as soon as they put on the sacred veil, immediately gave birth happily, without feeling any distress.[23]

Morigia does, moreover, instruct his readers on how to appeal to the Virgin for assistance, suggesting a hymn, the Ave Maria, and an antiphon, the Salve Regina, which might be used to address her. As might be expected because of its role in the original miracle of the veil, the Ave Maria occupies pride of place among these. Calling on earlier writers such as Anselm and Bernard, Morigia theorizes that this salutation with which Gabriel greeted Mary and revealed the mystery of the Incarnation is vested with the greatest power over evil and, if intoned sincerely, is a nearly infallible means of attaining grace.[24] However, Morigia also highly recommends praying the Salve Regina during illness, pregnancy, other storms, and at the moment of death. By 1594, in fact, the singing of the Salve seems to have become, at least in the minds of the public, the centerpiece of what the documents reveal to be a well-attended Saturday evening "Salve" service. In what is perhaps the most frequently quoted passage from Morigia's *Historia,* it is described as the church's primary drawing card:

> They have introduced a very beautiful devotion deserving of praise, that is that every Saturday evening at the hour of Compline the Salve Regina is sung with certain verses and responses, with several prayers to honor Saturday, the day dedicated by the Holy Church to the glorious Mother of God; at the appointed hour, therefore, one finds the Music and the Organist, and the vested priests, and after they have lighted many candles around the balustrade of the altar of Our Lady, the singing begins and the organ responds, and now the organ

and the singing united with great sweetness and most beautiful harmony that generates in the hearts of the listeners a holy devotion towards the mother of God. [It is] of such a manner that there is not a person devoted to that holy site who is not found present for such a sweet and devotional symphony, unless he has a legitimate impediment, because all these are excused; but I say with authority that many nobility congregate there.[25]

This impressive Saturday evening service, along with Vespers and High Masses sung on other occasions throughout the year, formed the nucleus of the Post-Tridentine cult of the Madonna of Miracles at Santa Maria presso San Celso. Even before the "Salve" service was initiated, however, the citizens congregated there. Giambattista Casale reported in his diary on almost every new development in the decoration of the church and the construction of its organ and choir that occurred between 1574 and 1598, and briefly described its celebrations for Cardinal Federico Borromeo's entry on 9 June as well as the feast of the Assumption in 1592.[26]

DEVOTIONS OF THE 1560S AND 1570S

Between 1998 and 2001 a good deal of scholarship on musical activity at Santa Maria presso San Celso was published,[27] and this work has demonstrated that the institution indeed boasted one of the strongest musical traditions in the city by 1600. Although most scholars agree that the polyphonic tradition at the church stretches back to the 1560s, our current understanding of how the musical chapel emerged and what relationship it had to the eighteen benefices founded by Filippo Maria Visconti and Lodovico Sforza has been murky, largely because the registers of the chapter meetings, which are by far the most informative of the sources with regard to music, are missing for most of the years before 1583, and the information must be pieced together from a variety of other sources. There is, however, a surprising amount of documentation about the early chapel in the Milanese archives that has yet to be mined, and this, along with a reexamination of some of the sources discussed in the earlier scholarship, provides a fairly clear, if not entirely complete, picture of how the cult developed musically.

There does seem to have been some interaction between the professional musicians and the eighteen benefices erected by Filippo Maria

Visconti and Ludovico Maria Sforza, as well as some overlap in the duties of at least some of them. An order formulated by the deputies in 1587 indicates that thirteen of the eighteen beneficiaries were then assigned to the choir and further specifies the duties of the chaplains and the singers. The order implies that these groups were seen as two separate yet interrelated bodies:

> These thirteen priests, in addition to the daily mass that each of them says in this church, take part every day in singing the High Mass and Vespers and also sing other votive masses in this church that they must celebrate for the devout, and such donations coming from these masses they divide amongst themselves, and this donation is another of those that is given them by an order as above.
>
> The singers attend Mass and Vespers on all the feasts ordered, and the organist in particular must attend the High Mass every Saturday.[28]

It is possible that that the thirteen chaplaincies instituted by Ludovico Maria were designated for the choir, while the five established by Filippo Maria Visconti were used to support singers who doubled as chaplains, or, alternatively, that some other similar division amongst the chaplains was made. Although it does not seem likely that all the chaplains participated in performing polyphony, a list of twelve choral chaplains from 1576 contains the names of at least one and perhaps two individuals who are described as singers in documents of the 1560s, so it is clear that some chaplains were considered proficient enough for such an enterprise.[29] Additionally, a note from a meeting of the deputies on 4 August 1585 reports that at least two of the chaplains doubled as singers that year.[30] Other documentation dating from 1598, however, indicates that while all eighteen ducal chaplaincies staffed daily masses in accordance with the stipulations originally set out by Filippo Maria Visconti, only those assigned to the choir were to sing plainchant masses individually on special feasts, Vespers as a choir daily in the summer and on all major feasts throughout the year, Compline as a choir during Lent, Masses for the dead, and any specially requested plainchant masses.[31] This suggests that a few of the beneficiaries were exempt from musical responsibilities, while the majority were assigned to the choir and sang plainchant. It is not clear exactly when the practice of assigning the majority of the chaplains to the choir was instituted, but the tradition was certainly at least sixty-five years old in 1598. An accord reached between the dignitaries at the adjacent Benedictine monastery of San Celso and the chaplains at Santa Maria presso San Celso in 1535 specified that the chaplains at Santa Maria presso San Celso were responsible for the performance of a High Mass and Vespers on the first Sunday of each month, for which they were to receive daily distributions of 12 and 8 soldi respectively.[32]

The first indications of singing polyphony at Santa Maria presso San Celso come from summer 1563, when an initiative on the part of the eighteen deputies to expand the musical content of the services seems to have converged with Archbishop Carlo Borromeo's desire to satisfy the efforts of his sister, Suor Corona Isabella, to secure a position for Simon Boyleau.[33] The extant registers from Santa Maria presso San Celso show that on 5 June 1563 the confraternity's current treasurer, Antonio Carcasola, received a sum of L1120 specifically for music. It is not clear from where the donation came, but the monies were to be dispersed over five years at a rate of 40 scudi per year: "And on 5 June because of a promise made to the Fabbrica to pay for the music an amount of 40 scudi per year beginning on the first of November at the rate of 10 scudi per quarter for five years which finish on the first of November 1567."[34]

Correspondence between Carlo Borromeo and his personal secretary, Tullio Albanese, during August of the same summer indicates that the archbishop's sister, Suor Corona Isabella, wrote him recommending Boyleau, a composer and former maestro from the Duomo whom she must have met at the Dominican convent of Santa Maria dell'Annunciazione alla Vecchiabbia in the Porta Ticinese, for the position of maestro di cappella at the Duomo, apparently unaware that Vincenzo Ruffo had already been nominated. Borromeo, who was at the time concerned that his best musicians be retained in the churches of the diocese, instructed Albanese to find something else appropriate for Boyleau.[35] The "something" Albanese found apparently was the post of maestro di cappella of a newly formed ensemble at Santa Maria presso San Celso.

The first archival references to singers (*cantori*) at Santa Maria presso San Celso occur around the same time that Boyleau was appointed. Between 1563 and 1567 the registers show remunerations of L56 per quarter for the singers[36] in addition to the L21 per quarter set aside for the organist Mortaro, who appears in the registers beginning in 1558[37] but may well have been employed for most of the previous decade. Unfortunately, however, the L56 for the singers was handed over to one of the deputies, so the pay registers neither list the names of the individual singers nor indicate how many singers were paid within a given quarter. The amount of L56, however, invites some speculation, as it is divisible by four at salaries of L14 per quarter, remunerations which would have been comparable to the L18 per quarter paid to most of the singers at the Duomo. Alternatively, the sum could have been divided across six to eight singers, as Kendrick suggests it may have been.[38] A document from 1563 lists daily distributions paid to six individuals, the composer and singer Simon Boyleau among them, for Masses and Vespers on Sundays and special feasts between February and April of that year.[39] A notation at the bottom of the page clearly identifies them as singers rather than chaplains, but the daily distributions (other than those for Boyleau) amount to soldi and denari, thus suggesting that the salaries of the singers were probably much lower than L10 to L14 per quarter. Moreover, a document from 7 November 1568 in which Boyleau requested his salary as maestro for November, December, and January of the year mentions that the amount owed him for the period was L30.[40] This, when considered in light of the aforementioned daily distributions and an overall outlay of L56 per quarter, suggests that the other five singers split the remaining L26. It is nonetheless impossible to determine with certainty from the surviving documents how many singers were used in the 1560s and how much they were paid; a summary for the expenses of 1566 indicates that L100 was paid to the organist and L280 for the rest of the music, thus leaving how the quarterly payments of L56 were divided and whether the maestro's salary was included in them unexplained.[41]

Although no documentation enumerating the responsibilities of the singers survives from the 1560s aside from the aforementioned list of daily distributions for Masses and Vespers on Sundays and special feasts in 1563, the 1563 accounting of the daily distributions corroborates to an extent later sources that divide the feasts for which the singers were responsible into three types: Sundays and those of selected saints; first Sundays of the month, episodes in the life of Christ and Mary, All Saints, and Requiems; and the Assumption with its two Vespers services. By 1612 all solemn feasts were marked by a Messa Grande and Vespers, the latter of which featured a motet after the Magnificat. Whether polyphonic mass movements and a motet after the Magnificat were sung in the 1560s is unclear, as the documentation shows only that Boyleau was reimbursed several times for donating and copying music.[42]

That the Magnificat was the musical centerpiece of the devotions held at Santa Maria presso San Celso in the 1560s and, further, that at least six singers were required to perform it seems clear, however, from Boyleau's five-voice *Modulationes in Magnificat ad omnes tropos* of 1566, which was printed in Milan during the composer's tenure at Santa Maria presso San Celso and dedicated to his patron, Carlo Borromeo.[43] The collection contains a Magnificat in each of the eight tones, as well as rubrics in each tone for singing the canticle in four-part falsobordone. As was typical of the period, only the even verses of the canticle are set polyphonically, leaving the odd ones to be rendered in plainchant. From both the structural and stylistic points of view, the *Magnificat 8 toni* is typical of those in the collection (see Appendix D, example 1.1). The plainchant recitation formulas underlie the construction of the cantus voice, while complementary imitation at the unison and fifth is introduced in the other four voices. The imitation is often not entirely systematic, but instead features either the simultaneous pairing of two different motives or overlapping entries of closely related melodic variants. An ongoing sense of motion is achieved not only through the succession of harmonies arising coincidentally from the counterpoint but also via the frequent insertion of scalar passages composed of successive semiminims. The "Sicut locutus est" section is distinguished by a reduction to four voices that is achieved by omission of the bassus, but this gives way to a full six voices for the closing of the Lesser Doxology through the addition of a *sexta vox*. The *sexta vox* is, interestingly, in this case in the bassus range, suggesting a cohort of singers that comprised a soprano, one or two contralti (depending upon the quality of the voice assigned to the quintus part), one or two tenors, and two basses.

Boyleau was a seasoned composer by 1566, having already published a collection of four-voice motets in 1544 and several books of madrigals, three of which are extant.[44] The Magnificats of the *Modulationes* display the influence of the midcentury madrigal in their approach to imitation and variety of texture, but they also show a clear grounding in certain rhetorical procedures taught in Italian schools of the period. As can be seen in the "Et exultavit" of the Magnificat 8 toni, each verse of the canticle is bisected into smaller segments, each of which is articulated and then repeated several times before being joined to a successive segment of the verse. The drive to the final cadence of the verse is achieved, in part, by further dividing the phrases into ever-smaller segments, each of which is also repeated several times. In his *Spiritual Exercises* of 1553, Ignatius of Loyola similarly suggests

praying by contemplating single words and repeating them as often
as is necessary to internalize them.[45] He even cautions against moving
through the text too quickly, observing that "if one is contemplating
the Our Father and finds in one or two words matter which yields
thought, relish, and consolation, one should not be anxious to move
forward, even if the whole hour is consumed on what is being found."[46]

Ignatius, in fact, devotes the first day of the second week of the
Spiritual Exercises to the incarnation, instructing the student first to
survey the history of the Annunciation by considering the perspective
of the Trinity as it looked down upon the state of the world prior to the
redemption and the succession of events as they are conveyed in Luke
1. The student is thereafter advised to visually "compose" the event
by actually placing it both in the world at large and in the rooms of
the Virgin in Nazareth. Finally, the student is to request an improved
knowledge and stronger love of the Lord as it relates to this event.
Ignatius goes on to explain that visualizing and listening are particularly significant factors in this contemplation, as the student can only
grasp the momentousness of the Annunciation by seeing and hearing
the "people walking in darkness," to borrow a phrase from Isaiah,
across the face of the earth, the Trinity looking down upon them in
mercy, and the Virgin submitting humbly to the stunning announce-
ment of Gabriel. Later in the week the student returns to the topic
of the Annunciation, first repeating the aforementioned contempla-
tive exercises and then applying all five senses to the imagining of
the event.[47] Thus, by splicing the text of the Magnificat into smaller
phrases, conjoining them gradually, and thereby dramatically slowing
the pace of its delivery, Boyleau was, in effect, aiding the congregants
at Santa Maria presso San Celso to hear, visualize, and internalize the
Annunciation. There is no evidence either supporting or refuting a
claim that Boyleau was familiar with the *Spiritual Exercises,* but his
personal experience with a particular method is far less significant than
the fact that musicians and listeners were being taught to think about
the viable strategies for meditating via grammar and rhetoric taught in
the gymnasia, the laude sung in the Christian Doctrine schools, which
were subjected to segmentation and repetition during the teaching process, and the proliferation of meditation books in the vernacular.[48]

Boyleau seems to have been absent from the post of maestro di cappella at Santa Maria presso San Celso for most of the year 1565, when
Pietro Taglia took his place,[49] and his name does not appear in any of
the registers or extant archival documents after 7 November 1568,
so scholars have assumed, on the basis of a pair of letters from his

son Orazio, that Filiberto Nantermi succeeded Boyleau at that time.[50] It actually is not entirely clear what steps were taken to sustain the music once the donation for five years made in 1563 had lapsed. The succeeding maestro Filiberto Nantermi first appears in the pay records on 15 November 1574, at which time he received an advance of L147 s10 of his salary for the year 1575.[51] A notary document from the following day indicates that his annual salary was actually set at L200,[52] and a further entry recording a payment of L2 s10 on 1 January 1577 confirms this with an addendum that the advance of L147 had been for three quarters extending from October 1574 to July 1575.[53] On 1 June 1577 Nantermi was paid another L150 without comment,[54] but the aforementioned evidence suggests that this remuneration was for the three previous quarters. Such a generous outlay for the maestro di cappella would suggest that several singers must have continued to be employed, but the archival evidence appears to report the opposite, at least for the 1570s. Beginning in 1571 a choral chaplain named Alberto Rosino donated L30 per year to sustain the music, and these annual donations are recorded through 1591.[55] During the 1570s modest remunerations of L7 s7, L4 s10, and L15 for the music were intermittently paid to Giovanni Antonio Brenna, who in several earlier documents was identified as an organist, but almost no mention is made of singers.[56] According to two letters written by Orazio Nantermi in 1605 and 1608, he began serving in the chapel around 1570, but he is never mentioned by name in the surviving registers from the decade.[57] The same is true of Giovanni Paolo Candiano, a singer who reportedly had been in the chapel for thirty years by 1603.[58] The only reference in the 1570s to specific musicians aside from Filiberto Nantermi and Giovanni Antonio Brenna occurs on 6 October 1574, when L12 s15 was paid to three musicians and three men responsible for lighting the candles on the altar for the feast of the Assumption. The musicians included Rev. Stefano Tortorino, who sang the High Mass and Vespers, and Father Hironymo Morono and the aforementioned Brenna, the musicians who assisted.[59] The evidence therefore suggests that during the 1570s there was a little money set aside to pay for singers, but most of the singing was done by the chaplains assigned to the choir. A report on the chaplains for 1576 indeed shows Brenna among them.[60]

DEVOTIONS OF THE 1580S AND 1590S

The apparent downturn in donations for singers around 1570 does not seem to have deterred the deputies in their quest to provide a singular devotional experience. Although Kendrick interprets a document of 1583 complaining of the behavior of the singers in the choir as indicative that the musical situation had deteriorated,[61] the same complaints are repeated several times in the succeeding decades when there is ample evidence of a strong musical tradition, so they should not necessarily be taken as evidentiary. Similar problems with the singers at the Duomo, moreover, are reported frequently across the sixteenth century.[62] Thus, it is likely that the deputies were dealing with typical management problems when it came to the behavior of the singers. Other archival evidence, moreover, points toward a flowering musical tradition. The extant registers show numerous payments in the 1570s and early 1580s to Cristoforo Valvasore, Paolo Gazza, and Heronymo and Battista Corbetta for the construction and decoration of a new organ and renovations to the choir under the cupola.[63] In addition, between September 1585 and August 1587 further attempts were made to improve the music. On 8 September 1585 the deputies decided to purchase five chant books for the choir from San Nazaro,[64] and between 1584 and 1586 they began raising salaries and making other concessions in order to retain the current singers.[65] On 9 August 1587, moreover, perhaps feeling somewhat flush and painfully aware of the competition from other emerging Marian cults such as the "Ave Maria in Duomo" and the Confraternity of the Rosary, the deputies further resolved to improve the music by hiring additional singers and augmenting their salaries.[66] If the deputies had encountered difficulties raising funds to support the music in the past, their fortunes must have turned by 1586; that year they spent an impressive L2663 on the musicians alone.[67] Of that sum, L500 was set aside for the current organist, Ottaviano Bariola, who was in his second year of a three-year contract,[68] while at least L200 was likely going to Filiberto Nantermi, thus leaving an ample L1963 for the singers. Such an amount should, in fact, have supplied salaries for at least eight to ten singers if the salaries of L185 assigned Marcantonio Secco in 1584 and Don Francesco della Rosa in 1586, or the L180 being received by Orazio Nantermi in 1590, are any indication of the standard.[69]

The deputies apparently followed through on their resolution to further improve the quality of the music by finding additional singers, for the registers of the chapter meetings mention any number of singers who served between 1584 and 1599. Some of these singers are discussed in the chapter because they had just been hired or were seeking salary increases, but many others are named because they were requesting permission to perform elsewhere, were being docked for not appearing at the appointed hour to sing, or had certain complaints (see table 1.1).[70] The acquisition of new singers must not have been enough, however, to compete with the other Marian cults around the city. On 30 May 1593, the deputies proposed the initiation of the famous Saturday evening "Salve" service, entrusting two among themselves to inquire into the cost of such an enterprise at other churches already holding similar devotions and, further, to find appropriate musicians:

> It is resolved that it would be a decent thing to persevere in having the prayer Salve Regina sung every Saturday in this church in the future, and having had consideration of the expenses that surround it had it been done in the past, and having reflected on it further, they have ordered that Sirs Giovanni Filippo Cavanesi and Carlo Brivio, custodians of the music, inform themselves of the cost in the other churches of this city in which the Ave Maria and Salve Regina is similarly sung and at the same time they make sure to find good musicians and then inform the aforementioned chapter, in order that it is able to put this very pious devotion into effect as soon as possible.[71]

This register entry is all the more interesting in that the Ave Maria is crossed out and the Salve Regina proposed in its stead, thus suggesting that the deputies perhaps originally had in mind imitating another extremely popular cult in the city, the Ave Maria in Duomo, in which the populace gathered every evening at the altar of the Madonna dell'Arbore in the Duomo for the polyphonic rendering of the Ave Maria.[72] Moreover, a memorial of 13 June 1593 regarding the opening of the bellows of the organ for the Saturday evening service specifies that it was to be for the singing of the Ave Maria, thus confirming that the deputies considered a Saturday Ave service at least for a time.[73] In the end, of course, a Salve service was instituted, and 1595 saw a series of reforms, many of which touched on the expectations that the deputies had of the singers, including the stipulation that the Salve was to be sung every day at the end of Vespers.[74]

With the institution of the Salve service, the cult of the Madonna of Miracles seems to have reached its zenith, offering, in addition to the Salve service on Saturdays, Terce, High Mass Vespers, and Compline on feasts, as well as low masses and Vespers daily.[75] The standard size of the cappella during the 1590s is not specified in the documents of the era, but Kendrick has supposed it to fall between seven and nine, and this estimation may be correct if the deputies indeed did consult with other institutions offering Ave and Salve services, such as the Ave

TABLE 1.1.
Musicians Mentioned in the Registers
of the Chapter Meetings, 1584–1599[1]

MUSICIAN	DATES OF REFERENCE
Marcantonio Secco	1584
Ottaviano Bariola, organist	1585, 1586, 1587, 1590, 1598
Don Mauro Pinto, capellano and cantore	1585
Don Francesco della Rosa, cappellano and tenore	1586
Gio. Paolo Candiano, cantore	1586, 1590, 1598
Cesare Vespolate, basso	1587
Dioniggi Rossi, cantore	1590
Orazio Nantermi, cantore	1590, 1594, 1595, 1598, 1599
D. Annibale Botigella, basso	1590, 1599
Francesco Lucino, cantore	1595 (attempt to recruit from Duomo)
Guglielmo Berti, maestro di cappella	1598
Michelangelo Nantermi	1598
Camillo Mazza	1598, 1599

Note:
1. Compiled from the ASDM, Archivio San Celso Amministrazione, Sedute, Registri 1583–1591 and Amministrazione, Sedute, Registri 1592–1599.

Maria in Duomo. The latter was typically performed with eight musicians. For at least part of the decade in which the Salve service was instituted, Orazio Nantermi unofficially assumed some of the duties of maestro di cappella from his father, an arrangement which reportedly caused some administrative confusion among the singers, but in 1598 Guglielmo Berti apparently was appointed maestro in his stead.[76]

During the last two decades of the sixteenth century, the chapel boasted at least five composers: the organists Gaspare Costa and

Ottavio Bariola, the maestri Filiberto Nantermi and Orazio Nantermi, and, after 1595, the organist Giovanni Paolo Cima. While Bariola was known primarily for his ricercari and capricci for organ and Filiberto Nantermi's extant output comprised primarily madrigals, both Costa and Orazio Nantermi contributed a number of motets, several of which are Marian in character, to the extant repertoire. Costa's *Primo libro de motetti et madrigali spirituali a cinque voci* of 1581 is dedicated to Jerzy Olelkowicz, third Duke of Slutsk (Georgius Slucensius), but its frontispiece identifies Costa as the organist at Santa Maria presso San Celso, a post he held from at least 1581 until 1584, and its dedication mentions that the Olelkowicz heard Costa's music in Milan.[77] The collection contains six motets, two of which are ceremonial in nature and address the duke, as well as seven spiritual madrigals, several of which recount the contributions of female biblical figures. If Lothar Schmidt is correct in arguing that Costa's spiritual madrigal *O sacro santo aventuroso chiodo* commemorates the feast of the sacred nail,[78] which was celebrated in Milan on 3 May 1576 with a series of penitential processions, one of which culminated in Santa Maria presso San Celso, then the four liturgical motets, which include a *Pater noster,* a Eucharistic motet, and two Marian pieces, arguably were also originally destined for devotional use at the church.

Of the two Marian motets, *Ave santissima Maria* is representative of what will come to be a standard for para-liturgical Marian motets at Santa Maria presso San Celso. It is grounded in the long tradition of polyphonic settings of the Ave Maria in that its text tropes the opening salutation of Gabriel and concludes with a series of invocations for intercession, but it otherwise departs from the textual model provided by Luke 1:28 by focusing primarily on enumerating Mary's many attributes. The motet hails the Virgin as the Gate of Paradise, the Queen of the Heavens, and a singularly pure vessel for the Christ Child (table 1.2). This cataloguing of Marian signifiers recalls both Marian litanies of the era and the essay on the Virgin found in Morigia's *Historia,* which, as was noted earlier, recommends invoking the Virgin with the Ave Maria and affords considerable space to describing the Marian attributes, odors, and virtues that clearly find their voice in Costa's *Ave Santissima Maria.* Like most Ave Marias of this sort, the style and structure of the text are modeled on the Litany of the Virgin. In keeping with the litany-like form and its increasingly personalized tone, textual (and therefore musical) repetition is reserved largely for the final requests for intercession. The motet is admittedly a little general

TABLE 1.2.

Text and Translation of Gaspare Costa, *Ave santissima Maria*

AVE SANCTISSIMA MARIA,	HAIL MOST HOLY MARY,
Mater Dei,	Mother of God,
Regina caeli,	Queen of the heavens,
Porta paradisi,	Gate of paradise,
Domina mundi pura singularis,	Mistress of the world, singularly pure,
Tu es virgo.	you are a virgin.
Tu concepisti Jesum sine peccato.	You conceived Jesus without sin.
Tu peperisti creatorem et salvatorem mundi.	You brought forth the creator and savior of the world.
In tu non dubito.	In you I do not doubt.
Libera me ab omni malo.	Save me from every evil,
Et ora pro peccatis meis.	and pray for my sins.

in its Marian content, but the references to the virgin birth would have rendered it appropriate for the "festa della Espettatione," or cult of the Madonna del Parto (Madonna of Childbirth), which was celebrated each year at Santa Maria presso San Celso in connection with the Annunciation and commemorated in the church with its own altar.[79] Descriptions of the altar indicate that it was located in one of the four chapels flanking the central cupola of the church (figure 1.3).[80]

The other Marian motet in Costa's *Primo libro* is a setting of the well-known antiphon *Virgo prudentissima*. Although the antiphon is not part of Ambrosian Vespers for the Assumption, nor for that matter of the feasts of the Visitation and Annunciation as they are outlined in the revised Ambrosian Breviary of 1582,[81] it does have a long association with Vespers for the Assumption. Costa's setting of the text (Appendix D, example 1.2) appears to follow a three-part rhetorical design similar, though certainly not identical, to that detected in other Marian motets of the post-Josquin generation:[82] an exordium featuring

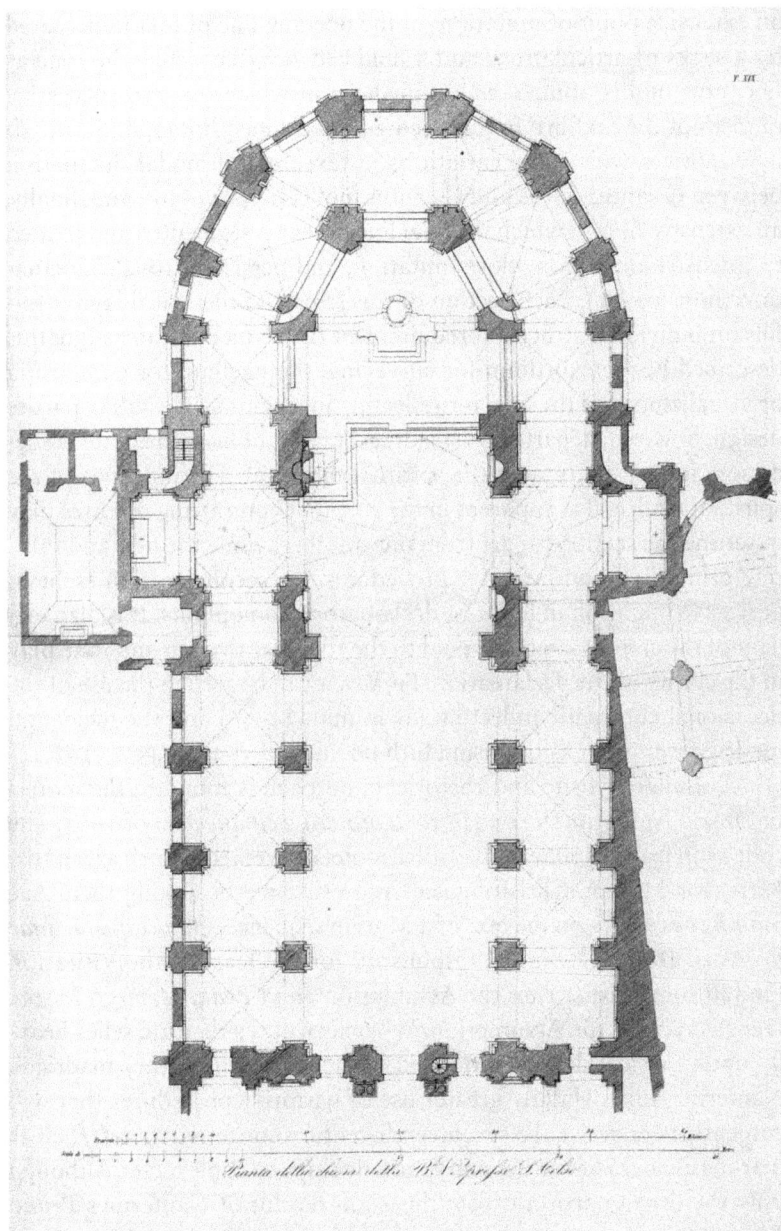

FIGURE 1.3. Ferdinando Cassina, Le fabbriche più cospicue a Milano
(Milano: Ferdinando Cassina e Domenico Pedrinelli, 1840), San Celso XIX,
Pianta della chiesa della Beata Vergine presso S. Celso, courtesy of Milano,
Biblioteca d'Arte. Copyright © Commune di Milano.

an extensive point of imitation on the opening line of text punctuated by a series of articulations and a final cadence that define the tone as G cantus mollis (mm. 1–23); a medium in which the two successive phrases of the text are fragmented and declaimed homophonically to new motives with some variations in texture and modal fluctuation between G cantus durus and G cantus mollis (mm. 23–36); and, finally, an extensive finis in which the final line of text is segmented and treated to intensive repetition, close imitation, and persistent tonal punctuation (mm. 36–61). Each section of this tripartite rhetorical layout fulfills an individual structural requirement of the meditation as Ignatius described it: the exordium for surveying, the medium for composing or visualizing, and the finis for reflecting in gratitude. Costa's tripartite design, however, departs stylistically from that of his immediate predecessors in its affinity with the spiritual madrigal. The influence of the spiritual madrigal is apparent in the role that contrasting textures play in setting the sections apart from one another; while the first and third rely primarily upon imitative procedures, the second section eschews pervasive imitation in favor of declamatory homophony. It is also evident in the careful attention paid to the role that rhythm and tone play in the clarity of the declamation. Finally, it can be seen in the use of the occasional chromatic inflection (as in mm. 35–36) and the incidental madrigalism (such as the rising fifth on "ut sol" in mm. 43–49).

A similar stylistic and rhetorical approach is found in the motets of Orazio Nantermi's *Primo libro di motetti a cinque voci* of 1601. The collection features sixteen five-voice motets (several of which are in two parts) for Marian, Christological, and other feasts, among them *Ave mundi spes Maria* on the text of a Marian sequence, *Quae est ista, quae processit* from the Matins responsory for the feast of the Visitation (and in some earlier rites the Assumption), and *Beata es, virgo Maria, Dei genitrix* for the Assumption. Whereas Costa's rhetoric relies heavily upon musical devices grounded in the sixteenth-century madrigal, Nantermi makes slightly greater use of narrative procedures that will come to characterize the seventeenth-century concerted motet, such as marked changes of texture and dramatic shifts to triple meter. Although only the organ partitura from the 1606 reprint of Nantermi's *Primo libro* survives, its dedication to the ecclesiastic Gasparo Maspero is dated 3 January 1601, thus suggesting that collection was first printed in the latter year as a sort of compendium of Nantermi's best work from his most successful years in the chapel.[83]

DEVOTIONS AFTER 1600

By 1600 musical devotions at the cult of the Madonna of Miracles at Santa Maria presso San Celso had reached their zenith, and were among the most celebrated that the city had to offer. In 1599 and 1600, in fact, visitors to the church included Marguerite of Austria and the Count of Fuentes, who was honored with the performance of a Te Deum.[84] The feast of the Assumption continued to be marked by the most elaborate festivities of the year, including a High Mass, first and second Vespers, and a procession to the Duomo featuring the city trumpeters, while the Saturday evening Salve service remained the core of the cult's identity. Documentation regarding the services from 1612 indicates that the musical forces performed High Mass and Vespers every Sunday rather than just on the first Sunday of the month as had been done in the sixteenth century, and, further, that the festal calendar had expanded to include a large number of days requiring special music. At the High Masses on Sundays and solemn feasts of this era, polyphony was reportedly performed by the singers during the Ingressa, Gloria, Credo, and Sanctus, while organ music was played during the Offertory and Sanctus. During Vespers on the same days, the singers provided the hymn, choral responses, psalms, and a motet after the Magnificat.[85] Lists of the singers recovered by Giuseppe Riccucci for the period show fifteen salaried musicians, including the maestro di cappella and organist, in 1604, fourteen in 1607, nine in 1610, twelve in 1611, thirteen to fourteen in 1613, seven in 1614, nine in 1615, and a steady eight between 1618 and 1630.[86] Riccucci ties the fluctuations in membership to economic factors, and, indeed, Kendrick argues, on the basis of certain archival evidence, that by 23 December 1607 the number of singers had been reduced to as few as four for Mass and Vespers and five for the Saturday Salve through drastic reforms that included the firing of the Nantermis, perhaps because so much had recently been spent upon decoration of the side chapels.[87] Fortunately, however, this reduction in forces appears to have been short lived, and the numbers were back to nine by 1610.

More information is available about the repertoire typically performed by the chapel during this period not only because of the presence of such composers as Giovanni Paolo Cima but also because one fairly detailed list of printed music owned by the chapel still exists. A receipt dated 21 December 1607 reveals that Cima, then organist and maestro di cappella, purchased eight music books for use in the chapel from the local printer and bookseller Giovanni Paolo Lomazzo at a price of L13 s10. The collections Cima chose, most of which appear to have been in Lomazzo's catalogue, included the four-voice masses of Enrico Radesca (1604), the five-voice masses of Giuseppe Belloni (1603), the five-and eight-voice masses and motets of Benedetto Regio (1607), the four-voice Magnificats of Simone Molinaro (1605), the five-voice Magnificats of Orfeo Vecchi (1603), small sacred concerti by Orazio Scaletta (1606) and Ludovico Viadana (from either 1602 or 1607), and an Ambrosian hymn collection of Orfeo Vecchi that is now lost.[88] Cima's purchase is informative on several fronts. First of all, the repertoire, when taken altogether, corresponds in content to the musical demands laid out for High Mass and Vespers in the documents of the period discussed above. Secondly, it shows that around 1607 when the chapel was reportedly at its largest, the singers at least aspired to attempt some double-choir music with Benedetto's Regio's *Missarum ac sacrarum cantionem quinque & octo vocibus conconcinendatum.* The collection contains not only two five-voice masses, but also an eight-voice mass and four eight-voice motets for double choir and basso continuo. Even if, as Kendrick maintains, the chapel employed too few singers in 1608 to perform the five-and eight-voice repertoire that Cima had just purchased,[89] by 1610 it did boast enough singers to perform all of the pieces with one singer assigned to each part. Finally, this list of books shows that while imitative polyphony in the Palestrina style was still being performed frequently, the chapel was beginning to embrace the new aesthetic of the small sacred concerto, a genre that likely came to dominate the repertoire performed at Vespers by the time that Giovanni Paolo Cima's *Concerti ecclesiastici* were issued in 1610.

Three of the four eight-voice motets in the newly purchased *Missarum ac sacrarum cantionem quinque & octo vocibus conconcinendatum* of Benedetto Regio are Marian, and the text of one of them, the sequence *Ave virgo gratiosa,* had at least some historical connections to celebrations of the conception of the Virgin.[90] Commemoration of the conception of the Virgin seems to have become increasingly important at Santa Maria presso San Celso during the final decades of the sixteenth century, when, as noted earlier, a feast and altar of the "Espettatione," or Madonna del Parto, were introduced in connection with the octave of the Annunciation. In 1606, moreover, the Italian painter Giovanni Battista Crespi, better known as il Cerano, executed cloth panels depicting the Annunciation and Visitation that were displayed on a triumphal arch in the interior of the edifice during the festivities associated with these two events of the liturgical calendar.[91] Regio's motet, then, provides an aural complement to Cerano's visual one. Its text, which, like that of Costa's *Ave sanctissima Maria,* catalogues the attributes of the Virgin and requests her intercession, is clearly divided, at least for Regio's purposes, into two parts, the second of which is repeated in its entirety (see Appendix D, example 1.3). The first section (mm. 1–29) comprises seven rhymed lines that enumerate well-known attributes of the Virgin, and, although they are largely declaimed homophonically, each line is set off from the next by changes in texture and clear articulations or cadences on different tones (see table 1.3). The opening *Ave virgo gratiosa* is further marked by brief shifts to triple meter, thereby calling attention to the actual act of saluting the Virgin, a practice recommended to the faithful in Morigia's *Historia.* The second section (mm. 23–54), which focuses upon requesting the Virgin's intercession amid continuing acclamations, is distinguished by the introduction of some brief imitative entries and ornamentation, but the procedure of delimiting the lines of the text through texture and cadence is never fully abandoned. The shifts in texture found throughout the motet are created primarily by alternating the first and second choirs, and the full eight voices are reserved for punctuation and marking off the division between the first and second sections of the text. The end of each section is further articulated by the introduction of motives featuring shorter rhythms, each of which is treated to some repetition. The decision to repeat the second half of the motet in its entirety, a format Regio favors elsewhere, places particular emphasis on the request for intercession, but since the cataloguing of Marian signifiers and the compositional process of using textural contrast and tonal articulation to frame the poetry govern the overall structure, the sense of rhetorical balance remains undisturbed.

The new aesthetic trend that is signaled by the 1607 purchase of the small sacred concerti of Viadana and Scaletta is perhaps best reflected in Giovanni Paolo Cima's *Concerti ecclesiastici a una, due, tre, e quattro voci* of 1610. By 1610 Cima had served the institution for fifteen years as an organist and for at least three years as maestro di cappella, and the collection can therefore be taken as a compendium of much of the repertoire he had prepared for use in the church over the past ten years. It features settings of numerous Marian texts, verses from the Song of Songs, selected Psalms, Eucharistic items, and a few antiphons and responsories associated with feasts of the sanctorale

TABLE 1.3.
Overall Design of Benedetto Regio, *Ave virgo gratiosa*

MEASURES	METER AND TEXT	VOICING	MUSICAL EFFECTS
1	₵ Ave	Cantus 1	solo
2–6	3 virgo gratiosa, 2	Choir 1	homophony, cadence F
7	₵ Ave	Cantus 2	solo
8–12	3 virgo gratiosa, 2	Choirs 1 & 2	homophony, cadence D
12–17	stella sole clarior, Mater Dei gloriosa,	Choir 1	homophony, articulation A
17–22	favo mellis dulcior, favo mellis dulcior.	Choir 1 Choirs 1 & 2	homophony, cadence C homophony, cadence D
22–25	Tu es illa speciosa, qua nulla est pulchrior,	Choir 2	homophony, cadence F
25–27	rubicunda plus quam rosa,	Choir 1	homophony, articulation A
27–29	lilio candidior, lilio candidior.	Choirs 1 & 2	homophony, repetition of triadic figures outlining, shorter rhythms, cadence on D //
30–37	Praesta misellis iuvamen, Regina clementiae	Choirs 1 & 2	homophony dissolving to short imitative entries, cadence on A
37–43	maerentibus ser solamen, aurora laetitiae,	Choir 1	homophonic, but with extensive ornamentation to cadence, cadence D
43–45	praedulcis fons pietatis,	Choir 2	homophony, elongated rhythms, cadence D

MEASURES	METER AND TEXT	VOICING	MUSICAL EFFECTS
45–46	dona nobis veniam,	Choir 1	homophony, shorter rhythms, cadence D
46–47	dona nobis veniam,	Choir 2	homophony, shorter rhythms, cadence A
47–53	et purgatos à peccatis duc ad caeli patriam.	Choirs 1 & 2	staggered entries of choirs, elongation of rhythms, plagal cadence D

that, according to the aforementioned calendar of 1612, had begun to populate the institution's busy festal calendar (Appendix C, table 1). It also includes a four-voice Mass and two four-voice Magnificats, as well as several capriccios and sonatas. Twelve of the concerti are inscribed with dedications to individual singers, several of whom were employed at the church, and two are actually by Giovanni Paolo's brother, Giovanni Andrea (as are two of the capriccios). The text of one of the motets for the feast of the Visitation duplicates that set by Nantermi nine years earlier, and one of those for the Assumption, *Beata es Virgo Maria,* is similar as well, thus suggesting the development of a specific textual tradition in the special music composed for the main feast days. There is further an *Assumpta es Maria* for eight voices, so it is obvious that resplendent double-choir repertoire still graced at least the most important celebrations of the year.[92]

Giovanni Paolo Cima's *Beata es Virgo Maria,* which is composed for two sopranos and bass and dedicated to the bass and vice-maestro at the Duomo Francesco Lucino, adheres to the three-part rhetorical structure found in other sixteenth-century motets emanating from the chapel, but the more transparent trio texture of the two sopranos with a single bass and the figuration that characterizes the finis render it at once more intimate and more theatrical.[93] An opening imitative trio in which the Virgin's blessedness is acclaimed clearly establishes the tone of G cantus durus (mm. 1–10). Throughout this section, two of the three voices are often paired and slightly set off against the remaining one, a characteristic which renders the imitative texture more transparent. Following a strong cadence on G, the medium or middle section expands on the opening declaration by explaining the Virgin's source of blessedness to be derived from her role in bearing the creator. The process of pairing two of the three voices found in the exordium is retained, but rather than entering in an overlapping fashion, the voices are increasingly set off from one another in an alternatim style (example 1.4). Articulations and cadences alternating between D and G intensify the excitement harmonically until all the voices are again brought together through more closely spaced imitative dialogue marked by increased figuration (mm. 10–34). The finis is devoted to a concluding Alleluia that is characterized by imitative and sequential repetition, as well as elaborate figuration (mm. 34–48).

That Cima was gearing his concerti to virtuoso singers is evident from not only the numerous dedications but also the frequent turns and scalar passages found throughout motets such as *Beata es Virgo Maria*. Such virtuoso singing brought a new element of theatricality to the liturgy. Yet along with this theatrical component came an increased intimacy that allowed the listener to visualize an earlier place and time and imagine himself there alongside the Virgin, experiencing her joy, her sorrow, and her ultimate glorification. This visualizing and imaging via liturgical and scriptural exegesis was the very technique upon which meditation books of the period relied, and it ultimately transformed both the sacred concerto and the spiritual madrigal into a primary vehicle for guided meditation within both the public and private spheres.

EXAMPLE 1.4. Giovanni Paolo Cima, *Beata es Virgo Maria,*
mm. 22–27.

Chapter 2

※

The Art of Lamenting

*The Cult of the Madonna Addolorata
at Santa Maria dei Servi*

"At the Cross her station keeping, stood the mournful
Mother weeping, close to Jesus to the last."

—*attributed to Jacopo da Todi*[1]

In his 1612 colloquy over the tears shed by the Blessed Virgin upon the death of her son, the Servite theologian Arcangelo Ballotino exhorts his readers to consider not only the suffering of Christ but also that of his mother. Ballotino gives voice to the Virgin's desire to perish with her son rather than endure the intense pain of watching him suffer, and invites his readers to simulate her anguish mentally:

> Christian Soul, consider how intense the sorrows that Jesus, the Son of God and the child of Mary, suffered in death, for the cry imitates the intensity of the pain; wherefore if Christ cried out in as loud a voice in death, it was because his sorrows were most intense. Consider still how painful were the troubles of Mary, who was not able to form a word for the great sorrows that consumed her heart. She repeated only these words: Child, my Jesus; Jesus, my son, would you allow me to die with you?[2]

The veneration of the Madonna Addolorata, or Virgin of Sorrows, was one of the most pervasive devotional practices of late Medieval and Renaissance Europe. The cult upheld the Blessed Virgin as the primary intercessor for mankind because of her special status as a partner in the redemption, a prestige earned through the sorrow she experienced in watching her son be subjected to the countless indignities of the crucifixion. By placing themselves in the proverbial shoes of the Madonna Addolorata, communicants imitated and experienced the agony of the Virgin in confronting the crucifixion, and thereby gained access to her mercy.

HISTORY OF THE CULT OF THE MADONNA ADDOLORATA

The cult of the Madonna Addolorata was introduced in late Medieval Europe largely through the writings of Anselm of Canterbury, Bernard of Clairvaux, Francis of Assisi, and Jacopone da Todi. As popular devotion to the Madonna Addolorata increased, altars devoted to her were erected in churches across late Medieval France and Burgundy, and canonical hours in honor of the feast, which was usually assigned to the Friday of Passion week, were cobbled together using both pre-existing and newly composed plainchant. In the 1490s Confraternities of the Seven Sorrows were established at three Flemish churches—Sts. Peter and Paul in Reymerswaele, St. Saveur in Bruges, and St. Gilles in Abbenbroeck—by Jan van Coudemburghe, a deacon from San Egidio of Abbenbroeck and secretary to Philip the Fair, thus providing the cult a certain social and political legitimacy.[3] Visual images, often in the form of crude woodcuts and engravings, played an important role in inspiring allegiance to the Madonna Addolorata across the region. Many of these depicted the Virgin's seven sorrows via a sword or group of seven swords penetrating her breast in direct reference to Simeon's prophecy in Luke 2:34–35: "Behold this child is set for the fall and for the rise of many in Israel; and for a sign which shall be contradicted. And thy own soul a sword shall pierce, that the thoughts of many hearts may be revealed."[4] Still other representations combined such depictions of the Madonna Addolorata with miniature scenes that elaborated upon her various trials.[5]

The cult of the Addolorata owed its popularity in Italy, however, largely to the efforts of the Servites, a mendicant order originating in Florence around 1233 that claimed the Madonna as its patron and established confraternities devoted to the contemplation of her seven sorrows across the peninsula. The Servites promoted the cult through the popularization of a Rosary of the Addolorata and the activities of their lay confraternities, as well as through the development of an official Vespers of the Seven Sorrows and the publication of meditation books devoted specifically to the topic.[6] By the late sixteenth century, the Vespers of the Madonna Addolorata were sung in Milan on Holy Saturday,[7] the feast dedicated to the Madonna Addolorata, and, with slight modifications, on all Saturdays not devoted to a festa duplex, despite the fact that a proposal for an official feast of the Addolorata was rejected by Julius II in 1506.[8]

THE CONFRATERNITY OF THE ADDOLORATA
AT SANTA MARIA BELTRADE

A confraternity dedicated to the Madonna Addolorata was founded at Santa Maria Beltrade in Milan on 22 November 1587, and the surviving documentation indicates that its membership typically included twenty-five to thirty local gentlemen.[9] There the confraternity's activities included attending the offices Matins and Vespers on holy days of obligation, celebrating both a sung mass in honor of the Madonna Addolorata and offices for the dead on the first Sunday of the month, visiting the sick and infirm, accompanying the bodies of deceased members to the sepulcher, and hearing the Office for the Dead on the first three feasts following the death of a former member,[10] as well as participating in the civic processions of the Sacred Nail, Blessed Sacrament, and the Ambrosian rite rogation days.[11] The festivities in honor of the Madonna Addolorata on the first Sunday of the month apparently were supported by a choir of musicians,[12] and all of the projects of the organization, including the renovation of the organs and acts of charity, were supported through donations that were collected by the members.[13] No other documentation regarding the activities of the Confraternity of the Madonna Addolorata at Santa Maria Beltrade is extant, but it is clear that the chapter was dwarfed in terms of both size and influence by the Confraternity of the Madonna Addolorata that was founded by the Servites at Santa Maria dei Servi in Milan on 16 April 1594.[14]

THE CHURCH OF SANTA MARIA DEI SERVI

One of three churches attached to influential Servite convents in Post-Tridentine Milan, Santa Maria dei Servi was constructed between 1290 and 1317 on property just northeast of the Duomo that formerly belonged to the Mozzaniga family and that is now occupied by the church of San Carlo al Corso.[15] Accounts from the late sixteenth and early seventeenth centuries reveal that some milk and a belt of the

Madonna, wood from the original cross, the ashes of the local saint Beato Angelo Porro, and at least thirty-six other minor items were among the relics housed in the Santa Maria dei Servi, and, further, that its decoration included both antique and more modern objects devoted primarily to Christological and Marian themes.[16] Although Santa Maria dei Servi was razed in 1837 to make way for the modern church and convent of San Carlo al Corso, the disposition of the altars and the appearance of the church at the outset of the seventeenth century can be gauged through consultation of an extant map of the church dating from 1594[17] and an etching of the obsequies for Prior Giovanni Maria Puricelli held in the church on 29 October 1658 (figure 2.1).[18] These sources reveal that as many as eighteen altars, many of which were located in the side chapels,[19] adorned the church, and, further, that the altar of the Confraternity of the Addolorata occupied a position of prominence second only to the main altar. Recent research on the sixteenth-century edifice contributed by Davide Maria Montagna[20] and Ermes Maria Ronchi,[21] when considered in light of additional archival documentation surviving from the period,[22] moreover, reveals that most of the altars were financed by local Milanese families (table 2.1). More families than those already identified likely occupied altars or chapels in Santa Maria dei Servi during the late sixteenth century, but some attempts appear to have been made to reorganize and reassign them. A branch of Urbano Monte's family, for example, had a family sepulcher in a chapel that he describes as that of St. Anthony, but as of 1581 the family had not paid its obligations to the foundation for over sixty years and wished neither to pay what was owed nor to continue donating, ostensibly because the occupiers were not his direct ancestors. The Monte family, therefore, vacated the chapel for a marked sepulcher, presumably in the floor space, on 17 February 1582.[23]

Although a few of the altars in question were dedicated to individual saints relevant to the interests of their patrons, the decoration of most of them contributed to a program in which the birth of Christ, the sorrows of his crucifixion, and the eventual translation of his mother figured prominently. In his three-volume chronicle of the architecture of Milan in 1674, Carlo Torre described the church as adjacent to the Palazzo Serbelloni and decorated not only with paintings of the Adoration, Agony in the Garden, and the Assumption, but also with an elaborate wood ceiling and numerous frescoes by the famed Giovanni Mauro della Rovere (c. 1575–1640), commonly known as il Fiamminghino:

FIGURE 2.1. Odeardus Ritius Delin, *Apparato fatto in Milano nella Chiesa di Nostra Signora del Sacro Ordine de suoi Servi per l'essequie del Reverendissimo Padre Maestro* GIROLAMO MARIA PURICELLI, *Milanese, Generale del medesimo Ordine, morto in Bologna alli 29 Ottobre 1658*, Triv. m. 6–7, by permission of the Civica Raccolta delle Stampe Achille Bertarelli, Castello Sforzesco—Milano.

"We have arrived at the church of the Servite fathers called S. Maria, and it is this that is found adjacent to the Palazzo Serbelloni . . . at the length of the public street, in a single Nave with a ceiling of wood painted by Fiamminghino in which was displayed a Virgin surrounded by flying spirits sowing black habits, devotion, and the particular sign of this order. Enter the ten chapels, half on each side and two further in the frontispiece attached to the main altar. Giovanni Paolo Lomazzo painted the panel of Christ in the Garden, and in that chapel admire also the slabs of marble, memorials of the house of Cossellina, but in particular of Giuliano, an erudite person and graceful poet of his time and a close friend of the aforementioned painter, as is clearly documented in his published writings. The chapel that follows is dedicated to the Servite S. Filippo

Benizzo and consecrated by Clement X, and there remained the panel painted by Daniele Crespi in which he is portrayed; the painting of the Adoration of the Magi in the chapel next to the door that opens onto the passage to the monastery is said to be by Bernardino Lovini, and Fiamminghino painted the last chapel near the threshold of the church. The panel containing the Assumption of the Virgin is an old, famous painting. I invite you moreover on another day to pay respects to the sacred body of Beato Angelo Porro, a Milanese Servite, that has remained unblemished and palpable within the noble sarcophagus for more than a century and a half although you will find it without breath. This church with monastery, which in its first years was a Palazzo with church adjacent of the noble family Mozzaniga, was consigned to the Servite fathers in 1290. And come still into the refectory bearing the mark of such a family, and in the choir admire the portrait in bas-relief on a marble slab of [Tommaso Mozzaniga]. These fathers enjoy a comfortable habitation, although it is positioned between narrow city dwellings. It is not lacking courtyards with columned porches painted by Fiamminghino representing the story of this order from the time of its founders.[24]

Aside from the panel by Daniele Crespi (c. 1600–1630) containing a likeness of S. Filippo Benozzi, which likely dated from around 1620–1625, and some of the surface decorations by Fiamminghino, Torre's description captures Santa Maria dei Servi much as it must have appeared around 1610. All of the individual images described by him survive in the church and convent of San Carlo al Corso in Milan[25] and several of them are also mentioned in later guides by Serviliano Latuada (1737)[26] and Carlo Bianconi (1787).[27] Thus, the Confraternity of the Addolorata at Santa Maria dei Servi spent even its nascent years in a centrally located edifice featuring sumptuous decorations by some of Milan's foremost artists.

THE CULT OF THE MADONNA ADDOLORATA AT SANTA MARIA DEI SERVI

By 1595 the Confraternity of the Addolorata at Santa Maria dei Servi had reportedly attracted nearly three thousand male and female members.[28] At least initially, however, the male and female members appear to have congregated separately. A document dated 21 August

Table 2.1.

A Reconstruction of the Chapels in Santa Maria dei Servi, c. 1600.

DATE OF FOUNDA-TION	ALTAR	FAMILY	DECORATION AROUND 1600
c. 1485	Main Chapel	Mozzaniga	Anonymous Lombard, *Madonna and Child Enthroned between Saints Vito and Modesto,* oil on cloth, second half of sixteenth century.
c. 1485	Crucifix	?	
c. 1485	Chapel of the Crypt	?	
1485	S. Anthony Abbot (alternatively the Assumption and S. Francis)	Mezzagora, Monte	
1491	SS. Sebastian and Benedict	Serbelloni	Anonymous Piedmontese, *Assunzione della Vergine tra i SS. Sebastiano e Benedetto,* oil on panel, c. 1580.
1491	S. Martin	Pagano	
c. 1500	Chapel of the Adoration	none	Anonymous Lombard, *Adorazione dei Magi,* oil on panel, 1550–1560.
1501	BVM	Gosellino/ Abignava	Ambrogio da Fossano called Bergognone, *Madonna in trono,* fresco, 1485–1490?
1501	unknown, later named S. Juliana Falconieri	Corte, later Tirchera	

DATE OF FOUNDA- TION	ALTAR	FAMILY	DECORATION AROUND 1600
1504	later Annunciation (1541–1544 Ashes of Beato Angelo Porro)	Porro	Terracotta of *L'Angelo e la Madonna?*
1513	Blessed Sacrament	none	
1529	Rabbia		
1554	Name unknown	Lomeno	
before 1561	Name unknown (at end on right)	Evangeli	
1571	S. Catherine	?	
1573	S. John the Evangelist (third on the right)	Gosselino	Giovanni Paolo Lomazzo, *Orazione nell'Orto*, oil on panel, 1572.
1579	Name unknown (near the main altar)	Vismara	
1594	Madonna Addolorata	none	A statue of the Madonna Addolorata?

1594 refers to the confraternity members as "brothers and sisters of this school" and further mentions that the female members were prohibited from going to the homes of gentlewomen to seek donations for the Madonna of the confraternity, as was already being practiced.[29] Another missive from the Prior General dated 18 February 1598, however, instructs Cesare Merlino to provide a copy of the confraternity's *Ordinationes* to the women. It indicates that the women wished to operate with twenty-four officers instead of twelve as did the men and, further, that they had not been observing the process for electing and maintaining offices that was used by the men,[30] thus suggesting that the women participated in a separate division that was modeled administratively upon that of the men.

From the outset of its founding, the Confraternity of the Addolorata at Santa Maria dei Servi was vigorously pursuing a liturgical program that incorporated the performance of plainchant and polyphony by both singers and instrumentalists.[31] The archival evidence indicates that its members attended Vespers and a procession of the Madonna on the fourth Sunday of the month and on Holy Saturday, as well as on other Saturdays during the year, particularly during Lent. A special guest was typically invited to preach a sermon at Vespers on the fourth Sunday of the month, thus adding to the service's prestige with the general public.[32] Confraternity members were further granted papal indulgences for attending Vespers on the feasts of the Assumption, the Nativity, the Conception, the Visitation, the Presentation, the Purification, and the Annunciation, as well as on the sanctoral feasts of SS. Fabian and Sebastian, S. Thomas Aquinas, SS. Peter and Paul, S. John the Baptist, S. Domenic, S. Philip, S. Michael the Archangel, S. Francis, All Saints, S. Nicholas, and the twelve apostles.[33] Of these, the Assumption, the Nativity of the Virgin, Holy Saturday, and the feast of Beato Angelo Porro on the fourth Sunday of October were reportedly among the oldest and most venerated.[34] Nevertheless, all seven primary feasts of the Virgin held particular significance for confraternity members. In his *Città di refugio a' mortali,* an extended commentary on devotional practices is seventeenth-century Milan, Ignazio Cornago observes that the Servites even promoted a practice of saying seven Ave Marias in contemplation of the seven feasts of the Virgin:

> Another devotion should be noted that the Servites of Maria must practice in this location, namely to commemorate frequently her seven feasts, the Conception, Nativity, Presentation in the Temple, Annunciation, Visitation to S. Elizabeth, Purification, and Assumption into the Heavens, by devotedly reciting seven Ave Marias while contemplating the mysteries of the aforementioned solemnities.[35]

Moreover, an undated archival document from the early seventeenth century in which the correspondent complains that a woman formerly of the order of the Virgins of St. Ursula was disrupting the activities of the confraternity further points to the importance attached to Vespers on solemn feasts, particularly those devoted to the Virgin.[36]

The extant breviaries and ceremonials used by the Servites reveal that a specific Vespers of the Madonna Addolorata had developed by the early seventeenth century. The Vespers of the Madonna Addolorata were celebrated on Holy Saturday, as well as on the sixth day of the month to which no other feast was assigned. Although not specified in the books, the Vespers of the Madonna Addolorata were also likely performed at the Vespers service attended by the Confraternity members on the third Sunday of the month. As can be seen from table 2.2,[37] the Vespers of the Madonna Addolorata differed only slightly from the Vespers BVM used on Saturdays, in that they featured an alternate antiphon for Psalm 109 ("Quo abiit dilectus tuus" in place of "Dum esset Rex"), a different Capitulum ("Cui comparabo te?" instead of "Ab initio et ante saecula"), a different hymn ("O quot undis lacrymarum" in place of "Ave maris stella"), and an alternate antiphon for the Magnificat ("Nolite me considerare" instead of "Beata Maria"). The hymn sung at the Compline service that immediately followed, however, was the same for both. . The Saturday Vespers BVM were sung on all Saturdays that were not assigned to a major feast, and were nearly identical to the Vespers of the Purification, the principal variation being the use of the Magnificat antiphon "Sancta Maria succurre miseris" in place of "Beata Maria." The psalm and antiphon group of the Saturday Vespers BVM, moreover, was used with minor modifications for Vespers on the feasts of the Assumption and the Nativity of the BVM.

Just where polyphony might have been inserted into the services is not clearly indicated in the surviving documents. Nor is it clear whether that polyphony was improvised or composed. The archival evidence suggests, however, that polyphony was most often employed, at least at the outset, on the fourth Sunday of the month, at Saturday Vespers during Lent, and at Solemn Mass on Holy Saturday. The archival documents from 1598, for example, report numerous remunerations made to Cesare Rossino, a singer at the nearby Duomo, on behalf of a group of singers from the same institution that regularly performed on the fourth Sunday of the month. Although the number of singers involved is not always indicated, one of the earliest entries describes it as four, while another from only a few months later mentions six.[38] The documents further list remunerations made for the same event to the church's organist, Felice Avogadro, as well as to an unnamed soprano, a violinist who played with the organ, a cornettist, trumpeters, and a

TABLE 2.2.
Vespers of the Madonna as Observed by the Servites

VESPERS OF THE MADONNA ADDOLORATA	SATURDAY VESPERS BVM
Ant. Quo abiit dilectus tuus	Ant. Dum esset Rex
Psalm 109	Psalm 109
Ant. Quo abiit dilectus tuus	Ant. Dum esset Rex (after Nativity: O admirabile commercium)
Ant. Recidite à me	Ant. Recidite à me
Psalm 112	Psalm 112
Ant. Recidite à me	Ant. Recidite à me
Ant. Non est ei species	Ant. Non est ei species
Psalm 121	Psalm 121
Ant . Non est ei species	Ant. Non est ei species
Ant. A planta pedis	Ant. A planta pedis
Psalm 126	Psalm 126
Ant. A planta pedis	Ant. A planta pedis
Ant. Fulcite me floribus	Ant. Fulcite me floribus
Psalm 147	Psalm 147
Ant . Fulcite me floribus	Ant. Fulcite me floribus
Capitulum: (Thren 2) Cui comparabo te?	Capitulum: (Eccl. 24) Ab initio et ante saecula creata sum.
Hymn: O quot undis lacrymarum	Hymn: Ave maris stella
	V. Diffusa est gratia
Magnificat with Ant. Nolite me considerare	Magnificat with Ant. Beata Mater (after Nativity: Magnum haereditatis mysterium and in Eastertide: Regina coeli)
———	———
At Compline: Jesu tibi sit gloria (Hymn)	At Compline: Jesu tibi sit gloria (Hymn)

regal player.[39] At least two singers, Fabritio Varese and an Impolitto who may be identified as the Ippolito Canova who sang at the Duomo during the feast of the Annunciation in 1598[40] performed for five Saturday Vespers services in 1597. A soprano from the Duomo, a soprano "a casa," a violinist, a cornettist, and a bagpiper, moreover, were employed during Lent, presumably for Saturday Vespers, in 1596, and two contraltos, a soprano, a bass, and a regale player were similarly contracted for Vespers on the six Saturdays of Lent during 1597. Finally, three sopranos, a violinist, a regal player, and two unspecified musicians performed on Holy Saturday during 1597.[41] The extant evidence suggests, in fact, that Santa Maria dei Servi, like other institutions in seventeenth-century Milan, had no established musical chapel, but rather relied upon the singers from nearby institutions such as the Duomo. Only the organist Felice Avogadro appears to have boasted a permanent appointment at Santa Maria dei Servi, and this appointment was financed by the confraternity. In response to a petition from Avogadro read on 1 January 1599, the deputies voted to raise his salary from twenty to thirty-five scudi per annum in recognition for three years of faithful service. In return, Avogadro was obligated to serve the confraternity for at least two more years.[42]

The earliest extant polyphony that is associated with the confraternity is Giovanni Battista Ala's *Secondo libro de' concerti ecclesiastici*, a collection of sacred concertos for one to four voices and continuo that was published by Filippo Lomazzo of Milan in 1621.[43] According to Mariangela Donà, the frontispiece of the print, which was once housed in the Biblioteca Capitolare in Vercelli but is now lost, identifies the composer as the organist at Santa Maria dei Servi.[44] Another Lomazzo print, the *Flores praestantissimorum viorum* of 1626, indicates that Ala was still there five years later.[45] Little else is currently known about Ala's career. A native of Monza,[46] he first emerged on the local scene in 1618 as an organist at the Collegiate Church in Desio.[47] Picinelli describes him as an excellent organist and a splendid composer, and suggests that he achieved a certain degree of local fame while serving at Santa Maria dei Servi.[48] A composer of canzonets and madrigals as well as of sacred concerti, Ala died a blind man at the tender age of thirty-two sometime after the publication of his third book of concerti in 1628,[49] but no record of him can be found in the Milanese *Registri Mortuari* for the years 1628 to 1630. The registers are incomplete for this period, however, and Mariangela Donà, relying on the circumstantial evidence found in the surviving prints, has suggested that Ala was a victim of the plague of 1630.[50]

Although the only copy of Ala's *Secondo libro* is now lost, its content can be recovered through an examination of Phalèse's *Pratum musicum* of 1634, where the collection is reprinted along with a few concerti by French composers (see Appendix C, table 2).[51] It reveals that the *Secondo libro* comprises eighteen concerti on texts derived from Marian and sanctoral liturgies, the Book of Psalms, and the Song of Songs, as well as a few other selected biblical texts. The Marian texts featured are appropriate to the feasts of the Assumption and the Addolorata, which were among the confraternity's primary observances, as well as to the feasts of the Visitation and the Madonna of the Rosary, which were also promoted vigorously by the confraternity. Several selections from the Song of Songs, including *Nigra sum, formosa sum, In lectulo meo,* and *Dilectus meus* additionally underscore the Virgin mother's long-touted role as the bride of Christ, and, by extension, as a party to both the tribulations and the ecstasies inherent in that spousal relationship.[52] The other concerti, which include settings of several psalms, two biblical texts, two additional antiphons, and a responsory for the Common of a Martyr, were likely intended for use either on the fourth Sunday of the month or on the other sanctoral feasts for which indulgences were granted the confraternity's members. The texts of several of these, moreover, had been incorporated into the theological essays and the meditation books as a means of expanding the Virgin's largely undocumented biography through reliance upon scriptural prophecy and exegesis.

MEDITATING THE MADONNA ADDOLORATA

As might be expected, the sixteenth-and early seventeenth-century visual images associated with the cult of the Madonna Addolorata do not, for the most part, focus upon literal representations of these texts. Instead, they emphasize three events in the life of the Virgin: the birth of Christ, the Crucifixion, and the Assumption. Pamela Jones has demonstrated that images of the Madonna and Child, the Passion, and the Assumption of the Virgin, were among those most valued by Post-Tridentine ecclesiastics as vehicles for the progressive meditation widely promoted by Ignatius of Loyola,[53] and this practice appears to have affected in some measure the decoration programs of institutions devoted to the Madonna Addolorata. In the case of Santa Maria dei Servi, renditions of the Madonna with Child enthroned and the Assumption are particularly numerous.[54] The association of both the infancy of Christ and the Assumption with the Madonna Addolorata is perhaps owed to the teachings of Bernard of Clairvaux, who argued that Mary was martyred in the spirit by the sword of redemption, as prophesied by Simeon in Luke 2: 34–35.[55] While early modern representations of the Assumption remained intertwined with related eschatological images such as the translated woman dressed in the sun of Revelation 12 and the second Eve implicit in I Corinthians 15,[56] sixteenth-and early seventeenth-century depictions of the Madonna and Child began to replace fifteenth-century cultic images of the Madonna Addolorata pierced by the seven swords of sorrow. In 1612, in fact, Servite Arcangelo Ballotino observed that the Madonna with Child Enthroned, an image of which decorated the main altar of Santa Maria dei Servi by 1567 (figure 2.2),[57] was one of three scenes that evoked the Madonna Addolorata for early seventeenth-century audiences. The other two were, of course, the Crucifixion and the Deposition.

> When it represents the martyrdom of a male or female saint, the Holy Church uses a portrait of his or her image, and places in hand the instrument of his or her martyrdom . . . your mother, o Christ, always is depicted with you her little son, now a live baby in her arms, now dying as she stands at your cross, now in the lap dead, signifying that you were the knife and sword of her martyrdom . . . [58]

Here the Virgin's love for her son effectually becomes the instrument of her martyrdom, and this love is communicated in the form of an intimate colloquy between mother and infant, between mother and her dying son, or between mother and her fallen child. For Ballotino, such depictions assisted the viewer in imagining the experiences and emotions of the subjects, thereby enhancing the meditation process.[59]

Several of the laude surviving from the period seemed to have served a function similar to that of the images in that they featured built-in mechanisms for role-playing on the part of the singers. These laude, which were well known to most communicants through the local Christian Doctrine schools,[60] likely were incorporated into the processions of the Madonna Addolorata held on the fourth Sunday of the month, and may also have been sung during certain other activities of the confraternity. Printed collections of laude had been issued in Milan by diocesan printer Pacifico Pontio in 1576[61] and again in 1586,[62] and similar ones published in Como, Torino, Venice, and Rome during the second half of the sixteenth century were likely circulating there as

FIGURE 2.2. Anonymous Lombard, *Madonna and Child Enthroned between Saints Vito and Modesto,* oil on cloth, Convento di San Carlo al Corso, Milano, courtesy of Padre Ermes Ronchi, Biblioteca dei Servi, S. Carlo al Corso, Milano.

well. Although both of Pontio's collections were intended primarily for the teaching of Christian Doctrine, they contain numerous laude devoted to the Virgin, one of which, "Giunto che fù quel giorno," from the 1586 collection, is dedicated specifically to Christ's departure from his Blessed Mother on the event of the Crucifixion. It includes an intimate dialogue between mother and son narrated from the perspective of the Virgin, who expresses the desire to die with her son rather than endure the pain of being parted from him by death. Here the singers are required to imagine themselves experiencing Christ's suffering on the cross, again reinforcing the importance attached to the exercise of imagining (table 2.3).

According to the rubrics provided, the song was to be sung to the fourth of five melodies used to sing all twenty-five laude in the collection. No melodies are provided in the print, thus suggesting that they were well known by their universal use in the doctrine schools, but an early owner of the copy now housed in the Biblioteca Braidense in Milan appended a manuscript containing simple, crudely copied versions of the five tunes. [63] The F mollis tune for "Giunto che fù quel giorno" comprises four phrases, the first and third of which are identical, to which all eleven stanzas recounting the Virgin's suffering are to be sung (example 2.1). Neither the melody nor the text appears in Serafino Razzi's well-circulated *Primo libro delle laudi spirituali* (1563),[64] but the text does appear with a slightly different version of the tune in Pontio's aforementioned *Lodi e canzoni spirituali* of 1576.[65]

Meditation books devoted to the Madonna Addolorata that survive from the period reveal that the internalization of the experiences of the Virgin, particularly when meditating the crucifixion, was central to the cult, for such internalization led not only to an appreciation for the humility, purity, and obedience with which the Virgin faced her sorrows, but also to an understanding of how she attained the role of principal intercessor. They reference the visions of noted figures who were reportedly moved to tears while contemplating the crucifixion, including St. Francis, St. Bernard, and St. Catherine, arguing that such transcendent meditation purified the viewer in the same way that the tears from the proverbial eyes of the dove in Song of Songs 6 purified the world as she witnessed the crucifixion.[66] These meditation books, although organized in very individual manners, utilize techniques not unlike those recommended to the "exercitants" in the *Spiritual Exercises* of Ignatius of Loyola, and they may well have drawn directly upon them, as the *Exercises* had been circulating in print since 1548.[67]

Table 2.3.
"Giunto che fù quel giorno."

Giunto che fù quel giorno, Nel qual nostro Signore Spinto dal grande amore Andò à la Morte.	The day arrived in which our Lord, Driven by great love, went to death.
Parlò con la sua santa, E benedetta Madre, Dicendole, il mio Padre Vuol ch'io moia	He spoke with his saintly and blessed Mother, saying to her "my Father wishes that I die.
Restate Madre in pace, Non posso far dimora; Perche venuto e l'hora Del partire.	Remain at peace, Mother; I am not able to remain because the hour of departure has come.
Cara madre io parto, E'l cor vi lascio in pegno, Che de l'amor sia segno, Ch'io vi porto.	Dear Mother mine I depart, and it pains my heart to leave you, which is a sign of the love that I bear for you.
Non da balestra, ò d'arco Disciolta una saetta Feri con tanta fretta Cerva mia,	An arrow shot neither from a crossbow nor from a bow could have wounded with such speed, my dove,"
Quanto'l cor di Maria Queste ultime parole Della diletta prole, Del suo ventre.	As did these last words of the beloved offspring of her womb [wound] the heart of Mary.
Volea darli risposta, Ma per cordoglio acerbo Formar non potea verbo In alcun modo.	She wished to respond. But because of her bitter affliction she was not able in any manner to form a word.
Poi respirando disse Tutta da'affano piena, Oime che grave pena, Mi da'l Cielo.	Then sighing she said with great anxiety, "Alas, what great pain the heavens have dealt me.
Donque posibil sia Dopò la sua parten[z]a Che possa viver senza Te mia vita?	Therefore, how is it possible that I will be able to live without you, my life, after your departure?

Chi potrà vita darmi,	Who will be able to give me life if I watch
Se te mio figlio, e Dio	you my son, and my God, vanish before
Vedrò nasconder'io	my eyes?
Da gli occhi miei?	
Se voule il Padre eterno	If the eternal Father wishes that you die, O
Che mori ò caro figlio	dear son, I also will leave my place of exile
Esca io ancora d'essiglio	and die with you."
E moia teco.	

Like the *Exercises,* they require the reader to be thoroughly schooled in the scriptural and theological history of the topic to be meditated, often providing a discourse based on intricately intertwined references excerpted from the scriptures, the liturgy, and earlier theological writings. Moreover, like the *Exercises,* they require the reader to imagine himself experiencing the seven sorrows of the Virgin, usually by mentally composing a specific scene and sometimes calling upon the five senses for assistance in doing so. Some make further use of Ignatius's technique of composition by visually translating the Virgin into a statue whose various body parts, each representing a specific attribute, can be meditated singly. Finally, like the *Exercises,* they feature colloquies, usually between either the reader and the Virgin or the Virgin and Christ.

Ala's *Secondo libro de' concerti ecclesiastici* effectively functions as a meditation book on the Madonna Addolorata in that, like the contemporary meditation books devoted to the subject, it gathers together and provides discourse on a number of liturgical and scriptural texts essential to the ecclesiastically sanctioned biography of the Virgin, which was itself cobbled together by Medieval scholars largely from prophetic texts of the Old Testament (see Appendix C, table 2). Each concerto, moreover, can be viewed as an individual meditation, not only because it elaborates a particular textual segment musically but also because in some degree it conforms structurally to the meditations found in contemporary sources of the period and assists the listener in the process of imagining and composing.

Ala's concerti for the Madonna Addolorata, *O Marias qui ploras* and *Consolare, o mater* rely largely on the process of colloquy, which

EXAMPLE 2.1. "Giunto che fù quel giorno," music.

Ignatius describes as "made, properly speaking, in the way one friend speaks to another, or a servant to one in authority." They share several structural characteristics with other early modern meditations on the Addolorata featuring the colloquy format, the most prominent of which is a shift of voice from third-person narration to a first-person soliloquy, assigned either to the reader or to the Virgin, when contemplating the crucifixion itself. In one such example from Arcangelo Ballotino's *Colloqui affettuosi del pianto che fece Maria,* the narrative gives way to a soliloquy in which the Virgin speaks directly to the reader:

> [T]his heart of mine is struck and pierced through with infinite punctures of sorrow. If you wish a sepulcher under an enclosed and locked garden, this heart of mine is your garden, planted by you, closed and locked with your hands, so that the envious serpent is never able to enter and spread his venom there. If you wish to be enveloped in a white sheet, here is my heart spotless in its virginal integrity and white in its innocent purity. If you wish to be anointed with myrrh and aloe, bitter mixtures, here is my heart, where the bitternesses of myrrh are my sorrows and anxieties . . . [68]

Further, they often conclude with an expression of transcendence or a request for intercession, if not both. Consequently, Ala chose a two-voice dialogue format for his concerti for the feast of the Addolorata, thus bringing to life the shifts in voice and concluding expressions of spiritual elation so characteristic of the meditations of the period.[69]

O Maria quid ploras (Appendix D, example 2.2),[70] a dialogue for two sopranos and continuo, opens by considering the weeping mother before the temple. The image of the Addolorata thereafter becomes the means by which the listener contemplates Christ's sacrifice and the salvation that arises from it. As the listener approaches the transcendent, the crucified Christ is repeatedly heralded as "my life" and "my soul" for eternity. At the outset of the concerto, the Cantus 1 voice functions as the narrative voice, while the Cantus 2 is assigned a soliloquy of the Virgin. Each voice initially presents an entirely separate text, and there is little textual or musical interaction between them. With the introduction of the text "O vita mea! Anima mea," (measure 22) however, the relationship between the two voices shifts, for they thereafter share the same text and participate in both homophonic pairing and imitative exchanges. This shift in the style of presentation suggests that the process of meditating upon the sorrow of the Virgin has elevated the narrative voice (Cantus 1) to a state of spiritual understanding equal to that of the Virgin.

The latter half of *O Maria quid ploras* (measures 22–41), moreover, makes use of the common meditative technique of repetition, which Ignatius of Loyola considered necessary "because the intellect, aided by memory, will without digressing reflect on the matters contemplated."[71] For Ignatius, repetition served to focus the mind and need not be hurried, even when applied to a single word or phrase, a method, as noted earlier, that he recommended for praying the Our Father and Ave Maria. Ignatius even goes so far as to suggest that the student might also pray the same text rhythmically "in such a manner that one word of the prayer is said between one breath and another. In between these two breaths one reflects especially on the meaning of that word."[72] Although the meditation books for the Madonna Addolorata do not recommend such techniques, it is not uncommon for such words as Mary and Jesus to be reused frequently in the texts and capitalized each time they appear, effectively calling the reader's attention back to the main object of meditation. They also frequently feature the repetition of a single line from a biblical text such as "Stabat Mater" or "Veni in hortum meum" throughout a given section much in the manner of the rhetorical device known as anaphora. In the first contemplation of the third chapter of his *Pietosi affetti di compassione sopra li dolori della B. V. Maria,* which is devoted to discussion of the fact that, according to John 19, St. John the Evangelist was the only apostle to remain standing with Mary at the cross, Ballotino repeats the word "Stabat" throughout, and three times within the first paragraph alone. In addition to being repeated incessantly, moreover, the word is set off typographically in the print:

> *Stands.* O God, give me the words, that I can recount the great bravery and singular strengths of Mary, with this word *Stands.* Come now, listen, I ask you, devoutly. If we speak entirely in the literal sense: *Stands.* She remained standing because the death on the cross was reckoned most ignominious. They were about to cry about the dead crucified sitting, as they did other honorable things . . . [73]

The modest length of Ala's concerti, all of which are self-contained entities on prose texts, does not temporally allow for the meditation of isolated words as recommended by Ignatius. Nonetheless, the moment of transcendence is reached musically through the imitative exchange and repetition of the final three phrases of the text, much in the way that the "exercitant" achieves transcendence by meditating on successive words or upon a designated line from a biblical text.

Consolare o mater, a dialogue for cantus, tenor, and continuo (Appendix D, example 2.3), is a sort of musical deposition in which the Madonna's fallen son cajoles her to gladness.[74] Its text, interestingly, is a slight variant of the one set for a single voice by Giulio Cesare Ardemanio, the organist at Santa Maria della Scala, in Francesco Lucino's *Aggiunta* of 1612 (reprinted 1616).[75] In Ala's two-voice setting, each voice is initially assigned its own distinctive material, thus differentiating the doleful speech of the mother from the exhortations of the Redeemer. Mary repeats the text "o my beloved son" a number of times before, at the Christ's coaxing, her desolation over his wounds gives way to joy for his triumph over the grave. As the Virgin's sorrow recedes, the two voices begin exchanging statements on the same text (measure 24). The moment of transformation is further marked by a shift to triple mensuration, and the two voices thereafter not only share the same text but also participate in imitative exchanges and homophonic duets. The listener is thereby transported from the contemplation of the crucifixion to the meditation of life eternal through the aural image of the disconsolate mother confronting the loss of her beloved son and basking in his final triumph. In this particular concerto, repetition of text and music is utilized throughout. Musical motives are restated either at the interval of the fifth, in sequence at the fourth or the fifth, or in imitation at the fifth, but the use of imitation is reserved for the point at which the Virgin achieves transcendence (measures 24–32).

As noted above, the meditation books of the period devoted to the topic of the Madonna Addolorata also contain numerous passing references to prophetic scriptures from Old and New Testament that serve to bolster the biography of the Virgin and underscore her singular position as the mother of Christ and the principal intercessor for mankind. Among the most important of these references are selections from the popular *Canticum Canticorum,* a book which, for scholars of the period, explored, at least in part, the spousal relationship to which the Virgin mother was entitled as Christ's earthly partner in the redemption plan. Ala set several texts from the *Canticum Canticorum* in the *Secondo Libro,* including the opening verse of chapter 3, *In lectulo meo* (Appendix D, example 2.4).[76] According to Ballotino, chapter 3 of the *Canticum Canticorum* unveils two so-called mysteries regarding Mary's relationship with Jesus, namely that, according to the Evangelists, Mary searched for Jesus three times as a wife searches for her husband, despite the fact that their souls were already united as the two proverbial doves, and that whenever Mary found him, he was about his Father's business.[77] In Ala's concerto *In lectulo meo,* the biblical text serves as a commentary on these mysteries, and Ala treats it accordingly. Although two voices are again used, it is obvious that dialogue techniques were seen to have no place in this setting. The shifts of poetic voice and subsequent expressions of transcendence found in the aforementioned concerti for the feast of the Addolorata are abandoned in favor of a straightforward presentation of the scripture in which both voices share the same text. Solo passages, imitative exchanges, homophonic duets, and brief shifts of meter abound, but any individuality of voice is subjugated in favor of a direct presentation of the prophetic text. Yet nearly every phrase of the text is repeated in full or in fragmentation, and this repetition is synchronized with sequential development, imitation, and increased figuration over a harmonically mobile bass so that the overall effect is of systematically tethering and releasing the musical tension as a means of progressing consistently toward the ultimate goal of the final cadence in D cantus mollis.

Given the variety of the Marian texts set in Ala's *Secondo libro,* it is rather surprising that a rather simple four-voice Magnificat with basso continuo in the fourth tone was chosen to represent him and his home institution of Santa Maria dei Servi in Filippo Lomazzo's *Flores praestantissimorum viorum* of 1526, a collection containing sacred concerti, a mass, and two Magnificats for one to four voices and organ (partitura) purportedly composed by the most talented composers currently employed in Milanese institutions.[78] Although other composers featured in the print took advantage of the opportunity for an expressive, concerted presentation implementing many of the musical devices discussed above, Ala chose to present the Magnificat text in a fairly straightforward, chordal style in which the emphasis is upon precise and accurate declamation of the Latin. It is possible that he saw the Magnificat, one of the only biblical moments in which the Virgin actually reveals something of herself by speaking, as a liturgical moment in which a clean delivery of the narrative supersedes the exegetical possibilities suggested by the text.

Whatever Ala's reluctance about applying the meditative techniques used in his small sacred concerti to the Magnificat, it is clear that Servite theologians prized images of the Passion, Assumption of the Virgin, and Madonna and Child in promoting the cult of the Madonna Addolorata. They wrote of their inspirational power in the meditation of the Virgin's sorrows and covered the walls of their institutions with them. For the three thousand members of the Confraternity of the Addolorata at Santa Maria dei Servi in Milan, however, aural stimuli were also integral to both the meditation of the sorrows of the Virgin and the assimilation of her biography. As a result, plainchant and ecclesiastical concerti promoting meditation of the personal sacrifices of the Madonna Addolorata and her attendant role in the redemption were presented against the backdrop of the graphic iconographical images. As they were juxtaposed with the images, the musical compositions unfolded the text in a manner that naturally conformed to the concepts of segmentation, repetition, suspended time, and internalization recommended in the meditation books, thereby leading the listeners to a state of transcendence.

Chapter 3

❧❧❧

Singing Before a Madonna
on the Pilaster

The Society of the Ave Maria in Duomo

"Holy Mary, Mother of God,
Pray for us now and at the hour of our death."

—attributed to Girolamo Savonarola

Like the Madonna of Miracles at Santa Maria presso San Celso, the
ancient cult of the Madonna del Pilone (the Madonna on the Pilaster),
more commonly known among the congregants at the Duomo as the
Ave Maria in Duomo, was a local one. It appears to have been entirely
unrelated to the better-known cult of the same name in Torino, which
dates to 29 April 1644. According to the surviving accounts of pastoral
visits made to the Duomo by Federico Borromeo, the singing of the Ave
Maria at the Vespers hour before a Madonna affixed to a Pilaster originated during the late fifteenth century when a mendicant friar known
as the "missionary from God" began preaching daily in the Piazza of
the Duomo. He exhorted the Milanese not only to repent their sins and
pledge to live in a Christian manner but also to enter the Duomo at the
sound of the Vespers bells and sing the Ave Maria. The public response
to this grassroots movement led certain gentlemen and merchants of
the city to form a Society of the Ave Maria to support the practice.
They apparently commissioned a painting of the Virgin, posted it on
a pilaster in the Duomo, and gathered the populace around it every
evening for the singing of the Ave Maria:

The devotion of the Ave Maria, which is sung every evening in the major church of the Duomo of Milan, originated around the year 1495 and is attributed to a foreign hermit who was called the "missionary from God" by the populace. This hermit was found late in the evening in the Piazza of the Duomo, and praying publicly, exhorted [the populace] to live in a Christian manner, leaving sin behind and serving the divine prefects. And since he heard the bell of the Ave Maria, he invited the listeners to enter immediately into the Duomo and pray and say the Ave Maria. In particular he exhorted several to convene and have the Ave Maria along with several laude sung in honor of the ever glorious Virgin Mary, thanking her for the benefits received and supplicating her to implore mercy of her beloved son for the time to come. Upon this exhortation, several gentlemen and merchants united under the name of the Most Holy Crucifix and initiated the singing of the Ave Maria at the third pilaster on the left-hand side when entering the Duomo (which pilaster would be the sixth when the church is finished), having for this reason placed [there] a painted image of the Glorious Virgin. Further they made a marble statue of the same Glorious Virgin, and in that location God, because of her merits, performed many miracles, for which reason the populace flocked to that devotion . . .[1]

In 1566 the singing of the Ave Maria was transferred from the aforementioned altar in the middle of the church to one on a nearby wall that served as the seat for the Christian Doctrine School for girls. Because Carlo Borromeo considered the image of the Virgin being used there indecent, he had it removed and commissioned another.[2]

Aside from the aforementioned documentation, which appears to have been widely circulated in early scholarship on Marian devotion in Renaissance Milan, very little information is extant regarding the activities of the society before the plague of 1576, when Carlo Borromeo reportedly first took an interest in the tradition of singing the Ave Maria at Vespers. In an effort to eradicate the city of the plague, he not only processed to various churches with the reliquary containing the sacred nail but also applied the practice of singing the Ave Maria to all seven of the canonical hours and extended participation in it to all the churches in the city:

> He also ordered that they construct altars in all of the quarters,
> in order that all of the people might at least see (if not hear)

the sacred sacrifice of the mass, and desired that the bells of the
Duomo, the parishes, and the monasteries sound the Ave Maria
seven times a day in order that the people, whether in their
homes or at their windows, set about praying the Ave Maria,
the Litanies, or Penitential Psalms, or Rosaries, or other pious
prayers all together seven times a day around the time of the
seven canonical hours; and that the populace respond from the
aforementioned windows, balconies, or doors to certain deputies in saying the litany, psalms or prayers from space to space
in every quarter, whether they come together in words (albeit
loudly), in song, or in sonorous and musical counterpoint, the
men, women, boys, and girls large and small and young and
old singing and responding devotedly from one part to the
other in alternatim and choir by choir of the aforementioned
quarters, so that the city seems the grand church of paradise.[3]

The young archbishop must have developed considerable confidence
in the grace attained by singing the Ave Maria at the Vespers hour,
for two years later he is still found promoting and even actively participating in it, now as a show of gratitude for the eradication of the
plague. In addition, he transferred the activity itself to the altar of the
Madonna dell'Arbore, which was later to become the seat of the prominent Confraternity of the Rosary and the location in which the image
of the Madonna used in the Confraternity of the Rosary's processions
would be housed.

Moreover, in the year 1578 Beato Carlo Borromeo, Cardinal
with the title of San Prassede and at that time our most vigi-
lant Archbishop, transported said devotion to the altar of the
Madonna dell'Arbore, which currently is that of Santa Tecla,
and several times there, for more decorum and convenience,
given that the enemies were usually at hand after the liberation
of the city from the plague of 1577, this Beato Carlo participated in said devotion at the main altar of the aforementioned
church every evening to say the litany with several prayers at
the aforementioned main altar in order to thank Our Lord
for the great benefit of that liberation, beseeching him to have
mercy on us and to preserve us in the future. Therefore, he
ordered that at the sounding of the Ave Maria, they meet
before the aforementioned main altar, that is at the first salutation of the Angelus, according to the custom, and while it
sounds subsequently, that they say the aforementioned litany

and prayers as usual, and immediately sing the Ave Maria, and
that one of the Ordinary Lord Canons always participate there
to say all of the aforementioned prayers. And in this way it is
always now performed, lighting the candles there before the
first balustrade of the choir, while one says the aforementioned
prayer and Ave Maria.[4]

Carlo Borromeo apparently was so enamored of the Ave service that
he extended the practice beyond the walls of the Duomo and into
other public spaces. In his diary of the most noteworthy events that
occurred in sixteenth-century Milan, for example, the Milanese noble-
man Urbano Monte reports that with the blessing of the Company of
the Sacred Cross on 6 February 1584, which was marked by a procession from San Babila, where Carlo Borromeo had presided over
a service that included music provided by professional singers, to a
makeshift altar set up at the Colonna, the Archbishop instituted the
practice of singing the Ave with the candles lit every evening at the new
altar of the Colonna.[5]

It is unclear whether the Ave Maria in the Duomo was sung in
plainchant or polyphony during Carlo Borromeo's tenure, for the documents indicate only that in 1585, the year following his death, L35 was
spent on musicians.[6] Under Federico Borromeo, however, the singing of
the Ave Maria at the Vespers hour became a distinctive liturgical and
musical moment, sometimes even sharing the stage with activities of the
Confraternity of the Rosary, and in this context it was likely rendered
polyphonically. On 13 September 1595, just shortly after Federico
Borromeo's appointment as archbishop and with him in attendance,
the Ave Maria appears to have been sung after Vespers and Compline
at the culmination of the procession of the Madonna of the Rosary
in the Duomo, which occurred on the first Sunday of the month and
on Marian feasts.[7] Some extant remarks from Federico Borromeo's
pastoral visit of 1595, moreover, note that the singing of the Ave on
these and other occasions was typically followed by the performance
of a motet.[8] By this point in the history of the cult, donations were
being collected during the singing of the Ave Maria, and maintaining
music of high quality and extending it to include additional polyphony
were considered the most significant means of increasing the size of the
donations collected.[9]

Most of the income amassed from the collections went first toward
paying the musicians and supplying candles to light the church ade-

quately enough for the singers to see their books during the service, although the documentation also suggests that the group took on other charitable causes. For such causes the society relied not only on the money collected during the singing of the Ave Maria but also on bequests left by deceased citizens.[10] According to the surviving records of the Banca di Sant'Ambrogio, most of the donations and bequests came from artisans and merchants living or active near Duomo, including the wheat merchants, greengrocers, vendors of swordfish and salted fish, and the judiciary officials, thereby reflecting the strong role played by the city's mercantile class in promoting the cult.[11] For these individuals, many of whom must have comprised the cohort of gentlemen and merchants described in the sixteenth-century documents, participation in the society served to increase their social mobility by extending and cementing their individual contacts, to improve their moral and financial image through association with a visibly charitable civic institution, and to fill their proverbial spiritual storehouses in preparation for paying down the debts of Purgatory incurred by themselves or members of their families. If the enumeration of the indulgences gained for participation in such Marian devotions is any indication, a stay in Purgatory for an indefinite period was a forgone conclusion among the majority of Catholics of the era. Financially supporting the daily devotions and donating to the poor, which were portrayed by mendicant preachers of the period as principal means of imitating Christ and thereby increasing grace, were pillars of the society's mission. While providing attractive avenues of worship for the public and caring for the indigent by accumulating alms for the society had social and spiritual rewards, the collection of donations was not likely the driving force behind the extraordinary success of the cult. The act of singing the Ave was itself a way of generating indulgences that could shorten a sentence to Purgatory, since praying the Ave Maria was an exercise that, from the time of Urban IV, earned members of the Confraternity of the Rosary thirty days of indulgences for every single instance.[12] In terms of its general social and spiritual constructs, therefore, the Society of the Ave Maria was not unlike the laudesi companies of fourteenth-century Florence, which emphasized meditation, collective worship, and the imitation of Christ as avenues for the improvement of the layman's moral and social status.[13]

In comparison to the laudesi of Florence and, in fact, to many of the other confraternities in Milan, the spiritual program of the Society of the Ave Maria was less complex and its agenda more straightforward, perhaps because the main goal of the society was to accumulate indulgences in the process of accessing the intercessory grace of the Virgin. The centrality of the Ave Maria in this regard is perhaps no better expressed than in a model Socratic dialogue between the teacher and the disciple of the Christian Doctrine School found in a the instruction book of the Jesuit Diego Ledesma:

M. Who first said the Ave Maria?

D. The Angel Gabriel, when he came to salute Our Lady, and S. Elizabeth and the Church added several words.

M. Whom does the Ave Maria address?

D. Our Lady.

M. Who is Our Lady?

D. She is the Mother of God, a Virgin full of grace and every virtue, the queen of the heaven and the earth, and our advocate . . .

M. Where is Our Lady?

D. In heaven.

M. Why then do we call her Our Lady of Mercy, of Remedy, of Consolation, and other names?

D. She is called by the many names for the many and diverse benefits that she grants as the Mother of God.

M. What does one say in the Ave Maria?

D. We salute her, praise her, and recommend ourselves to her.[14]

Here then is found, in simple and direct prose, the theology behind the Ave Maria as it was taught and received by the masses in Post-Tridentine Italy; the Virgin was a conduit for grace, a model of virtue, and an advocate for the faithful in every ill encountered during the journey to salvation. Paolo Morigia more eloquently echoes the same sentiment when he paraphrases St. Bernard, saying, "The heavens respond, the angels rejoice, the world exults, and the demons tremble when I say Ave Maria."[15] The mere simplicity of the theology and the applicability of the practice of saying the Ave Maria to the daily experience of ordinary citizens are likely what rendered the Ave Maria in Duomo one of the most popular devotions in Counter-Reformation Milan.

Under Federico Borromeo the Society of the Ave Maria was integrated into a School of the Sacred Cross, which assumed responsibility for managing the daily devotions and providing eight of the "best singers in the city" for the singing of the Ave Maria.[16] This was a fairly typical Milanese solution for cults, particularly grassroots ones, that had either spiraled out of control or were in danger of becoming unmanageable because of the sheer number of devotees flocking to the devotions. It had, in fact, been successfully employed at Santa Maria presso San Celso at the end of the previous century. In the case of the Ave Maria in Duomo, the reorganization of the society, particularly in terms of its directives for fiscal and organizational oversight, seems to have been motivated, at least in part, by certain recurring problems with the singers, including tardiness, inattentiveness, frequent absences, and irreverence, for the statutes that were drawn up suggest that the authorities were responding to these very indiscretions:

> The Prior is to see to the things of the School, most importantly of the aforementioned devotion of the Ave Maria, that they go according to his direction, and that the singers are found at the lectern where they usually are to sing the laude at the appointed hour of the sounding of the Ave Maria, in order that they don't have reason to hurry in order to be on time to sing, wherein they are not able moreover to be available to answer the need, nor the maestro di cappella able to know for how many voices to prepare if he does not first see the singers present; taking care also that the aforementioned singers stand there with modesty and devotion, and that the aforementioned maestro di cappella is always found there before the others in order to prepare the books.
>
> The aforementioned prior also appoints one of the servers, or another whom he prefers, to make note in a little quinternion of the days in which the aforementioned singers fail to appear in order to then retain that portion of their payment, and also in order to see if the absences continue in such a manner that it be better to put another in his place according to what seems best to the chapter.
>
> He likewise is responsible for seeing that the servers are present every evening to carry the candles to the usual location before the main altar and to see that they are all lit at the first sound of the Ave Maria, which candles they remove after the Ave Maria is finished to take care of them, and that they are

careful to keep track of them, as also they are to do with the
books of music, and that while the music is sung, they go as
usual about the church with the offering plate to collect the
donations . . .[17]

As I have noted elsewhere, by 1604 eight singers—two sopranos, two
contraltos, two tenors, and two basses—were being paid to sing the
Ave Maria daily, and the distribution of the voices used supports the
theory that four-voice polyphony was usually performed.[18] A number
of the pay records for the singers of the Ave Maria from the years 1605
to 1623 recently surfaced in the Archivio dei Luoghi Pii Elimosinieri in
Milan, moreover, and these demonstrate that this four-part voicing was
more or less maintained throughout the first two decades of the seventeenth century (see Appendix B).[19] They further show that during the
first decade of the seventeenth century a maestro di cappella was additionally employed to lead the ensemble at a salary of L100 per year, but
between 1606 and 1611 this duty was reassigned to a tenor or a bass
from among the eight regular singers in order to reduce the expenses.
At least one, and usually two, of the singers participating in the Ave
service at any given time were members of the cappella musicale of the
Duomo: the Ave singers Alessio Brioschi, Giovanni Antonio Picenardi,
Hieronymo Vimercate, and Giovanni Antonio Blancino were all concur-
rently members of the Duomo choir.[20] Between 1628 and 1633, moreover, both Vimercate and Blancino were released by the Fabbrica on
numerous occasions to perform at other churches in the diocese.[21] Thus,
the Ave singers clearly did represent the best that the city had to offer
and were apparently in great demand throughout the region.

The availability of such skilled singers and the growing popularity
of the small sacred concerto may have been the motivations behind a
thoughtfully debated proposal to hire an organist and retain four solo
singers in place of the larger choir. The proposal was advanced sometime around 1608, at roughly the same time that the number of singers
in the Salve service at Santa Maria presso San Celso was temporarily
reduced to four.[22] This coincidence suggests that attempts to downsize
may have been driven not only by economic factors but also by the
availability of new types of repertoire. In 1608 the Milanese firm of
Tini and Lomazzo released Francesco Lucino's *Concerti di eccellentissimi autori,* a collection of sacred concerti for two to four voices featuring, among others, several concerti by the Duomo's current maestro di
cappella, Giulio Cesare Gabussi.[23] The first decade of the seventeenth

century in Milan, in fact, saw the publication of thirteen such collections, all of which were issued by Tini and Lomazzo and document the rising interest in the small sacred concerto in the city.[24] To the members of the society and perhaps even to the singers, such repertoire must have offered the opportunity to showcase what they repeatedly claimed were the best voices in the city. In the end, however, it would seem that most of the members of the society were not sufficiently moved by the newly fashionable aesthetic and its virtuosic potential, as most of the discussion on whether or not to hire an organist and four soloists in place of the eight-member choir centered upon the financial exigency of such a plan. The proposal was defeated when put to a chapter vote, apparently because of the added expense of approximately L130 per annum that was expected to be incurred, and the eight-voice polyphonic model was retained instead.[25]

Interestingly enough, the choirbooks in the musical archives of the Duomo contain only a few polyphonic settings of the Ave Maria. Polyphonic Ave Marias are entirely absent from Libroni 10, 10 bis, 25, and 26, all of which were printed or copied during the latter half of the sixteenth or the early seventeenth century. Yet all four sources include numerous arrangements of the Pater Noster, as well as a wide variety of hymn settings for various feasts celebrated throughout the year, including those of locally important saints.[26] Two four-part settings of the Ave Maria are found in the third Milan Choirbook (Milan 2267): the anonymous one with the rather macaronic text on folios 182v-183r and the widely circulated setting of the text from Luke 1 by Loyset Compère.[27] Two others dating from roughly the same era are preserved in the badly damaged fourth choirbook (Milan 2266). These include the well-known four-voice *Ave Maria . . . virgo serena* of Josquin and an anonymous five-voice *Ave Maria spiritus sancti*.[28] The three aforementioned four-voice settings feature a texture in keeping with the SATB vocal distribution suggested by the society's payment notices, and the five-voice *Ave Maria spiritus sancti* could have been performed with one singer per part. Moreover, at least two of the four-voice settings enjoyed a certain amount of staying power. Compère's *Ave Maria* appears in at least eleven Italian, German, and Spanish sources printed or copied between 1498 and 1549[29] and was reportedly still being sung at the papal chapel as late as 1568,[30] while Josquin's *Ave Maria . . . virgo serena* was circulated in some twenty-seven print and manuscript sources, twenty of which date from between 1502 and ca. 1560 and include among them the *Dodecachordon* (1547) of

Glareanus.[31] It has been argued that both settings reflect a distinctively Milanese style that dominated the sacred compositions emanating from Sforza chapel of the 1470s, a style with which Compère would have been familiar through his membership in the chapeland which Josquin assimilated upon his arrival in Milan in 1484.[32] More recently, however, David Fallows suggested that Josquin's *Ave Maria . . . virgo serena* emulates a style already familiar to the composer in the 1470s through northern sources. While fully acknowledging certain textual and musical affinities between the two works and their shared reliance on the so-called Milanese style, Fallows demonstrates that these common features may be traced to the influence of plainchant sources from around Cambrai and the international currency of the Milanese style.[33] Regardless of the dating and origins of Josquin's *Ave Maria . . . virgo serena* and its relationship to Compère's motet on a similar text, both settings were copied in the Milan choirbooks and also circulated widely in other sources during the first half of the sixteenth century, so were undoubtedly well known and readily available to Milanese musicians of the period. Despite their apparent popularity in the first three quarters of the sixteenth century, however, both settings must have seemed rather stylistically antiquated to audiences of the early seventeenth century, who were more accustomed to double choir music, the small sacred concerto, and the still-popular imitative polyphony of Giovanni Pierluigi da Palestrina.

One print still housed in the Duomo archives contains a four-voice setting of the Ave Maria by Palestrina. The collection is a reprint issued by the heirs of Francesco and Simone Tini in 1587, and features motets from the composer's second book of four-voice motets first published in 1584.[34] Given Palestrina's continued authority across the peninsula during the first three decades of the seventeenth century, it is, of course, possible that this Ave Maria setting was among those performed at the Duomo's "Ave services." It would, at the very least, have been considered more musically current than those from the Milan choirbooks. Yet there is no conclusive evidence to suggest that settings found in prints such as the aforementioned were used by the singers of the Ave Maria in Duomo. The archival evidence does indicate that the society had its own sets of books, and these apparently were kept separate from those being used by the cappella musicale of the Duomo, for a request to house them in two empty benches in the shape of chests found in the pulpit from which the singing was done was endorsed by the Duomo's maestro di cappella, Giulio Cesare Gabussi, on 19 April 1606.[35] One

would expect such a group of books to contain numerous settings of
the Ave Maria in addition to the motets that were to follow it, but no
manuscript or print has surfaced as a likely candidate to date.

A number of extant manuscripts and prints contain more than one
setting of the Ave Maria, but only one source from the period, Ljubljana,
N 207 (c.1590) seems to have been expressly destined for an organization such as the Ave Maria in the Duomo. Ljubljana, N 207, which
is now housed in the National and University Library in Ljubljana,
Slovenia, contains eighteen settings of the *Ave Maria gratia plena* along
with sixty-eight other motets. Although motets for a number of diverse
feasts are included, the content of the manuscript is decidedly Marian in
character. Particularly impressive, aside from the group of eighteen Ave
Marias, is the large number of Marian antiphons: twenty-one settings of
the Salve regina, eleven of Regina caeli, six of Alma redemptoris mater,
and three of Ave regina caelorum. Ljubljana N 207 is thought to have
been copied in Ljubljana or Gormji Grad by the same scribe responsible
for Ljubljana N 285, a compilation of twelve masses, three mass prop-
ers, and one motet by Jacob Händl, Christian Hollander, Jacobus de
Kerle, Orlando Lassus, Philippe de Monte, and Jacob Regnart, a constel-
lation of composers active in Austria, Bavaria, and Bohemia during the
sixteenth century. Although Ljubljana N 207, in contrast to Ljubljana
N 285, is dominated by Italian composers, Northern composers are
also represented, so it does not seem likely, given the scribal relationship
between the two sources, that Ljubljana N 207 originated in Milan.
Nonetheless, the implications for the content of Ljubljana N 207 are
intriguing.[36] It would seem that the singing of the Ave Maria and other
motets at the Vespers hour was practiced elsewhere by the turn of the
century, and, further, that Ljubljana N 207 had a particular devotional
function within the context of that practice, one perhaps associated with
the cathedral church of St. Nicholas in Ljubljana.

Since the 1604 statutes specify that "the singers are found at the
lectern where they usually are to sing the laude at the appointed hour
of the sounding of the Ave Maria,"[37] it is possible that the books in
question included actual collections of laude, and, further, that the
Ave Maria itself was performed as improvised falsobordone or in a
simple four-voice homophonic texture according to a "cantasi come"
designation along with other Marian laude contained in the books.[38] In
1576 and 1586 respectively the diocesan printer Pacifico Pontio issued
collections of standard laude recommended for use in the Schools of
Christian Doctrine, and these include a number of songs dedicated to

the Virgin.[39] Although only the 1576 collection contains notated music, the rubrics provided in the texts of both collections clearly indicate that all of them were to be sung to one of five or six well-known melodies. The texts in both volumes are further grouped according to the melody with which they were to be performed, thus suggesting that the first song in each group was the melodic source for those that followed. Every song in the collections had a designated didactic purpose or was associated with a specific feast.[40] Similar collections were issued in Torino in 1579[41] and Como in 1596.[42]

The Duomo archives do contain several printed collections dating from 1526 or before that contain other Maria motets with Ave invocations and Litanies of the Virgin, including a reprint of the third book of five-voice motets of Palestrina (1587), the five-and eight-voice masses and motets of Benedetto Regio (1606), the fourth book of two- and three-voice motets of Agostino Aggazzari (1606), the first book of eight-voice motets by Nicola Pisani (1620), a collection of masses, Magnificats, motets, and Marian litanies for two choirs by Guglielmo Arnone (1625), and the litanies for two choirs by Giovanni Francesco Anerio (1626).[43] It is, however, unlikely that any of these were used by the society, as all of them, save the Palestrina, feature basso continuo parts.

Whatever the repertoire performed at the Ave service during the early seventeenth century, it clearly served as a sonic backdrop for the collection of alms from the local merchants, artisans, and other wealthy families resident in the immediate vicinity of the Duomo, whose generous gifts to the poor all but insured a shortened stay in Purgatory for themselves and their relatives. Just how the donations amassed in this period were distributed and the specific purpose they were to serve, aside from supporting the music itself, is not made clear in the documents that have surfaced to date. It is known that the society gave six donations of fifty lira for the dowries of poor girls in Milan beginning in 1699, and these could be used either toward matrimony or religious vocation.[44]

In 1784 the Ave Maria in the Duomo was integrated with the altar of the Quattro Marie.[45] The society appears to have been facing financial difficulties far earlier, however, for on 31 December 1620 the deputies met to discuss how they should address a pressing debt of L170. It was decided that each member would immediately donate L8 to the cause.[46] This action appears to have staved off the collapse of the devotions, and the pay records reveal that the singers and ushers continued to receive their regular salaries. In 1622 and 1623, however, the pay records show a slight decrease in the outflow of funds, with the vocal forces reduced from eight regularly salaried singers to six regular singers and one unidentified soprano. Moreover, no pay records for the singers seem to be extant after 1623.[47] A single entry from 1648 does note, nonetheless, that two deputies are normally delegated to select the musicians, thus suggesting that at least a few singers continued to be hired to sing the Ave Maria after the plague of 1630.[48]

For Carlo Borromeo, the Ave Maria in the Duomo appears to have served as a prelude for what was to become a much more important personal endeavor, namely the establishment of a Confraternity of the Rosary. Following its second transfer in 1578, the Ave Maria in Duomo was situated at the altar of the Madonna dell'Arbore, the Duomo's main altar and the one that soon was to become the home of the equally visible Confraternity of the Rosary. There Carlo Borromeo vigorously promoted the singing of the Ave Maria by the city's most prominent singers by lending his auspicious presence to the occasion. If the diaries of the period are any barometer, the zealous archbishop needed only appear at a spiritual function for it to acquire immediate significance among the local communicants. From the Ave Maria, then, it was only a small step to the institution of a Confraternity of the Rosary, the first in the city associated directly with him rather than with its traditional custodians, the Dominicans.

Chapter 4

꙰꙰꙰

Invoking the Mulier Fortis

The Confraternity of the Rosary

Hail Mary, full of grace, the Lord is with thee

—*Luke 1:28*

For inhabitants of Post-Tridentine Italy, no instrument associated with the Blessed Virgin possessed more spiritual force than the Rosary. Also commonly known as the *corona* or garland, the Rosary was the primary means of accessing the intercessory power of Mary as Mulier Fortis, the virtuous woman who crushed the head of the proverbial serpent.[1] Praying the Rosary while meditating upon its fifteen mysteries allowed the devoted communicant to realize the miraculous potential of the Virgin's influence and demonstrate its use in overcoming the ills of the world, and the activity was encouraged through the publication of Rosary books that described various techniques of praying the Rosary, as well as through volumes that recounted the numerous legends that had developed in connection with them. Bernardo Giunti's 1587 *Miracoli della sacratissima Vergine [Maria . . . del santissimo Rosario]* relates at least thirty well-known stories in which a communicant tapped into the Virgin's intercessory power while praying the Rosary and was thus saved from recurrent sins or imminent danger. Perhaps the best known of them was one associated with the founder of the Confraternity of the Rosary itself:

> Mister Alain [de la Roche] of the Valley of Coloata in Brittany near the city of Douai, going to fight against the Albigensian

heretics near Toulouse under the standard of the Magnificent Count Simon of Montfort, at the time in which St. Dominic preached and persuaded the Count to say the Rosary every day, indefatigably said this Rosary on his knees, meditating the incarnation, passion, and glorification of Jesus Christ. And as he was combating a great multitude of heretics with few companies and being surrounded by them in such a manner that he could not escape death, the glorious Virgin Mary appeared to him and threw 150 stones at those heretics and all were thrown to the ground. And he was liberated with his company.[2]

In the years immediately following the Council of Trent, Alain del la Roche's rescue via the Rosary had a particular resonance for Italian Catholics, for it was considered emblematic of the Christian League's 1571 victory over the Turks at Lepanto, a triumph which supposedly was garnered through the concerted efforts of members the Confraternity of the Rosary who prayed and processed on the day of the battle. The significance of this victory for all Christendom is reflected in the diary of Giambattista Casale, who, in a rare foray into current political events, recorded the moment among the most important of the year 1571:

> Memorial how on October 7 the total and unutterable providence of God Our Lord, after many calamities and travails on account of our sins, today wished to show all Christianity his immense good will and mercy in visiting and favoring his holy church with the marvelous and unprecedented victory that his Most Serene Lord Don Juan of Austria has reported against the conceit and tyranny of the Turk, enemy of the Christian name, in the Gulf of Lepanto . . .[3]

In attributing the victory at Lepanto to the special invocations to the Virgin made by Confraternity of the Rosary members, Rome publicly endorsed membership in an organization heretofore primarily controlled by the Dominicans, and the added political clout that might be accrued in erecting a chapter of his own was, as usual, not lost on Archbishop Carlo Borromeo.

HISTORY OF THE CONFRATERNITY OF THE ROSARY IN MILAN

Most historical accounts claim that the Confraternity of the Rosary itself was founded around 1460 by the aforementioned Alain de la Roche, a Dominican friar who organized the local citizens of Douai into congregations that prayed the corona on a regular basis. Similar companies were thereafter formed in Brittany, the Netherlands, France, Spain, and, finally, Italy.[4] Although the Confraternity of the Rosary was confirmed in a breve of Alexander V as early as 1479,[5] membership in it achieved popularity relatively late in Northern Italy, perhaps not only because of the added impetus of the victory at Lepanto but also because permission to form new companies was restricted to the Dominican Prior general and his deputies until 1569.[6] In any case, membership was open to individuals of both sexes and any social class, and the requirements for maintaining it were few.[7] Members were merely expected to confess, take communion, and pray at least one third of the Rosary upon their induction, and thereafter to pray it at least once a week. Those who prayed the Rosary at least three times per week; participated in the masses and processions held on Marian feasts, on the feast of the Rosary, on the first Sunday of the month, and on anniversaries of the dead; visited an altar of the Rosary on the feasts in which the fifteen mysteries were represented or the feast of the Rosary; visited the five altars of the Virgin held equal to the Stations in Rome; and attended the singing of the Salve at Compline in churches that hosted a Confraternity of the Rosary earned extra indulgences.[8]

Milanese enthusiasm for the Confraternity of the Rosary can be attributed largely to the efforts made by Carlo Borromeo to promote it during the last year of his tenure as Archbishop of Milan, but as Carlo Marcora has demonstrated, active chapters of the Confraternity of the Rosary were already in place at Sant'Eustorgio and Santa Maria della Rosa when Borromeo established the chapter in the Duomo that he trumpeted as a new diocesan initiative. In fact, the day after he founded the Confraternity of the Rosary at the Duomo of Milan, Borromeo wrote Cesare Speciano in Rome describing the festivities and acknowledging the fact that the Dominicans at Sant'Eustorgio and Santa Maria della Rosa had voiced strong objections to the erection of the Confraternity of the Rosary in the Duomo on the basis of long-standing papal privileges that gave their order, at least in their view, the sole right to establish such chapters.[9] Borromeo argued that while he had no intention of impeding the pre-existing chapters at Sant'Eustorgio and Santa Maria della Rosa, Sant'Eustorgio was too far from the city center to sustain active participation of the general population and Santa Maria della Rosa was not sufficiently staffed to handle the activities of the organization.[10] If the reactions of ordinary Milanese citizens are any indication, Borromeo may have been partially justified in his initial skepticism of the efficacy of the chapters at Sant'Eustorgio and Santa Maria della Rosa. On 25 March 1584 Giambattista Casale recorded the founding of the Confraternity of the Rosary at the Duomo in his diary, noting that a large segment of the population was present for the event, and eight days later he inscribed himself, his wife Catelina, and his children, David and Angela, in the chapter at the Duomo, despite that fact that they were already members at Santa Maria della Rosa.[11]

Although Borromeo does not mention it in his letter to Speciano, a Confraternity of the Rosary was also in place at the Spanish church of San Protasio in Campo (al Castello or al Porto Giovio) from at least 1582. An extant document regarding this company, which filed a protest against the confiscation of its candles during Carlo Borromeo's tenure, indicates that it was founded with the permission of the Dominican Prior General and had been in place for two years prior to the filing of the supplication.[12] No documentation of the founding itself has been uncovered, but it is noteworthy that the congregation at San Protasio was Spanish and, further, that the Confraternity of the Rosary had an especially strong following in late fifteenth-and early sixteenth-century Spain. Borromeo likely was less concerned about this organization because it was not directly associated with the Dominican order as were the chapters at Sant'Eustorgio and Santa Maria della Rosa.

As Maria Cecilia Visentin has observed, there is some iconographical evidence of a strong Rosary tradition at the basilica of Sant'Eustorgio dating from as early as 1444.[13] Yet the earliest extant archival document associated with the Confraternity of the Rosary at Sant'Eustorgio dates from 1568 and pertains to the sale of property belonging to Antonio Clerici in order to provide for a benefice in the basilica; how this benefice related specifically to the activities of the Confraternity itself remains unclear and, thus, it is not possible to establish a founding date for the Confraternity from it.[14] In his description of the church published in 1737, moreover, Serviliano Latuada mentions that its Rosary chapel with frescoes by Federico Macagni and Andrea Porta was then undergoing enlargement and redecoration commissioned by the Confraternity of the Rosary, and further notes that the original chapel was finished in 1575 through donations of the faithful.[15] The surviving records of the donations and expenditures of the Confraternity of the Rosary at Sant'Eustorgio depart from 1604, and these demonstrate that between 1603 and 1662 the organization raised funds for charity by auctioning clothes and jewelry. The only entries for music are payments to trumpeters, and these payments appear directly related to the auctions, as several of them include the lists of "things sold to the [sound of the] trumpet."[16] According to the extant printed evidence, Jacopo Filippo Cabiago was the organist at Sant'Eustorgio in 1626, but nothing is known of his connection, if any, to the Confraternity of the Rosary.[17]

The earliest extant archival reference to a Confraternity of the Rosary at Santa Maria della Rosa is found in the aforementioned diary of Casale. It reports that on 25 March 1578 Casale enrolled his son David in the Confraternity of the Rosary at Santa Maria della Rosa.[18] A register of the notarial instruments and other archival documents housed in the confraternity's archive as of 1716, moreover, departs from 7 February 1581 with an accord between the "Scuola of Santa Maria del Santissimo Rosario" and Prete Paolo, Priore of Santa Maria delle Grazie, who was to celebrate a daily mass, and contains a number of additional entries for the 1580s.[19] Perhaps the most interesting of these is note of the expenses to be covered through donations by various benefactors in constructing two sepulchers, two sacristies, four altars, and two walls near the pulpit of the church dated 10 January 1583.[20] It not only suggests that the major renovations to the interior of the church undertaken in the 1590s originated in the previous decade but also confirms, to a certain extent, Carlo Borromeo's observation on 12 July 1584 that "those of the aforementioned [Santa Maria della] Rosa had so large a donation in the past year in that church that they considered returning most of it to the Covent of [Santa Maria delle] Grazie."[21] The donations collected by the chapter of the Confraternity of the Rosary at Santa Maria della Rosa, were, in fact, a major point of contention between the chapter and Borromeo, for it had gone over his head and secured a license to collect donations from the public at large, an activity prohibited of confraternities by the archiepiscopal offices, from the Magistrate of Health of the city of Milan.[22] Public donations were, from the point of view of the Confraternity, essential to the completion of the structure that housed it, and Borromeo's persistent opposition to the collection of them may have been the impetus for the establishment on 11 February 1585 of a sister confraternity at Santa Maria della Rosa under the title Society of the Most Holy Name of God. Although a copy of the foundation instrument for this organization of approximately thirty male scholars was retained in the archive of the Confraternity of the Rosary at Santa Maria della Rosa,[23] the instrument itself specifies neither the relationship between the Society of the Most

Holy Name of God and Confraternity of the Rosary nor the role this confraternity played within the church itself.[24] The body of surviving documentation does suggest, however, that with the founding of this sister organization the decoration and appointment of Santa Maria della Rosa's interior was undertaken in earnest, and, further, that this sister organization likely played a role in retaining the church's prominence as a primary seat of the Confraternity of the Rosary in Milan.

The erection of Borromeo's competing Confraternity of the Rosary in the Duomo on 25 March 1584 was announced via a printed copy of a pastoral letter in which the particulars of the erection, the basic purpose and activities of the organization, and the significance of the Rosary and its mysteries were discussed. The letter included an invitation to participate and an order that the letter be read on the first Sunday of the month, the day on which the Confraternity held its monthly procession, for the next six months.[25] The letter continued to circulate in print well after Borromeo's death, for an elaborate printed version featuring a miniature woodcut of the Virgin and child handing a Rosary to a kneeling Archbishop Carlo Borromeo was issued by Filippo Ghisolfi, a printer active in the second quarter of the seventeenth century (figure 4.1). The figures in the woodcut are posed beneath a tree and the portrait is encircled by a garland of flowers.[26]

In addition to serving as a reference to the tree of Jesse, the tree that shelters the figures in the woodcut is emblematic of the Madonna dell'Albore, the altar in the Duomo to which Borromeo assigned the Confraternity and that reportedly housed an image of the Madonna that was carried in procession on the first Sunday of the month.[27] At the outset of Borromeo's tenure, this altar, which from 1517 had been devoted to the Madonna and Child, was situated to the immediate left of the main altar. In 1577, however, it was transferred to the *capocroce* of the left transept underneath of the newly constructed organ. The idea of installing a Confraternity of the Rosary at this altar may well have been related to another tradition already established in the Duomo of which Borromeo took advantage both during and immediately following the plague of 1576, namely the singing of the Ave Maria at the altar of Santa Maria del Pilone at the beginning of the Vespers hour.

All of Carlo Borromeo's efforts to promote the singing of the Ave Maria and the Confraternity of the Rosary in the Duomo clearly were intended to bolster the practice of praying the Rosary throughout the diocese, and Federico Borromeo further elevated the latter activity by promoting Rosary processions during the early part of his tenure in

FIGURE 4.1. Woodcut from the pastoral letter of Carlo Borromeo printed by Filippo Ghisolfi. ASDM, Archivio spirituale X, Metropolitana LXXX (Visite pastorali e documenti aggiunti), fasc. 24, by permission of Milano, Archivio Storico Diocesano.

Milan, perhaps in an effort to underscore his title, Cardinale "Santa Maria degli Angeli." On 3 September 1595, for example, Casale recorded in his diary that upon Federico Borromeo's entrance into the city as archbishop, he accompanied the Madonna del Rosario in procession throughout the Duomo:

> Memorial how the first time that he entered into the Duomo after his entry, the aforementioned cardinal said low mass in the alley behind the entrance into the choir. And there he remained for the prayers and the high mass. And after dining he came to the Duomo and remained there for Vespers and Compline. And immediately after the Madonna del Rosario was carried in the Duomo. And he accompanied her in procession with the banner of the Madonna because in that day the Madonna in relief known as dell'Arbore is not carried.[28]

Casale further reports that ten days later, on the feast of the Nativity of the Virgin, Federico Borromeo led another procession of the Madonna del Rosario in the Duomo, this time with the clergy of the Duomo and the seminary, and he further suggests that in this case the Cardinal was particularly impressed by the singing of the Ave Maria that occurred at the close of the event:

> Memorial how on the 13th after his entrance, which was the feast of the Nativity of the Madonna that is held in the Duomo, the aforementioned Cardinal sang the first high mass that he sang in Milan . . . and many were the ceremonies made at that mass, as many as were possible. And Vespers and Compline were done similarly after dinner. And immediately after the procession of the Madonna of the Rosary called dell'Arbore, actually the one of relief in her tabernacle, was held. And there was the Cardinale himself with all of the Seminary and all of the clergy only of the Duomo. At the aforementioned Mass, Vespers, and procession there was an infinite number of people. And at the sounding of the Ave Maria he complimented everything.[29]

Such references show that the Ave Maria in Duomo and the Confraternity of the Rosary, although separate organizations with distinct devotional activities, were linked in practice by the shared central reliance on the Ave Maria.

Under Federico Borromeo, the aforementioned pastoral letter of Carlo Borromeo announcing the erection of the Confraternity in the Duomo was reprinted and circulated several times[30] along with printed copies of the indulgences earned for activities associated with the Rosary and its Confraternity.[31] In addition to those at the Duomo, San Protasio in Campo, Sant'Eustorgio, and Santa Maria della Rosa, moreover, new companies were established in San Nazaro in Barona in 1595,[32] and San Lorenzo Maggiore by 1527,[33] as well as in a number of parish churches outside the city walls by 1630. There was even some heated competition among these groups. In 1627 Sant'Eustorgio lodged a complaint against nearby San Lorenzo, arguing that the erection of a Confraternity of the Rosary in the latter church was illegitimate because it lacked the authorization of the Dominican prior general.[34] Although the Dominicans at Sant'Eustorgio were initially supported by local authorities in their efforts to abolish the Confraternity of the Rosary at San Lorenzo and continued to vigorously oppose its erection, the dignitaries at San Lorenzo persisted, and by 1659 the controversy had found its way to the Congregation of Sacred Rites and Rituals in Rome, which apparently suggested a simple compromise of asking San Lorenzo's organization to celebrate the feast of the Rosary on a different day.[35] It was likely a bittersweet victory for both groups. The Dominicans at Sant'Eustorgio never entirely succeeded in preventing the authorities at San Lorenzo Maggiore from accomplishing what Carlo Borromeo had succeeded in doing at the Duomo, and neither Confraternity of the Rosary ever quite achieved the civic status of the one sponsored by the Dominicans at Santa Maria della Rosa.

THE CONFRATERNITY OF THE ROSARY
AT SANTA MARIA DELLA ROSA

Despite some initial competition from the chapter at the Duomo, the Milanese church of Santa Maria della Rosa boasted the strongest Rosary tradition in seventeenth-century Milan. Founded by the Dominicans of Santa Maria delle Grazie in 1480, Santa Maria della Rosa was intended as a central location in which the Milanese populace might congregate for the administration of the sacraments, the praying of the Rosary, and the singing of the Salve on Saturdays and principal Marian feasts throughout the year.[36] The church was situated immediately southwest of the Duomo and its basic structure completed around 1495.[37] Little is known about the activities of its Confraternity of the Rosary before 1585, but with the establishment of the sister Society of the Most Holy Name of God, its deputies began collecting relics and arranging for the decoration of the interior.[38] Between 1585 and 1600, they reconstructed the main chapel and the chapel of S. Georgio (to the left of the main altar), replaced the ancona on the altar of the Rosary with an even larger one, placed a balustrade and an iron grate before the main altar, decorated the vault of the church, constructed an organ, and began work on the choir lofts.[39]

Although Santa Maria della Rosa was razed during the early nineteenth century, the extant documents reveal that the organ was central to its interior decoration from the outset. A map of the interior space dated c. 1574 from the Raccolta Bianconi in Milan (figure 4.2) shows that the church was constructed in the German Gothic style with a single nave over a basic cruciform. Four side chapels lined each side of the nave, with the main altar positioned in the apse opposite the south door and the altar of the Rosary in the first chapel on the right.[40] It should be noted, however, that the orientation of the edifice itself is shown inconsistently in extant maps of the surrounding area dating from 1603 to 1722, as some show the altar on the northwest end and others on the southeast.[41] In any case, the organ, which was commissioned by the Confraternity of the Rosary and constructed by Cristoforo Valvasore, was, according to most early accounts, placed directly behind the main altar. The contract for the instrument, which is dated 31 May 1588 and preserved in the fondo Notarile of the Archivio di Stato in Milan, describes an organ of fifty keys and eleven ranks "with that high finish, beauty, and burnish like that [of Sant'Angelo in Milan] and with six mantle covers of Bulgarian leather from Russia."[42]

That the organ was intended as an integral part of a visual program that would inspire visitors of the church to the meditation of the Mulier Fortis is clear not only from the contract but also from surviving descriptions of the church by Milanese historians writing in the two successive centuries. All of them mention the organ, describing in particular detail the organ screens of Graziano Cossali of Brescia and the surrounding frescoes by the Fiamminghini brothers depicting the 1571 naval victory of the Christian League against the Turks at Lepanto, a triumph that, as noted above, was attributed to the processions held by the individual chapters of the Confraternity of the Rosary on the day of the battle, and, because of her favorable response, to the Mulier Fortis in turn. In 1666, for example, Galeazzo Gualdo Priorato described the interior of the church as follows:

> The church is finely squared and fully painted from top to bottom by Giovanni Battista and Marco Fiamenghi. On the façade near the organ is depicted the naval battle against the Turk given by the Catholic League on the feast of S. Giustiziana in 1572 [sic.] with the victory of the Christians. The doors of the organ are in the hand of the Brescian Grazio Cosselle. There are pictures by Ambrosio Figino and Camillo Proccacino, and two statues over the door by Annibale Fontana.[43]

Some seventy years later Serviliano Latuada described the instrument and its surrounding frescoes in even greater detail:

> In facing the main altar one sees a most beautiful organ of considerable size, supported by several columns of vivid stone over which rests the balconies of ornamented wood, and [the organ] is concealed by the guides, on which was depicted a bit before by the Brescian Cossali the triumphs of David on one side

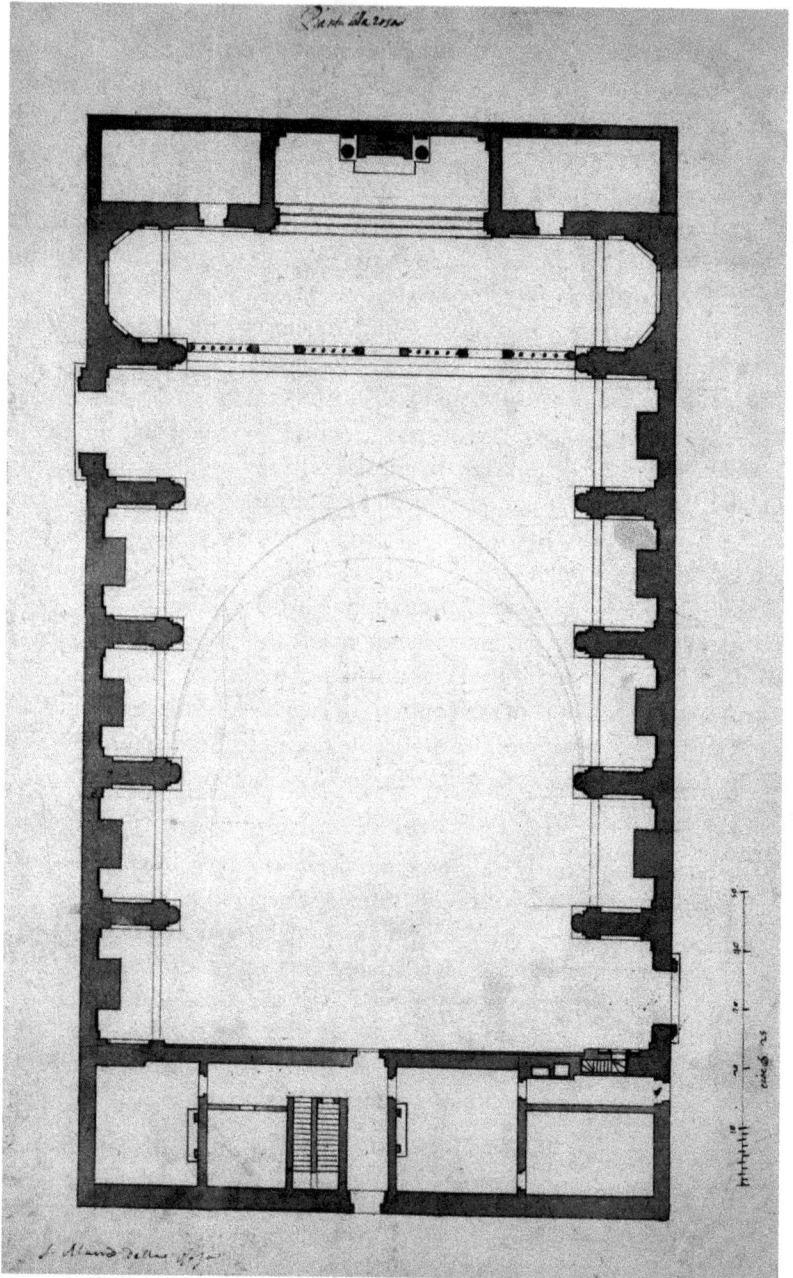

FIGURE 4.2. Map of Santa Maria della Rosa, c. 1574, Raccolta Bianconi V.24–25, courtesy of Milano, Archivio Storico Civico e Biblioteca Trivulziana. Copyright © Commune di Milano.

and those of Judith on the other . . . all [the antique pictures], as we would write, that dress this church are the works of the Fiamminghini brothers; those on the wall beside the organ presented in a lifelike manner the naval victory achieved by the Catholic forces against the Turks near the Gulf of Lepanto during the Pontificate of Saint Pius V. And truthfully they are so lifelike, portraying ships, trawlers, galleys, onslaughts, pillaging, fires, murders, and shipwrecks, that one is not able to withdraw from them immediately, the eye gazing in wonder at such a well-expressed victory.[44]

The contracts for the frescoes and the screens have not been located, but other registers and notary documents indicate that the former were well underway, if not finished, by 1603,[45] while the latter were completed on 1 July 1597 at a cost to the Confraternity of lire 1.200,000.[46] Casale reports that the organ was first played on 25 November 1590,[47] while the choir lofts, which were positioned to the immediate left and right of the main altar, were not begun until July 1598.[48] It is not likely that work on the frescoes preceded the construction of the choir lofts.

MUSIC FOR SANTA MARIA DELLA ROSA

Although the decoration of the organ fulfilled certain visual requirements in the adoration of the Mulier Fortis, its primary purpose was to support a sounding scriptural exegesis that expounded on the biography of Mary, the related mysteries of the Rosary, and the power of the Mulier Fortis. The first composer known to have been associated with the institution was Agostino Sodarini, who is identified as the organist there in the frontispiece to his *Canzoni à 4 & 8 voci* of 1608.[49] The *Canzoni* themselves are primarily instrumental, but the last five works in the collection are eight-voice motets and canzona-motets [50] on texts from the Song of Songs,[51] Psalms 95 and 65, and *Salve virgo et mater*. According to the dedication, many of the canzonas contained were performed at the palazzo of Soderini's patron, Luca Francesco Brivio, several years prior to their publication.[52] Yet the texts of at least three of the motets and canzone-motets, namely the two settings of the Song of Songs and *Salve virgo et mater* are entirely characteristic of the Marian scriptural exegesis promoted at Santa Maria della Rosa.

Salve virgo et mater, in fact, addresses the Mulier Fortis.[53] It hails the Virgin as chief among women, as the most chaste, beautiful, and blessed, and as the vessel for the conception and bringing forth of the

Son of God. The text of the motet can be seen as bipartite, since the first half catalogues the attributes and contributions of the Virgin while the second describes the various choirs that have been called upon to praise her.[54] The motet itself, however, is divided temporally into three sections. Across these sections the text is redistributed into a three-part rhetorical structure similar to that of Costa's *Virgo prudentissima:* an opening exordium that acclaims the Virgin (mm. 1–32), a central section in which a chorus of Angels and Archangels celebrate her (mm. 33–47), and a final Alleluia section (mm. 48–67). The second of these, which describes the heavenly choir, is set apart from the first and third by a shift to triple meter. Although the motet is, like Benedetto Regio's *Ave virgo gratiosa,* for eight voices divided into two CATB choirs, it relies somewhat less on the technique of creating a dialogue of alternation between the two choirs and instead makes greater use of the full eight voices through the frequent overlapping of the entries of the two groups. Some alternatim passages, however, are found, and these, which are often set off by clearly articulated cadences, seem to be systematically linked to parallel repetitions of short phrases of the text. Even when an alternatim texture is introduced, however, it often disintegrates into pseudo-polyphony through the sudden staggering of the entrances of the two choirs. Such staggering of the entrances seems to be a byproduct of the accelerated repetition that marks the close of the individual sections, a rhetorical device that simulates the rhythmic meditation described by Ignatius and seen in the finis of many works of this nature. Equally noteworthy from a meditational point of view, moreover, is the constant shifting between the G cantus mollis and the B-flat durus tonalities, which serves to re-engage the listener as he mentally processes the numerous repeated phrases. A striking foray into the third-related B-flat durus tonality also serves to distinguish, along with the shift to triple meter, the aforementioned heavenly choir that comprises the second section.

Soderini's five motets invite, in the absence of other documentation about musicians, some speculation regarding the forces that may have performed in the two lofts that reportedly flanked the organ in early seventeenth-century Santa Maria della Rosa. They are voiced for a cohort of eight singers comprising two sopranos, two altos, two tenors, and two basses that could have been assigned one or two to a part. Such a distribution of the voices seems to have been common in the choirs of other Marian cults in early seventeenth-century Milan, including the Madonna of Miracles at Santa Maria presso San Celso and the

Ave Maria in Duomo. There is, of course, no indisputable proof that Soderini's motets and canzona-motets were ever performed at Santa Maria della Rosa while he was the organist there, but the likelihood that he attached these five motets to the 1608 collection of *Canzoni* because he had recently prepared them for use in the church is strengthened by the fact that three of them are designated as "motetti di canzon." The development of this distinctive, yet liturgically functional genre in which aspects of the instrumental canzona are adapted to the imitative motet was particularly associated with well-known organists working in major North Italian churches, especially those in Milan.[55]

The collection most closely associated with Santa Maria della Rosa during this period is Andrea Cima's *Il secondo libro delli concerti* of 1627.[56] Its title page identifies the composer as the organist at Santa Maria della Rosa and Santa Maria delle Grazie, and its dedication, which was addressed to the Milanese senator Giovanni Battista Arconato, describes the collection as a "memoir or catalogue of [Cima's] spiritual thoughts." The dedication further notes that the composer had drawn musical inspiration for the collection from Arconato's sister, Suor Paola Maria, of the Monastery of Santa Maria del Vetere.[57] An examination of the contents (Appendix C, table 3) uncovers an emphasis upon settings of Marian texts, texts from the Song of Songs, and the Psalms, and, as Robert Kendrick has already noted,[58] reveals that three concerti were individually dedicated to local nuns known for their singing abilities. Not all of the Marian texts can be attached to a specific feast, but *Vocem Mariae* seems clearly intended for the Visitation,[59] one of the five Marian feasts celebrated by the Confraternity of the Rosary. Other Marian texts seem to have a more ubiquitous usage. The dialogue *O Quam humilis,* for example, expounds upon the humility, benignity, and purity of the virgin, making all the usual allusions to the fragrant odors emitted by the garden of her spotless soul, while *O Domina nostra Sanctissima Maria* supplicates the Virgin for intercession. *Una es. O Maria* pays homage to the woman dressed in the Sun and standing on the moon of Revelation 12:1, a passage associated with the Virgin's fecundity and often interpreted as referring the Immaculate Conception in meditation books and artistic representations of the period, but in this particular case, the woman severs the head of the dragon, a direct reference to the Mulier Fortis.[60] Homage to the Mulier Fortis is perhaps most strongly present, however, in *Gaudete filiae sion,* a concerto specifically designated in the print for the celebration of the feast of the Rosary (figure 4.3). Here the daughters of Zion, which commentators of the period variously identified with the Jewish nation, the Scribes and Pharisees, the adolescent sons of Jerusalem, and the church triumphant[61] are exhorted to rejoice in the fact that Mary, queen of the Rosary, has destroyed the hydra and the dragon.[62] In keeping with the *Gaudete*'s exhortation to rejoice, the collection includes other laudate-type texts, such as Psalms 150, 80, 65, and 95, as well as songs of supplication, such as Psalms 122, 70, and 87. All of these might easily have found a place in the celebrations held on the first Sunday of every month.

Paolo Morigia's *Calendario volgare* reveals that in addition to the confraternal mass and procession on the first Sunday of the month, Santa Maria della Rosa was by 1620 the principal civic site for the celebration of six feasts annually: the Circumcision on January 1, the Visitation on July 2 and the Assumption on August 15, both of which were among the five principal Marian feasts observed by the Confraternity of the Rosary, the feast of St. George the Warrior on April 24, the feast of the Rosary on the first Sunday in October, and the procession commemorating the 1571 Victory over the Turks on October 7.[63] Therefore, Cima's inclusion of a concerto in honor of San Carlo Borromeo, canonized in 1610, appears to be somewhat of an anomaly. It likely found its way into the collection because the former archbishop was a revered local saint who, along with St. Ambrose, occupied a position of particular prominence among those assigned to the Ambrosian calendar.

That settings of the Song of Songs also figure prominently in Cima's collection is not at all surprising, considering the enthusiasm with which the biblical text was embraced during the late sixteenth and early seventeenth centuries and the role that it had played in the Marian *historia,* particularly with regard to the Assumption.[64] Scores of commentaries were issued by European printers, some of them multiple times, which dissected its various chapters in great detail. This was not, of course, an entirely new phenomenon, as most of these commentaries drew on a host of earlier sermons and tracts by such scholars as Ambrose, Bernard, Jerome, Bede, and Rupert Abbatus. Most of the commentaries seem to recognize three primary interpretations of the beloved pair in the Song of Songs, namely Christ and the church, Christ and the soul, and Christ and the Virgin. Yet the church, the soul, and the Virgin were often seen as symbolically somewhat synonymous. In a commentary that enjoyed at least four editions during the second decade of the seventeenth century, Michele Ghisleri systematically dis-

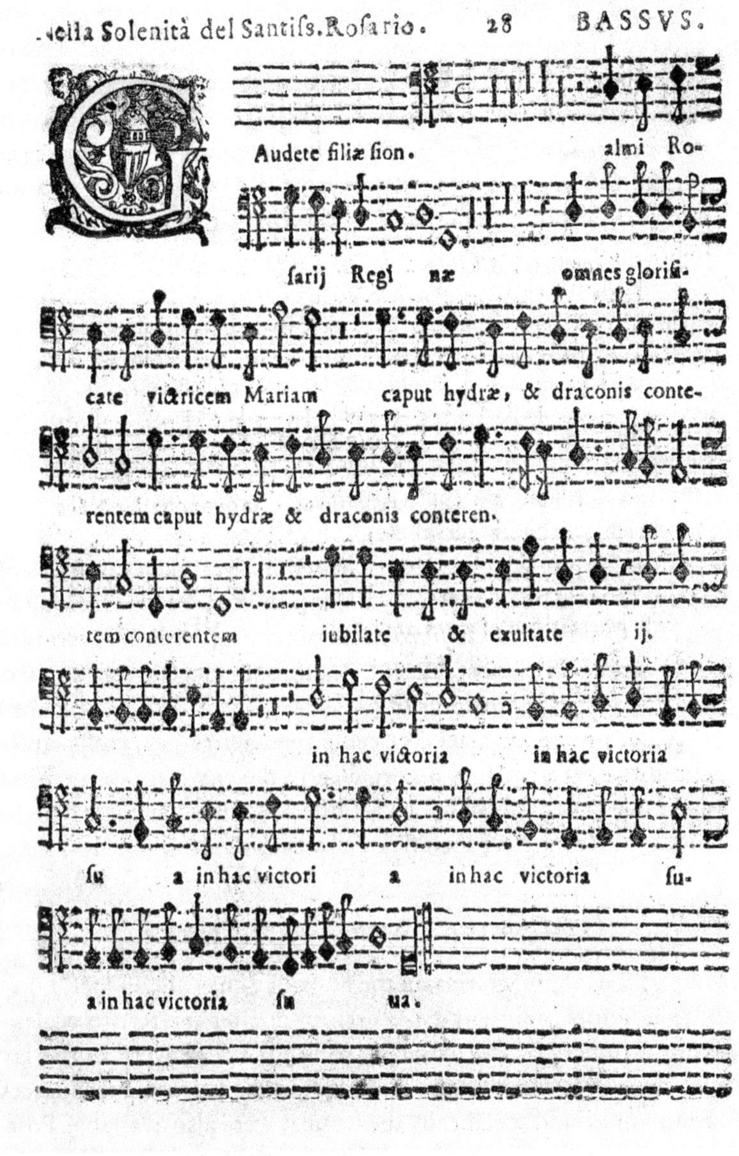

FIGURE 4.3. Giovanni Andrea Cima, *Il secondo libro delli concerti, a due, trè, & quattro, voci* (Milano: appresso Filippo Lomazzo, 1627), bassus, f. 28, Milano, Biblioteca Nazionale Braidense, musica B.4, by permission of the Ministero per i Beni e le Attività Culturale.

sected the Song of Songs in its prophetic relevance to the church, the soul, and the Virgin by considering the interpretation of each line of the text separately and providing documentation from earlier writers to support his analysis.[65] According to Ghisleri, the text of Cima's motet *Audi dulcis amica me, nigra sum sed Formosa* (Songs 1: 4–5) contrasts the impurity of the flesh with the purity of the Virgin's soul, thereby explaining the purification of the daughters of Jerusalem as prophesied by Isaiah (Isaiah 4:4).[66] *Indica mihi* (Song 1:7) is the Virgin's lamentation on the death of her son. It is prophesied in David's lament on the death of Jonathan (II Kings 1) and Jesus's temporary disappearance at the age of twelve during the return from Jerusalem (Luke 2).[67] *Quam pulchra es* (Song 4) elaborates on the Virgin's virtue and spotless nature, giving particular emphasis to her faith, humility, and charity, and confirming the doctrine of the Immaculate Conception.[68] In such commentaries, biblical references to the Israelites are often interpreted as metaphorical of the universal church, while the joys, trials, and triumphs of the Virgin, which are represented in the fifteen mysteries of the Rosary, are explained as synonymous with those of the church and soul.[69] Thus, Cima's *Secondo libro delli concerti* represents, in terms of its textual content, the most current theological concepts of the time. Whether this so-called "memoir of his spiritual thoughts" was shaped by the study of religious tracts, or came together rather haphazardly through his ongoing work as an organist in the city[70] and some passing contact with meditation books is difficult to ascertain, but there is undoubtedly a strong hermeneutic cast to the collection.

MEDITATING THE MADONNA OF THE ROSARY

Most of the commentaries on the Song of Songs are, in fact, fairly technical in nature, and may have been of greater interest to ecclesiastics and members of the monastic sects than they were to the lay audience. However, many other less intimidating hermeneutic sources on Marian topics, and specifically the Rosary, were also available. Post-Tridentine devotion to the Rosary not only encouraged the production of books that recounted Rosary legends and miracles or the life of the Virgin but also inspired Latin and vernacular texts that expounded upon each Pater Noster and Ave Maria of the Rosary via short poetic or prose meditations. The latter volumes usually are organized according to the fifteen mysteries of the Rosary into three large sections of fifty meditations, each of which was seen as constituting a single Rosary or *corona:* one for the five joyful mysteries, another for the five sorrowful ones, and, finally, a third for the five glorious ones.

Some of the meditation books, such as the *Novo Rosario della Gloriosissima Vergine Maria* published in Venice by Bernardo Giunti in 1588, feature vernacular meditations arranged in simple standard poetic structures such as ottava rima.[71] This approach seems intended to reach the audience by appropriating common literary and dramatic formats that can be tailored to the sort of intimate meditative dialogue made popular by Ignatius of Loyola while still allowing for narrative in an accessible style. Although the individual meditations in some measure define a specific event or theological construct for meditation, at some point in each stanza the Virgin usually is addressed in the second person or familiar voice and asked to intercede on the part of the faithful. Moreover, references to prophetic texts from the bible typically are mixed with those from popular mythology, as can be seen in the sixth meditation on the mystery of the Assumption from the aforementioned *Novo Rosario.* It makes reference not only to the woman dressed in the sun of Revelation 12:1, but also to Cerberus, the multi-headed beast of Greek mythology who guards the gates of Hades and, in this particular context, stands in for the great dragon of Revelation 12:

Maria del Sol vestita,
      e i piedi adorna
	Mary dressed in the sun
	      and with feet

Del bel globo argentino,
      apri in noi gli occhi;
	resting on the silver globe,
	      open our eyes:

Ecco Cerbero,
      ancor ch'erge le corna,
	Here is Cerberus,
	      who still raises his horns

Per far che'l servo tuo fidel trabocchi:	*to confound your faithful servant.*

Deh benche'n Cielo
      sei con noi soggiorna,
	Ah, although in the heavens,
	      you remain with us,

Che caggiam' senza te misteri,
      e sciocchi,
	for without you we contrive
	      mysteries and foolishness.

& dal superno Throno in noi
      ti degna,
	And from the celestial throne
	      you deign to

Mirar, ch'un sol tuo sguardo
      il Ciel n'insegna.
	gaze at us, because a single one
	      of your glances instructs us
	      of heaven.[72]

Still other meditation books appear to have been initially intended for clerical or monastic use, but thereafter were introduced into the secular sphere. One such volume is Bartolomeo Scalvo's *Rosario preces ad gloriosam Dei genetricem Mariam Virginem,* a collection of 150 prose meditations in Latin that was first published in Milan by diocesan printer Pacifico Pontio in March 1569[73] and reissued in the vernacular under the title *Le Meditationi del Rosario della Gloriosa Maria Vergine* the same year.[74] Like the meditations of the *Novo Rosario,* Scalvo's are divided into three sections of fifty meditations according to the respective classifications of the fifteen mysteries. They also include a few decorative woodcuts to illustrate selected mysteries, but these are rather crude and offer only limited visual interest. In 1583, however, the vernacular edition of Scalvo's meditations was reprinted by Domenico and Giovanni Battista fratelli della Guerra of Venice, this time with a woodcut to illustrate every single mystery. (See, for example, figure 1.2 of the Introduction.)[75] The addition of the illustrations is highlighted in the title of the volume, thus suggesting that the visual elaborations were considered an important meditative tool. Maria Luisa Gatti Perer has argued, in fact, that the illustrations brought together the depiction of familiar scenes in the life of the Virgin and visual symbols associated with the Madonna of the Rosary that can be traced back to earlier iconographical representations, and, in particular, to those in Alberto de Castello's *Rosario della gloriosa Vergine Maria* of 1522.[76] The illustrations were clearly intended to assist the reader in holding the mental images so important in the popular Counter-Reformative systems of meditation described by such writers as Ignatius of Loyola and Federico Borromeo, both of whom suggest that the stimulation of the senses was imperative in helping humans maintain a heightened level of spiritual contemplation.[77] To this end Scalvo's meditations themselves are fairly formulaic in structure and feature an exordium that introduces the subject of the meditation followed by a second section that expands on it, partly via references to scriptural passages that had been appropriated to reinforce the biography of the Virgin. Moreover, they almost invariably close with a request for intercession. In a manner similar to that employed in the illustrations, therefore, the verbal depiction of familiar scenes is combined with traditional literary symbolism drawn from the scriptures, and these facets are intertwined in a manner that triggers and sustains the desired mental image, as can be seen in Part II, Meditation 40, which is devoted to the sorrowful mystery of Mary encountering her son on Calvary:

MARY, most sainted mother, setting out towards the city of Jerusalem with all alacrity and speed in order to meet your most sweet son, quite tearful and sorrowful because of the past afflictions and pains of that most precious body, yet much more distressed because of the future travails, in fact because of the very instant his death was forecast by all: Alas, how many lamentations were sent to the heavens from the street? How may tears? How many sobs? And how many sighs? How many wretched visions of your most amiable son before the eyes such that you seemed to have the countenance of a woman somewhat removed from herself? And how miserable was that cross, [was] that beating of your most sainted hands when having arrived in the city you found yourself blocked from being near your most beloved son by the large mob. And finally how incomparable and extreme was that sorrow which transfigured your soul like the most pungent knife, the heart having seen that most tormented body under the weight of such a mighty cross, violated by those dogs at the ascent of the Mount. That JESUS, the son of God, so disfigured and tormented, enduring with the greatest compassion the falsehoods themselves, and the exhibition of being led so ignominiously, like the most simple Lamb, to the extreme torture of the cross, near to whom, O MARY, most sainted Mother, intercede for us sinners. Amen.[78]

If the texts and illustrations of the meditations were intended to assist the reader visually in holding particular mental images even as they reinforced traditional symbols, then the music must have served a similar auditory function. Like the individual meditations for each Ave Maria or Our Father found in Rosary meditation books of the period, Cima's *Gaudete filiae Sion* (Appendix D, example 4.1) for the feast of the Rosary is divided into two parts: a short exordium that introduces the subject of the meditation and a longer section that expands on it, partly via references to related scriptural passages (table 4.1). The opening section (measures 1–20), which exhorts the daughters of Zion to rejoice and congratulate the victorious queen of the Rosary,[79] features a tenor solo firmly grounded in the tonality of G cantus durus that is punctuated with a short trio containing several medial articulations on A and D followed by a strong cadence on G. The lengthy expansion on the exordium that follows (measures 21–70) opens with solos for the cantus, altus, and tenor voices followed by passages of four-voice imitation flanked by short homophonic tuttis. Textual references to Zechariah 2:10, Psalm 9, Psalm 48, Isaiah 61, which the meditations of Scalvo associate with the glory of the Virgin,[80] and Revelation 12, a biblical text considered emblematic of the Virgin's dominion over evil, abound throughout. As in the Rosary meditations of Scalvo, repetition is confined primarily to the closing line of text, and this repetition is underscored by an increase in the harmonic rhythm and a subsequent prolongation of the G tonality, thus driving the exhortation to rejoice to a proverbial fever pitch.

Cima's *Vocem Mariae* (Appendix D, example 4.2) for the feast of the Visitation, another of the major events celebrated by the Confraternity, departs slightly from the standard structure found in the meditational literature in that rather than developing a tightly constructed exordium that specifies the subject matter of the meditation, the first part of the piece is devoted to graphically recounting the well-known meeting between the Virgin and her cousin Elizabeth.[81] Only after the exchange between the two women has been fully reported is the momentous declaration "Blessed art thou among women and blessed is the fruit of thy womb" introduced, and this is real the subject of the meditation, albeit delayed until almost the end of the piece (table 4.2). Robert Kendrick justifiably described this concerto as a showpiece especially suited to the voices of the nuns to whom it is dedicated,[82] but the alternate voicing provided by the composer in the table of contents suggests that he intended the piece to be useful in a variety of venues. Cima announces this musical meditation in G cantus mollis by declaiming the opening phrase "Vocem Mariae" homophonically twice in a rising sequence over a descending bass. He then draws the listener into the narration via a highly ornamented imitative duet featuring several voice exchanges, followed by a series of figurative solos that cadence alternately on D, G, and the occasional C. A heightened musical tension is achieved throughout the aforementioned solos by using the cadences on D, G, and C to demarcate a systematic unfolding of the text in which each successive phrase is first presented in the cantus and then echoed at the fourth or fifth below by the tenor. In addition, the most significant moments in the narrative are underscored by shifts of meter. The seesawing tonal centers and metrical shifts are brought to a halt with the advent of Elizabeth's much anticipated utterance "benedicta tu in mulieries" (blessed art thou among women), which is marked by the introduction of extensive text repetition. Ignatius of Loyola argued that such repetition was essential to eliminating distractions and focusing

TABLE 4.1.
Formal Layout of Giovanni Andrea Cima, *Gaudete filiae Sion*

TEXT	VOICING	MUSICAL EVENTS
Section 1: Gaudete filiae Sion, jubilate virgines Hierusalem, laetamini populi fideles	tenore	solo cadence A
et congratulamini gloriosae victrici Mariae,	tenore, cantus, altus	trio begins
almi Rosarij Reginae;	tenore, cantus, altus	trio, articulations on A & D, cadence on G
Section 2: afferte rosas, et liliae ex conuallibus syon,	cantus	solo with sequence
diem festum agite in psalterio et cantico,	altus	solo, cadence D
date magnificentiam nomini eius et in voce laudis,	tenore	solo, cadence G
omnes glorificate victricem Mariam	cantus, altus, tenore, bassus	all homophonically
caput hydrae, et draconis conterentem.	cantus, altus, tenore, bassus	imitation a 4
Jubilate et exultate in hac victoria sua.	tenore, altus, cantus	imitation a 3, followed by cadence on G
Jubilate et exultate in hac victoria sua,	cantus, altus, tenore, bassus	all homophonically [G, V/A, A, D, V/G, cadence G]
in hac victoria sua.	cantus, altus, tenore, bassus	prolongation of G [paired imitation, imitation a 4, cadence G]

the intellect, so Cima's application of it here underscores the point at which the movement toward transcendence was intended to occur. In addition to the use of extensive repetition, the "benedicta tu in mulieries" section is characterized by a sudden reversion to the imitative duet texture and voice exchanges that opened the concerto. Aside from a cantus solo that marks the closing "Alleluia," this imitative texture is retained throughout the remainder of the work, and although a few cadences on alternate tones are found, cadences on G are far more predominant. Despite its stronger anchoring in G cantus mollis, however, the second half of the concerto is not without intensity. As Kendrick has noted, the imitation, overlapping sequences, upward resolving dissonances, and extensive figuration add considerable excitement,[83] and these musical devices, when paired with the gradually increasing rate of text repetition employed throughout, must certainly have transported the listener to the desired state of transcendence. Thus, although the text of *Vocem Mariae* appears a continuous narrative, the standard division into two sections, with the second one focused solely on the meditation of a well-known phrase from the Ave Maria, is clearly articulated by the music. An increasing sense of transcendence is achieved musically in the second section through extensive repetition, as well as through the simultaneous implementation of common contrapuntal devices such as imitation, sequence, and upward resolving dissonances, all of which are articulated within the context of a fairly static harmonic background. The increasingly elaborate figuration executed by the soloists, moreover, would only have heightened the intensity of aforementioned musical effects considerably, and the potential aural impact of experiencing a live performance should not be underestimated, despite the possibility that viewing the singer might have detracted somewhat from the meditative atmosphere of the piece.

OTHER MUSICAL ROSARIES

Cima's *Secondo libro* was not the only musical Rosary to appear on the market in Milan during the 1620s. Another Rosary-inspired collection was published by printer Filippo Lomazzo just one year before Cima's *Secondo libro* was issued. Entitled *Flores praestantissimorum virorum* and dedicated to the accomplished young Polish singer and organist Constantine Czirenberg, the collection contains concerted sacred works, many of which are also on Marian texts, for one to four voices and instruments by Milan's most eminent composers (Appendix C, table 4). In its dedication, Lomazzo enumerates Constantine's musical virtues, comparing her to a variety of Greek gods and goddesses.[84] Katarzyna Grochowska has suggested that Lomazzo learned of Constantine through Prince Władysław, who visited the home of her father in Gdansk and heard her perform there just prior his 1624 voyage to Milan. According to the extant royal diaries, the prince attended services in a number of the Milanese churches during his visit there in order to partake of the current sacred literature. Although the content of the *Flores* cannot be tied to a particular church or cult, it most certainly represents the best music and musical talent that the city's churches had to offer at the time of the prince's visit. Prince Władysław's role in the compilation of the collection admittedly remains unclear, as there is no extant documentation connecting him directly with Lomazzo.[85] What is clear, however, is Lomazzo's obvious allusion to another well-known Rosary legend in Constantine's garland of "flowers collected by me" from "the most excellent men."[86] Second in popularity only to the account of the victory of Alain de la Roche, this legend, in its most familiar form, tells of a knight who was saved from a vengeful assailant when his attacker came upon him as he was praying the Rosary. The assailant was so mesmerized by a vision of the Virgin collecting the roses that emanated from the prayerful knight's mouth that he was divested of his anger.[87]

Rosary collections such as the *Flores* were not, of course, peculiar to Milan. In 1619, for example, the Roman publisher Luca Antonio Soldi issued a volume of twenty-two concerted motets by Giovanni Francesco Anerio under the title *Ghirlanda Di Sacre Rose Musicalmente Contesta, & Concertata*. The five-voiced motets contained include settings of Marian texts, psalms, and texts based on the Song of Songs. Anerio, then maestro di cappella at the recently constructed titular church of Santa Maria dei Monti and a musician in the household of the Avila family in Rome, dedicated the collection to his pupil and patron Isabella Avila.[88] Two years prior Isabella had been the dedicatee of Anerio's *Selva armonica,* a collection of concerted motets, spiritual madrigals, canzonette, dialogues, and arias intended as spiritual exercises in the style of the oratorian Agostino Manni.[89] That she, like Suor Paola Maria Arconata and Constantine Czirenberg, was a proficient musician seems evident considering the attention that Anerio lavished on her. The association of such collections with female patronmusicians is suggestive not only of the dominant role that women, who were generally prohibited from holding offices in the Confraternity of

TABLE 4.2.
Formal Layout of Giovanni Andrea Cima, *Vocem Mariae*.

MEASURE		VOICING	MUSICAL EVENTS
1–5	*Section 1:* Vocem Mariae	C, T, Basso	Homophonic declamation.
5–13	audivit Elisabeth et factum est	C, T, Basso	Ornamented imitation and voice exchange at the fifth.
13–18	ut audivit salutationem	C, T, Basso	Cantus solo cadencing on D, repeated as tenor solo at fifth cadencing on G.
19–39	exultavit infans in utero eius	C, T, Basso	*Mensural shift to 3.* Ornamented cantus solo cadencing on D, repeated as ornamented tenor solo at fourth below cadencing on G; ornamented imitation at the fourth below cadencing on D.
40–49	et repleta est de spiritu sancto	C, T, Basso	*Mensural shift to C.* Cantus solo cadencing on D, repeated as tenor solo at fifth with half cadence on C; imitation at fifth.
49–57	et voce magna exclamavit	C, T, Basso	Ornamented cantus solo, repeated as ornamented tenor solo at fourth below cadencing on G.
57–60	et dixit	C, T, Basso	Ornamented cantus solo cadencing on G, repeated as ornamented cantus solo cadencing on D.
60–88	*Section 2:* benedicta tu inter mulieries et benedictus fructus ventris tui.	C, T, Basso	Voice exchange at unison, imitation at fifth cadencing on C, imitation at fifth cadencing on G, imitation at fifth cadencing on F + extension to cadence on D, imitation at fifth cadencing on G.

MEASURE		VOICING	MUSICAL EVENTS
89–114	Alleluia.	C, T, Basso	***Mensural shift to 3.*** Cantus solo followed by sequential imitation cadencing on G, ornamented imitation at the unison cadencing on D, ornamented imitation at the fourth below cadencing on G, ornamented imitation at fifth disintegrating into ornamented homophony cadencing on G.

the Rosary, played in the social development of Rosary meditation, but also of the manner in which the church may have utilized such meditations to shape Post-Tridentine conceptions of motherhood and female virtue.

Several other musical Rosaries printed in Milan, in fact, appear intended primarily for private domestic use, which was entirely in keeping with the aims of the Confraternity of the Rosary, for no restrictions were placed on where the required weekly Rosary was to be prayed. What is especially fascinating about them, however, is that they, like Angelo Tignosi's 1605 collection of meditations entitled *Statua di Maria Vergine*,[90] are dedicated to female patrons on the occasion of the birth of a son, thus suggesting that they were intended as musical *deschi da parto*, or confinement-period presentation plates. Roberta J.M. Olson[91] and Maria Luisa Gatti Perer[92] have discussed the relationships in form and content between the *desco di parto* and the Rosary, and, indeed, the imaging of the Virgin in Rosary meditations and iconography overlaps considerably with that of another Marian cult that was among the most significant for the city's expectant mothers—the cult of the Madonna del Parto.

Chapter 5

❦

Clothed in the Sun
and Standing on the Moon

Meditating Motherhood
in the Cult of the Madonna del Parto

"A certain Jewish woman, very tired from labor and unable
to do anything but cry, and not expecting anything other than to
give up the spirit immediately, having given up on the midwife
and her pain and anguish nevertheless increasing, saw a great
light come from above when between many pains of the soul
and body and at the same time heard a voice from this light
which said "invoke the name of Mary and you will be saved."
The woman, all of a faithful heart and full of confidence
in the Lord, invoked the name of Mary with a loud
voice and immediately gave birth to a baby boy."[1]

—Silvano Razzi, pub. 1587

In her seminal study *Women of the Renaissance,* Margaret L. King
asserts that the lives of most Renaissance women were defined by
motherhood.[2] While women who nourished their own babies gave
birth every twenty-four to thirty months, those who sent out their
children to nurse conceived and brought children to term at an even
faster rate.[3] Infant mortality rates were relatively high and the pressure
to produce an heir fairly intense. The Milanese tradesman Giambattista
Casale, for example, reports that his first wife, Angela da Riva, brought
four children, including a set of twins, to term between 1553 and 1557,

only one of whom lived beyond the age of seven, while his second wife, Catelina d'Aqua, bore four children between 1562 and 1573, only two of whom survived infancy. In all, only three of Casale's eight children, one son and two daughters, lived to adulthood.[4] Casale does not mention whether or not his children were sent to nurse, but he does note that his son David's first male child was tended by his mother for a time before being sent to a nurse.[5] It has long been assumed that the poor nursed their own children, a phenomenon that, although not well documented, seems to be true considering the costs involved. Recent studies devoted to nursing practices in Florence between 1300 and 1530 show, however, that not only the nobility but also many established middle-class fathers, including successful artisans, merchants, notaries, and doctors, put children out to nurse. Those who could afford or otherwise arrange it (by using a slave or other household servant) hired a nurse in the home, especially if the child in question was a male heir, while many others sent their children out to the nearby countryside.[6] Despite the evident popularity of wet nursing—particularly among the noble classes—humanists, physicians, and theologians had long opposed the practice, arguing that the birth mother's milk was physically and morally essential to the development of the infant. This line of thinking was particularly prevalent during the Counter-Reformation, when both Protestant and Catholic theologians emphasized nursing as a moral responsibility of the birth mother. Thus, the Post-Tridentine church found itself in the difficult position of championing lactation by the mother, which had the effect of retarding birthrates, while fighting the parents' tendency to turn to natural contraception as a means of slowing infant birth, and, in turn, mortality rates.[7] Such a paradoxical message required a unifying theme, and the Post-Tridentine church found it in the already well-established cult of the Madonna del Parto.

HISTORY OF THE CULT OF THE MADONNA DEL PARTO

The cult of the Madonna del Parto first emerged in Italy around 1320. It owed its proliferation, in part, to the teachings of the Franciscans, which stressed the importance of the virtues of poverty, humility, and obedience. These and other graces were largely seen as monastic or feminine attributes in the Mediterranean cultures, and, thus, they quickly became associated with the Virgin, who, in submitting to the Virgin birth, demonstrated unsurpassed obedience and humility. Mendicant preachers, including Franciscans Bertold von

Regensburg (d. 1272) and San Bernardino of Siena (d. 1444), exhorted women to imitate the Virgin, and their admonitions took on a social, rather than a merely spiritual dimension. Books of hours, images of the Virgin, and Marian-themed songs, although overtly religious in their outward trappings, became instruments for social education, at the center of which was the feminine ideal of a virtuous, gentle, docile, and devoted mother.[8]

Visual representations of the Madonna del Parto had their origins in the Byzantine Maria Platytera or Madonna "more ample than the heavens," which in early iconography was depicted as the Virgin standing prayerfully with her hands on her chest, on her breast or otherwise near a clypeus that contained an image of the child organically aligned at the half breast.[9] According to Gianfranco Ravasi, the Maria Platytera itself derived from Egyptian art and mythology in which the womb was depicted as a potter's wheel or wood-turning lathe, an image that is referenced in Job 10: 8–11, where God is imagined as a potter inside the womb of the mother.[10] Other biblical references associated with the Virgin birth, including Galatians 4:4, Wisdom 7:1–2, Psalm 139: 13–16, and the Song of Songs 4 and 7, as well as certain Islamic and cabbalistic readings,[11] appear to have influenced the fourteenth-century transformation from Maria Platytera to Madonna del Parto in which the Virgin, usually clothed in the white of purity, the red of the mystical rose, and the blue of obscurity, is typically depicted standing and holding a book that symbolizes knowledge over her swelling womb.[12]

SHRINES FOR THE MADONNA DEL PARTO IN MILAN

Although iconographical depictions of the Madonna del Parto were especially popular in Tuscany and date primarily from the fourteenth and fifteenth centuries,[13] the cult also was popular in Milan between the fourteenth and sixteenth centuries and experienced a doctrinal revival of sorts during the Counter-Reformation at the hands of ecclesiastics who wished to promote the sanctity of both motherhood and lactation. At least four major institutions in Post-Tridentine Milan sponsored altars dedicated to the Madonna del Parto: Santa Maria dei Servi, Santa Maria presso San Celso, Santa Maria della Scala, and the Duomo. Interestingly enough, all of these churches, save the royal ducal chapel of Santa Maria della Scala, promoted popular Marian cults discussed in the previous chapters. Unfortunately, however, the images of the Madonna del Parto associated with them are more difficult to reconstruct because the altars devoted to the cult in all four institutions were either transferred to other locations or otherwise transformed during the succeeding centuries. Nonetheless, it is evident that the cult was visually manifest similarly in each. At Santa Maria dei Servi, which was razed in 1837, the cult was associated primarily with two relics, the girdle and the milk of the Virgin,[14] both of which were likely kept at the main altar, one of three devoted to the Virgin in the sixteenth-century church. By the second half of the sixteenth century this altar was decorated with an anonymous painting of the Madonna and Child flanked by Saints Vito and Modesto (figure 2.2).[15] In this image the Virgin is not nursing, but the relic of the milk preserved at the altar implies an association between the Madonna del Parto and Maria lactans.

In Santa Maria presso San Celso, a chapel was set aside for the Madonna del Parto as early as 3 September 1567, when a payment of L94 s8 was made to the sculptor Angelo Curiano for a sculpture to decorate the altar,[16] and, as noted earlier, a "festa della Espettatione" was celebrated there in her honor from at least 1573.[17] According to Serviliano Latuada, who authored a guide to the monuments of Milan that was published in 1737, the Madonna del Parto at Santa Maria presso San Celso was depicted "sitting in a rose-colored statue covered with glass and flanked by two paintings, that on the right portraying Sant'Anna with her most sainted infant daughter by Federico Panza and the other of San Carlo carrying the sacred nail in procession to this church (an event which took place in 1576 at the time of the plague and which obtained liberation from the plague through the intercession of Our Lady)."[18]

Carlo Torre, writing some sixty-five years earlier, describes the painting of the Virgin and St. Anne as similar to the one by Leonardo in Paris, but mentions neither the painting of San Carlo, which likely was executed after his canonization in 1610, nor the statue.[19] Yet Latuada's description of the Virgin as seated suggests that the statue depicted the Madonna and Child. Little else is known about the chapel itself, but it may have been the one known during the sixteenth century as the chapel of Our Lady.[20] At Santa Maria della Scala, mothers reportedly left gifts of candles equal in weight to their newborn infants before a fresco of a "Madonna del Latte" executed sometime before 1311.[21] The only known image that seems to fit this description even slightly is a Madonna and Child by Bernardino Lovino that Latuada identifies as an Assumption and Torre calls a Madonna del Rosario. It is now commonly known as the Madonna della Scala and was transferred to

San Fedele without the flanking Saints Michael and John the Baptist when Santa Maria della Scala was demolished, and Italian art historians have dated it to the fifteenth century (figure 5.1).[22] The Madonna depicted in it, however, is not nursing. Finally, a belt, some breast milk, some hair, and a piece of the sepulcher of the Virgin were among the most important relics reportedly held by the Duomo of Milan,[23] and in 1737 Latuada reported that "there is still a devoted image of Our Lady vulgarly called of the Parto . . . before the image of the Madonna del Parto there was once an altar under the invocation of Saints Mary and Elizabeth, and there several daily masses and other devotions were instituted, and then, when the altar was demolished on the orders of Carlo Borromeo, as it is told, its pieces were transferred to the nearby altar of St. Agnes."[24]

Latuada's claims are supported by the extant archival documentation, which reveals that in 1511 one Matteo Retondo de Serono provided the foundation for a sung Mass along with first and second Vespers on the feast of the Visitation and a Lady Mass every Saturday at the altar of the Visitation of Mary to St. Elizabeth, more commonly known as the Parto.[25] Although Carlo Borromeo ordered this altar dismantled and its foundations moved to the altar of St. Agnes in 1566,[26] a fresco of a nursing Madonna is still found in the altar's original location (figure 5.2). It has been attributed, on the basis of a single and somewhat nebulous entry in the Duomo pay registers, to Jacopo Sormani and dated 1566.[27] This nursing Madonna does, however, appear to be the "Madonna del Parto" that was venerated in the Duomo during the late sixteenth and early seventeenth centuries. As the extant documentation regarding all four of these images shows, in Post-Tridentine Milan the Madonna del Parto was visually represented by the Madonna and Child, sometimes accompanied by saints and sometimes nursing. The intimate tone of the images combines a celebration of motherhood with traditional iconography suggesting either the Madonna Addolorata, which in the late sixteenth century was communicated, according to religious commentators on the subject, in sacred conversations,[28] or with the Virgin as intercessor, a notion signified by the lactating Madonna.[29]

MEDITATING THE MADONNA DEL PARTO IN PUBLIC SPACES

The aforementioned shrines to the Madonna del Parto were, of course, public spaces, but the cult's intersection with private life was facilitated through meditation books devoted to the subject. The

Figure 5.1. Madonna della Scala, San Fedele, photograph by Giovanni dell'Orto, WikiCommons.

Figure 5.2. attr. Jacopo Sormani, Madonna dell 'Aiuto, 1566, fresco, Duomo of Milano, Copyright © Veneranda Fabbrica del Duomo di Milano.

majority of these were vernacular translations or imitations of Jacopo Sannazaro's *De partu virginis,* a Latin poem in three cantos dating from 1526 that celebrates the Annunciation, Visitation, and Birth of the Christ Child. Like the Sannazaro poem that functioned as their model, the Post-Tridentine meditations are almost invariably divided into three books, one for the Annunciation, another for the Visitation, and a third that recounts the Birth.[30] Each book contains as many as fifty stanzas in ottava rima or versi toscani, and the predominance of these popular verse forms, along with decorative woodcuts depicting the primary Marian themes (figure 5.3),[31] suggest a secular readership. Yet the meditations are rife with tropes of hymns and antiphons, references to Biblical passages that define the Marian hagiography, symbols from classical mythology, and Marian signifiers such as *Mulier fortis, hortus conclusus* and *civitatus dei* that elucidate the Virgin's special status as a temple, a bride, a mother, a protectoress, and an intercessor. In the following excerpt from the Visitation section of Castor Durante's *Del parto della Virgine* of 1573, for example, Greek and Roman mythology is employed to amplify all three of the aforementioned Marian symbols.

Salve patria mia dolce amata, e cara	Hail my sweet, beloved and dear country,
Madre di tanti Eroi, di tanti Regi,	Mother of many heroes, of many kings,
Nido di stirpe gloriosa, e rara	Nest of glorious and rare descendants
Quant'altra, c'hoggi al mondo più si pregi;	How much more you are honored by the world today;
Città, che la progenie illustre, e chara,	City, who will rush to aid the illustrious and
Dentro accorrai; perche t'adorni e fregi,	shining progeny within because you adorn and
Il gran Figliuol di Dio, che'n carnal velo	decorate the great son of God, who from carnal
Involto darà legge al mondo, e al Cielo.	obscurity will rule the earth and heavens.
Non havran Creta, o Tebe hor più cagione	Neither Crete nor Thebes will any longer have
Di si pregiarsi, e gloriarsi al mondo,	reason to esteem and glorify itself to a world

Quella per Giove altera, *e per Giunone,*	distorted by Giove and by Juno.
E questa per lo suon tanto giocondo	And this through the very joyous sound
De la soave Lira d'Anfione,	Of the sweet lyre of Anfione,

Che la cinse di muro alto,
     e profondo;
	by which the high and deep
	     enclosure

Che la tua Gloria, e la tua gran
     Ventura
	of your glory and your great
	     fortune

Fà d'ogn'altra Città la fama oscura.[32]	renders every other city of dim reputation.

The two strophes declare that all other locations, even the ancient and influential Greek city Thebes and the large and populous island of Crete, pale in comparison to Mary, the city of God and the mother of heroes. Mary's union with God is described as superior in strength to the marriage between the Roman gods Jupiter and Juno, and her power as an intercessor therefore deemed to overshadow theirs. Finally, the enclosure that surrounds the sacred garden of the Virgin's soul is rendered higher and deeper than that of any other city, a fact evoking a joyful response in the allegorical sound of the lyre of Anfione, one of the twins born out of wedlock to Antione and Zeus who avenged the subsequent wrongs done his mother through the magic of his playing. The two strophes, which are part of a larger section of fifty, are presented in the ottava rima typical of the genre, but the opening acclamation to the Virgin, the rhymed verse, and the Marian symbolism allude topically and stylistically to well-known Marian hymns such as *Ave maris stella* and *Salve sancta parens matris*.

The troping and allusion to relevant passages or images from the Bible, the liturgy, and classical literature was certainly not peculiar to poetic meditations on the Madonna del Parto. Rather, it was a typical feature of Post-Tridentine meditation books, and often occurred, in the case of biblical and liturgical quotes, in the form of Latin interpolations into an otherwise vernacular text.[33] For vernacular readers who were unschooled in Latin, such interpolations must have provided free associations to the liturgy that served to enhance their understanding of the ritual. In the case of the meditations of the Madonna del Parto, however, the reinforcement of liturgical and theological concepts also appears interlaced with explicit messages about femininity. Mary, the most divine of all women, is repeatedly shown in three defining

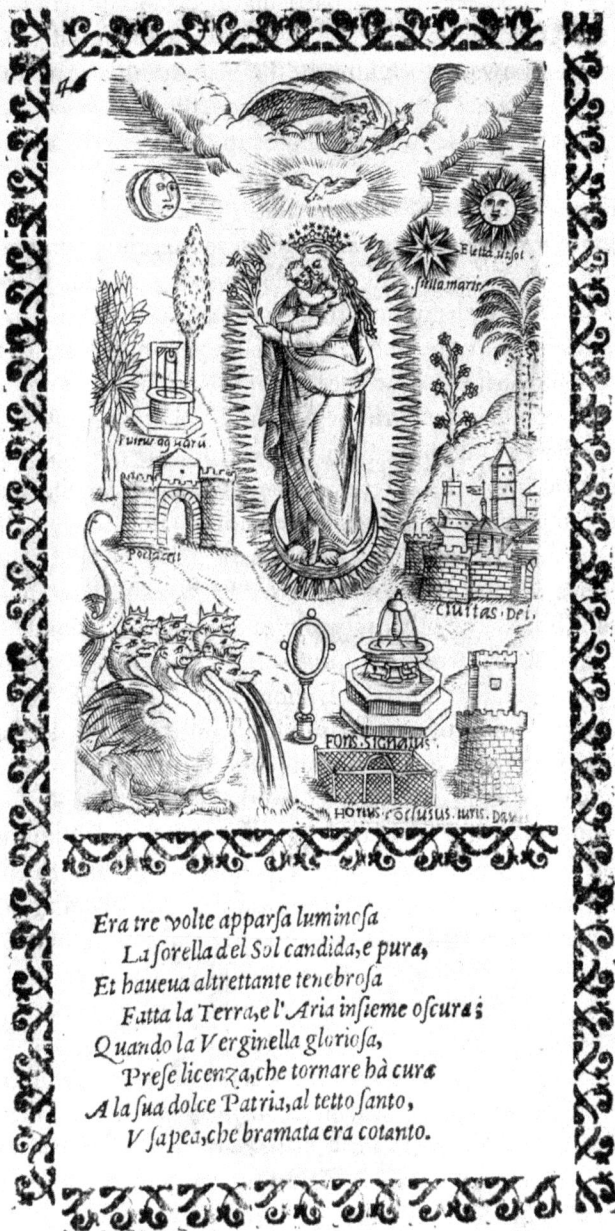

Figure 5.3. Castore Durante, *Del parto della Vergine libri tre di M. Castore Durante da Gualdo ad imitatione del Sanazaro con gli argomenti di M. Ieronimo Pallantieri* (In Roma appresso Gio. Battista de Cavalleri, 1573), 46, by permission of Roma, Biblioteca Nazionale Centrale Vittorio Emmanuele.

moments of her career that had particular resonance for contemporary writers of tracts on maternal duty: in submission to the will of God (the Annunciation); awaiting childbirth (the Visitation); and as a new and nursing mother (the Nativity).[34] To this end, illustrative woodcuts that visually captured these three events for the reader were also included (figure 5.4).[35]

A Roman Vespers of the Expectatio Partus that did not include the famous O Antiphons appears in the seventeenth-century breviaries (table 5.1),[36] but was not likely widely used in Milan, where every effort was made to bring institutions into some level of conformity with the Ambrosian rite, particularly following the release of the new Ambrosian Breviary in 1582. Since celebrations of the Expectatio Partus occurred in conjunction with the Annunciation in the Ambrosian calendar, the feast would have been celebrated using the Vespers for the Annunciation (table 5.2). Yet even the indications for the Vespers of this feast found in the 1582 Breviary cannot be taken too literally, given the variations of the liturgy, both monastic and ecclesiastical, used in Milan even after the release of the revised Breviary.[37] The content of the Milan choirbooks and other sacred prints emanating from the Duomo such as Matthias Werrecore's *Cantuum quinque vocum* of 1555 has shown, moreover, that where polyphony was concerned, there was no established tradition of placing emphasis on the ritual derivation of texts, so motets featuring texts from either of the rites or from other passages considered significant to the theology of the Madonna del Parto would also have been appropriate to public celebrations of the feast. These include not only the aforementioned biblical passages from Job 10: 8–11, Galatians 4:4, Wisdom 7:1–2, Psalm 139: 13–16, and Song of Songs 4 and 7, but also at least five antiphons from the Ambrosian rite, including *Ecce iam aperti sunt caeli*, *Venite et videte in Bethlehem*, *Placuit Deo castitas et immaculata verginitatis*, *Beatus uterus Mariae Virginis*, and *O santa Maria di Dio*.

At least one large-scale sacred concerto on a para-liturgical text, Benedetto Regio's *Quam dulces et misterijs pleni sunt tui partus*, appears to have been used in celebrations of the Expectatio Partus at both the Duomo and Santa Maria presso San Celso, two of the earliest Milanese institutions to adopt variant observances of the feast. The concerto, which is dedicated to the "noble and virtuous" Caterina Assandra, was first published in *Missarum ac sacrarum cantionum quinque et octo vocibus concinendarum. Liber primus*, a volume of the Regio's sacred works published in 1607 by Simone Tini and Filippo

Figure 5.4. *Del parto della Vergine del Sanazaro. Libri tre. Tradotti in versi Toscani da Giovanni Giolito de' Ferrari* al. Ser. Signor Don Vincenzo Gonzaga, Duca di Mantova, e di Monferrato, & c., Annunciation. (In Venetia, appresso I Gioliti M.D.LXXXVIII), Milano, Biblioteca Nazionale Braidense 25.13.0.19, by permission of the Ministero per i Beni e le Attività Culturale.

TABLE 5.1.
Roman Vespers of the Expectatio Partus

Antiphon Quo abiit dilectus tuus/Psalm 109.

Antiphon Recidite à me/Psalm 112.

Antiphon Non est ei species/Psalm 121.

Antiphon A planta pedis/Psalm 126.

Antiphon Fulcite me floribus/Psalm 147.

Capitulum: Thren 2. Cui comparabo te?

Hymn: O quot undis lacrymarum.

Antiphon Nolite me considerare/Magnificat.

Capitulum: Isa 11. Egredietur virga da radice Jesse.

Hymn: Creator alma siderum.

V. Ave Maria, gratia plena. R. Dominus tecum.

Antiphon Spiritus Sanctus in te descendet, Maria.

*During Advent, Compline Hymn: Virtus, honor, laus, gloria.

Lomazzo of Milan.[38] The archival records indicate that a copy of the *Missarum* was among several music prints purchased by the deputies of Santa Maria presso San Celso for use in their services in 1608, and an extant copy of the volume is still found in the Archivio della Veneranda Fabbrica del Duomo in Milan.[39] All of the motets in the collection receive individual dedications, but just why Regio dedicated *Quam dulces et misterijs pleni sunt tui partus* to Caterina Assandra is not entirely clear. She apparently studied composition with him, but was likely a young novice when the *Missarum* was published, since the dedication of her own *Motetti a due e tre voc . . . opera seconda* of 1609, also printed by Tini and Lomazzo of Milan, indicates that she took her vows shortly after its publication.

In any case, the text of *Quam dulces et misterijs pleni sunt tui partus* is presented in the second person, a technique frequently used in meditation books of the era to evoke an atmosphere of intimacy

TABLE 5.2.
Ambrosian Vespers of the Annunciation

Lucernarium: Quoniam tu.

Ant. in Coro. Ex Sion species decoris.

Hymn. Mysterium ecclesiae.

V. Dominus Vobiscum.

R. in Coro. Sicut cedrus exaltata sum.
V. Myrrha, gutta, & cascia.

Ant. Ave virgo.
Ps. 114 Dilexi V. Dominus vobiscum quia
Ps. 133 Ecce nunc.
Ps 116 Laudate dominum omnes sub uno. Gloria
Ant. Ave virgo Maria, gratia plena Dominus tecum.

Kyrie x 3

V. Dominus vobiscum.

Oratio 1. Aspice de coelo Deus.

V. Dominus vobiscum.

In Magnificat. Ant. Ecce ancilla Domini.

Kyrie x 3

V. Dominus vobiscum.

Oratio 2. Conscientias nostras que sumus.

Psall. Spiritus sanctus in te descendat Maria.

Compl. 1. Quoniam tu illumines.

Compl 2. Benedictus es Domine.

Oratio 3. Protégé quaesumus Domine.

---

between the student and the Virgin (table 5.3). Although it is focused primarily on the moment of the birth of Christ, it ties the event to the Annunciation, the encounter in which the Virgin first submits to the will of God and is hailed as blessed among women, as well as to the Crucifixion, which was seen by commentators of the period to be the Virgin's ultimate sacrifice of submission, and the Resurrection, the final triumph effected by the birth.[40] Despite the fact that the feasts attached to these events are now generally separated on the liturgical calendar, this conflation is not as problematic from a liturgical point of view as it might at first seem, as the Annunciation and the Expectatio Partus were virtually synonymous in the Pre-Tridentine Ambrosian rite, which did not allow for the celebration of joyful Marian feasts during Lent. In the Pre-Tridentine Ambrosian rite, in fact, the Annunciation and the Expectatio Parto were often celebrated simultaneously on 18 December and its octave, whereas in the Roman rite that was observed at certain churches in Milan prior to the publication of the Ambrosian Breviary of 1582, the Expectatio Partus was essentially celebrated twice, namely on the traditional 18 December and on the 25 March in connection with the Annunciation. After the Ambrosian rite was revised and somewhat Romanized by Carlo Borromeo in 1582, the two feasts appear to have used the same liturgy but were at least nominally separated on the calendar, the Expectatio Partus remaining on 18 December and its octave and the Annunciation falling on 25 March. The latter feast, incidentally, is the one to which the pay registers at Santa Maria presso San Celso actually refer when they mention the "festa della Espettatione." Thus, *Quam dulces et misterijs* links several consecutive yet interrelated events in the life of the Virgin that historically had been celebrated either synonymously or in close succession on the liturgical calendar, namely the Annunciation, the final gestation period, and the birth itself.

Quam dulces et misterijs is for eight voices and basso seguente, and its texture could perhaps have been reduced to fewer voices by combining the basso seguente with selected upper parts. However, the motet likely would have been less effective musically with reduced scoring, for the articulation of its text is largely dependent upon the division of the eight voices into two distinct four-voice choirs that sing in combination, alternation, and close imitation, sometimes reiterating specific phrases through repetition in varying textures (table 5.4). The work is harmonically rather static, diverting from the F cantus mollis tonality only briefly on occasion, and featuring numerous cadential articulations on F. Thus, the musical rhetoric is primarily sonic rather than

TABLE 5.3.
Text of Benedetto Regio, *Quam dulces et misterijs*

Quam dulces et misterijs pleni sunt tui partus, O beatissima Maria,	How sweet and mysterious are the riches of your labor, O most blessed Maria.
summum Sacerdotem sine dolore peperisti, qui pro nobis Deo patri in cruce se obtulit,	You brought forth without travail the highest priest, whom God the father offered for us on the cross.
Hodie novum paris Sacerdotem ut sacrificij filij tui memoriam saepissime renovet.	Today you give birth anew to the priest in that [today] renews most frequently the memory of the sacrifices of your son.
Gaudeamus igitur de tanto partu et gaudenter clamemus,	We rejoice, therefore, in such a labor and we cry aloud joyfully
Surrexit Christus de sepulchro, Alleluia.	Christ is raised from the grave, Alleluia.

tonal, and is predicated upon the alternation of the aforementioned four-voice textures with full eight-voiced ones (Appendix D, example 5.1), although one line of the text is unfolded in high- and low-voiced duets. Meter also plays a significant rhetorical role in that the two liturgical tropes that tie the Expectatio Partus to the Annunciation and Crucifixion, "O beatissima Virgo Maria" and "Surrexit Christus de sepulchro, alleluia," respectively, are set homophonically and in triple meter, thus distinguishing them from the remainder of the text.

Also particularly pertinent to the veneration of the Madonna del Parto in the Duomo is the cult's connection to the feast of the Visitation, which not only is established by the meditation books of the era, but also, as noted earlier, was commemorated in the Duomo with an altar of the Visitation of Mary to St. Elizabeth that was colloquially known as the Madonna del Parto until 1566. Even after the foundation associated with the altar of the Visitation was transferred to that of St. Agnes and a fresco of the Madonna del Parto substituted

Table 5.4.

Formal Layout of Benedetto Regio, *Quam dulces et misterijs*

METER	TEXT	VOICING	TEXTURE
¢	Quam dulces et misterijs pleni sunt tui partus,	Choir 1	homophony
3 2	O beatissima Maria,	Choirs 1 and 2	homophony
¢	Quam dulces et misterijs pleni sunt tui partus,	Choir 2	homophony
3 2	O beatissima Maria,	Choirs 1 and 2	homophony
¢	summum Sacerdotem sine dolore peperisti, sine dolore peperisti, sine dolore peperisti,	Choir 1 Choir 1 Choir 2 Choirs 1 and 2	
	qui pro nobis Deo patri in cruce se obtulit,	Choir 1	homophony
	Hodie novum paris Sacerdotem, Hodie novum paris Sacerdotem	Cantus 1 and Altus 1 Bassus 1 and Bassus 2	imitative duet imitative duet
	ut sacrificij filij tui memoriam saepissime renovet.	Choirs 1 and 2	close imitation
	Gaudeamus igitur de tanto partu	Choirs 1 and 2	close imitation
	et gaudenter clamemus,	Choirs 1 and 2	imitation/ alternating
3 2	Surrexit Christus de sepulchro, Alleluia. Surrexit Christus de sepulchro, Alleluia.	Choir 1 Choir 2	homophony homophony
	Alleluia.	Choirs 1 and 2	imitation/ alternating

in its original location, the feast of the Visitation apparently continued to be significant enough to warrant the composition of special
polyphony for certain of its canonical hours. An anonymous four-voice
setting of Matins and Vespers polyphony for the feast of the Visitation
is included, for example, in Librone 23 of the Duomo choir books.
It has been dated by Claudio Sartori to the second half of the sixteenth century on the basis of the remaining contents of the book,[41]
which include a *Missa Christus Resurgens* and a *Missa Beatus vir* by
Petrus Colini, a *Missa Pape Marcelli* by Pierluigi da Palestrina, and
a *Missa Ne timeas Mariae* by Giovanni Giacomo Gastoldi, all also
for four voices. However, Librone 23 more likely dates from the first
two decades of the seventeenth century, for the *Missa Papae Marcelli*
attributed to Palestrina is the version arranged for four voices (from the
original six) by Giovanni Francesco Anerio and published by Soldi of
Rome in 1619, while Gastoldi's *Missa Ne timeas Mariae* was included
in his first book of four-voice masses printed by Amadino of Venice
in 1602.[42] The two masses of Pierre Colin admittedly first appeared
in the *Libro octo missarum, quarum priores, quae numero sex sunt,
quatuor vocum concentu compositae sunt* by Jacques Moderne of Lyon
as early as 1541, and thus likely were the basis for Sartori's somewhat
earlier dating. However, the *Libro octo missarum* was subsequently
reprinted in Venice as the third book of four-voice masses in 1544,
1567, and 1580,[43] and, given the dating of the concordant sources for
the other works, the 1580 edition of Colin's masses probably served
as the source for Librone 23. In any case, the content and condition of
Librone 23, which is distinguished by cutting, rebinding, the pasting
of page reinforcements along the bindings, inexplicable irregularities
in the pagination, and the absence of font matter and a table of contents, suggests that it actually comprises the remains of two separate
volumes, a book of four-voice masses and a collection of Marian office
polyphony, that were at some point united for the sake of convenience.
The latter includes four-voice Vespers polyphony for the feast of the
Visitation and for the feasts of female matrons (table 5.5).[44]

   Although not designated for Matins in the print, the polyphony for
the feast of the Visitation that precedes the material clearly designated
as accompanying the Magnificat is based on the lectiones and a responsory with verse from the Ambrosian Matins for the Visitation. The
polyphony provided for the Magnificat at First and Second Vespers,
however, does not conform liturgically to the antiphons stipulated for
the Magnificat on the feast of the Visitation in the Ambrosian Breviary

TABLE 5.5.
Four-Voice Marian Office Polyphony in Librone 23

IN VISITATIONE B.V.M.	IN FESTO SANCTARUM MULIERUM
Exurgens Maria. Abijt in montana cum festi natione in civitatem Juda. Intravit Maria. In domum Zacharie et salutavit Elisabeth. Ut audivit. Salutationem Marie Elisabeth exultavit infans in utero eius repleta est spirit sancto alleluia. Benedicta tu. Inter mulieres et benedictus fructus ventris tui. Es quo facta est vox. Salutationis tue in auribus meis exultavit infans in utero meo. Alleuia.	Ad Magnificat in Primis Vesperis. Simile est regnum celorum nomini negotiatori querenti bonas margaritas inventa una precisa dedit omnia sua et comparavit eam.
Ad Magnificat in Primijs Vesperis. Beata es Maria, Que credisti perficientur in te que dicta sunt tibi a domino alleluia.	Ad Magnificat in Secondis Vesperis. Manum suam Apervit inopi et palmas suas extendit ad pauperum et panem otsiosa non comedit.
Ad Magnificat in Secundis Vesperis. Beatam me dicent Omnes generationes quia Ancillam humilem respexit deus alleluia.	

of 1582, thus suggesting that the pieces were not meant to replace specific responsories or antiphons from the canonical hours. Since some of the polyphony is specified for the Magnificats and the texts themselves form a coherent linear narrative, it appears likely that all the polyphony provided actually was intended for use during Vespers. The polyphony on the texts derived from the lectiones and a responsory for the Ambrosian Matins of the Visitation recounts in a slightly abbreviated, straightforward fashion the Visitation of the Virgin to Elizabeth as narrated in Luke 1. The settings provided to accompany the Magnificat at First Vespers and Second Vespers thereafter abandon the narrative to comment on the consequences of the event for each participant in the story.[45] The polyphonic elaboration for the Magnificat at first Vespers encapsulates Elizabeth's recognition of the magnitude of the Virgin in a declaration derived from Luke 1:45, while that for second Vespers captures the entirety of the Magnificat itself in miniature through a four-part setting of Luke 1:48. This particular distribution of the text does not, of course, preclude the possibility that the narrative passages were sung at Matins as an elaboration of the lessons, while the commentary passages were performed at Vespers as indicated in the source. Yet all the texts seem to belong together, as the settings designated to accompany the Magnificat are rather short and lose some of their rhetorical force when widely separated from the preceding narrative.

All of the pieces, regardless of their intended placement in the liturgy, essentially are harmonizations of plainchant melodies, and these plainchant melodies are assigned to the bass voice, which intones the plainchant evenly in breves throughout while the three upper voices weave imitative counterpoint above it (Appendix D, example 5.2). There is considerable crossing of the altus and tenor voices, which are assigned to relatively the same range (as the cleffing is $C_1C_3C_3C_4$), but the thicker inner texture that results is offset by the superius voice, which moves, for the most part, in an ambitus encompassing the fifth above the altus and tenor.

The approach of shifting from narrative to commentary found in the polyphony for the Visitation in *Librone* 23 is not dissimilar to that found in the meditations for the Madonna del Parto, which typically feature an argument that sets the stage by recounting the appropriate biblical story at the opening of each book or section, followed by numerous stanzas that imagine dialogues between the characters involved and comment, primarily through tropes of the liturgy, of pertinent ecclesiastical writings, and of biblical passages, on the argument and its related theological implications. This multi-faceted mode of presentation is intended to evoke empathy in the reader while at the same time instructing her in the theological precepts associated with the argument. The four-part polyphony for the Visitation in Librone 23, however, presents the texts in a rather straightforward manner, save for the use of a sort of parallel rhetorical epizeuxis in which the final phrases of each section are repeated for the purposes of cadential emphasis (Appendix D, example 5.3). It relies far less on the temporal and spatial effects that distinguish the *Quam dulces et misterijs,* and is also devoid of the myriad of Marian references invoking the theologies of the Virgin birth and Immaculate Conception found in the Visitation sections of meditations on the Madonna del Parto.

MEDITATING THE MADONNA DEL PARTO IN PRIVATE SPACES

A motet such as *Quam dulces et misterijs,* with its large-scale scoring and antiphonal effects, and the four-part polyphony for the Visitation in Librone 23, with its foundation in plainchant formulas, clearly were intended for use in the ritual, but the cult of the Madonna del Parto was also forwarded through at least two Milanese collections dating from the first decade of the seventeenth century that were intended for domestic use. Both collections commemorated the birth of an infant son, and functioned in a manner similar to the *desco da parto,*[46] a decorative confinement-period presentation plate that was often laden with fruit or gifts for the expectant mother. Unlike the *desco da parto,* which generally depicted scenes from the lives of male heirs from the Bible such as David, Jesus Christ, and John the Baptist, the adventures of strong female biblical characters such as Susannah or Judith, or allegories from mythology in which women were sexually dominant, glorify the Virgin. The first of these, Orfeo Vecchi's *La donna vestita di sole* of 1602 (figure 5.5), was presented to Hippolita Borromea Sanseverino Barbiana, the Countess of Belgioioso, upon the birth of her son, Giovanni Battista.[47] It contains twenty-one spiritual madrigals for five voices that expand upon twelve virtues of the Virgin, the seven principal Marian feasts celebrated in Milan, each of which corresponds to a joyful event in the Virgin's life, including the Annunciation, Visitation, and birth of Christ, and the text of Revelation 12:1,[48] which in the sixteenth century was interpreted as referring prophetically to both the Virgin's fecundity and to the Immaculate Conception, a doctrine which was beginning to gain currency in the late sixteenth century even among the Dominicans, its greatest detractors.[49] A well-defined thematic organization, although entirely unique in this case, is a characteristic that the collection shares with others of its ilk such as Angelo Gardano's *Musica spirituale di ecellentissimi autori* (1586)[50] and Giovanni Francesco Anerio's *Ghirlanda di sacre rose* (1619),[51] but the tonal plan is somewhat extraordinary (Appendix C, table 5). Part I, which expounds on the twelve stars or virtues of the Virgin's crown, features madrigals in G cantus durus. Part II, which is dedicated to two madrigals that elaborate on the text of Revelation 12:1, is set in A cantus durus, a tonal type outside the standard church key system that was perhaps chosen precisely because of its otherworldliness. Part II, which is dedicated to the seven Marian feasts that mark the principal events of the Virgin's life, is comprised of seven madrigals, four of which are in F cantus mollis and three of which are in G cantus mollis, the point of division occurring with the birth of Christ.[52] The overarching program clearly was intended as an educational one, as the dedication of the collection specifies that the five-part madrigals contained were to be sung in a domestic setting by Hippolita and her children as they reflect on the Virgin. In order to facilitate the meditation process, and perhaps even to offer the opportunity to meditate on the texts without music, the text is printed on the facing page of its respective madrigal in the cantus partbook (figure 5.6). Although singing the texts with her children actually may not have been immediately possible, given that Hippolita's fourth child has just entered the world, it may have been at least figuratively viable from the perspective of voicing, for the extant documentation shows that she had at least two daughters and one other son.[53] Even so, the alto voice lies in the range of the tenor part more often than in that of the higher quinto part, thus suggesting a singing cohort of three men and two women. Such an interpretation does not, of course, take into consideration some sort of arrangement with keyboard (or another appropriate instrument) in which the basso, which does often take the role of providing a harmonic foundation, is combined with one or two voices sounding the melodies.

Vecchi, a mansionarius and maestro di cappella at the royal ducal chapel of Santa Maria della Scala in Milan from approximately 1586 until his death in 1603, was a prolific composer of sacred polyphony, but *La donna vestita di sole* seems to have been his first foray into composition in the vernacular, and, indeed, his first attempt at a madrigal collection. That Vecchi was preparing pieces intended for domestic use by amateurs seems not to have influenced him toward musical simplification, and he appears to have been somewhat aware of the Milanese madrigal tradition that preceded him. As can be seen in the madrigal "Del parto," the carefully spaced imitative counterpoint that characterizes Vecchi's sacred polyphony alternates with a rhythmically pliable declamatory homophony typical of the mid-century Milanese madrigal of such composers as Hoste da Reggio and Giuseppe Caimo (example 5.4).

The individual lines of poetry are further delineated through strategically placed cadences and tonal articulations that define the perimeters of the G cantus mollis tone in terms of its final and dominant relationships (table 5.6). Alternating trio and quartet textures are explored, with the most prominently offset trio reserved for the declaration "Meraviglio Cielo, Vergine siete voi" (Marvel of the Heavens,

LA DONNA
VESTITA DI SOLE,
CORONATA DI STELLE,
CALCANTE LA LVNA,

In 21. Madrigali cantata da Orfeo Vecchi.

Corona ſtellarum duodecim,

Mulier amicta Sole, & in capite eius

Et Luna ſub pedibus eius.

Apoc. 12.

IN MILANO,

Per l'herede di Simon Tini, & Gio. Franceſco Beſozzi.

ℳ. DCII.   A

Figure 5.5. Orfeo Vecchi, *La donna vestita di sole* (Milano: erede di Simone Tini e Giovanni Francesco Besozzi, 1602), frontispiece, courtesy of the Sibley Music Library, Eastman School of Music, University of Rochester.

Del Parto.

Oggi dal Ciel' vn lampo
   Chiarißimo riluce,
   Che col feren' ogni confort' adduce.
Merauigliofo Cielo
   Vergine fete voi,
   Lampo Dio ftefs' afcoſt' in human velo,
   Che da voi nafce, e fi difcopr' à noi,
   Egli rimen' il già bandito rifo,
   In terr' il Paradifo.

Figure 5.6. Orfeo Vecchi, *La donna vestita di sole* (Milano: erede di Simone Tini e Giovanni Francesco Besozzi, 1602), cantus, Del Parto, courtesy of the Sibley Music Library, Eastman School of Music, University of Rochester.

Virgin are you). Some madrigalisms on words such as "Cielo" and "riso" are found, but text painting takes a backseat to the clarity of the text declamation and the use of chromatic inflections to accentuate certain syllables of the text. The madrigal texts themselves, however, are more straightforward than those of the meditation books for the Madonna del Parto in that they rely far less on a network of liturgical

EXAMPLE 5.4. Orfeo Vecchi, *La donna vestita di Sole,* "Del Parto,"
mm. 15–17.

and mythological tropes than they do obvious gestures and sweeping theological themes. The author of the texts has not been identified, so it is unclear whether or not the poems stand as presented by Vecchi or comprise a part of some larger literary work. If the texts are part of some larger whole, it can be argued that Vecchi combined them into a theologically effective and tonally logical cycle in which the feminine virtues, the text of Revelation 12:1, and the principal Marian feasts are systematically contemplated via the carefully crafted counterpoint for which he was well known. In short, these madrigals may have been intended for domestic use, but they are by no means easily performable by mere amateurs.

Although seemingly directed at Hippolita and her children, the composer's invitation to sing the pieces contained while meditating the Virgin was really extended to all those who acquired the print simply by virtue of its inclusion in the introduction to the collection. The frontispiece of the collection further suggests, in fact, that the cycle was to function as a sort of musical Rosary,[54] for it is not unlike the Rosary woodcuts found in both Bartolomeo Scalvo's widely circulated meditations on the Rosary (figure 5.7)[55] and Castore Durante's meditations on the Madonna del Parto (figure 5.8),[56] which depict a Madonna enthroned and encircled by a garland or Rosary, in the former case dressed in the sun and standing on the moon, and in the latter overshadowed by them. The relationship between the cults of the Rosary and the Madonna del Parto actually appears to have been quite fluid. Post-Tridentine prints in the vernacular aimed at forwarding the Rosary and other devotions to the Virgin recount in great detail miracles in which women in danger were brought to safe delivery by saying the Rosary, reciting the Salve Regina and Ave Maria, or simply invoking the name of the Virgin. Bernardo Giunti's *Miracoli della Sacratissima Vergine Maria* of 1587, for example, reports that a pregnant Spanish noblewoman who was captured, tortured by infidels, and then held alone in a stall during the fall of Granada said the Rosary and was thereafter personally assisted by the Virgin in the successful delivery of her son,[57] while Sivano Razzi, in his *Dei miracoli della Gloriosa Vergine Maria* of 1612, relates several cases in which pregnant women in extreme pain or danger of losing a child during labor purportedly were saved by reciting the Salve Regina, the Ave Maria, or merely invoking the name of the Virgin. It is perhaps worth noting that these women were reportedly of both the Christian and the Jewish faith.[58] The intersections between the cults of the Madonna del Parto and the Madonna del

TABLE 5.6.
Formal Layout of Orfeo Vecchi,
Del Parto from *La donna vestita di sole*

TEXT	TEXTURE	CADENTIAL STRUCTURE
Oggi dal Ciel un lampo chiarissimo riluce, oggi dal Ciel un lampo chiarissimo riluce, (un lampo chiarissimo riluce,)	five-voice imitation (CQATB); four-voice imitation over A pedal tone in bass	successive cadences on D
Che col seren'ogni conforto adduce,	five-voice imitation	cadence on D
ogni conforto adduce,	four-voice homophony (CQTB)	cadence on G
Meraviglio Cielo,	three-voice homophony (ATB)	articulation on B-flat
Vergine siete voi.	three-voice homophony (ATB)	articulation on D
Lampo Dio stesso ascosta in uman velo,	three-voice imitation (CQA) dissolving to homophony	articulation on A
che da voi nasce, e si di scopra a noi,	four-voice homophony (CQTB)	cadence on D
Egli rimena il già bandito riso,	four-voice imitative entry (CATB) dissolving to five-voice homophony	articulation on B-flat
In terra il paradiso, in terra il paradiso.	four-voice homophony (QATB) expanding to five voice-imitation	cadence on D
Egli rimena il già bandito riso,	four-voice imitation (CQAT);	articulation on F
egli rimena il già bandito riso,	three-voice homophony (QTB) expanding to five-voice imitation	articulation on B-flat

TEXT	TEXTURE	CADENTIAL STRUCTURE
In terra il paradiso,	four-part homophony (CATB)	cadence on D
in terra il paradiso, in terra il paradiso.	four-voice imitation (CQAT) expanding to five-voice imitation	cadence on G

Rosario arise somewhat naturally from the fact that the Annunciation, Visitation, and Nativity were among the joyful mysteries of the Rosary. The connection between the cult of the Madonna del Parto and that of the Madonna Addolorata is founded, on the other hand, in ecclesiastical tracts of the era that claimed a delivery without travail for the Virgin while acknowledging that her suffering eventually came at the hands of her son during the Crucifixion. In his *Pietosi affetti di compassione sopra li dolori della B. V. Maria* of 1612, for example, the prolific Servite author Arcangelo Ballotino cites the scriptures and the writings of Saints Cyrus, Anselm, Bernard, and Damasceno, to name only of few, in arguing that the Virgin experienced a sort of double delivery, the second of which occurred during the Crucifixion and dealt her more sorrow and pain than that experienced by any other martyr.[59]

Ballotino's perspective appears to define the other Milanese collection associated with the Madonna del Parto, Stefano Limido's *I Regii Concenti Spirituali* of 1605. Dedicated to Philip III of Spain and his wife Marguerite of Austria upon the birth of their firstborn son,[60] it features vernacular settings of both Italian and Castilian texts (Appendix C, table 6) for four to six voices.[61] These not only honor the Madonna Addolorata and the woman of Revelation 12:1, they also enumerate her virtues and request her mercy. San Francesco di Paola, the founder of a mendicant order known as the Minims that was the Spanish counterpart to the nuns of Las Descalzas Reales, is also invoked via a villancico alluding to a miracle in which the saint reportedly sailed the Strait of Messina on his cloak in a manner not entirely dissimilar to Elijah's crossing of the Jordan. The centerpiece of the collection, however, is a five-voice madrigal cycle on Angelo Grillo's *Le braccia aperse*, a nine-stanza poetic meditation of the Virgin at the cross that underscores the aforementioned theological construct of the Crucifixion as the Virgin's second, and more painful delivery. In its nine-section structure and raw,

Figure 5.7. Bartolomeo Scalvo, *Meditationi della Gloriosa Maria Vergine* (Venezia: Domenico e Giovanni Battista fratelli Guerra, 1583), frontispiece, courtesy of Milano, Biblioteca Nazionale Braidense Braidense Gerli 2313, by permission of the Ministero per i Beni e le Attività Culturale.

Figure 5.8. Castore Durante, *Del parto della Vergine libri tre di M. Castore Durante da Gualdo ad imitatione del Sanazaro con gli argomenti di M. Ieronimo Pallantieri* (In Roma: appresso Gio. Battista de Cavalleri, 1573), 59, by permission of Roma, Biblioteca Nazionale Centrale Vittorio Emmanuele.

gritty portrayal of the Virgin's emotional response to the Crucifixion, *Le braccie aperse* mimics symbolically the novena of the Expectatio Partus that enjoyed extensive popularity in the Mediterranean cultures, and, in particular, in Spain.

The feast of the Expectatio Partus was especially revered in Spain, particularly in Toledo, and seventeenth-century documentation from the royal court shows that it was among the most important celebrated in the Spanish queen's chapel. There the feast and the novena of the Expectatio were faithfully observed before an image of Our Lady of Hope in order to ensure successful royal deliveries and preservation of the line.[62] After her marriage and shortly before the birth Philip III, in fact, Marguerite of Austria reported that she had great hope of bearing a son in the near future because both she and her spouse had made a petition in the sanctuary of Our Lady of Hope in Valladolid.[63] Marguerite's devotion to the Virgin and her novena apparently were well known as far away as Italy. In his tract on Marian cults and devotion in seventeenth-century Milan, the capuchin monk Ignazio Carnago alludes to the importance of the novena of the Expectatio Partus at the royal court in stating that the queen faithfully observed the nine major Marian mysteries and had nine masses said during the advent of her delivery:

> Marguerite of Austria, wife of Philip III King of Spain, was devoted to the principal mysteries that concern the life of Mary, which are nine in number: the Immaculate Conception, Nativity, Presentation, Marriage, Annunciation, Visitation, Birth of the Christ Child, Purification, and Assumption; however when the time of her deliveries approached, she had nine masses, one after the other, said in honor of the aforementioned principal mysteries of the life and death of the of the Blessed Virgin, which assisted her greatly. On the day of the Annunciation, she served nine poor women with her own hands in honor of the aforementioned mysteries, in memory of which they set about saying nine Ave Marias.[64]

Marguerite actually took on the role of the Virgin in at least two paintings by Spanish court artist Juan Pantoja de la Cruz in order to assert her fecundity, sanctity, and the divine authority of the Hapsburg line. In the foreground of the first, the *Nacimiento de la Virgen* of 1603,[65] Marguerite's mother, the Archduchess of Bavaria, and a servant wash a newborn in a basin as Marguerite's two sisters look on, while a woman in childbirth is attended in the background. Magdalena S. Sanchez suggests that the woman on the bed is Marguerite of Austria,[66] but it is equally likely, given the subject matter, that the baby is intended to represent Marguerite. In the second painting, the *Annunciation* of 1605, the Infanta Anna, taking the role of the angel Gabriel, announces the Virgin birth to her mother, Marguerite, who appears in the role of the Virgin.[67] An archival document dated 8 April 1605 regarding a commission for Juan Pantoja de la Cruz in anticipation of the birth of the future Philip IV further reveals that she twice requested an image of the Expectatio Partus on the eve of the birth of a child.[68]

Further, there is musical precedent for the concept of composing an aural *desco di parto,* and, indeed, one containing a structural novena of sorts, in honor the queens of Spain. An archival document associated with the birth of princess Maria Eugenia on 21 November 1625 reports that it was the custom in Spain for the singers of the royal chapel to assemble in the Capilla of the Palacio Real and begin singing the Matins of the Nativity of Christ at the onset of labor and, if the baby had been brought forth by its close, to conclude with a Te Deum in celebration. If, on the other hand, the queen's labor continued beyond the conclusion of the singing of the Matins of the Nativity, the chapel singers were to remain on hand until the delivery, after which they reassembled to sing the Te Deum. The same documentation mentions, moreover, that a litany by Antonio de Cabezón composed in honor of Mary Tudor at the time of her betrothal to Philip II was sung in the corridors of the palace throughout the queen's ninth month.[69] This litany may have been the five-voice *Sancta Maria ora pro nobis* found on folio 107 of the Cancionero de la Casa de Medinaceli and attributed to Cabezón.[70] In any case, Limido, who is identified in a document dated 13 November 1608 as the supervisor of the violins of the Capilla Real and an employee of the Capilla for the past nine years,[71] would have been familiar with these practices at the Spanish court.

Although only four of the five partbooks of Limido's *I Regii Concenti Spirituali* are extant, it is possible to glimpse the character of *Le braccia aperse* by examining a transcription of the remaining four voices of the opening madrigal. In choosing to set the poetry of the currently fashionable Grillo, with its terse diction and stark imagery,[72] Limido clearly set for himself the task of relying primarily on textural contrast and tonal articulation rather than conventional compositional devices such as text painting in articulating the text, and this is a characteristic that the collection shares with Vecchi's *La donna vestita di sole*. Text painting on isolated words such as "ciel" (heaven) and "riv-olse" (turns again) admittedly is found (Appendix D, example 5.5), but the successive lines of text are unfolded according to a scheme in which points of imitation and passages of declamatory homophony freely alternate, often set off by clearly articulated cadences (table 5.7). Rhetorical amplification, which is neither a predominant literary feature in the meditations for the Madonna del Parto nor of Grillo's poetry, is liberally applied to specific phrases, each of which is repeated in a similar texture but with a different configuration of the voicing or disposition of motives. The purpose of reiterating such phrases as "Le braccia aperse, e gl'occhi al Ciel rivolse" ("Her arms opened, and she turned her eyes towards heaven"), according to Ignatius of Loyola, is to assist the communicant in internalizing the text, and, therefore, in a case such as this one, the plight of the Virgin. Thus, the fact that the technique is not frequently applied in meditation books for the Madonna del Parto does not negate its validity as a musical adaptation of typical meditational processes. What the setting does share stylisti-cally with published meditations for the Madonna del Parto, however, is the perspective of the one meditating, who typically views the events experienced by the Virgin as an onlooker whose empathy is aroused through the graphic detail of the text. In the case of Limido's setting, the music assists this process by providing not only an aural component that enhances the visual one, but also a participatory dynamic in which the communicant is able to further internalize the meditation by physi-cally reproducing the visual and aural images. A similar observation can be made about the madrigals of Vecchi's *La donna vestita di sole*.

As in *La donna vestita di sole*, the theological constructs presented in Limido's *I Regii Concenti Spirituali* are interwoven with more gen-eral messages of the relative value of feminine virtue and motherhood. Whereas meditation of the virtues and principal feasts is approached systematically in *La donna vestita di sole*, however, it is embedded intermittently within certain of the pieces, especially the Castilian ones, of *I Regii Concenti Spirituali*. The latter collection's intended audience, aside from the Spanish royals and their courtiers, was likely the large Spanish community in Milan (where the print was published), which congregated at the church of San Protasio in Campo. The central mad-rigal cycle on Grillo's poem is, of course, in Italian, and would have been accessible to the musically literate Milanese public at large, while the Castilian polyphony would have been of particular interest to San Protasio's Spanish bourgeoisie.

TABLE 5.7.
Formal Layout of Limido, *Le braccia aperse,* stanza 1[1]

Le braccia aperse, e gl'occhi al Ciel rivolse	point of imitation at fifth on G, cadences on D
Le braccia aperse, e gl'occhi al Ciel rivolse	point of imitation at fifth on G, cadences on D and G
Le braccia aperse, e gl'occhi al Ciel rivolse	point of imitation at fifth on G, cadence on D
Mestissima MARIA,	declamatory homophony, articulation on A
Quando sotto'l gran peso de la Croce,	declamatory homophony, articulation C
Stanco anhelante il Figlio	quasi homophony in reduced scoring, articulation on F
Stanco anhelante il Figlio	quasi homophony in reduced scoring, articulation on D
Stanco anhelante il Figlio	quasi homophony in reduced scoring, cadence on G
S'offerse à lei per via,	two to three repetitions per voice in staggered entries
Con sanguinoso ciglio:	declamatory homophony, articulation on D
E mentre, ohimè, la voce	declamatory homophony, cadence D
Lasse proferir volse,	declamatory homophony in reduced scoring
proferir volse,	declamatory homophony, articulation D
Il duol la voce	imitation at third (and fifth?) on B-flat, articulation on D
ed il vigor le tolse,	imitation at fifth on D, articulation D
ed il vigor le tolse.	series of imitative entries on D, G, C, G, articulation on G followed by cadence on D.

Note:
1. Her arms open and eyes again turned toward heaven, most sorrowful Mary tries to express, turns to express the pain, the voice and the vigor torn from her when her Son tired, gasping, under the great weight of the cross appeared before her on the road with a bloody brow.

Altars and street-corner shrines devoted to the Virgin continued to thrive throughout Italy during the sixteenth and early seventeenth centuries, so it is highly likely that the musical practices associated with the Madonna del Parto in Milan represent in microcosm those across the peninsula. Although beginning in fourteenth-century Italy the cult itself was manifest to the public primarily through visual imagery, it clearly was redefined and expanded for the secular audience of the Counter-Reformation through the circulation of texts in the vernacular that glorified feminine virtue, pregnancy, and motherhood by upholding the Virgin, the most revered of all Christian mothers, as a mirror for the early modern woman. These texts were not limited to commentaries and meditation books that drew upon the Bible, the liturgy, mythology, and ecclesiastical essays for inspiration, but also included motets and spiritual madrigals that relied on extra-musical programs, literary allusions, and musical rhetoric to propagate the gendered religious, social, and moral agendas espoused by the Post-Tridentine theological scholars who advocated for the Roman church's agenda on family.

Epilogue

The Case of Santa Maria Segreta

Blessed art thou among women,
and blessed is the fruit of thy womb!

—*Luke 1:42*

If Paolo Morigia was correct in observing that the city of Milan boasted at least forty-two Marian cults by 1594, then we have but begun to scratch the surface in understanding the role that Marian devotions played in the fabric of Post-Tridentine civic life there, and we yet have much to discover about the place of the numerous collections of polyphony composed by the city's musicians within the dynamic of its Marian cults of the late sixteenth and early seventeenth centuries. Some of these cults, such as the Compagnia dell'Abito of Santa Maria del Carmine, seem to have been directly associated with the institutions themselves, while many others, like Santa Maria della Neve in the Duomo and the Madonna della Passione at Santa Maria della Passione, were situated at altars within the city's churches, a number of which were themselves Marian. To properly identify and understand them rests in uncovering a happy conflation of archival and musical sources that sufficiently reveal the story. This is particularly true of the Marian cults that resided at specific altars within larger institutions. Perhaps most illustrative in this regard are the Marian cults at Santa Maria Segreta, a church dating back to the ninth century that stood just west of the Duomo and adjacent to the Piazza de Mercanti and the Orefici in the heart of city's commercial center.

Santa Maria Segreta was founded under the pontificate of the Archbishop Angilberto around 833 via the contributions of one Damigella de' Conti Fulcorino e Pedo and at some point thereafter passed under the supervision of the Humiliati. Upon the expulsion of the Humiliati in 1570, Carlo Borromeo placed the church under the supervision of the local priest Giovanni Battista Bagarotto, who administered as pastor of the parish until 1586 when it was awarded to the Somaschi. The edifice was razed in 1911 to make way for the Palazzo delle Poste in the Piazza Cordusio, and with it much of the documentation regarding the original church was lost.[1] According to Serviliano Latuada, the church consisted of a single nave with four lateral chapels, one of which was devoted to Saint Ambrose and another of which honored the "Angelo Custode" (Guardian Angel). At the time of Latuada's report in 1737, the former chapel was decorated with an oil of Saint Ambrose by the Milanese artist Bernardino Lovino as well as a cycle of frescoes recounting his life, while the latter featured an oil of the "Angelo Custode" by Jacopo Taurini. The wall opposite the main altar boasted a fresco cycle of the life of the Virgin, and one of the more bizarre relics housed below it was the arm of a young girl bound in strands of coral that had been cannibalized by a local woman who was miraculously caught in the act.[2] An archival document dating from around 1586 makes no mention of the altar of the "Angelo Custode," and instead indicates that the altars included the Maria Assumpta (main altar), Sant'Ambrogio, Santa Maria Pissina, and Santa Maria Annunziata.[3] In any case, Latuada describes the church as a popular destination for local devotees and attributes its popularity to the efforts of the Somaschi, who very zealously attended to the cult and administered the sacraments there.[4]

It is not clear however, to which cult Latuada refers. The archival documents reveal that at least two cults, both of them Marian, flourished at Santa Maria Segreta during the sixteenth and seventeenth centuries: Santa Maria della Pissina and Santa Maria Annunziata. The early history of both cults has been discussed by Paola Curatolo, who was able to view extant documents pertaining to them in the private archive of the parish of Santa Maria Segreta in the early 1990s. According to Curatolo, the Scuola della Pissina was founded on 8 January 1527 through an agreement of the parish of Santa Maria Segreta, the parish priest Vincenzo Vimercate, and several noble Milanese, and centered around devotion to a miraculous image found on the wall of a nearby house. In the agreement, the Scuola, which was populated by the nobility (not all of whom were from the parish) and governed by twelve deputies, was given permission to complete an external cappella especially for the cult, administer the bequests, celebrate masses, elect a chaplain, sell candles and little images for the benefit of the chapel and oratorio, and construct a cemetery behind the church for their dead. In the end, however, the chapel was never completed and the image was moved into Santa Maria Segreta, so the confraternity congregated there. Its two main obligations for the year included a high mass on the feast of the Annunciation and a high mass on the feast of the Nativity of the Virgin,[5] but elsewhere mention of daily masses is found. The orders from a pastoral visit of Carlo Borromeo dated 5 May 1582 mandate that the confraternity begin having them sung from the Ambrosian missal within fifteen days.[6]

The cult of the Santa Maria Annunziata was founded in 1516 around an image of the Madonna Annunziata affixed to the exterior of the church that had been credited with many miracles. Its membership drew from the parish, and its twelve officials were elected by the parish; at its founding fifty-two parishioners, among them several women, were present. Although the image around which the cult was originally organized was externally located, in 1582 Carlo Borromeo ordered it moved indoors into the chapel of Sant'Ambrogio until a proper chapel could be built. He further ordered that the confraternity be united with the Santissimo Sacramento, a frequent fate of Marian confraternities in Milan and elsewhere during the period, and appointed Giovanni Battista Bagarotto its rector. From at least 1586 the confraternity displayed the Blessed Sacrament on the altar every month, said Vespers, and processed about the church. It also set about financing the construction of the vault, a loft for sermons and "concerti di musica," confessionals, and the cappella of the Madonna, as well as the decoration of the vault and the cappella. Around that time the confraternity also adopted as its charitable work the care of the infirm and the provision of dowries for poor girls.[7]

A document dating from as early as 18 November 1565 reports that the church itself employed an organist at a salary of L22 per year and spent L100 on the feast of the Assumption,[8] but two later musical references discovered by Curatolo, which mention a procession featuring trumpets and other sounds of music to celebrate the transfer of the image of the Annuziata to the interior on 18 November 1582 and a funeral mass in music for Bagarotto on 24 June 1586,[9] point toward Santa Maria Annuziata as the more musically influential confraternity of the two, and other archival sources seem to confirm that view. A register kept by Bagarotto, which is also of interest for its information on his activity as a singer in many of the city's churches between 1570 and 1580, contains several notations for the years 1577, 1578, 1580, and 1588 regarding musical activity at Santa Maria Segreta. It reveals that by 1577 the organist was receiving an annual salary of L25 and that special music was featured at Vespers on the Nativity in 1577 and on the feast of the Assumption in 1578. The former involved four singers, and while the number of singers in not specified for the latter, the outlay for candles and music totaled L44 s10.[10] Although music is not specifically mentioned, large sums were also spent for the Nativity BVM in 1586 and the feast of Sant'Alessio in 1586 and 1587.[11] None of the aforementioned references indicates which group was responsible for funding these activities, but additional ones for 1580 and 1588 clarify the division of financial responsibilities. A list of obligations for 1580 indicates that the Pissina financed one daily and one annual mass (with no mention made of their annual celebrations on the Annunciation and Nativity BVM), while the Santissimo Sacramento/Santa Maria Annuziata sponsored a sung mass on the first Sunday of the month.[12] Finally, an entry for 1588 notes that the Santissimo Sacramento/Santa Maria Annunziata was responsible annually for the monthly sung mass in the chapel of the Madonna, the high mass in the chapel on the feast of the Annunciation, the feast of St. John the Baptist, an annual donation to the foundation for Giovanni Battista Bagarotto, the feast of Corpus Christi, the oil for the lamps, and the annual salary of L25 for the organist.[13]

A contract reported by Kendrick between Santa Maria Segreta's provost, Gabriel Bracco; the musician Giuseppe Gallo, who perhaps was serving as some sort of maestro or cleric in the church; and the organist Enrico Fiammengo for the year 1593 both sheds further light on the musical obligations and muddies the water with regard to the individual contributions made by each confraternity in the succeeding years. It specifies that Fiammengo is to play the organ at mass and Vespers on all the feasts of the year; at Compline on the feasts of Easter, Christmas, Pentecost, the Assumption, and St. John the Baptist; at processions on and during the octave of Corpus Christi; and at Vespers on the feasts of Saints Hugo and Alessio. Fiammengo's remuneration for these services was to be 20 scudi.[14] It would seem then that either a single organist paid by the Santissimo Sacramento/Santa Maria Annuziata had subsumed all the duties in the church and these had expanded markedly, or that the Santissimo Sacramento/Santa Maria Annuziata hired an organist of its own in addition to one employed by the Somaschi.

Giuseppe Gallo's participation in the aforementioned contract suggests that he had some sort of musical responsibilities at Santa Maria Segreta during the early 1590s, but at present we can only speculate about what these might have been. His *Sacri operis musici alternis modulis concinendi liber primus* (1598) of which only the altus part of the first chorus and the cantus part of the second chorus are extant, features a nine-voice mass, eight motets for double chorus (8vv), and three instrumental canzonas.[15] If the works contained were intended for Santa Maria Segreta, then double-choir music surely graced some of the aforementioned feasts, although it is not clear whether these feasts would have been the ones celebrated by the Somaschi, those observed by the Marian confraternities, or both. One of the eight-voice motets, "Veni in hortum meum," found its way into several northern sources, including the encyclopedic Pelplin tablature,[16] perhaps because it is a rearrangement of Lasso's five-voice motet from 1562 of the same title. Kendrick has noted that Gallo designates it for the feast of Corpus Christi, and he accordingly gives it an Christological reading, a rather interesting turn of events given the usual role of texts from the Song of Songs in defining Mary's *historia*.[17] The motet's designated association with the sacrament, nonetheless, offers the tantalizing possibility that it may have been composed expressly for use at the Corpus Christi celebration of the cult of the Santissimo Sacramento/Santa Maria Annuziata.

Other polyphony definitely emanated from Santa Maria Segreta after 1625. The *Flores praestantissimorum viorum* of 1626 (Appendix C, table 4), a collection of thirty-six works compiled by printer and bibliophile Filippo Lomazzo that was intended to showcase abroad the work of the city's most prominent composers, contains four sacred concerti, one concerted Magnificat, and an instrumental canzona by Lorenzo Frissone, who is identified in the print as the current organist at Santa Maria Segreta. Of the four sacred concerti, two are settings of texts from the Song of Songs, "O quam pulchra es amica mea" (Song of Songs 4:1) and "Qualis est dilectus" (Song of Song 5: 9–10), that are commonly found in the liturgies of the Assumption and Nativity BVM respectively, while a third, "Una ex o Maria," celebrates the Mulier fortis.[18] That Frissone contributed one-sixth of Lomazzo's collection places Santa Maria Segreta in a position of relative musical prominence with respect to the other churches represented, which include the Duomo, Santa Maria della Scala, Santa Maria presso San Celso, San Sepolchro, Sant'Ambrogio, and Santa Maria della Rosa, to name a few. Moreover, the four sacred concerti he contributed are textually and liturgically appropriate to feasts celebrated by both the Pissina and Santissimo Sacramento/Santa Maria Segreta, although, interestingly, they exhibit no overtly explicit textual ties to the Annunciation, the only primary feast celebrated by both. In any case, with the destruction of Santa Maria Segreta in 1911, the architecture, imagery, and much of the archival documentation that would contextualize these four concerti within the two different Marian cults at the institution was unfortunately largely lost. Also lacking is a clear explanation of the theological precepts on which the two cults themselves were founded, conceptual principles that would surely also help us to understand how the music enhanced the meditation process. Both cults apparently arose from the formalization of devotion to local street images, and seem not to have relied heavily upon the sort of systematically developed theological exegesis and culture of meditation books that supported such cults as the Madonna Addolorata, the Rosary, and the Madonna del Parto, or even, for that matter, the Madonna of Miracles at Santa Maria presso San Celso. Instead, their beginnings suggest that each developed individually along lines similar to that of the Ave Maria in the Duomo. If such is the case, then the polyphony that was performed for their observances was likely conceived and received according to the same general principles of meditation fostered in the cults discussed in the preceding chapters.

The case of the two Marian cults at Santa Maria Segreta represents a situation that is repeated for many other Marian cults that existed in Post-Tridentine Milan. Thus, the five Marian cults that were discussed in the previous chapters—the Madonna of Miracles at Santa Maria presso San Celso, the Madonna Addolorata, the Ave Maria in the Duomo, the Confraternity of the Rosary, and the Madonna del Parto—offer a window, albeit a modest one, into the Post-Tridentine devotional culture of the Virgin that fired the imagination and served as touchstones for the catechistic instruction of ordinary citizens in early modern Milan.

Appendix A

Documents

Document 1.1

ASDM, Archivio San Celso Amministrazione, Sedute, Registri 1583–1591, 46v (new 94).

8 Settembre 1585

Havendo il Reverendo sacrista di questa chiesa proposto il bisogno ch's'ha de libri per servigio del choro di detta chiesa, et exhibita nota de libri che li Reverendi Canonici di S. Nazaro di questa città hanno di vendere con liberi prezzi del tenere che segue

Nota della stima fatta delli cinque libri di carta connotta di canto di S. Nazaro di Milano

un' salterio carte numero 275 la seraitura et ligatura in tutto

Libro del Advento carte numero 260.

Libro dominicale carte numero 258.

Libro della quadregessima carte numero 263.

Hanno ordinato che li sodetti signori Gian' Battista Archinto, et Fossani s'informano del bisogno de questa chiesa qualità, et vero prezzo d'essi libri, è, poi, referiscanno.

Baldesar Adda Priore

September 8, 1585

The Reverend sacristan of this church, having related the need of books for use by the choir of this church, and been shown a list of books, which are as follows, that the Reverend Canons of San Nazaro of this city have for sale at liberal prices.

Note of the appraisal made of the five books in paper with musical notation from San Nazaro in Milan:

Psaltery, 275 pages in paper, with fastening and binding throughout.
Advent book, 260 pages in paper.
Sunday service book, 258 pages in paper.
Liturgy of the Saints, 258 pages in paper.
Book for Quadrigesima, 263 pages in paper.

They have ordered that the above-mentioned gentlemen Gian'Battista Archinto and Fossani investigate the need of this church, the quality, and the real price of these books and thereafter report back.

Baldesare Adda, prior

Document 1.2

ASDM, Archivio San Celso Amministrazione, Sedute, Registri 1583–1591, 47v (new 96).

26 September 1585

Intesa la relacione fatta per il sod*etto* si*gno*r Fossano s*opr*a il bisogno che q*ue*sta chiesa hà delli libri de canti de quali se fa mentione nel ordinat*ione* fatta nel pros*s*imo passato cap*itolo* co*n* la qualità, et vero prezzo d'essi libri,

Hanno ordi*n*ato del d*etto* si*gno*r Fossano col si*gno*r Gian' Batt*ist*a Archinto gia eletto co*m*mettano che d*etti* libri se compra*n*no per quel prezzo che à d*etti* sig*no*ri parerà, et si puotra co*n*venire co*n* gli venditori dando à d*etti* si*gno*ri ogni facoltà de fare fare, et fermare ogni oppor-tune mandato al si*gno*r Th*e*sau*r*o per il pagame*n*to d'essi,

Baldesar Adda P*ri*ore

26 September 1585

Understanding the report made by the above-mentioned Mr. Fossano about the need that this church has of the music books of which was made mention along with the quality and real price of these books in the order made in the previous chapter,

they have ordered that the aforementioned Mr. Fossano, with the previously elected Mr. Gian' Battista Archinto, determine whether the aforementioned books can be purchased for that price which seems appropriate to the aforementioned gentlemen, and if it is possible to reach agreement with the sellers. They give the aforementioned sirs every authority to do it, and to sign every appropriate order for pay-ment to the Lord Treasurer for the payment of them.

Document 1.3

ASDM, Archivio San Celso Amministrazione, Sedute,
Registri 1583–1591, 98v (new 100).

26 November 1585
. . . il R*evere*ndo m*esser* prete Annibale Campioni sacrista di q*ue*sta
chiesa eti*am* confessa havere recevuto quà presencialme*n*te dalli sod*etti*
st*essi* Sig*n*ori Priore, et Deputati p*re*senti [detti libri] . . . tutti coperti
d'asse perservirsene in choro, è quali libri d*etto* R*evere*ndo confessa
come s*op*ra havergli ricevuto in consegna co*n* prometta de riconsignarli
in q*ue*l med*esi*mo modo, è, stato che li suono consignati . . .

26 November 1585
The Reverend priest Mr. Annibale Campioni, sacristan of the
church, now confesses to having received here at present from the
above-mentioned same Lord Prior and Deputies present [the aforementioned books] . . . all bound in board for use in the choir, and the
aforementioned Reverend confesses as above to having received those
books into custody with the promise to return them in the same manner and state in which they were delivered.

Document 1.4

ASDM, Archivio San Celso Amministrazione, Sedute, Registri
1592–1599, 56r–59r (excerpts from reforms of 29 May 1595).

57r:
Che ogni giorno si canti la messa ordiniaria, et vespero seconda
l'ordine del calendario. Le feste terza, messa, vespero et compieta, assig-
nando li ponti alla messa del piano habere, et al vespero il resposo in
choro.
    That every day the regular mass and vespers according to the order
of the calendar are sung. On feasts, Terce, Mass, Vespers, and Compline
[are sung], assigning to the days in between the low mass and at Vespers
service in the choir.
    57r:
Che non si trovarà le feste à tempo di cantare la messa perderà
soldi diece, et il medesimo perderà non trovandosi al vespero. Et chi
non si troverà alle messe cantate, et alli vesperi dalla festa di pasca

di resurrettione sino alle calende di novembre di ciascuno anno delli giorni feriali perderà tutti l'emolumenti del giorno seguente et vogliono che nel fine di ciascuno vespero si canti la salve.

That he who is not found on feasts at the time of the singing of the mass will lose ten soldi, and he not found at Vespers will lose the same. And whoever is not found at sung masses and Vespers from Easter to the calends of November on the ferial days of each year will lose all the extra income of the following day, and they wish that at the end of every Vespers the Salve be sung.

57v:

Che quando si andarà in choro per cantar messa overo vespero, ogn'uno seguiti con decoro et divotione unitamente il sacerdote apparato, et che non vi andarà sotto pretenso di qualche senza perderà tutti l'utili di quel giorno,

That when going into the choir to sing mass or Vespers, each one will follow the sacerdote dressed with decorum and devotion, and that none will go there under any other pretense without losing all the income of that day.

57v:

Che mentre si stara in choro se gli stia con decentia cleriale servando silencio per non dare scandalo al popolo, et per non disturbar i compagni, et dirano le salmi

distintamente et pontualmente ne uscirano dal choro se non per qualche suo bisogno necessario senza licenza del Reverendo Prefetto.

That when in the choir each will be there with clerical decency serving quietly in order to avoid scandalizing the populace and disturbing the members of the company, and they sing the psalms distinctly and unfailingly, and they do not leave the choir without the permission of the Reverend Prefect unless for some necessary reason.

58v:

Che li musici non introduchino à cantare in chiesa figliuoli ne altri poco pratichi di musica per insegnarli, o, per qualche altro loro dissegno, ma solamente entrino in choro li musici stipendiati della madona, eccetto se vi introducessero qualche buon sugietto qual sorte per dare ornamento alla musica, et non per disturbarla.

That the musicians not introduce children nor others little practiced in music to sing in the church in order to instruct them, or for some other intention of their own, but only the salaried musicians of the Madonna enter in the choir, except if they introduce some good subject for the purpose of ornamenting the music, and not for disturbing it.

Document 2.1

ASDM, Arichvio spirituale X, San Carlo XXIII (Visite pastorali e documenti aggiunti: Santa Maria dei Servi), fasc. 2, f. 5.

Aurelia Gialda altre volte della compagnia delle Vergini di S. Orsula ma puoi p*er* commandamento di Monsig*n*or Ill*us*triss*im*e Cardinale fu cassata et privata di detta compagnia, et hora si diporta ta*n*to scadalalosamente che è causa di grandiss*im*a mormoratione non solo di se stessa, ma ancora de tutto de Vergini di S. Orsola, poscia che p*er* il colarino, et habito che ella porta, è stimata vergine di S. Orsola, et p*er* li suoi mali diporti da occasione che le persone dicono pocho bene delle Orsoline, anzi agiongono che stupiscono essendo ella tollerata.

Pratica scandalosam*en*te nella chiesa de servi sotto pretesto d'esser della scola della Madonna, e d'haver carico d'adornar l'altare della qual occasione se ne serve malamente poiche se ne sta'in d*ett*a Chiesa molto tempo, a certe hore particolari diportandosi molto familiam*en*te con li frati, accomodando insieme l'altare, hora piegando et dispiegando palij, tovaglie et simili altre cose p*er*tinenti all'ornamento di d*ett*o altare, sempre burlando, et facendo atti molto scandalosi.

Nell'hora che si celebrano li divini offitij et particolarm*en*te nelle feste solenne, et feste della Madona, sta' in chiesa con il capo scop*er*to portando il velo sopra le spale a fogia di banda, vagando, et passegiando p*er* chiesa, ridendo, burlando, hor'con questa gintildona hor con quel'altra, et nel tempo delle processioni della Madona si diporta p*er* le strade in modo tale che pare un sergente de soldati . . .

Aurelia Gialda, once of the society of the Virgins of St. Ursula but then removed and expelled from said society by order of the Illustrious Monsignor Cardinale, now arrays herself so scandalously that it is cause for great gossip not only about herself, but also about all of the Virgins of St. Ursula, because by the clerical collar and habit that she wears, she is regarded as a Virgin of St. Ursula. And on account of her sinful behavior persons speak ill of the Ursulines; in fact, they seem surprised that she is being tolerated.

She practices scandalously in the church of the Servites under the pretense of being a member of the Confraternity of the Madonna, and of having the responsibility of adorning the altar, on which occasion she serves it badly, as she remains in the aforementioned church for a long time, at certain particular hours behaving very familiarly with the friars, making herself comfortable at the altar, now folding and unfolding banners, linens, and similar other things pertinent to the decoration of said altar, always jesting and performing very scandalous acts.

During the hour in which they celebrate the divine offices, and particularly during the solemn feasts and feasts of the Madonna, she remains in the church with her head uncovered wearing the veil over the shoulders in the style of a vagrant, roving and strolling through the church, laughing, jesting, now with this gentlewoman, then with that other, and during the time of the processions of the Madonna she comports herself on the street in a manner similar to that of a quarter-master of soldiers . . .

Document 2.2

Milano, Archivio di Stato. Fondo di Religione 679 (Milano, Confraternità, S. Maria dei Servi, Addolorata, Fondazione).

Illustrissimi Signori

Felice Avogadri il quale ha già dui anni servito nella loro chiesa delli servi per organista con provisione solo di vinti ducatoni l'anno, ma con la speranza datagli che sicuramente si sarebbe fra poco tempo accresciuta la sudetta sua provisione conforme alli meriti suoi, et alla buona servitù che havesse fatto al sudetto suo officio di sonar l'organo. La qual speranza però non ha mai sortito effetto alcuno. Per il che essendo hormai il terzo anno che serve, et havendo più volte lasciate andare assia migliori occasioni di questa per la promessa che se gli è sempre fatta di acrescrere il suo salario; Ricorre dalle Signori Vostre.

Supplicandole ad esser servite che questo loro promessa sia esse-guita, et si accresca la provisione dell'organo almeno à trenta scudi l'anno; acciò possa il detto Felice trattenersi, et habbia occasione di servire più volontieri et ingegnarsi per far' il debito honore all'officio suo. Il che per esser giusto et conveniente spera facilmente ottenere dalle Signori Vostre, alle quali non cessa di pregare da Dio ogni desid-erata prosperità, et contento.

Al primo Genaro 1599. Letto il presente memoriale nella Congregatione fatta il detto d'ogi nel solito loco della Sagreteria è statta detto e stabilito che si acreschi il salario al sudetto signor Felice organista in tutto sino la somma de ducati numero 15 dico quendici per la parte spetante ala scola cominciando il giorno d'ogi con che il detto *sign*or Felice organista sia obbligato servire doi anni intiere. Con ogni diligentia et cura et no*n* altrimente. Giovanni Stefano Stancho priore. Giuliano Pozzobonello Cancelliere.

Most Illustrious Gentlemen:

Felice Avogadro already has served as organist for two years in your church of the Servites with a remuneration of only twenty ducats per year, but with the expectation that his aforementioned provision would be increased shortly according to his qualifications and the good service that he would give in the aforementioned office of playing the organ. That expectation, however, has never been fulfilled. Given that it is now his third year of service, and many better occasions than this have been allowed to pass in which to fulfill the promise that is always made to increase his salary, he now returns to your lordships, supplicating you that their promise to the fellow Servite be executed, and that the remuneration for the organ be raised to at least thirty scudi per year, in order that the aforementioned Felice be able to remain and have occasion to serve more willingly and to strive to give proper honor to his office. This which is just and convenient he hopes to obtain easily from your lordships, for who he does not cease to pray to God for every desired prosperity and contentment.

On 1 January 1599 the present memorial was read in the congregation and on the same day in the usual location of the secretary's office it was suggested and agreed to increase the salary of the aforementioned Mr. Felice, organist, by 15 ducats in all, that is fifteen due on the part of the Scuola beginning today, in return for which the aforementioned organist Mr. Felice is obligated to serve two full years. With every diligence and solicitude and not otherwise. Giovanni Stefano Stancho, prior. Giuliano Pozzobonello, chancellor.

Document 3.1

Milano, Archivio dei Luoghi Pii Elimosinieri 289/8
(Ave Maria: Uffici A–Z, Musici), s.d., Insert 2.

Si propone se saria bene per avanzare dinaro, di fare cantare l'Ave Maria ad organo con Quattro voci sole.
Il conto è tale   L616_
Di presente importo a il salario delli musici <u>486</u>

Avanzano   L130
Con l'organo importarebbe
Al organista L100
Ali mantieri L40
et forse meno, poiche le tiene, et potrà servire in occasione di mancamento
del organista per infirmità o altro, oltre che ha da battere.
A Hippolito tenore   L100
Alto   L70
Basso   L96
Soprano   L50
Nella quaresima si potranno pigliare musici et acordarli per quel tempo, che sarà non più de 30 giorni L30
L486

It is proposed that it would be a good idea by advancing money to arrange to sing the Ave Maria with the organ and four solo voices.
The cost is such   L616__
Of the current total to the salary of the musicians 486
They advance   L130
With the organist it would total:
To the organist   L100
To the bellows pumpers   L40
and perhaps less, since he supports them, and can serve on the occasion of the absence of the organist because of illness or other. Besides, he has to conduct.
To Hippolito tenore L100
Alto   L70
Basso   L96
Soprano   L50
During Lent they could take musicians and contract them for that time, which will be not more than 30 days L30
L486

Document 3.2

Milano, Archivio dei Luoghi Pii Elimosinieri 289/8
(Ave Maria: Uffici A-Z, Archivio).

Illustri et molto __
Li scolari che hanno cura di mantener' la musica de l'Ave Maria
che si canta in questa chiesa maggior,' si trovano in necessità di haver
'in essa chiesa. luogo o cassa commoda per riponer'li libri. et altre cose
pertinent a la musica, et havendo visto che nel pulpito istesso ove si
canta, sono duoi banchi in foggia di cassette quali siano continuamente
aperti, et niuno se ne serve, ne il maestro di capella del istesso Domo
intende in alcun modo servirsene. Però essi scolari
Supplicando *Vostro Signor* Illustre et m*olta* R*everen*da darli licenza
che possano usar' d'essi banchi, a quali possono anco far' metter' ser-
rature per maggior' sicurezza, per il detto effetto solamente; che lo
riceveranno per gracia, con promessa che in ogni evento di bisogno che
ne potesse haver' la chiesa, li restituirano protanm*en*te.
Io Giovanni Jacomo de Clerici
Io Giulio Cesare Gabussi m*ae*stro di capella mi consento quanto
di sopra si contiene.
—un ordine del molto Ill*ust*re et R*everen*do Monsig*nore* Proposito.
data A di 19 aprile 1606 istesso. ric*omen*do Priore.

Illustrious and very __
The scholars that have the responsibility of maintaining the music
of the Ave Maria that is sung in this largest church find themselves
needing a place or case in this church convenient for putting away the
books and other things pertaining to the music, and having seen that
in the same pulpit from which one sings there are two benches in the
form of chests that are continually open and serve no one, nor does the
maestro di cappella of the same Duomo intend for them to serve him
in any manner. But these scholars
[are] supplicating Your Illustrious and Very Reverend Lord to
give them license to use these benches, for which they also are able to
construct locks for greater security, for the aforementioned belongings
only. [And they request] that they receive it as a favor, with the promise
that in any case in which the church has need, they will return them
promptly.
Giovanni Giacomo de Clerici

I Giulio Cesare Gabussi, maestro di cappella, consent to that which is contained.

An order of the very illustrious and Reverend Monsignor Preposito dated 19 April 1606 of the same.

I recommend, Prior.

Document 3.3

*Milano, Archivio dei Luoghi Pii Elimosinieri 289/8
(Ave Maria: Uffici A-Z, Musici, 1605–1629).*

Deliberò il venerando Capitolo della divotione dell'Ave Maria che si canta ogn'sera nella Metropolitana chiesa di Milano Adì 31 decembre 1620-in osservatione d'una serra già sottoscritte dalli signori deputati ò sia contribuenti, d'essa divotione Che per estintione dil debito che ha detta divotione quale assende alla somma de-L 170-In circa, si mandasse da tutti quelli non si troviorno al Capitolo Accio s'accontentino soccorere con l'ellemosine per estintione dil sudetto debito, Atteso che quelli hevano presenti tutti sboriorno un' ducate cioè L8 per ciascuno restorno al signor tesoriero.

The venerable chapter of the devotion of the Ave Maria that is sung every evening in the Metropolitan church of Milan deliberated on the day of 31 December in observation of a compact already undersigned by the Lord deputies or rather contributors to said devotion that for the elimination of the debt that the aforementioned devotion has accrued, which has now risen to around the sum of L170, all those not present at the chapter be sent a dispatch in order that they fulfill their obligation in assisting to eliminate with a donation the above-mentioned debt, all those present having attended to it by shelling out a ducat, that is L8 each left with the Lord treasurer.

Document 4.1.

*ASDM, Archivio spirituale X, S. Lorenzo IX
(Visite pastorali e documenti aggiunti), fasc. 4.*

Pro societate Santissimi Rosarij 1627
Illustrissimo Signore

Dalla *lette*ra di *Vicario Prefetto Reverendissi*ma, è dal *Priore* Provinciale della Provincia di S. Pietro Martire dell'Ordine suo più diffusamente ancora ho inteso la difficoltà che viene fatta sopra l'erettione della Compagnia della B.V. del Rosario nella Collegiata di S. Lore*nz*o in questa Città, come che'à ciò ortino ha concessio in A*pplichazione* fatta alla sua Religione, è non possa se giurare pregiudicio alla Chiesa di S. Eustorgio vicina à quella di S. Lorenzo; E perchè non intendo ne voglio che sia pregiudicato in cosa benche minima, non alle sue Chiese, overo à cioè Privilegi suoi, quando sufficentemente sarò informato, che ha sudetta Compagnia non possa sussisceri di ragione, vi porrò qual remedio che converrà, è che sarà di soddisfattione alla P.V. *Reverendissi*ma alla quale dal *sig*n*o*re prego il colmo della sua santa gratia. Milano di 21 Agosto 1627

On behalf of the Society of the Most Holy Rosary 1627.
Most Illustrious Sir
From the letter of Your Most Reverend Vicar Prefect and from the Provincial Prior of the Province of San Pietro Martire of his order I understand more fully still the difficulty that has arisen over the erection of the Company of the Blessed Virgin of the Rosary in the collegiate church of San Lorenzo in this city, so that to that end it has conceded the little garden in an application made to his order, and I am not able but to vow prejudice toward the church of Sant'Eustorgio near to that of San Lorenzo. And because I neither intend nor wish to be prejudiced, even the slightest bit, against its churches nor those which are its privileges in this thing, and because I am not able to gossip about motives, when I am sufficiently informed that it has the aforementioned company, I will take that measure that will be expedient, and that will be satisfactory to the Most Reverend Vicar Prefect for whom I ask the Lord the full measure of his blessed grace. [In] Milan [on] 21 August 1627.

Document 4.2.

ASM, Notarile 14363 (Francesco Tessera q. Bartolomeo 17/10/1587–10/02/1589), 3 Junij 1588.

Al nome de dio adi 31 maggio 1588 in milano
Conventione pacti et acordio facti fra li infras*cri*pti *ma*gi*n*i*fi*ci si*gno*ri priore et scolari dilla scola dil *santissi*mo rosario nella chiesia

dilla rosande milano per una parte et D. Cristoforo Valvasore per l'altra parte dil efetto infrascripto e primo.

Che detto messer Cristoforo sia tenuto come per tenor di la presente Instromente sotto obbligo di se et suoi beni presenti et futuri pegno ali detti infrascripti signori priore et scolari presenti et che aceteno di far uno organo bello et bone sonor et corista di tuto ponto nella sudeta chiesia dilla rosa conforme al stato di detta chiesa che sia di la qualita et forme infrascripta et alia le infrascripte cosse ben facta et durabile cioe-

Sia de piedi numero dodese conli registri infrascripti cioe il principale tuto di stagno con la prima cana in faciata

La ottava dil principale di piombo

La quintadecima

La decima nona

La vingiesima secondo

La vingiesima sesto

La vingiesima nono

La tregiesima terzo

dil flauto in ottava con il principale

un flauto in quintadecimo

una registra in duodecimo a imitacion di corneti

il somercione sechreta dil vento cioe che sia facto a vento conli soi registri de rame et la sua maestra di noce per la faciata et il crivello che tien impiedi le cane con la sua cadenzatura, cioe reducione dil somero con la tastatura de tasti numero 50 et pedali con le sue cane del vento

Et che la faciata di deto organo sia de cinque campi de come che soneno et dui campi de come morte simile al organo di Sant'Angelo de milano con quella polideza et beleza come quello et imbronitura con sei montesi coperti de bulgori di rossia grandi alla porcione di esso organo

Che tute le cosse mobilli siano tenuto il detto messer Cristoforo farle per lo infrascripto precio convenuto qui da basso

Et li sudeti signori scolari sieno tenuti alor spese farli far la cassa di deto organo con il suo pogiolo et pontili con la sua comodita da condare lorgano et il castelo da la pondare sopra il somero di detto organo-

Et piu fare la cassa da logare li mantesi con il cavalo da pondare le stange delli mantesi et il locho comodo da logare detto organo et montesi

Il qual organo il detto messer Cristoforo promete farlo bono et qui valente di tuta bonta a giudicio de quarto amici periti cioe dui per parte uno maestro da organi et uno suonatore per banda li quali abieno da giudicare incosciencia sua se tal organo sara perfetto et casa che altramente giudicasero che non poseno tratare di niuno accordo salvo che lorgano abia da restare ad detto messer Cristoforo et che lui sia tenuto a restetuire tuti li dinari che avera avuto da detti signori scolari prontamente abia a dare sigurta idonea qui in milano per la restitucione delli dinari che segli pageramo per deto organo et per li obligi che si contiene in questo caso che lui non desse la deta opera nel modo sopradetto il qual organo sia tenuto il detto messer Cristoforo darlo dil tuto ben formito et conzio perfetto et posto in opera nella sudeta chiesa nel termine de mesi disdotto prossimi avenir

Et che si possia compitamente sonare et non dandolo nel modo et tempo sudetto che sia tenuto et obligato a restetuire li dinari et altra cossa che avesse avuto da deti signori scolari con ogni dano spese et interesse che sara giudicato dal signor prior con doi altri amici comuni se cossi pero piacere del deto signor prior overo che sia in arbitrio delli deti signori prior et scolari di poterne far fare un altro simile da qual maestro che a loro piu piacera a spese et doni di deto messer Cristoforo

Et di piu deto messer Cristoforo se obliga et promete di mantenere deta opera et acordarlo per anni tri da poi facta et posta in opera che non abia a fare ne bustare difetto alcuno che sia de dano mentre pero che essi signori lo guardeno da aqua da rovina et malignita de dalcuno che vi potesse fare dano che per causa et pagamento di detta opera nella sudeta qualita et forma et bonta li deti signori scolari sieno tenuti come per tenore dilla presente il magnifico signor alessandro Lombardo priore et li magnifici signori bartolomeo sacco francesco cantone soto priore nicolo agudi tuti scolari et alor nome et deli altri scolari per quali prometeno che averano ratto e fermo sotto obligo delli soi bene dare al detto messer Cristoforo per detta opera come di sopra scuti trecento setanta doro da lire sei per scuto imperiale nelli termini infrascripti cioe scuti cento in termine de otto giorni da poi dato la sigurta quale sigurta se obliga darlo in termine de giorni otto prossimi avenire nelle mane dil signor francesco tesera notaro publico di milano e sindico di essa scolla et altri scuti cento a la mita di deta opera la qual sia pero vista da uno de detti signori scolari et altri scuti cento da poi ferita lopera et messa in opera et il restante che sarano

scuti setanta in termine di uno anno da poi ferita della opera con ogni
dano et spesa non pagandoli li detti dinari nelli termini sudeti per
le qual tute cosse dete parte valgieno poter esser convenute avanti a
qual giudice in forma di camera in milano et volendo che il presente
abia forza de publico istrum*en*to come se fusse fatto et rogato da
publico notaro con le clause solite et p*er* fede dette parte ano soto-
scri*p*to la presente di lor propria mane a la presentia delli infras*cri*pti
testimoni . . .

In the name of God on 31 May 1588 in Milan

A covenant reconciled and an accord made between the undermentioned magnificent Lord Prior and gentlemen scholars of the
Confraternity of the Most Holy Rosary in the church of the Rosa
in Milan on the one hand and D. Cristoforo Valvasore on the other
hand to the underwritten and above effect that the aforementioned Mr.
Cristoforo has agreed and is obliged according to the present instrument, through secure bond of his present and future property to the
aforementioned undersigned Lord Prior and scholars present, to build
a beautiful and good-sounding organ and a diapason entirely of scaf-
folding in the aforementioned church of the Rosa in conformity to the
state of said church, that is of the quality and form stated below, and
otherwise well made and durable according to the understated condi-
tions which are as follows:

It is of twelve ranks with the underwritten registers, namely the
principal all of tin with the first pipe on the façade

The octave of the principal of lead

The fifteenth

The nineteenth

The twenty-second

The twenty-sixth

The twenty-ninth

The thirty-third

Of the flute at the octave with the principal

A flute at the fifteenth

A register at the twelfth in imitation of cornetti

The recessed chest of the wind, that is wind operated with its registers of copper, and its guide of walnut for the façade, and the sieve
that holds the pipe standing [in place] with its downward extension,
namely the reduction of the wind-chest with the keyboard of fifty keys
and pedals with their windpipes.

And the façade of the aforementioned organ is of five audible fields and two inaudible ones similar to the organ of Sant'Angelo of Milan with the high finish, beauty, and burnish of that [instrument] and with six mantle covers of Bulgarian leather from Russia equal to the size of said organ.

That the aforementioned Mr. Cristoforo is to make all the mobile things for the undermentioned price agreed here below.

And the aforementioned gentlemen scholars are to pay for the construction of the case of said organ, with its balcony and bays making it convenient to handle the organ, and the tower from the scaffold over the wind-chest of said organ.

And also to make the case to lodge the bellows, with the horse on which to rest the beams of the bellows and the comfortable location to lodge said organ and bellows.

Which organ the aforementioned Cristoforo promises to construct well and be here judged expert in all quality by four expert friends, that is two for a part, a maestro of organ, and a player from a company, each of whom is to judge according to his conscience whether such organ is perfect, and in the case that it is otherwise judged, they will not be able to reach any accord save that the organ will remain with the aforementioned Mr. Cristoforo and that he is obligated to return all of the money that he has been given by the aforementioned gentlemen scholars and immediately give suitable security here in Milan for the restitution of the money. And if we pay him for the aforementioned organ and for the requirements contained and in this case he does not execute the aforementioned work in the manner mentioned above, Mr. Cristoforo is obligated to see that that organ is well formed and in perfect dimension and placed in working condition in the abovementioned church in the period of eighteen months to come.

And if it can be politely played and it is not provided in the abovementioned manner and time, that he is held and obligated to return the money and other thing that he has had from the aforesaid Lord scholars with every fine, expense, and interest that will be determined by the Lord prior with two other mutual friends. If, however, such is the pleasure of the aforesaid Lord Prior or if it is the will of the aforesaid Lord Prior and scholars, they can have another similar one made by that maestro who seems the best to them at the expense and donation of the aforesaid Mr. Cristoforo.

And, further, said Mr. Cristoforo obligates himself and promises to maintain said work and tune it for three years after it is finished and installed. And he does not have to fix nor enclose any defect that is from damage, however, while these gentlemen guard it from water, from ruin or malignancy of any sort that is able to damage it there. For cause and payment of said work in the above-mentioned quality, form, and excellence, the said gentlemen scholars are obligated according to the present terms, the magnificent Lord Alessandro Lombardo, prior, and the magnificent Lords Bartolomeo Sacco, Francesco Cantone sub-prior, and Nicolo Agudi promising in the name of all the scholars by ratifying and signing under obligation of their property, to give the aforementioned Mr. Cristoforo for said work as described above three hundred and seventy scudi of gold at six lire per Imperial scudo according to the above written terms, that is one hundred scudi given as security within a period of eight days, which security must be placed in the hands of Sir Francesco Tessera, notary public of Milan and auditor of this school, and another one hundred scudi at the halfway point of the work, which work, however, will be seen by one of the said Lord scholars, and another hundred scudi when the work is cut and installed, and the rest, which will be seventy scudi, in the term of a year from when the work was cut with every loss and expense not paid the said money being in the above-mentioned terms, every part of which they validate by convening formally before that judge in the chamber in Milan. And wishing that the present have the force of a public instrument as was made and notarized by a public notary with the usual clauses and by faith, said part is underwritten in their own hand in the present year in the presence of the above-written witnesses . . .

[Witnessed by Cristoforo Vavalsore, Alessandro Lombardo priore, Giovanni Battista Casella notaio publico di Milano (in the name of Francesco Cantono sotto priore), Bartolomeo Sacco, Nicolo Agudo, Alessandro Trada.]

Appendix B

Pay Records for the Singers of the Ave Maria in Duomo[1]

1 April 1605 for first three months of the year.

94 à D. Giovanni Maria Negri, maestro di cappella	L 23 s12
50 à Mons. Prete Agostino Costa	L12 s1 d9
50 à D. Cesare Vespolate	L11 s16 d3
50 à D. Camillo Mazza	L11 s10 d6
50 à D. Ottavio Verdere	L10 s8 d6
50 à D. Niccolo Pelizzone	L11 s19
50 à D. Giovanni Battista Negri	L10 s19
50 Alli duoi soprano	L12 s10
144 Alli duoi huomini che espongono li cilostri	L36

1606. Annual salaries beginning on 1 April 1606.

Hercule Cuneo, Maestro di Capella	L100
Bassi: Li Reverendi Prete Agostino	L60
Prete Alessio	L96
Tenori: M. Ottavio	L70
M. Hippolito	L70
M. Camillo	L50
Alti: Reverendo Vittoriano	L70
M. Nicolò	L50
Soprani: Antonio de Picinardi	L40
Melchior Reina	<u>L32</u>
	L630

4 December 1611 for last six months of 1611.

D. Hippolito Canova	L50
Prete Agostino Costa	L30
Prete Alessio Briosco	L48
D. Giovanni Battista Bonhomo	L35
D. Giovanni Battista Crespi	L35

R. Prete Vittoriano Sodarini	L35
D. Alvisio Rabastello	L25
D. Pietro Maria Giussani	L25
Alli duoi huomini che espongono li Cilostri	<u>L72</u>
	L355

June 1612 for first six months of 1612.

D. Hippolito Canova maestro di cappella	L50
All'istesso Hippolito canova per tanto ha detto	
il s. Aurelio facino esserci speso in libri de Canti	L3
R. Prete Agostino Costa	L30
R. Prete Alessio Briosco	L48
D. Giovanni Battista Bonomo	L35
D. Giovanni Battista Crespi	L35
R. Prete Vittoriano Sodarini	L35
D. Alvisio Robastello	L25
D. Giovanni Maria Giussani	L25
Alli duo huomini che espongono li cilostri	<u>L72</u>
	L358

2 January 1613 for six months.

D. Hippolito Canova	L50
R. Prete Alessio Briosco	L48
R. Prete Cesare Cappi	L35
Aurelio Mazani	L35
D. Giovanni Battista Crespi	L35
D. Antonio Pizinardi	L35
D. Alvisio Rabastelli	L25
m. Battista Angosciola et Paolino Molatore	L25
Alli doi huomini che espongono li cilostri	<u>L72</u>
	L360

8 July 1613 for six months.

D. Hippolito Canova	L50
R. Prete Alessio Briosco	L48
R. Prete Cesare Cappi Pavese per tre mesi	L17.10
D. Giovanni Battista Bononio	L35
D. Giovanni Battista Crespi	L35
R. Prete Vitoriano Sodarini	L35
D. Alvisio Rabastello	L25
D. Pietro Maria Giussani	L25
Alli duo huomeni che espongono li cilostri	<u>L72</u>
	L342.10

2 January 1614 for six months.

D. Hippolito Canova	L50
R. Prete Alessio Briosco	L48
R. Prete Cesare Cappi Pavese per tre mesi	L35
D. Giovanni Battista Bononio	L35
D. Giovanni Battista Crespi	L35
R. Prete Vitoriano Sodarini	L35
D. Alvisio Rabastello	L25
D. Pietro Maria Giussani	L25
Alli duo huomeni che espongono li cilostri	<u>L72</u>
	L360

1 July 1614 for six months.

D. Hippolito Canova	L50
R. Prete Alessio Briosco	L48
R. Prete Cesare Cappi Pavese per tre mesi	L35
D. Giovanni Battista Bononio	L35
D. Giovanni Battista Crespi	L35
R. Prete Vitoriano Sodarini	L35
D. Alvisio Rabastello	L25
D. Pietro Maria Giussani	L25
Alli duo huomeni che espongono li cilostri	<u>L72</u>
	L360

2 January 1615 for six months.

D. Hippolito Canova	L50
R. Prete Alessio Briosco	L48
R. Prete Cesare Cappi	L35
D. Aurelio Mazano	L35
D. Giovanni Battista Crespi	L35
D. Antonio Picenardi	L35
D. Alvisio Rabastello	L25
Pietro Antonio Vigentijs	L25
Alli duo huomeni che espongono li cilostri	L72
Al maestro di cappella per tanti spesi in libri doi cantiis	<u>L5</u>
	L365

30 June 1616 for six months.

D. Hippolito Canova	L50
R. Prete Cesare Cappi Pavese	L40
R. Prete Alessio Briosco	L48
D. Giovanni Battista Crespi	L35
R. Gio. Battista Larotione for the service of Aurelio Mazza	L17.10

D. Hieronymo Vimercato	L17.10
D. Antonio Picenardi	L35
D. Alvisio Rabastello	L25
D. Hippolito Canova per pagare soprani	L25
Alli duo huomeni che espongono li cilostri	<u>L72</u>
	L365

29 July 1616 for six months.

D. Hippolito Canova	L50
R. Prete Cesare Cappi Pavese	L40
R. Prete Alessio Briosco	L48
D. Giovanni Battista Crespi	L35
R. Gio. Battista Larotione for the service of Aurelio Mazza	L17.10
D. Hieronymo Vimercato	L17.10
D. Antonio Picenardi	L35
D. Alvisio Rabastello	L25
D. Hippolito Canova per pagare soprani	L25
Alli duo huomeni che espongono li cilostri	<u>L72</u>
	L365

5 January 1617 for six months.

D. Hippolito Canova	L50
R. Prete Alessio Briosco	L48
R. Prete Cesare Cappi	L40
D. Hieronymo Vimercato	L35
D. Giovanni Battista Crespi	L35
D. Antonio Picenardi	L35
D. Alvisio Rabastello	L25
Al putto che canta il soprano	L25
Alli duo huomeni che espongono li cilostri	<u>L72</u>
	L365

28 June 1617 for six months.

D. Hippolito Canova	L50
All'istesso *per* pagare un soprano	L25
R. Prete Alessio Briosco	L48
R. Prete Cesare Cappi	L40
D. Hieronymo Vimercato	L35
D. Giovanni Battista Crespi	L35
D. Antonio Picenardi	L35
D. Alvisio Rabastello	L25
Alli duo huomeni che espongono li cilostri	<u>L72</u>
	L365

21 March 1618. Mandato to pay the singers for 1 January to 14 March of 1618 with their usual salaries, noting that Francesco has taken the place of Alvisi.

2 tenors and 2 contraltos at 2.5 months of their L70 annual stipend=<u>L14.11.8</u>

For all four=L58.6.4

Reverendo Prete Alessio for same portion of his L96 annual salary=L20

Reverendo Cesare Pavese for same portion of his L80 annual salary=L16.13.4

To the sopranos for that time at the rate of L50 aside from the one from S. Maurizio=L10.8.4

2 July 1618 for April, May, and June of 1618.

D. Hippolito Canova	L25
R. Prete Giovanni	L14.11.9
D. Hieronymo Vimercato	L17.10
D. Gio. Battista Crespi	L17.10
D. Antonio Picenardi	L17.10
D. Francesco detto il filatorello	L17.10
D. Hippolito Canova, maestro di cappella per pagare un soprano	L12.10
et alli duo huomini che espongono li Cerei ogni sera	<u>L35</u>
	L194.1.9

7 January 1619 for six months.

D. Hippolito Canova	L50
R. Giovanni Blaccino	L35
D. Pietro Paolo Antoniani	L35
D. Hieronymo Vimercato	L35
D. Giovanni Battista Crespi	L35
D. Antonio Picenardi	L35
D. Francesco [ferari]	L35
Al sude*tto* Canova p*er* dare à un soprano	L25
Et alli huomini che espongono li cilostri	<u>L72</u>
	L357

30 December 1620 for six months.

D. Hippolito Canova	L50
R. Giovanni Blaccino	L35
D. Pietro Paolo Antoniani	L35
D. Hieronymo Vimercato	L35

D. Giovanni Battista Crespi	L35
D. Antonio Picenardi	L35
D. Francesco [ferari]	L35
Al sudetto Canova per dare à un soprano	L25
Et alli huomini che espongono li cilostri	<u>L72</u>
	L357

7 July 1621 for six months.

D. Hippolito Canova	L50
R. Giovanni Blaccino	L35
D. Pietro Paolo Antoniani	L35
D. Aurelio Mazano	L35
D. Giovanni Battista Crespi	L35
D. Antonio Picenardi	L35
D. Francesco [ferari]	L35
Al sudetto Canova per dare à un soprano	L25
Et alli huomini che espongono li cilostri	<u>L72</u>
	L357

4 March 1622 for six months.

D. Hippolito Canova	L50
R. Giovanni Blaccino	L35
D. Pietro Paolo Antoniani	L35
D. Francesco Bernardo Crespi	L35
D. Giovanni Battista Crespi	L35
D. Antonio Picenardi	L35
D. Francesco [ferari]	L35
Al sudetto Canova per dare à un soprano	L25
Et alli huomini che espongono li cilostri	<u>L72</u>
	L357

1 July 1622 for six months.

R.Prete Giovanni Blancino	L45
D. Pietro Paolo Antoniani	L35
D. Giovanni Battista Crespi	L45
D. Francesco Bernardo Crespi	L35
D. Antonio Picenardi	L35
D. Francesco Ferrari	L35
a soprano	L25
Et alli duo huomini che espongono li cilostri	<u>L72</u>
	L327

15 January 1623 for six months.

R.Prete Giovanni Blancino	L45
D. Pietro Paolo Antoniani (basso)	L35

D. Giovanni Battista Crespi	L45
D. Francesco Bernardo Crespi	L35
D. Antonio Picenardi	L35
D. Francesco Ferrari	L35
a soprano	L25
D Aurelio Mazano for singing tenor in July & August 1621	L11.13
Et alli duo huomini che espongono li cilostri	<u>L72</u>
	L330.13

6 July 1623 for six months.

R.Prete Giovanni Blancino	L45
D. Pietro Paolo Antoniani (basso)	L35
D. Giovanni Battista Crespi	L45
D. Francesco Bernardo Crespi	L35
D. Antonio Picenardi	L35
D. Francesco Ferrari	L35
a soprano	L25
Et alli duo huomini che espongono li cilostri	<u>L72</u>
	L319

Note: 1. ALPM, 289/9 (Ave Maria: Uffici A-Z, Musici, 1605–1629). By 1620 the Scuola was experiencing difficulty in meeting the annual expenses associated with music through general donations, and, as a result, each member was required to donate L8. ALPM 289/9 (Ave Maria: Uffici A-Z, Musici, 1605–1629), 13 dicembre 1620.

Appendix C

Contents of Selected Collections
by Milanese Composers

TABLE C.I.
Vocal Works in Giovanni Paolo Cima,
Concerti ecclesiastici a una, due, tre, e quattro voci . . .
(Milano: gl'heredi di Simon Tini, & Filippo Lomazzo, 1610.)

TITLE	VOICING (WITH CONTINUO)	LITURGICAL USAGE OR TEXT SOURCE
Adiuro vos filiae	C or T	Song of Songs 5: 8–10
O dulcedo meliflua	C	Marian votive
Nativitas tua Dei genitrix	C	Nativity of the Virgin
Confitemini Domino	C or T	Psalm 105: 1; De Judith (Responsory Verse, Matins)
Veni sponsa Christi	A solo	Common of Virgins (Responsory Verse for Matins, Vespers Antiphon)
Cantantibus Organis	A solo	St. Cecilia
Iubilate Deo, ded. Gio. Battista Lambrugo, maestro di coro at S. Maria presso S. Celso	C & A	Psalms 65: 1–2, 16
Quam pulchra es	C & A	Assumption (Antiphon or Responsory Verse, Matins)
Benedicam Dominum	C & T	Feria 2 (Responsory Verse, Matins)

TITLE	VOICING (WITH CONTINUO)	LITURGICAL USAGE OR TEXT SOURCE
Exaudi Domine	C & T	Psalm 26: 7, 9; Pro Defunctis (Lauds Antiphon)
Surge propera, ded. D. Paola Ortensia Serbellona in S. Vincenzo	2C in Ecco or T	Song of Songs 2: 10, 14; Visitation (Antiphon or Responsory Verse, Matins)
O sacrum convivium, ded. D. Paola Ortensia Serbellona in S. Vincenzo	2C in Ecco or T	Corpus Christi (Antiphon, 2nd Vespers)
Cantate Domino, ded. D. Matteo Ferrari, basso in S. Maria presso S. Celso	2B	Psalm 97: 1–2; Eastertide
Iustus ut palma, ded. Sigr. Pietro Paolo Maderno	2B	Psalm 91: 13–14
O Domine	C & B	Adoration of the Cross?
O vos omnes	C & B	Lamentations of Jeremiah 1: 12; Holy Saturday (Matins Responsory)
Beati qui habitat in domo	C & B	Psalm 83:5; Dedication of the Church (Matins Versus or Antiphon)
Ad te desiderat	C & B	Marian votive
Gio. Andrea Cima Voce mea	C & B	Comm. Martyrs (Matins Antiphon)
Gio. Andrea Cima Quam pluchrae sunt	C & B	Song of Songs 4: 10–11
Cor mundum, ded. S. Battista Corrado, sop. in Duomo	C & B	Psalm 50: 12–13; Dom. 1 Quadregesima (Lauds Antiphon)
Gustate, et videte, ded. Sigr. Giulio Maleardo, tenore S. Maria presso S. Celso	2C & B	Psalm 33: 9–10
Ardens est	C, T & B	Eastertide (Lauds or 2nd Vespers Antiphon)

TITLE	VOICING (WITH CONTINUO)	LITURGICAL USAGE OR TEXT SOURCE
Vidi speciosam	2S & T	Assumption (Matins Responsory or Vespers Antiphon)
Quae est ista	2S & T	Song of Songs 3:6
Exaudi Deus	C, A & B	Psalm 63:2–3; Feria 4 (Matins Versus)
Non turbetur, ded. M.R. Iacomo Antonio Fasolo contralto	C, A & B	John 16: 16–17?; Comm. Martyrs (Matins Versus)
Vulnerasti cor meum, ded. R. S. D. Francesco Lucino	C, T & B	Song of Songs 4: 9–10; Nativity of the Virgin, Assumption (Matins and 2nd Vespers Antiphon)
O altitudo divitiarum	C, A & T	Romans 11:33
Beata es Virgo MARIA, ded. R. S. D. Francesco Lucino	2S & B	Assumption, All Saints (Matins Responsory)
Laudate Dominum	a 4	Psalm 116: 1–2; Feria 2 (2nd Vespers Antiphon)
Haec dies	a 4	Psalm 117:24; Resurrection (Lauds Gradual) and Octave of Nativity (Matins Versus)
Mirabile mysterium, ded. Sigr. Francesco Gradignano	a 4	Octave of Nativity (Lauds Antiphon)
Ecce MARIA, ded. Sigr. Francesco Gradignano	a 4	Nativity and Octave (Lauds Antiphon)
Gio. *Andrea Cima* Cantate Domino	a 4	Psalm 95: 1–3; Feria 6, 2nd week Advent (2nd Vespers Antiphon)
Gio. *Andrea Cima* Vadam, et circuibo	a 4	Song of Songs 3:2; Purification (Antiphon for Magnificat)
Egrediamur omnes	a 4	St. Francis

TITLE	VOICING (WITH CONTINUO)	LITURGICAL USAGE OR TEXT SOURCE
Confitebor	a 4	Psalm 137:1–2; Sundays (2 Vespers Antiphon)
Gaudeamus omnes in Domino	a 4	St. Stephen (Matins Responsory?)
Assumpta es MARIA a 8	a 8	Assumption (Lauds Antiphon)
Missa	a 4	
Magnificat. Quinto tono	a 4	
Misericordias	a 5	Psalm 88:2; Feria 6 (Matins Responsory)
Ornaverunt	a 5	Machabees 4:57–58; Machabees (Matins Responsory or Versus)
Magnificat. Sesto tono	a 4	

TABLE C.2.

Giovanni Battista Ala, *Secondo libro de' concerti ecclesiastici a una, due, tre, e quattro voci . . . opus 3.* Milano: Filippo Lomazzo, 1621.

CONCERTO	VOICING	TEXT SOURCE(S)
Deus, Deus meus	2C	Antiphon Feria 3
Nigra sum, formosa sum	C	Song of Songs 1:5; Magdelene, Assumption, and Octave; BVM
Bonum est confiteri Domino	C	Psalm 91
O Maria quid ploras	2C	Addolorata
In lectulo meo	2C	Song of Songs 3:1
Quare tristis es Anima mea	CA	Psalm 42
Gaude Hierusalem	CA	Zech 2:10
Fili quid fecisti	CT	Antiphon, 1st Sunday after Epiphany
Consolare o Mater	CT	Addolorata
Gaude virgo Maria	AT	Antiphon, Assumption
Laudate Dominum in Sanctis	CB	Psalm 148
Desiderium Animae eius tribuisti ei Domine	CB	Psalm 20:3 Responsory, Comm. unius Mart.
Gaudent in celis	CB	Antiphon, Comm. Plur. Mart.
Ab initio, et ante saecula creata sum	CTB	Eccl. 24 Lectio, Presentation Capitulum, Purification and Saturdays BVM
Surge propera amica mea	CAT	Antiphon, Visitation
O Felix supernae	CATB	Madonna of the Rosary
De profundis clamavi	CATB	Psalm 129
Dilectus meus	CATB	Song of Songs 6:1
Laetentur caeli	CATB	I Chron 16: 31

TABLE C.3.
Contents of Giovanni Andrea Cima, *Il secondo libro delli concerti* (Milan: Filippo Lomazzo, 1627).

TITLE	VOICING	TEXT SOURCE
Dialogo A 2. O quam humilis & benigna est facies tua Maria	C&B	BVM
Dialogo A 2. Indica mihi	C&B	Songs 1:7; Songs 4
A2. Decantabat populus Israel & universa multitudo Iacob	C&B	Easter Antiphon
A 2. Audi dulcis amica me, nigra sum sed formosa	C&B	Songs 1:4–5
A 2. Ad te levavi oculos meos qui habitas in caelis	A&B	Psalm 122
A 2. O Iesu Fili mi. *(ded. Suor Paola Maria Arcontata, S. Maria del Vetere)*	A & C ò T	Adoration N.S.
A 2. Vocem Mariae. *(ded.Anna Clemenza Tetoni e Suor Giramma, S. Bernardo)*	A,&C ò T	Luke 1:41–42 (Visitation)
A 3. Beatus iste sanctus qui confisus est in Domino. *Di Gio. Paolo Cima.*	CAB	Antiphon Comm. Conf.
A 3. Domine qui ingreditur sine macula & operatur iustitiam.	CTB	Psalm 14
A 3. In te domine speravi. Duoi C & B si placet. *(ded. Rev. D. Angiola Maria Clerici, S. Radegonda)*	Duoi C&B si placet	Psalm 70
A 4. Laudate dominum in sanctis eius.	CATB	Psalm 150
A 4. Exultate Deo adiutori nostro.	CATB	Psalm 80
A 4. Quam pulchra es.	CATB	Songs 4
A 4. Una ex ò Maria aureo clarior.	CATB	BVM
A 4. O Domina nostra Sanctissima Maria.	CATB	BVM
A 4. *Nella Solenità del Santissimo Rosario.* Gaudete filiae Sion.	CATB	Rosary

TITLE	VOICING	TEXT SOURCE
A 4. O felicissimus dies.	CATB	St. Carlo Borromeo
A 4. Ad te Domine clamavi deus meus. *Di Gio. Battista Cima.*	CATB	Psalm 87
A 4. Jubilate Deo omnis terra servite Domino in laetitia.	CATB	Psalm 65
A 4. Cantate Domino canticum novum.	CATB	Psalm 95
A 4. Letanie [della Vergine] a 4. Kyrie Eleison.	CATB	Litany of the Virgin

TABLE C.4.
Content of the *Flores praestantissimorum viorum*
(Milano: Filippo Lomazzo, 1626).

COMPOSER	INSTITUTION	TITLE	VOICING	TEXT SOURCE
Francesco Rognoni di Taegio	Royal Ducal Instrumental Chapel	I. Ave Virgo benedicta stella	C	BVM
Vincenzo Pellegrino	Maestro, Duomo di Milano	II. O quam pulchri sunt gressus tui	C, à duoi co'l basso	Songs 7:1; Maria Aegyptiacae (Verse, Mattutino)
Ignazio Donati	Maestro, Cathedral of Novara	III. O Gloriosa Domina Caelorum (à modo di Ecco)	2C o 2T o C/T con strumento	Hymn BVM; Assumption?
Ignazio Donati	Maestro, Cathedral of Novara	IV. Bonum certamen certavi cursum consumavi	2C o 2T	II Tim 4: 7–8; S. Paul (Antiphon, Mattutino)
Lorenzo Frissone	Organist, S. Maria Segreta	V. O quam pulchra es amica mea	C&A	Canti 4:1; Assumption (Antiphon, Vespers)
Lorenzo Frissone	Organist, S. Maria Segreta	VI. Hi sunt quos habuimus	A&T	Proverbs 5: 3–5
Federico Coda	Maestro, Cathedral of Dertona	VII. Beatus vir qui inventus est	2C	Comm. Martyrs and Apostles (Responsory, Mattutino)
Iacopo Filippo Biumi	Organist, Duomo of Milan	VIII. O Sanctissima Maria	C&B	BVM

COMPOSER	INSTITUTION	TITLE	VOICING	TEXT SOURCE
Lorenzo Frissone	Organist, S. Maria Segreta	IX. Qualis est dilectus	ATB	Songs 5: 9–10; Nativity BVM (Antiphon Mattutino)
Io. Domenico Rognoni di Taegio	Maestro, Royal Ducal Chapel	X. Tu Gloria Hierusalem	A, C o T & violino	Marian gloss on Judith 15:10
Gio. Paolo Cima	Organist, S. Maria presso S. Celso	XI. Gaudeamus omnes	3C	Assumption (Antiphon, Mattutino)
Giulio Cesare Ardemanio	Organist, S. Maria della Scala and Maestro, Royal Ducal Chapel	XII. Quo abijt, quo declinavit dilectus meus	2C & T	Gloss of Songs 5: 17; Mater dolorosa, Nativity BVM and Assumption
Andrea Cima	Organist, S. Maria della Rosa	XIII. Heu me misera	CTB	Gloss on Songs 3
Michelangelo Grancino	Organist, S. Sepolcro	XIIII. O Maria Dei genitrix	CTB	BVM
Guglielmo Arnone	Organist, Duomo di Milano	XV. Laetamini cum Hierusalem	CAT	Feria 5 Heb. 3 Adv. Antiphon, Vespers (also Feria 6 Heb. 3 Adv Antiphon, Mattutino)
Pietro Maria Giussano	Organist, S. Ambrogio	XVI. Deus, Deus meus	2C&B	Psalms 62:2–3
Pietro Maria Guissano	Organist, S. Ambrogio	XVII. Cantemus filiae Sion	CAB	Gloss on Zeph. 3:14

COMPOSER	INSTITUTION	TITLE	VOICING	TEXT SOURCE
Vincenzo Pellegrino	Maestro, Duomo di Milano	XVIII. Levavi oculos meos	CATB	Psalm 120; Feria 2 per annum, Vespers
Lorenzo Frissone	Organist, S. Maria Segreta	XIX. Una ex O Maria	CATB	BVM (Mulier fortis)
Gio. Domenico Rognoni di Taegio	Maestro, Royal Ducal Chapel	XX. Confitebor tibi Domine in toto corde meo	CATB	Psalm 9: 2–3; Sunday Antiphon, Vespers
Federico Coda	Maestro, Cathedral of Dertona	XXI. Venite, & fruamur	2C&TB	?
Gio. Paolo Cima	Organist, S. Maria presso S. Celso	XXII. Vox dilecti mei	CATB	Songs 2: 8–10; Nativity BVM (Verset and Antiphon)
Giulio Cesare Ardemanio	Organist, S. Maria presso S. Celso and Maestro, Royal Ducal Chapel	XXIII. Quam pulchra es	CATB	Gloss of Songs 4: 1, 2, 7; Nativity and Assumption BVM (Antiphon)
Iacopo Filippo Biumi	Organist, Duomo di Milano	XXIIII. Florete flores quam florete	CATB	Ecclesiastes 39: 19–20; Sundays Advent (Versus, Mattutino)
Andrea Cima	Organist, S. Maria della Rosa	XXV. Ave summi patris filia chiarissima virgo	CATB	BVM
Michelangelo Grancini	Organist, S. Sepolcro	XXVI. Gustate, & videte	CATB	Psalm 33: 9–10

COMPOSER	INSTITUTION	TITLE	VOICING	TEXT SOURCE
Andrea Cima	Organist, S. Maria della Rosa	Messa a 4 Concertata	CATB	Mass
Giovanni Battista Ala	Organist, S. Maria dei Servi	Magnificat Quarto Tono a 4 Concertato	CATB	Magnificat
Lorenzo Frissone	Organist, S. Maria Segreta	Magnificat Secondo Tono a 4 Concertato	CATB	Magnificat
Francesco Rognoni di Taegio	Royal Ducal Instrumental Chapel	Canzone prima	2 violini o cornetti	*Instrumental*
Francesco Rognoni di Taegio	Royal Ducal Instrumental Chapel	Sonata Seconda	2 violini o cornetti	*Instrumental*
Giovanni Domenico Ripalta	Organist, Collegiate Church of Modoctia	Canzone Terza a 4 ridotta a 2 da Gaspare Zanetta	Not specified	*Instrumental*
Iacomo Filippo Cambiago	Organist, S. Eustorgio	Canzone Quarta a 4 ridotta a 2 da Gaspare Zanetta	Not specified	*Instrumental*
Lorenzo Frissone	Organist, S. Maria Segreta	Canzone Quinta a 3	2 violini o simili	*Instrumental*
Gio. Paolo Cima	Organist, S. Maria presso S. Celso	Canzone Sesta a 4	Not specified	*Instrumental*
Lorenzo Frissone	Organist, S. Maria Segreta	Canzone Settima a 4	Not specified	*Instrumental*

TABLE C.5.
Tonal Organization of Orfeo Vecchi, *La donna vestita di sole*
(Milano: erede di Simone Tini e Giovanni Francesco Besozzi, 1602).

TITLE	OPENING PHRASE	TOPIC	CLEFFING	SYSTEM	FINAL
Prima stella: Bellezza	Più bella donna	Beauty	$G_2G_2C_2C_3C_4$	♮	G
Seconda stella: Sapienza	Più saggia donna	Wisdom	$G_2G_2C_2C_3C_4$	♮	G
Terza stella: Fortezza	Più mag-nanima donna	Fortitude	$G_2G_2C_2C_3C_4$	♮	G
Quarta stella: Purità	Più pura donna	Purity	$G_2G_2C_2C_3C_4$	♮	G
Quinta stella: Liberalità	Più liberal, più pia	Generosity	$G_2G_2C_2C_3C_4$	♮	G
Sesta stella: Tranquilità	Più pacifica in terra	Tranqui-lity	$G_2G_2C_2C_3C_4$	♮	G
Settima stella: Taciturnità	Più quieta donna il nostro	Taciturnity	$G_2G_2C_2C_3C_4$	♮	G
Ottava stella: Humilità	Più grave donna, e mite	Humility	$G_2G_2C_2C_3C_4$	♮	G
Nona stella: Santità	Più stret-tamente unita	Sanctity	$G_2G_2C_2C_3C_4$	♮	G
Decima stella: Carità	Più fervo-rosa donna	Charity	$G_2G_2C_2C_3C_4$	♮	G
Undecima stella: Perseveranza	Più stabil donna	Persever-ance	$G_2G_2C_2C_3C_4$	♮	G
Duodecima stella: Perfettione	Più preghi-ata non visse	Perfection	$G_2G_2C_2C_3C_4$	♮	G

Vestita di sole	Non di porpora ò d'oro	Rev 12:1	$G_2C_2C_3C_3F_3$	♮	A
Calcante la luna	Se fan coron'al crine	Rev 12:1	$G_2C_2C_3C_3F_3$	♮	A
Della Natività di Maria Vergine	Al vostro nascer nacque	Nativity BVM	$C_1C_1C_3C_4F_4$	♭	F
Della Presentatione	Allor ch'al sacro Tempio	Presentation BVM	$C_1C_1C_3C_4F_4$	♭	F
Dell'Annonciatione	Spiegò veloce il corso	Annunciation	$C_1C_1C_3C_4F_4$	♭	F
Della Visitatione	Pieno di Dio sen poggia	Visitation	$C_1C_1C_3C_4F_4$	♭	F
Del Parto	Oggi dal Ciel un lampo	Nativity N.S.	$C_1C_1C_3C_4F_4$	♭	G
Della Purificatione	Qual gentil Colomba	Purification	$C_1C_1C_3C_4F_4$	♭	G
Dell'Assontione	Questa che spiega il volo	Assumption	$C_1C_1C_3C_4F_4$	♭	G

TABLE C.6.
Contents of Stefano Limido, *I Regii Concenti Spirituali*
(Milano: Tradate, 1605).

TITLE	SUBJECT	VOICES
Vergine tu (prima parte) Basti in tanto (seconda parte)	Madonna Enthroned	5

Le braccia aperse (prima parte; text by
  Angelo Grillo)
  E tra le braccia (seconda parte)
  E ritornato (terza parte)
  O miei crin d'oro (quarta parte)
  Gionta al fin (quinta parte)
  O cara imago (sesta parte)
  O dolor per pietà (settima parte)
  E voi ministri (ottava parte)
  Fate che io moia (nona ed ultima
    parte)
	Madonna
	Addolorata
		5

O de l'eterno Sol (prima parte) Questo de la mia mente (seconda parte)	Rev 12:1	5
Virgen Hermosa (primiera parte) Virgen discreta (segunda parte)	Virtues	5
Mestissima mia vita	Madonna Addolorata	6
Pues nauegays (primiera parte) Y para mas (segunda parte)	Mulier Fortis	6
Deten el carro (primiera parte) Llagas de amores son (segunda parte)	St. Francesco di Paola	6
Et è per vero, ohime.	Penitence	6

Appendix D

Musical Examples

EXAMPLE 1.1. Simon Boyleau, *Magnificat 8 toni*

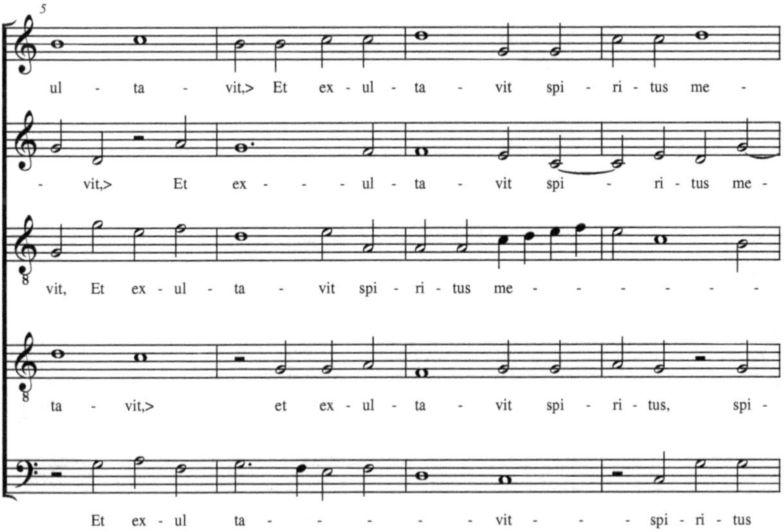
5
ul - ta - vit,> Et ex - ul - ta - vit spi - ri - tus me -
- vit,> Et ex - - - ul - ta - vit spi - ri - tus me -
vit, Et ex - ul - ta - vit spi - ri - tus me - - - - - - -
ta - vit,> et ex - ul - ta - vit spi - ri - tus, spi -
Et ex - ul ta - - - - - - vit - - - spi - ri - tus

9
us, spi - ri - tus me - - - - - us, spi - ri - tus me - - -
- - us, spi - ri - tus me - - - us in
us, <spi - ri - tus me - us,> spi - ri - tus me -
ri - tus me - - - us, spi - ri - tus me - us,
me - - us, spi - ri - tus - me - us, <me - - - -

13
us in De - o, in De - o sa - lu - ta - ri me - o,
Deo - o, in De - o sa - lu - ta - ri me - o, sa -
us in De - o, in De - - - - o sa - lu -
in De - o sa - lu - ta - ri me - o, sa -
us,> in De - o sa - lu - ta - ri me -

17
in De - o, sa - lu - ta - ri
lu - ta - ri me - - - o, in De - o sa -
ta - ri me - o, in De - o sa -
- lu ta - ri me - - - - - - - o, in De - o sa -
- - o, in De - o, in De - o

21
— me - o, sa - lu - ta - ri me - o, sa - lu - ta - ri me - - -
tu - ta - ri me - - - - - o, sa - lu - ta - ri me -
lu - ta - ri, sa - - lu - ta - ri me - o, me - - -
- lu - ta - - - ri me - o, sa - lu - - - ta - ri me -
— sa - lu - ta - ri me - - -

25
o. Qui - a fe - cit - mi - hi ma - - - - -
o. Qui - - - a fe - cit
o. Qui - a fe - - - - - - - - -
o.
o. Qui - - - a

29
- - - - gna, qui - a fe - cit mi -
— mi - hi ma - - - - - gna, <qui - a fe - cit mi - hi ma -
cit, - qui - a fe - cit, — qui - a fe - cit> mi - hi ma - gna, —
Qui - a fe - cit mi - hi ma - - - - - gna,
fe - cit mi - hi ma - gna, qui a fe - cit mi - hi ma -
33
- - hi ma - gna qui — po - tens est, qui po - - -
gna, qui - a fe - cit — mi - hi ma - gna,> qui po - - - tens
— mi - hi ma - gna qui - po - - - tens est, qui
qui - a fe - cit mi - hi ma - gna qui po - tens est, qui —
gna, mi - hi ma - gna qui po -

37
- - tens ___ est, et ___ san - ctum, et ___
___ est ___ et san - ctum no - men ___ e - - - - - - ius, ___
po - tens ___ est, et san - ctum no - men e - ius, <et san -
___ po - tens est, et san - ctum no - men e - - - - ius, no -
tens ___ est,

41
___ san - ctum ___ no - men e - ius, <et ___
___ e - - - - - - ius, et - san - ctum no - men, no - men -
ctum no - men e - ius,> ___ et san - ctum no - men e - ius, no -
- - - men e - ius, et san - ctum no - men,
et san - ctum no - men e - ius, no -

45
— san - ctum no - men e - ius,>
- - e - - - - ius, et san - ctum no - men e - ius, no - - - -
men e - - - - - - ius, et san - - - tum no -
no - men e - ius, et san - ctum no -
men e - ius, et san - ctum no -

49
et san - ctum no - men e - ius, no - men
men e - - - ius, et san - ctum no - men e -
- - men c - ius, <et san - ctum no -
men e - - - ius, et san - ctum no - men e - ius no - - -
- - men e - ius, et san - ctum no -

53
e - - - - - ius. Fe -
ius.
men e - ius. Fe - cit po - ten - - - ti -
men e - ius. Fe - cit po -
men e - ius. Fe - cit po - ten -
57
cit po - ten - - - ti - am, fe - cit po -
Fe - cit po - ten - - - ti - am, fe - cit po - ten -
am, po - ten - ti - am, fe - cit po - ten - - - - - - ti -
ten ti - am, fe - cit po - ten - ti - am, po -
- - ti - am, fe - cit po - ten - - - ti - am, fe - cit po -

61
ten - - - ti - am, po - ten - ti - am in bra - chi - o su - o di -
- - ti - am in bra - chi - o su - o, in bra - chi - o su - o di -
am in bra - chi - o su - o di - sper -
ten - ti - am in bra - chi - o su - o di -
ten - ti - am in bra - chi - o su - o, di -

65
sper - sit su - per - bos, men - te cor -
sper - sit su - per - bos men - te cor - - - - - - - -
sit su per - - - bos men - te cor - dis su - - -
sper - sit su - per - bos, su - per - bos,
sper - sit su - per - bos, men - te cor - - -

69
- dis su - i, men - te cor - dis, men - te cor - dis su -
- dis su - i men - te cor - dis
- - - - - i, men - te cor - - - - - dis su -
men - te cor - - - - - - - dis su -
- - - - dis su - i,
73
- - i, <men - te cor - dis su - i.>
su - i, men - te cor - - - dis su - i.
- - i, men - te cor - dis su - - - i.
i, men - te cor - - - - - dis su - i.
men - te cor - - - - - - dis su - i.

77
E - su - ri - en -
E - su - ri - en - tes, <e - su - ri -
E - su - ri - en - tes, <e - su - ri - en - tes>
E - su - ri - en - tes, - - - <e - su - ri -
E - - - su - ri - en - tes, <e - su - ri - en - - - tes im -
81
tes im - ple - - - vit bo - nis, im - ple - vit bo -
en - tes im - ple - vit bo - nis, im - ple - vit bo -
im - ple - vit bo - - - - - - nis, im - ple - vit, im -
en - tes> im - ple - vit, im - ple - - - vit, <im -
ple - vit bo - nis, <im - ple - vit bo - nis,> im - ple - vit

85
- - - - - nis, et di - vi - tes, et
- - - - - nis et di - - - - vi - tes, et di - vi - tes
ple - vit bo - nis, et di - - - - vi - tes, et di -
ple - vit,> et di - vi - tes, <et di - - - - vi -
bo - - - - - nis et di - vi - tes
89
di - - - vi - tes di - mi - sit i - na - nes,
di - mi - - - sit i - na - nes, di - mi - sit
- - - vi - tes di - mi - sit i - na - nes, di - mi - sit
tes,> et di - - - - vi - tes, di - mi - sit i -
et di - - - - vi - tes, et di - - - - vi - tes di - mi - sit

93
et ___ di - vi - tes di - mi - sit i - - - - - -
i - - - - - - na - nes, et di - vi - tes di -
___ i - na - nes, di - mi - - - - - sit i - na -
na - nes, et di - vi - tes di - mi - sit i - na - nes, di -
___ i - na - - - - - nes, et di - vi - tes di -
97
- - na - nes di - mi - - - - sit i - na - nes, di - mi - sit
mi - sit i - na - nes, di - mi - sit i - na - nes, di - mi - sit
nes, i na - nes, di - mi - sit
mi - sit i - na - nes, di - mi - sit i - na - nes, ___ <di -
mi - sit i - na - nes, di - mi - sit

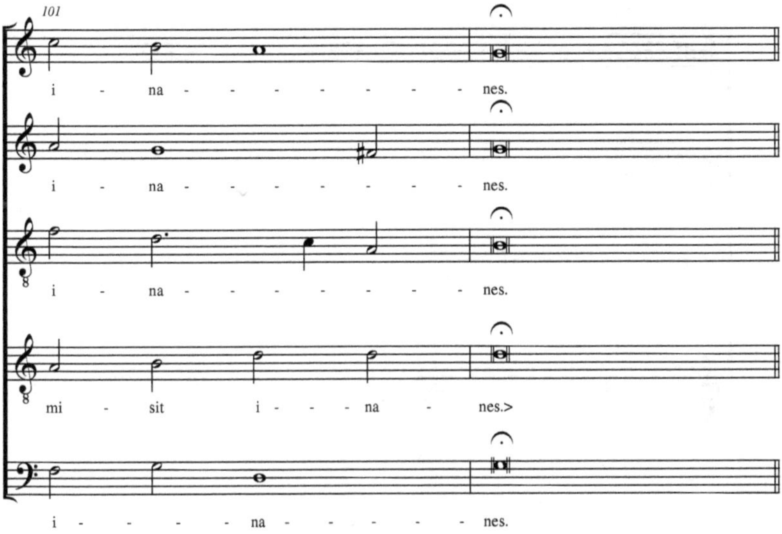
101
i - na - - - - - - - nes.
i - na - - - - - - - nes.
i - na - - - - - - - nes.
mi - sit i - - - na - nes.>
i - - - - na - - - - - nes.

Cantus
Altus
Quintus
Tenor
107
Si - - - cut lo - - - - cu - - - tus
Si - cut lo - cu - tus est, <si - cut lo -
Si - cut
Si - cut lo - cu - tus est, si - cut lo -

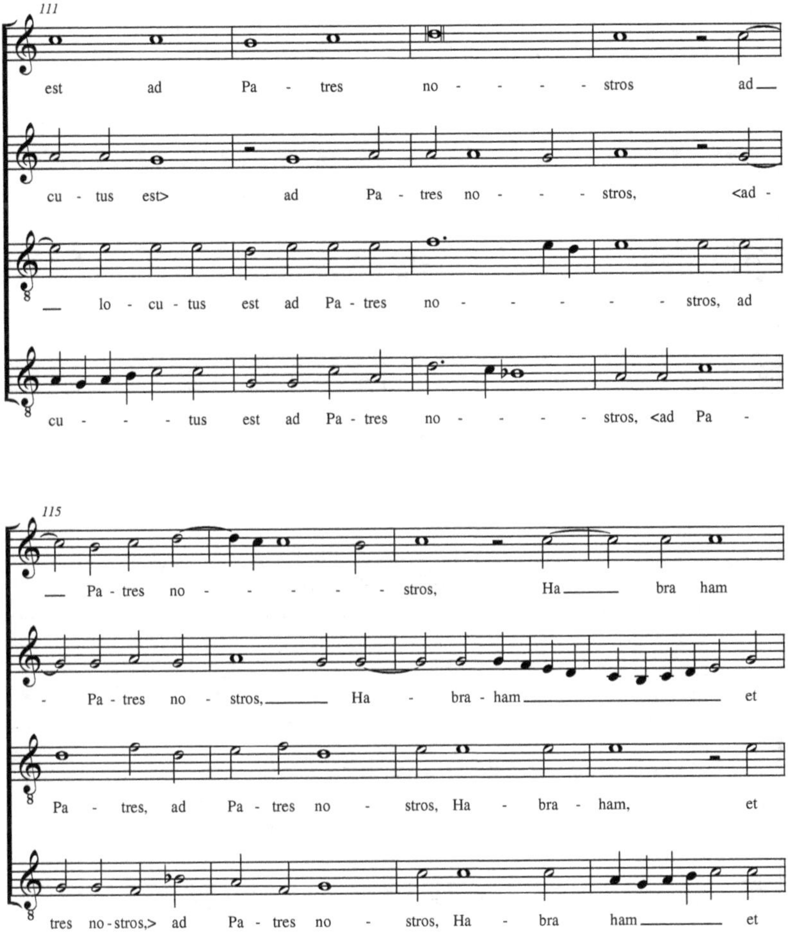
111
est ad Pa - tres no - - - - - stros ad
cu - tus est> ad Pa - tres no - - - - stros, <ad -
lo - cu - tus est ad Pa - tres no - - - - - - stros, ad
cu - - - - tus est ad Pa - tres no - - - - - stros, <ad Pa -
115
Pa - tres no - - - - - - stros, Ha bra ham
- Pa - tres no - stros, Ha - bra - ham et
Pa - tres, ad Pa - tres no - stros, Ha - bra - ham, et
tres no - stros,> ad Pa - tres no - stros, Ha - bra ham et

et se - mi - ni e - ius in se - cu - la,

se - mi - ni e - ius in se - cu - la, et se - mi - ni e - ius in

se - mi - ni e - ius in se - - - cu - la, e - ius

se - mi - ni e - ius, e - ius in se - cu - la, Ha -

Ha - bra - ham et se - mi - ni e - ius in se - cu -

se - cu - la, et se - mi - ni e - ius in

in se - - - cu - la, et se mi - ni, et se - mi -

bra ham et se - mi - ni e - ius

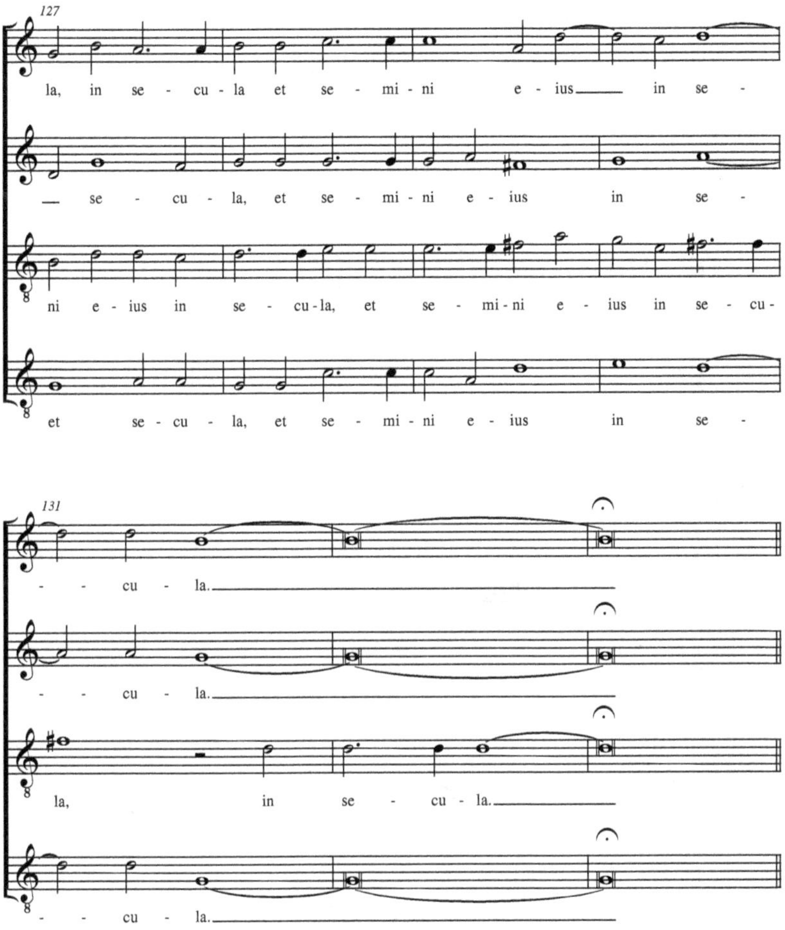
127
la, in se - cu - la et se - mi - ni e - ius in se -
se - cu - la, et se - mi - ni e - ius in se -
ni e - ius in se - cu - la, et se - mi - ni e - ius in se - cu -
et se - cu - la, et se - mi - ni e - ius in se -
131
- - cu - la.
- - cu - la.
la, in se - cu - la.
- - cu - la.

Cantus
Altus
Quintus
Tenor
Bassus
Sexta pars
Si - cut e - - - -
Si - cut e - - - - - - - - - - - - rat, si -
Si - - - cut e - rat, e - rat, si -
Si - cut e - - - - - - - - rat,
Si - cut

138
rat, <si - cut e - rat, si - cut e - - - - rat,> in
cut e - rat, e - rat, si - cut e - rat, <si - cut e - rat> in
- - - cut e - rat, si - cut e - rat, <si - cut e - rat> in
si - cut e - rat, <si - cut e - rat, si - cut e - rat>
e - - - - - - - rat, si - cut e - rat in prin -
Si - cut e - - - - - rat, si - cut e - rat in

142
prin - ci - pi - o et nunc et sem - per,
prin - ci - - pi - o, et nunc et
prin - ci - pi - o et nunc et sem - per, et
in prin - ci - pi - o et nunc et
ci - pi - o, <in prin - ci - pi - o et nunc et
prin - ci - pi - o et nunc et sem - per, et nunc et

146
et nunc et sem - per,
sem - - - - per,
nunc et sem - per, <et nunc et sem - per,>
sem - per, <et nunc et sem - - - - per,>
sem - - - - per,
sem - - - - per, et nunc et sem - per,

150
Et in se - cu - la, <et in se - - - cu -
Et in se - cu - la, se - cu - la, se -
Et in se - - - cu -
Et in se - cu - la, et in se - - - -
Et in se - - - cu -
Et in se - - - cu -

154
la,> se - cu - lo - rum A - men, se - cu - lo -
cu - lo - rum A - men, se - cu - lo - rum A - men, <se - cu - lo -
la se - cu - lo - - - - rum A - men, se - cu - lo -
- - cu - la se - cu - lo - rum A - men, A - men, se - cu - lo -
la se - cu - lo - rum A - men,
la se - cu - lo - rum A - - - - men, se - cu -

158
- rum A - men, <se - cu - lo - rum A - men.>
rum A - - - men.>
rum A - - - men, <se - cu - lo - rum A - men.>
rum A - men, se - cu - lo - - - rum A - - - - - -
se - cu - lo - rum A - men.
lo - rum A - men, <se - cu - lo - rum A - men,>

161
men.

EXAMPLE 1.2. Gaspare Costa, *Virgo prudentissima*

5
vir - - go pru - den - tis - - - - - - si - ma,
ma, <vir - - - go pru - den - tis - si - ma,>
tis - - - - si - ma, <vir - go
pru - den - tis - si - ma, <vir - go pru - den - tis - si - ma,> vir - go
tis - - - - - - si - ma,> vir - go pru - den - tis - si -

9
<vir - go pru - den - tis - si - ma,> quo pro -
vir - - go pru - den - tis - si - ma,
pru - den - tis - si - ma,> vir - go pru - den - tis - - - - - - si -
pru - den - tis - si - ma,
<vir - go pru - den-
ma,
quo pro -

13
gre - de-ris, quo pro - gre - de - ris, <quo pro - gre - de-
quo pro - gre - de-ris, <quo pro - gre - de - ris,>
ma, quo pro - gre - de-ris, pro - gre - de-ris, quo pro -
tis - si - ma,> quo pro - gre - - - de - ris,
gre - de-ris, <quo pro - gre - de-ris,>

17
ris, quo pro - gre - de - ris,>
quo pro - gre - de-ris, <quo pro - gre - de - ris,> quo
gre - de-ris, <quo pro - gre - de - ris,> quo pro - gre - - - de -
quo pro - gre - de - ris, <quo pro - gre - de-ris,>
quo pro - gre - de-ris, <quo pro -

21
quo pro - gre - de - ris, qua - si au - ro - ra, qua - si au - ro -
pro - gre - - - de - ris, qua - si au - ro - ra, qua - si au - ro -
ris, <quo pro - gre - de - ris,> qua - si au - ro - ra,
quo pro - gre - de - ris, qua - si au - ro - ra, qua - si au - ro -
gre - de - ris,> qua - si au - ro -
25
ra, qua - si au - ro - ra, <qua - si au - ro - ra> val - - - de ru -
ra, <qua - si au - ro - ra,> qua - si au - ro - ra val - de ru - - - ti -
qua - si au - ro - ra val - de ru - - - ti -
ra, qua - si au - ro - ra val - de ru - - - ti -
ra, qua - si au - ro - ra val - de ru - - - ti -

29
- - ti - lans, fi - li - a Si - on, fi - li - a Si - on to - ta for -
lans, fi - li - a Si - on, fi - li - a Si - on to - ta for -
lans, fi - li - a Si - on, fi - li - a Si - on to - ta for -
lans, fi - li - a Si - on, fi - li - a Si - on, to - ta for -
lans, fi - li - a Si - on, fi - li - a Si - on,
33
mo - sa, <to - ta for-mo - sa> et su - a - vis es: pul -
mo - sa, <to - ta for-mo - sa> et su - a - vis es: pul -
mo - sa, <to - ta for-mo - sa,> to - ta for-mo - sa et su - a - vis es: pul -
mo - sa, <to - ta for-mo - sa> et su - a - vis es:
to - ta for-mo - sa, <to-ta for-mo - sa> et su - a - vis es:

37
chra ut lu - na, pul - chra ut lu-na, <pul - chra ut lu-na,> pul -
chra ut lu - na, pul - chra ut lu - na, pul - chra ut lu-na, <pul - chra ut lu-na,> pulchra ut lu - na, pul - chra ut lu - na, pul - chra ut lu-na, <pul - chra ut lu-na,>
pul - chra ut lu - na, pul - chra ut lu-na, <pul -
pul - chra ut lu - na, pul - chra ut lu - na, <pul -

41
chra ut lu - na, <pul - chra ut lu - na,> e - lec - ta ut sol, e - lec -
chra ut lu - na, <pul - chra ut lu - na,> e - lec - ta ut sol, e - lec - ta ut
e - lec - ta ut sol. e - lec - ta ut sol,
chra ut lu - na,> pul - chra ut lu - na, e - lec - ta ut sol,
chra ut lu - na,> pul - chra ut lu - na, e - lec - ta ut sol,

45
ta ut sol, e - lec - ta ut sol, e - lec - ta,
sol, e - lec - ta ut sol, e - lec -
e - lec - ta ut sol, <e - lec - - - ta ut sol,> e - lec - ta, e -
e - lec - ta ut sol, ut sol, e - lec - ta ut sol,
e - lec - ta ut sol, e - lec - ta ut
49
ut sol, ut sol, al - le - lu - - - ia, al - le -
ta ut sol, ut sol, al - le lu - - - ia,
lec - ta ut sol, al - le - lu - ia, al - le -
e - lec - ta ut sol, ut sol, al - le - lu -
sol, ut sol, al - le - lu - ia,

53
lu - ia,
al - le - lu - ia, <al - le - lu - ia,>
lu - ia, <al - le - lu - - - - ia,> al - le - lu - ia,
ia, al - le-lu - ia, al - le - lu - ia, <al -
al - le - lu - ia, <al - le - lu - ia, al - le - lu - ia,>
57
61
al - le - lu - ia, <al - le - lu - ia.>
al - le - lu - ia, <al - le - lu - - - - ia,>
<al - le - lu - ia, al - - - le - lu - ia.>
le - lu - ia, al - le - lu - - - ia.>
al - le - lu - ia.

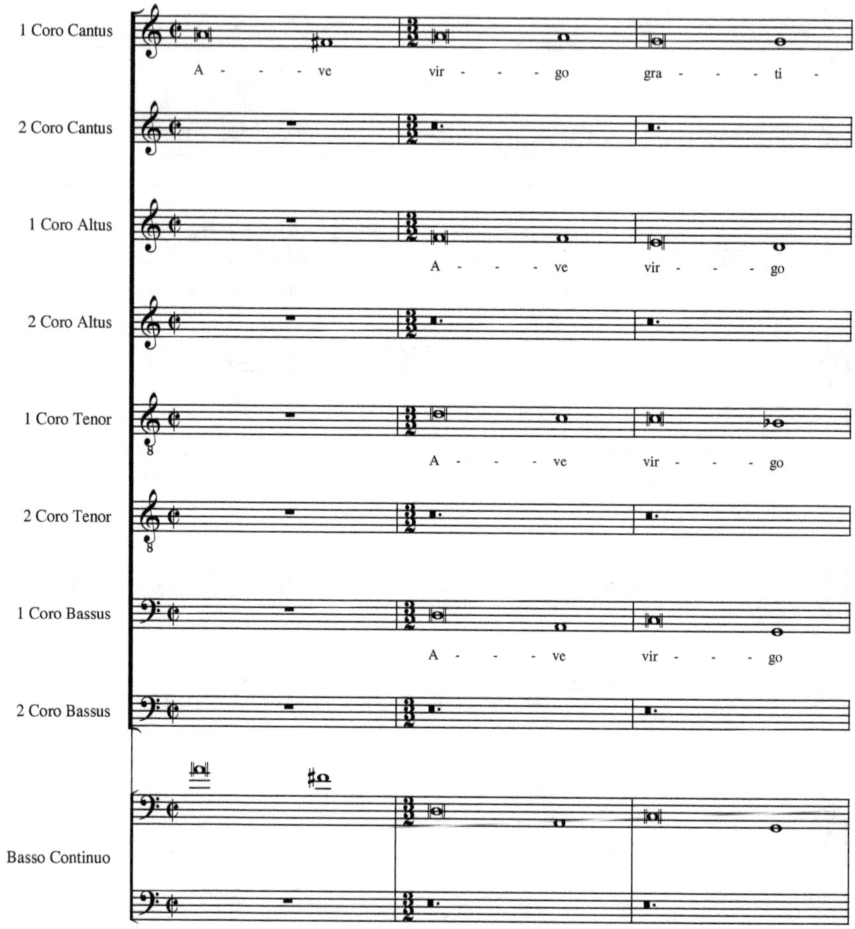

EXAMPLE 1.3. Benedetto Regio, *Ave virgo gratiosa*

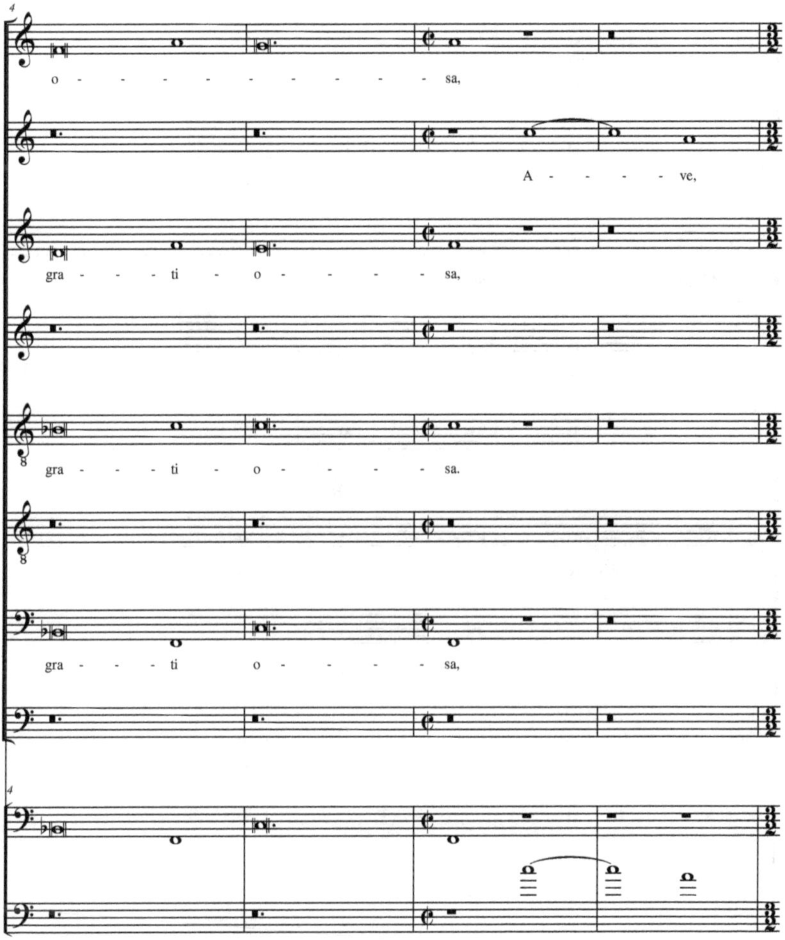
4
o - - - - - - - - - sa,
A - - - - ve,
gra - - - ti - o - - - - - sa,
gra - - - ti - o - - - - - sa.
gra - - - ti o - - - - - sa,
4

Appendix D

11
o - - - - - - sa, stel - la so - le cla - - ri - or, Ma -
o - - - - - - sa,
o - - - - - - sa,> stel - la so - le cla - ri - or, Ma -
o - - - - - - sa,
o - - - - - - sa,> ste - - la so - le cla - ri - or, Ma -
o - - - - - - sa,
o - - - - - - sa,> stel - la so - le cla - ri - or, Ma -
o - - - - - - sa,
11

15
- - ter De - i glo - ri - o - sa,
fa - vo mel - - - - lis
- - ter De - i glo - ri - o - sa,
fa - vo mel - - - lis dul -
- - ter De - i glo - ri - o - sa,
fa - vo mel - - - lis
- - ter De - i glo - ri - o - sa,
fa - vo mel - - - lis
15

18
fa - vo mel - lis dul - - - ci -
— dul - ci - or,
fa - vo mel - lis dul - - - ci -
- - - - ci - or,
fa - vo mel - lis dul - - - ci -
dul - - - ci - or,
fa - vo mel - lis dul - - - ci -
dul - - - ci - or
18

20
or, fa - vo mel - - - - lis dul - - - - ci - or,
fa - vo mel - - - - lis dul - - - - ci - or, Tu est il - la
or, fa - vo mel - - - - lis dul - - - - ci - or,
fa - vo mel - - - - lis dul - - - - ci - or, Tu es il - la
or, fa - vo mel - - - - lis dul - - - - ci - or,
fa - vo mel - - - - lis dul - ci - or. Tu es il - la
or, fa - vo - mel - - - - lis dul - - - - ci - or,
fa - vo mel - - - - lis dul - - - - ci - or, Tu es il - la
20

23
ru - bi -
spe - ci - o - sa, qua nul - la est pul - chri - or,
ru - bi -
spe - ci - o - sa, qua nul - la est pul - chri - or,
ru - bi -
spe - ci - o - sa, qua nul - la est pul - chri - or,
ru - bi -
spe - ci - o - sa, qua nul - la es pul - chri - or,
23

26
cun - da plus quam ro - - - sa, li - li - o can - di - di - or, li - li-
li - li - o can - di - di - or, li - li - o can - di - di-
cun - da plus quam ro - - - sa, li - li - o can - di - di - or, li - li-
li - li - o can - di - di - or, <li - li - o can - di - di-
cun - da plus quam ro - - - sa, li - li - o can - di - di - or, li - li-
li - li - o can - di - di - or, <li - li - o can - di - di -
cun - da plus quam rro - - - sa, li - li - o can - di - di - or, li - li-
li - li - o can - di - di - or, <li - li - o can - di - di-
26

29
o can - di - di - or. Prae - - sta mi -
or, can - di - di - or. Prae - - sta mi -
o can - di - di - or. Prae - - sta mi -
or,> can - di - di - or. Prae - - sta mi -
o can - di - di - or. Prae - sta mi - sel -
or,> can - di - di - or. Prae - - sta mi -
o can - di - di - or. Prae - - sta mi -
or,> can - di - di - or. Prae - - sta mi -
29

32
sel - - - - - - - lis iu - va - - - - men, Re -
sel - - - lis iu - va - - - - men, Re - gi - - - - -
sel - lis iu - va - men, Re - gi - - - - - -
sel - - - lis iu - - - - va - men
- - - - - - - - lis iu - va - - - - men, Re -
sel - - - lis iu - va - men, Re - gi - - -
sel - lis iu - va - - - - men Re - gi -
sel - - - lis iu - va - - - - - - men, Re - - -
32

35
gi - - - na cle - men - - - ti - ae, mae -
- - na cle - - - men - - - - - ti - ae,
na cle - - - - - - men - - - ti - ae, mae -
Re - gi - na cle - men - - - ti - ae,
gi - - - na cle - men - ti - ae, mae -
- - na cle - - - men - - - - - ti - ae,
- - - - - - - na cle - men - - - ti - ae, mae -
gi - - - na cle - men - - - - - - - ti - ae,
35

38
ren - ti - bus ser so - la - men, au - ro - ra lae - ti - - - - - - - -
ren - ti - bus ser so - la - men, au - ro - ra lae - ti - ti - - - - - - -
ren - ti - bus ser so - la - men, au - ro - ra lae - ti - - - - - ae, au -
ren - ti - bus ser so - la - men, au - ro - ra lae - ti - - - - - - - -
38

42
- - - - - - ti - ae,
prae - dul - - - - - cis fons
- - - - - - ti - ae,
prae - dul - - - - - cis fons
ro - ra lae - ti - ti - ae,
prae - dul - - - - - cis fons pi -
- - - - - - ti - ae,
prae - dul - - - - - cis fons
42

44
do - na no - bis ve - ni - am,
pi - - - e - ta - tis, do - na no - bis ve - ni -
do - na no - bis ve - ni - am,
pi - e - ta - - - - - tis, do - na no - bis ve - ni -
do - na no - bis ve - ni - aam,
- - e - ta - - - tis, do - na no - bis ve - ni -
do - na no - bis ve - ni - am,
pi - e - ta - - - - - tis, do - na no - bis ve - ni -
44

47
et pur - ga - tos à pec - ca - - - - - - tis duc
am, et pur - ga - tos à pec - ca - - - -
et pur - ga - tos à pec - ca - - tis duc ad
am, et pur - ga - tos à pec - ca - - - -
et pur - ga - tos à pec - ca - - tis duc
am, et pur - ga - tos à pec - ca - - - -
et pur - ga - tos à pec - ca - - tis duc
am, et pur - ga - tos à pec - ca - - - -
47

49
— a cae - - - - - li pa - - - - - tri - am,
tis duc - ad cae - - - - - - - - - - li
cae - - - - - - - - - li pa - tri - am,
tis duc ad cae - - - - li pa - - - - -
— ad cae - - - - - - - - - - - - - - li
- - - - tis duc ad cae - - - - li pa -
— ad cae - - - - - - - - - - - - - - li
tis duc ad cae - - - - - - li pa -
49

52
ad cae - - - - li pa - tri - am am.
pa - - - - - - - tri - am. am.
pa - - - tri - am.
tri - - - am. am.
pa - - - - - - tri - - - - am. am.
- - - - - - - tri - - - - am. am.
pa - - - - - - - tri - am. am.
- - - tri - - - - - - - am. am.
52

EXAMPLE 2.2. Giovanni Battista Ala, O *Maria quid ploras*

7
cau - sa do-lo - ris,
Cru - ci-fi-xe-runt A-mo-rem me - um et oc-ci-de - runt e -
6
10
um, Cru - ci-fi-xe-runt A-mo-rem me - um et oc-ci-de - runt e -
6
13
Ab-ster - ge ca -
um, qui mi - hi de - dit vi-tam, <qui mi - hi de - dit vi - tam,>

16
den-tes la - cry-mas, in - vi - tis per - fi-dis iu - dae - is, Il-le vi - vet et vi-vet in ae-

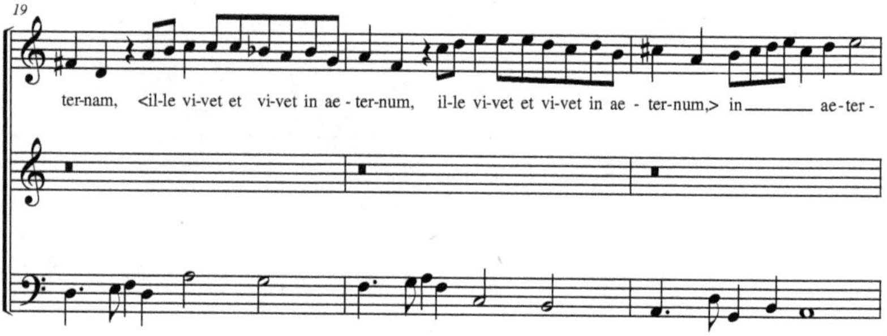
19
ter-nam, <il-le vi-vet et vi-vet in ae - ter-num, il-le vi-vet et vi-vet in ae - ter-num,> in ae - ter -

22
num,
O vi - ta me - a, A - ni-ma me - a, Gau - di-um cor - dis me -

25
O vi-ta me-a A - ni-ma me-a, Gau - di-um cor-dis me - i,
i,
28
O vi-ta me-a, A - ni-ma me-a, Gau - di-um cor-dis me-i,
O vi-ta me-a, A - ni-ma me-a, Gau - di-um cor-dis me - i, u-bi
31
u-bi te in-ve-ni-am di - ci-to mi - hi,
te in-ve-ni-am di - ci-to mi - hi, ut te de
4 3 6

34
ut te de o - scu-ler, et fru-ar in ae-ter - num,
o - scu-ler, et fru-am in ae-ter - num,
ut te de
37
<ut te de o - scu-ler, et fru-ar in ae - ter-num,> et fru - ar in ae-ter - num
o - scu-ler, et fru-ar in ae - ter - num, et fru - ar in ae - ter - num.
3 4 3
40

EXAMPLE 2.3. Giovanni Battista Ala, *Consolare o mater*

7
- - si - me Ie - su,
sur - re - xi, sur - re - xi, sur-re - xi glo - ri - o -
7 6
9
o mi fi-li, o-mi fi-li, o mi fi-li, o-mi fi-li, o fi-li, fi - li mi,
sus,laetare,lae-tare, laetare,lae-tare, laetare, laetare O ma-ter mea, O ma-ter
4 3 9
11
<o fi-li, fi - li mi,> Vul - ne-ra tu - a, fi-li, fi - li,
me - a, lae - ta - re O ma-ter me - a,
6 5 6 4 3:

13
fi - li, fi - li cor me - um, - Vul - ne - ra tu - a, fi - li, fi - li, fi - li, fi - li cor me - um,
15
Vul - ne - ra - - - - - - runt, Vul - ne - ra - - - -
17
- - - - - - runt, Vul - ne - ra - - - - -

19
runt,
Nunc vi - des, nunc vi-des tri-um-
6 3 4
21
phan - tem pri-mo-ge - ni-tum tu - um, nunc vi - des, nunc vi - des tri - um -
6
23
o lae - ti - ti - a,
phan-tem pri-mo-ge-ni-tum tu-um, o lae -

25
<o lae - ti - ti - a, o lae - ti - ti - a,>
ti - ti - a, <o lae - ti - ti - a, o lae - ti - ti - a,>
5 6 5
27
O gau-di-um ve-rum, o gau-di-um ve-rum, o gau - di - um ve - rum.
O gau-di-um ve-rum, o gau-di-um
6 8 6 5
29
<o gau - di-um ve-rum, o gau - di-um ve-rum, o gau - di-um ve -
ve-rum, <o gau - di-um ve - rum,> <o - gau - di-um

30
rum, o gau - di-um ve-rum, o gau - di-um ve-rum, o gau - di-um ve-rum,> o gau - di - um
ve-rum,> o gau - di-um ve-rum, O gau - di-um ve - rum, <o gau - di - um
6 7 6 6 5:
31
ve - rum, <o gau - di - um ve - rum.
ve - rum,> o gau - di - um ve - rum.
7 6 7 6 6

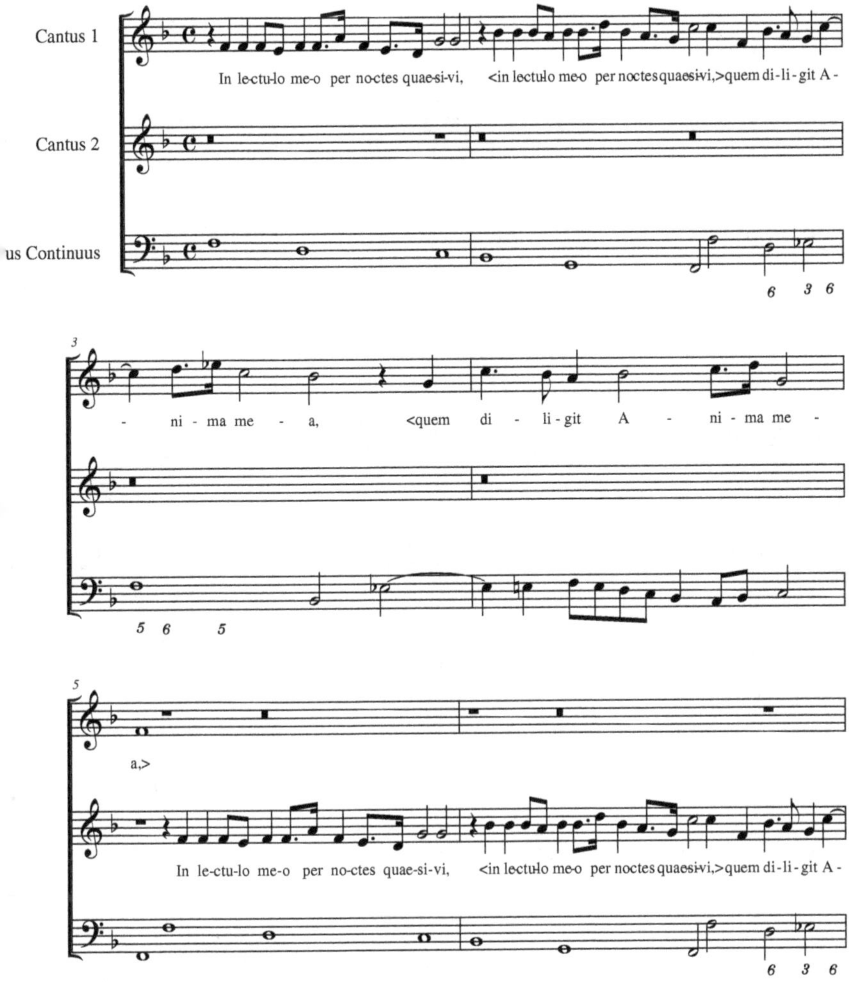

Example 2.4. Giovanni Battista Ala, *In lectulo meo*

7
quae - si - vi il - lum
- ni - ma a, <quem di - li-git A - ni - ma me - a, que - si - vi il - lum
5 6 5 6
10
et non in - ve - ni, <quae - si - vi il - lum et non in-ve-ni, quae - si - vi il - lum et non in-ve-
et non in - ve - ni, <quae - si - vi il - lum et non in-ve-ni, quae - si - vi il - lum et non in-ve-
6 6 6
12
ni,> sur - - gam, <sur - gam,> sur -
ni,> sur - gam, sur - gam,

15
gam et cir - cu - i - bo, cir - cu -
6
16
i - bo ci-vi-tatem per vi-cos et pla - teas, per vi-cos et pla - te-as,
sur - gam et cir-cu-i-bo, cir-cu-i - bo ci - vi-
6
19
circu-i-bo ci-vi-tatem, <circu-i-bo ci-vi-tatem,>
tatem per vi-cos, et pla - teas, per vi-cos et pla - teas, circu-i-bo ci - vi-tatem, <circu-i-bo ci-vi-

22
per vi-cos, et pla-te-as, per vi cos et pla-te - as, que - ram quem
ta-tem,> et pla-te-as, per vi - cos et pla - te - - - as,
7 6 6 6
25
di - li - git, quem di - li - git, quem di - li - git A - ni-ma-
quem di - li-git A - ni-ma me - a,
28
me a, <quem di-li-git A-ni-ma me-a,> A-ni-ma me-a, <A - ni-ma me -
quem di-li-git, A-ni-ma me-a, <A-ni-ma me - a, A - ni-ma me-
3 4 3
31
a,> quem di - li-git A - ni - ma me - a.
a,> quem di - li-git A - ni - ma me - a.

EXAMPLE 4.1. Giovanni Andrea Cima, *Gaudete filiae Sion*

6
ni po - pu-li fi-de - les et con-gra-tu - la - - - mi - ni glo-ri - o - sae vic-
6

10
Al - mi Ro - sa-rij Re-gi -
tri - ci Ma-ri - ae, al - mi Ro - sa-rij Re-gi - nae, et con - gra - tu - la - mi-
10

15
na, <Al - mi Ro-
Al - mi Ro - sa - rij Re - gi - nae, <al - mi Ro - sa - rij
ni glo - ri - o - sae vic - tri - ci Ma - ri - ae, Al - mi Ro - sa - rij, al - mi Ro-
Al - mi Ro - sa - rij Re -
15

19
sa - rij Re - gi - nae;> af - fer - te ro - sas, et li -
Re - gi - nae;>
sa - rij Re - gi - nae;
gi - nae;
19

-li-a ex co - nual -li-bus sy - on,

di - em fe-stum a - gi - te in psal-te - ri - o et

can - ti - co,

da - te ma-gni - fi - cen - ti - am no - - - - mi-ni e -

28
om - nes glo - ri - fi - ca - te - vic - tri - cem Ma-
om - nes glo - ri - fi - ca - te vic - tri - cem Ma-
ius et in vo - ce lau - - - dis, om - nes glo - ri - fi - ca - te vic - tri - cem Ma-
om - nes glo - ri - fi - ca - te vic - tri - cem Ma-
28

31
ri - am ca - put hy - dre, et dra - co - nis con - te - ren - tem,
ri - am ca - put hy - dre, et dra - co - nis con - te - ren - -
ri - am ca - put hy - drae, et dra -
ri - am ca - put
31

34
ca - put hy-drae, et dra-co-nis con-te-
tem, <ca - put hy-drae, et dra - co-nis con-te-ren - tem,>
co-nis con-te-ren - - - tem,
hy-drae, et dra-co-nis con-te - ren - tem, ca - put hy-drae, et dra-
34

37
ren - - - - - - - - - - - - - - - - - -
ca - put hy-drae, et dra - co-nis con-te-ren - tem, con - te-ren - - -
ca - put hy-drae, et dra - co-nis con-te-ren - tem, con - te - ren -
co-nis con-te-ren - - - - - - tem, con - te - ren -
37

40
tem.
tem.
Ju-bi - la - te
tem. Ju-bi - la - te et e-xul - ta - te in hac vic - to - ri-a su - - a,
tem.
40

45
Ju-bi - la - te et e-xul - ta - te in hac vic-
et e-xul-ta - te in hac vic-to - ri a su - a,
45

50
to - ri - a su - a, ju - bi - la - te et e - xul - ta - te, <ju-bi - la - te et e - xul -
Ju - bi - la - te et e - xul - ta te, <ju-bi - la - te et e - xul -
Ju - bi - la - te et e - xul - ta - te, <ju-bi - la - te et e - xul -
Ju - bi - la - te et e - xul - ta - te, <ju-bi - la - te et e - xul -
50

55
ta - te,> in hac vic - to - ri - a su - - - a, in hac vic - to - ri -
ta - te,> in hac vic - to - ri - a su - - - a,
ta - te> in hac vic - to - ri - a, - - - -
ta - te> in
55

59
a, in hac vic-to - ri-a,
in hac vic-to - ri-a su - - - - a, in hac vic - to - ri -
in hac vic-to - ri-a su - - - - a,
hac vic - to - ri - a, in hac vic-to - ri-a su - - - -
59

64
in hac vic - to - ri -
a, in hac vic - to - ri-a su - - - - - a, in hac vic-
in hac vic - to - - - - ri - a, in hac vic-to - ri - - - - - a,
a, in hac vic-to - - - - ri - a, in hac vic-to - ri-a su - a, in hac vic-
64

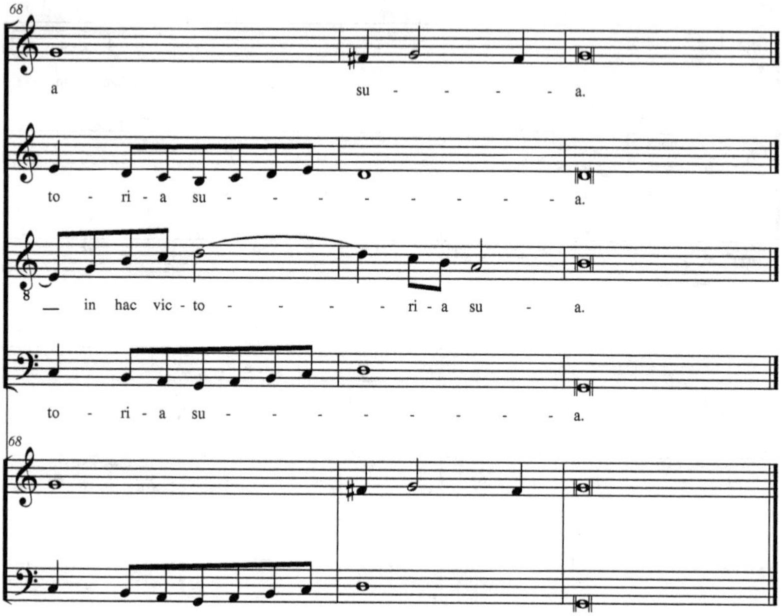
68
a su - - - - a.
to - ri - a su - - - - - - - - a.
— in hac vic - to - - - - ri - a su - a.
to - ri - a su - - - - - - - - a.
68

EXAMPLE 4.2. Giovanni Andrea Cima, *Vocem Mariae*

13
ut au - di - vi sa - lu - ta - ti - o - - - - - nem
est ut au -
17
e - xul - ta - vit in - fans in
di - vit sa-lu-ta-ti - o - nem
21
u - te-ro e - - - - - - - - - - - - -

25
ius
e - xul - ta - vit in fans in u - te-ro e - - - - - -
29
e - xul - ta - vit in -
- - - - - - - - - - ius e - xul-
33
fans in u - te-ro e - - - - - - - - - - - - - -
ta - vit in - fans in u - te-ro e - - - - - - - -

37
ius, et re-ple-ta
ius
41
est de spi - ri-tu san - cto
et re-ple-ta est de spi
45
et re-ple-ta est de spi - ri - tu san -
ri-tu san - cto, et - re-ple-ta est de spi - ri-tu

49
- - cto et voce mag-na ex - - cla-ma - - - - - - vit
san - cto et
53
vo-ce mag - na ex - - - - cla - ma - - - - - - -
57
et di - - - - - xit be-ne-dic-ta
vit, et di - - - - - xit

61
tu in-ter mu-li - e - res et be-ne-dic-tus fruc-tus ven-tris tu - i,
et be-ne - dic-tus fruc-tus ven-tris tu - i be - ne - dic - ta
65
<et-be - ne-dic-tus fruc-tus ven - tris tu - - - i,> be - ne - dic - ta tu in-ter mu-
tu in - ter mu - li - e - res et be-ne-dic-tus fruc-tus ven-tris tu - i,
69
li - e - res et be - ne - dic-tus fruc - tus ven-tris tu - i, <et be-ne-
et be-ne-dic-tus fruc-tus ven-tris tu - i be - ne-dic - ta tu in-ter mu-li - e -

73
dic-tus fruc-tus ven - tris tu - i,> be - ne dic - ta tu in-ter mu-li - e -
res, et be-ne - dic-tus fruc-tus ven-tris tu - i be - ne - dic - ta tu in-ter mu-
77
res, <be - ne - dic - ta tu in-ter mu-li - e - res> et be-ne-dic-tus fruc-tus ven - tris tu -
li - e - res, <be - ne - dic-ta tu in-ter mu-li - e res,> et be-ne-dic-tus fruc-tus
81
- - - - i, et be - ne dic - tus fruc-tus ven - tris tu -
ven - tris tu - i, et be - ne - dic - tus fruc-tus ven - tris tu - - - -

85
i.
i.
89
Al - le - lu -
al - le - lu - ia, al - le - lu - ia,
93
ia, al - le - lu - ia, <al - le-lu - ia, al - le-lu -
<al - le-lu - ia, al - le-lu - ia,

97
ia, al - le - lu - ia, al - le - lu - ia,> al - - - -
al - le lu - ia,> al - le - lu - ia, al - - - - - - -
101
- - - - - - - le - lu - ia, al - - - - - -
- - - - - - - le - lu - ia, al - - - - -
105
- - - - - - - - - - - le - lu - ia,
- - - - - - - - - - - le - lu - ia, al - -

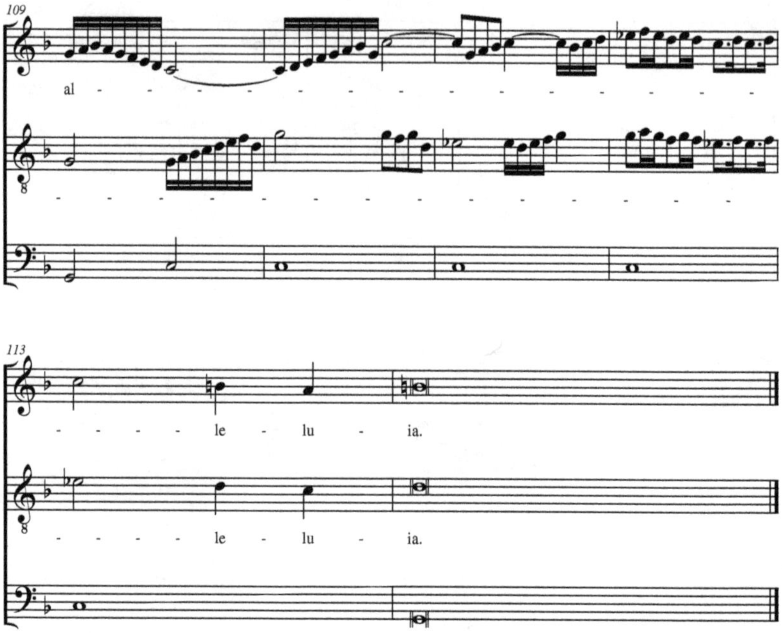
109
al - - - - - - - - - - - - - - - - -
113
- - - - - le - lu - ia.
- - - - - le - lu - ia.

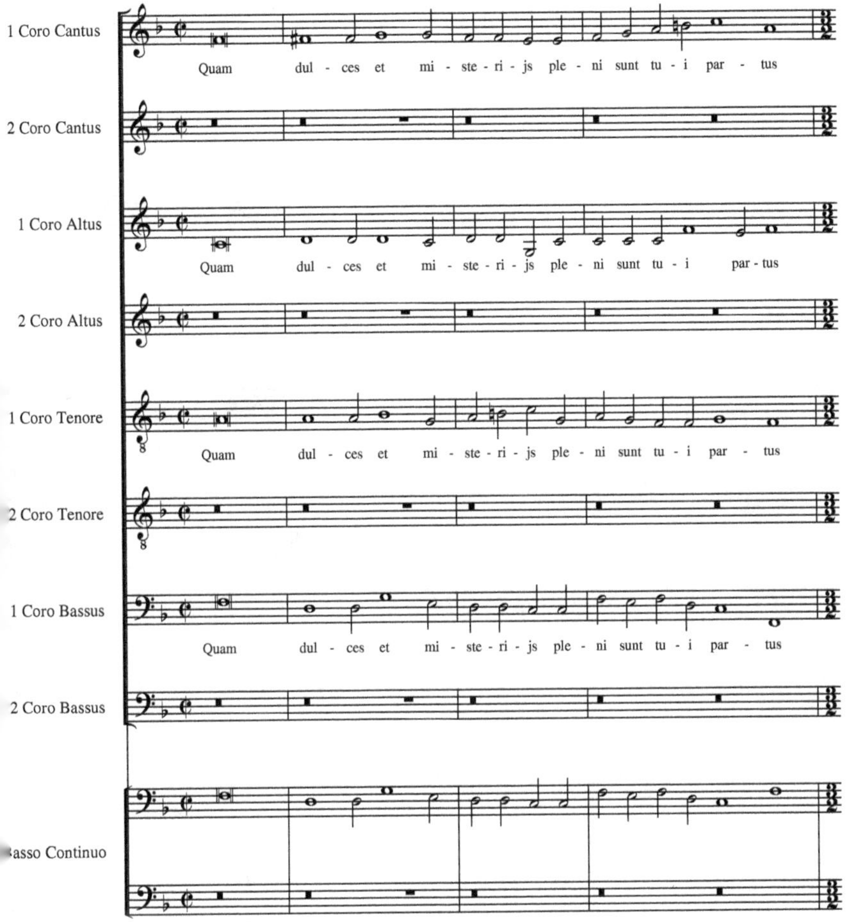

Example 5.1. Benedetto Regio, *Quam dulces et misterijs*

5
O be - a - tis - si - ma Vir - go Ma - ri - - - - a,
O be - a - tis - si - ma Vir - go Ma - ri - - - - a, Quam
O be - a tis - si - ma Vir - go Ma - ri - - - - a,
O be - a - tis - si - ma Vir - go Ma - ri - - - - a, Quam
O be - a - tis - si - ma Vir - go Ma - ri - - - - a,
O be - a - tis - si - ma Vir - go Ma - ri - - - - a, Quam
O be - a - tis - si - ma Vir - go Ma - ri - - - - a,
O be - a - tis - si - ma Vir - go Ma - ri - - - - a, Quam
5

9
dul - ces et mi - ste - ri - js ple - ni sunt tu - i par - tus,
dul - ces et mi - ste - ri - js - ple - ni sunt tu - i par - tus,
dul - ces et mi - ste - ri - js ple - ni sunt tu - i par - tus,
dul - ces et mi - ste - ri - js ple - ni sunt tu - i par - tus,
9

13
<O be - a tis - si - ma - Vir - go Ma - ri - - - - a, sum - mum Sa-cer do -
O be - a - tis - si - ma Vir - go Ma - ri - - - - a,
<O be - a - tis - si - ma Vir - go Ma - ri - - - - a,> sum - mum Sa - cer - do-
O be - a - tis - si - ma Vir - go Ma - ri - - - - a,
<O be - a - ti - si - ma Vir - go Ma - ri - - - - a,> sum - mum Sa - cer - do-
O be - a - tis - si - ma Vir - go Ma - ri - - - - a,
<O be - a - tis - si - ma Vir - go Ma - ri - - - - a,> sum - mum Sa - cer - do-
O be - a - tis - si - ma Vir - go Ma - ri - - - - a,
13

17
tem si - ne do - lo - re pe - - - pe - ri - sti,
si - ne do -
tem si - ne do - lo - re pe - pe - ri - - - sti,
si - ne do - lo - re,
tem si - ne do - lo - re pe - - - pe - ri - - - sti,
si - ne do - lo -
tem si - ne do - lo - re pe - pe - ri - - - sti,
si - ne do - lo -
17

21
si - ne do - lo - re pe - - - - pe - ri -
lo - re pe - pe - ri - - sti, si - ne do - lo - re pe - pe -
si - ne do - lo - re pe - pe - ri - sti, pe -
si - ne do - lo - re pe - pe - ri - sti, si - ne do - lo - re pe - pe - ri -
si - ne - do - lo - re pe - - - pe - ri -
- - re pe - - - pe - ri - sti si - ne do - lo - re pe - - - pe - ri -
si - ne do - lo - re pe - - - pe - ri -
- re pe - pe - ri - - sti, si - ne do - lo - re pe - pe - ri -
21

25
- - - - - sti, qui pro no-bis De-o pa - tri in cru - ce se ob - tu - lit,
ri - - - - - sti,
- - pe - ri - sti, qui pro no-bis De-o pa - tri in cru - ce se ob - tu - lit,
- - - - - sti,
- - - - - sti, qui pro no-bis De-o pa - tri in cru - ce se ob - tu - lit,
- - - - - sti,
- - - - - sti, qui pro no-bis De-o pa - tri in cru - ce se ob - tu - lit,
- - - - - sti,
25

Ho - di - e   no - vum   pa - ris   Sa - cer - do - tem

no - - - vum   pa - ris   Sa - cer - do - tem

33
ut sa-cri-fi - ci - j
ut sa-cri-
ut sa-cri-fi - ci - j
ut sa-cri-
ut sa-cri-fi - ci - j
ut - sa-cri-
Ho - di - e no - vum pa - ris Sa - cer - do - tem ut sa-cri-fi - ci - j
no - vum pa - ris Sa - cer - do - tem ut sa-cri-
33

37
fi - li - i tu - i me - mo-ri - am sae-pis - si - me re - - - no - vet.
fi - ci - j fi - li - j tu - i me-mo-ri - am sae - pis - si - me re - - - no-vet.
fi - li - j tu - i me - mo-ri - am sae-pis - si - me re - no - vet.
fi - ci - j fi - li - j tu - i me-mo-ri - am sae - pis - si - me re - no - vet.
fi - li - j tu - i me - mo-ri - am sae-pis - si - me re - - - no - vet.
fi - ci - j fi - li - j tu - i me-mo-ri - am sae - pis - si - me re - no-vet.
fi - li - j tu - i me - mo-ri - am sae-pis - - - si - me re - - - no-vet.
fi - ci - j fi - li - j tu - i me-mo-ri - am sae - pis - si - me re - - - no - vet.
37

41
Gau-de - a-mus i - gi-tur, <gau-de - a-mus i - gi-tur> de tan-to par - tu, <de tan-to par -
Gau-de - a mus i - gi-tur, gua-de - a mus i - gi - tur de tan-to par - tu, <de tan-to
Gau-de - a mus i - gi-tur, <gau-de - a-mus i - gi-tur> de tan-to par - tu, <de tan-to par -
Gau-de - a-mus i - gi-tur, <gau-de - a-mus i - gi-tur> de tan-to par - tu, <de tan-to
Gau-de - a-mus i - gi-tur, <gau-de - a-mus i - gi-tur> de tan-to par - tu, <de tan-to par -
Gau-de - a-mus i - gi-tur, <gau-de - a-mus i - gi-tur> de tan-to par - tu, <de tan-to
Gau-de - a-mus i - gi-tur, <gau-de - a-mus i - gi-tur> de tan-to par - tu, <de tan to par -
Gau-de - a-mus i - gi-tur, gau-de - a-mus i - gi - tur de tan-to par - tu, <de tan-to
41

45
- - tu> et gau-den-ter cla-me - mus, et-gau - den - ter, <et gau-
par - tu,> et gau-den-ter cla-me - mus, et gau-den - ter,
- - tu,> et gau-den-ter cal-me - mus, et gau - den - ter, <et gau-
par - tu,> et gau-den-ter cla-me - mus, et gau-den - ter,
- - tu,> et gau-den-ter cla-me - mus, et gau - den - ter, <et gau-
par - tu,> et gau-den-ter cla-me - mus, et gau-den - ter,
- - tu,> et gau-den-ter cla-me - mus et gau - den - ter, <et gau-
par - tu,> et gau-den-ter cla-me - mus, et gau-den - ter,
45

49
denter> cla - me - mus Sur - re - xit Chri - stus de se - pul - chro,
et gauden - ter cla - me - mus
denter> cla - me - mus Sur - re - xit Chri - stus de se - pul - chro,
<etgauden - ter> cla - me - mus
den-ter cla - me - mus Sur - re - xit Chri - stus de se - pul - chro,
<etgauden-ter> cla - me-mus
denter>clame - - - - - mus Sur - re - xit Chri - stus de se - pul - chro,
<etgauden-terclame - mus
49

53
Al - le - lu - ia, al - le - lu -
Sur - re - xit Chri - stus de se - pul - chro, Al - le - lu - ia,
Al - le - lu - ia, al - le - lu -
Sur - re - xit Chri - stus de se - pul - chro, Al - le - lu - ia,
Al - le - lu - ia, al - le - lu -
Sur - re - xit Chri - stus de - se - pul - chro, Al - le - lu - ia,
Al - le - lu - ia, al - le - lu -
Sur - re - xit Chri - stus de se - pul - chro, Al - le - lu - ia,
53

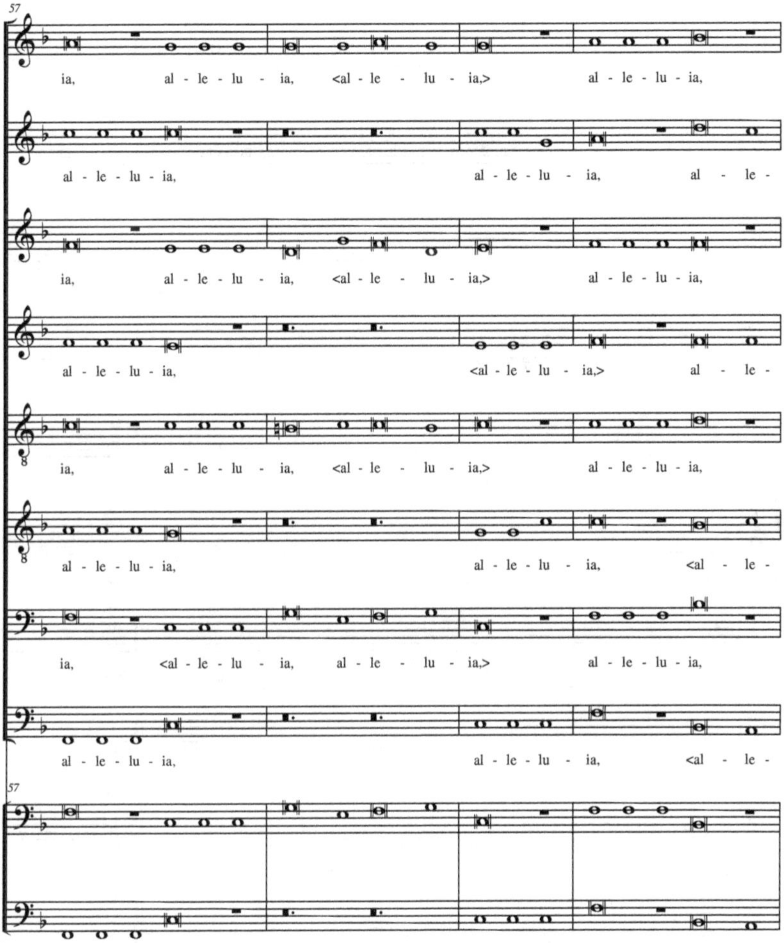
57
ia, al - le - lu - ia, <al - le - lu - ia,> al - le - lu - ia,
al - le - lu - ia, al - le - lu - ia, al - le -
ia, al - le - lu - ia, <al - le - lu - ia,> al - le - lu - ia,
al - le - lu - ia, <al - le - lu - ia,> al - le -
ia, al - le - lu - ia, <al - le - lu - ia,> al - le - lu - ia,
al - le - lu - ia, al - le - lu - ia, <al - le -
ia, <al - le - lu - ia, al - le - lu - ia,> al - le - lu - ia,
al - le - lu - ia, al - le - lu - ia, <al - le -
57

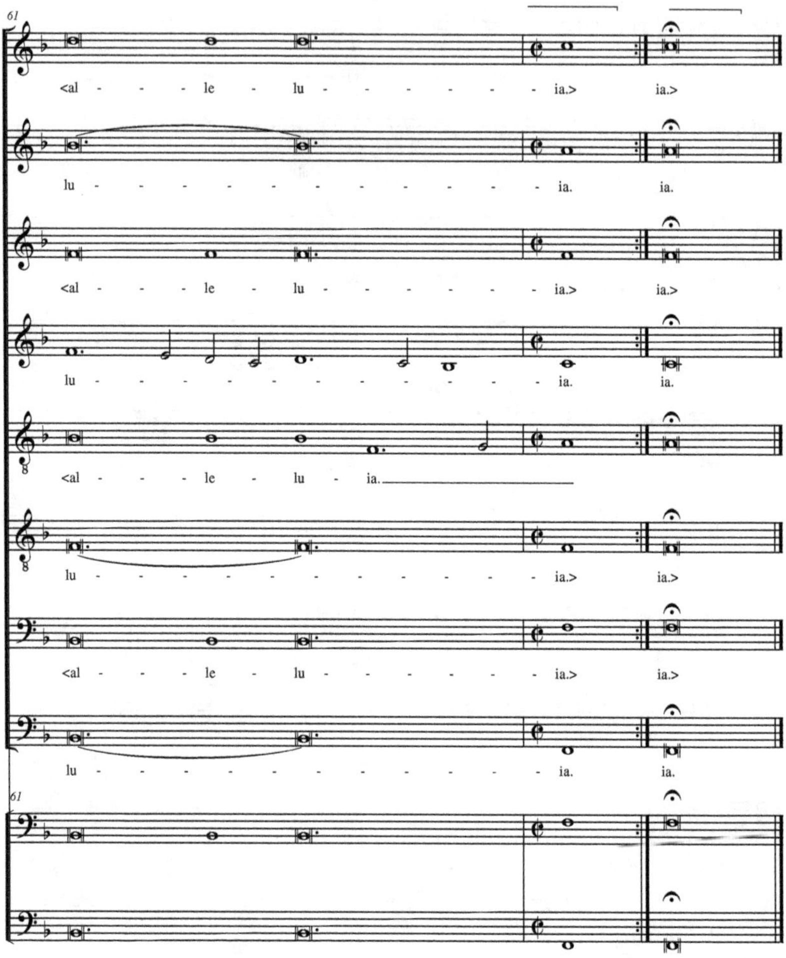
61
<al - - - le - lu - - - - - - - ia.> ia.>
lu - - - - - - - - - - - - ia. ia.
<al - - - le - lu - - - - - - - ia.> ia.>
lu - - - - - - - - - - - - ia. ia.
<al - - - le - lu - ia.
lu - - - - - - - - - - - - ia.> ia.>
<al - - - le - lu - - - - - - - ia.> ia.>
lu - - - - - - - - - - - - ia. ia.
61

EXAMPLE 5.2. Anonymous, Librone 23, Ad Magnificat. In Primis Vesperis. Beata es Maria

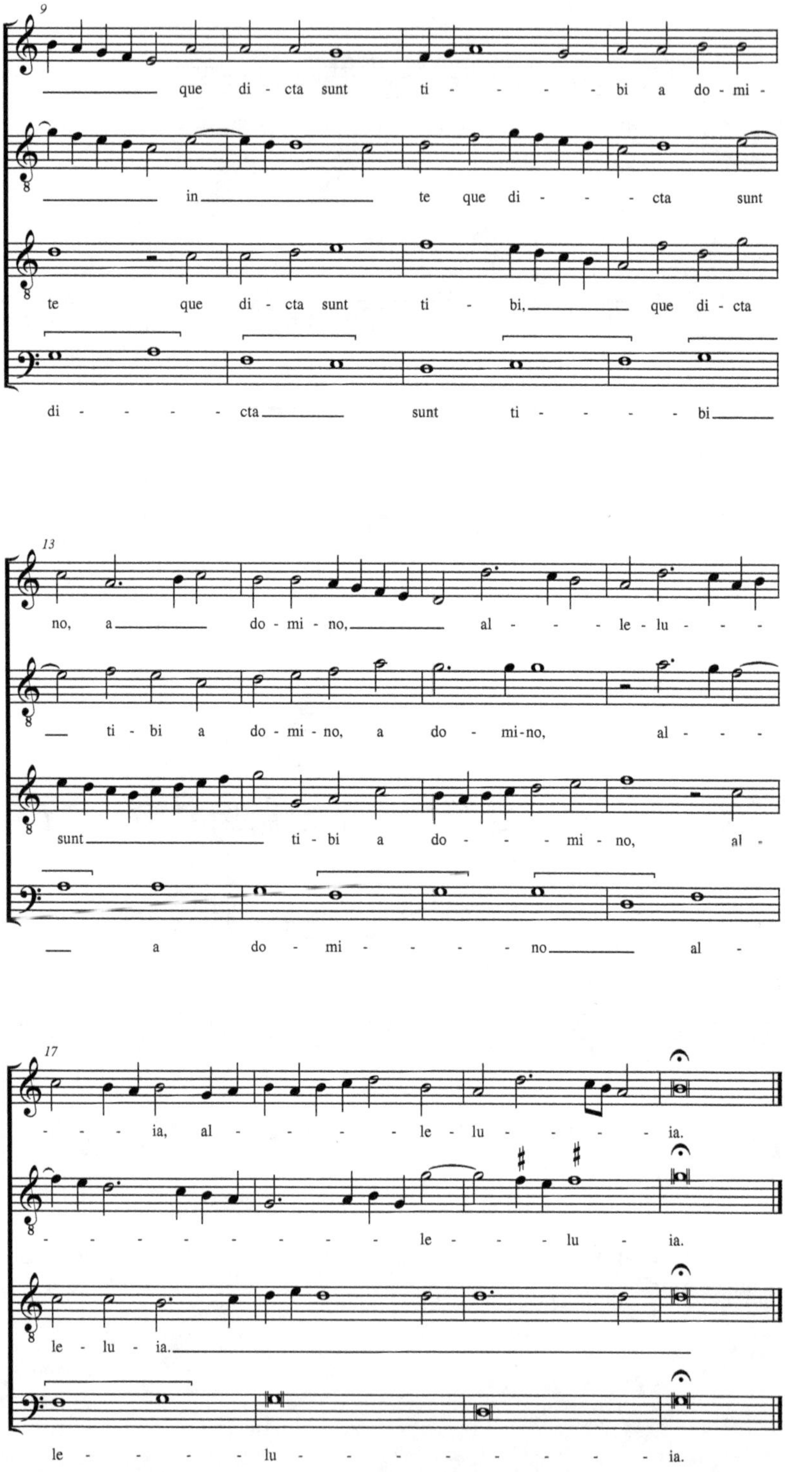
9
que di - cta sunt ti - - - - - bi a do - mi -
in te que di - - - - cta sunt
te que di - cta sunt ti - bi, que di - cta
di - - - - cta sunt ti - - - - bi
13
no, a do - mi - no, al - - - - le - lu - - -
ti - bi a do - mi - no, a do - mi-no, al - - -
sunt ti - bi a do - - - mi - no, al -
a do - mi - - - - - no al -
17
- - - ia, al - - - - - le - lu - - - - ia.
- - - - - - - - - le - - - lu - ia.
le - lu - ia.
le - - - - lu - - - - - - - - - - ia.

EXAMPLE 5.3. Anonymous, Librone 23, Ad Magnificat. In Secundis Vesperis.
Beatem me

9
a an - cil - lam hu - mi - lem re - - - - -
cil - lam hu - mi - lem
hu - - - - mi - lem re - spe - - xit,
cil - lam - - - hu - - - - - - - - - - - -
13
spe - - - - xit de - - - - - - us, re -
re - - - spe - xit de - - - - - - - us
re - spe - xit de -
mi - - - - - - - lem re - - - spe - - - -

spe - - - xit de - - - - - - - - - - us
re - spe - xit de - - - - - - - - us, al -
- - - - - - - - - - us al - le lu -
xit de - - - - us al - - - - - - le -
17
al - le - lu - ia, al - - - - - le - lu -
le - - - - lu - ia, al - - - le - - - - - lu -
- - - - - - - - - ia, <al - le - - - lu -
- - - - - - - lu - - - - - - - - - - -
ia.
ia.
ia.>
ia.

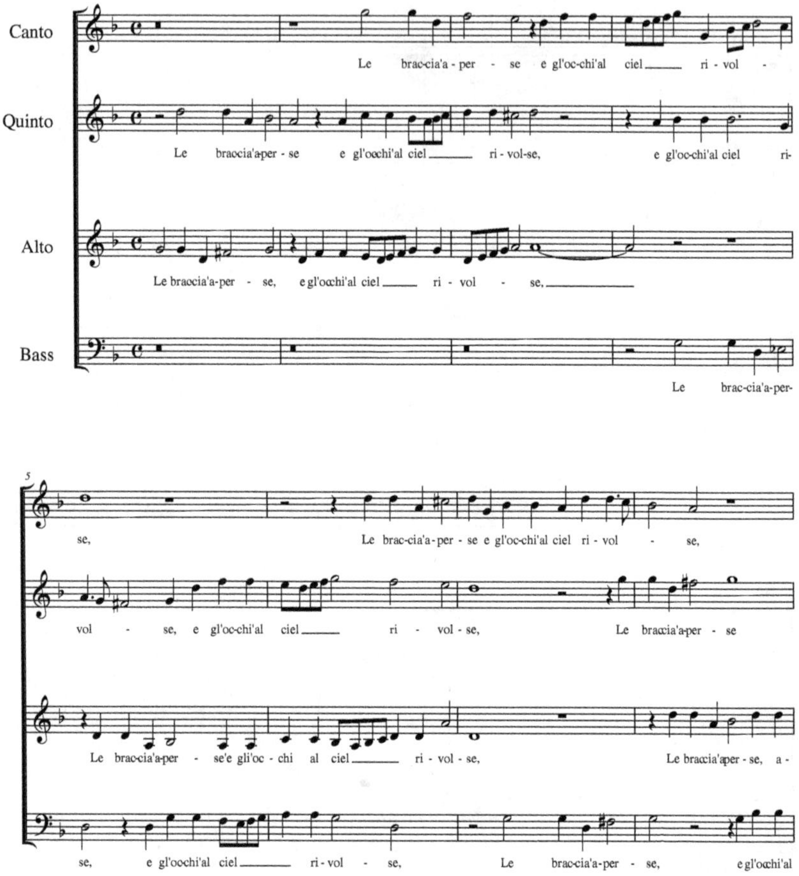

EXAMPLE 5.5. Stefano Limido, *Le braccia aperse*

9
e gl'oc-chi'al ciel ri - vol - - - - se, Me - stis - si -
e gl'oc-chi'al ciel ri - vol - se, e gl'oc - chi'al ciel ri - vol - se, Me - stis - si -
per - se, e-gl'oc-chi'al ciel ri - vol - se, Me - stis - si -
ciel ri - vol - se, e gl'oc - chi'al ciel ri-vol - se, Me - si -

13
ma Ma - ri - - - a, Quan - do sot - to'l gran pe - so de la Cro - ce,
ma Ma - ri - a, Quan - do sot - to'l gran pe - so de la Cro - ce,
ma Ma - ri - - - a, Quan - do sot - to'l gran pe - so de la Cro - ce,
ma Ma - ri - - - a, Quan - do sot - to'l gran pe - so de la Cro - ce,

17
Stan - co - an - he - lan - te'il
Stan - co'an - he - lan - te'il Fi - glio,
Stan - co'an - he - lan - - - - - te il Fi -
Stan - co'an - he - lan - te'il Fi - glio, Stan - co'an - he - lan -
21
Fi - - - - - - - glio s'of - fer - se'à lei
Stan - co'an - he - lan - te'il Fi - glio, S'of - fer - se'à lei per
glio, Stan - co'an - he - lan - te'il Fi - glio, S'of - fer - se'à lei per vi - a, S'of -
te'il Fi - glio,

25
per via, s'of - fer - se à lei, s'of - fer - se à lei per vi -
vi - a, S'of - fer - se'à lei per vi - - - - - -
fer - se'à lei per vi - a, S'of - fer - se'à lei per
29
- - a, Con san - gui - no - so ci - glio: E - men - tre'ohi -
a, Con san - gui - no - so ci - glio: E men - tre'ohi -
vi - a, Con san - gui - no - so ci - glio: E men - tre'ohi -
Con san - gui - no - so ci - glio: E men - tre'ohi -

33
me la vo - ce Las - - - - - sa pro - fe - rir vol - se, pro - fe - rir vol -
me la vo - ce Las - - - - - sa pro - fe - rir vol - se, pro - fe - rir vol -
me la vo - ce Las - - - - - sa pro - fe - rir vol - se. pro - fe - rir vol -
me la vo - ce Las - sa pro - fe - rir vol -
37
se, Il duol la vo - ce ed il
se, Il duol la
se, Il duol la vo - - - - - ce ed il
se, Il duol la vo - ce ed il vi -

41
— vi - gor — le tol - se, ed il vi - gor —
vo - ce ed il vi - gor — le tol -
— vi - gor — le tol - se, ed
gor le tol - se,

45
— le tol - se, ed il —
se, ed il vi - gor, - ed il — vi - gor —
il vi - gor — le tol - se, ed il — vi - gor le -
ed il vi - gor le tol -

49
vi - gor le tol - se, ed il vi - gor le
le tol - se, ed il vi - gor le tol -
tol - se, ed il vi - gor le tol - - -
se, ed il vi - gor le
53
tol - - - - - se.
- - - - - - - se.
- - - - - - - se.
tol - - - - - - se.

Notes

Introduction

1. "Et mentre di fresco sete amaestrati a riparare, colpi della Divina Ira, non lasciate irruginir l'arme le quale havete sin qui adoprate, esercitatevi continuamente nella frequenza de santisacramenti, nell'orationi, ne i divini, nelle elimosine, nelle processioni, nel visitar le chiese et altari e finalmente perseverate in tanti altri cristiani esercitij ne quali, gratia del signore sete gia cosi bene incaminati, acioche possiate con quest'arme valorosamente combattere." From a letter written by Sfondrato and recorded in Milano, Biblioteca Ambrosiana (hereafter BAM) P. 249 sup (Urbano Monti, *Delle cose più notabili successe alla città di Milano, seconda parte, 1578–1581*), 2v–3r.

2. For a general economic and social history of Milan in this period, see Domenico Sella, *Lo stato di Milano in età spagnola* (Torino: UTET Libreria, 1987).

3. See, for example, Gaspare Bugati, *L'aggiunti dell'Historia universale et delle cose di Milano . . . dall 1566 fin'al 1581* (Milano: Francesco ed heredi Simone Tini, 1587), 154–155; Carlo Marcora, "Il diario di Giambattista Casale (1554–1598)," *Memorie storiche della diocese di Milano* XII (Milano 1965), 286–300; and BAM, P. 249 sup (Urbano Monti, *Delle cose più notabili, seconda parte, 1578–1581*), 104r-105v.

4. On Carlo Borromeo and his reform programs, see Sella, 86–97; Hubert Jedin, *Carlo Borromeo* (Rome: Istituto della enciclopedia Italiana, 1971); Domenico Maselli, "I concilii provinciali nella prassi di S. Carlo e i loro rapporti con il Concilio di Trento," *Studia borromaica* 7 (1993), 71–81; and John B. Tomaro, "San Carlo Borromeo and the Implementation of the Council of Trent" in *San Carlo Borromeo: Catholic Reform and Ecclesiastical Politics in the Second Half of the Sixteenth Century*, ed. John M. Headley and John B. Tomaro (London and Toronto: Associated University Presses, 1988), 67–84.

5. BAM, P. 248–251 sup (Urbano Monti, *Delle cose più notabili successe alla città di Milano*).

6. BAM, P. 249 sup (Urbano Monti, *Delle cose più notabili successe alla città di Milano, seconda parte, 1578–1581*), 58v.

7. BAM, P. 251 sup (Urbano Monti, *Delle cose più notabili successe alla città di Milano, quarta parte, 1585–1587*), 105r-112r and 117v.

8. Carlo Marcora, "Il diario di Giambattista Casale," 209–210, 220–221, 249–250, 271, 348, and BAM, Trotti 413 (Diario Giambattista Casale), 30r, 46r, 110r, 115r.

9. BAM, Trotti 413, 2r-v.

10. BAM, Trotti 413, 5r.

11. Carlo Marcora, "Il diario di Giambattista Casale," 209–210.

12. BAM, Trotti 413, 75r-81r.

13. BAM, Trotti 413, 96r and 128v.

14. BAM, P. 248–251 sup and BAM, Trotti 413.

15. Paolo Morigia, *Historia dove si narra l'origine della famosa divotione della Chiesa della Madonna, posta vicina à quella di S. Celso di Milano* (Milano: Pacifico Pontio, 1594), 27–28.

16. On this general phenomenon in sixteenth-century Italy, see Edward Muir, "The Virgin on the Street Corner: The Place of the Sacred in Italian Cities" in *Religion and Culture in Renaissance and Reformation*, ed. Steven Ozment (Kirksville: Sixteenth Century Journal Publishers, 1989), 25–40.

17. "il primo fà, che sendo solito una giovane Ivi vicina qual' era gobba a metter a piedi di detta figura ogni sabato una candela, et bisognando percio alzarzi un poco con forza, detta gobba volendo arrivare al loco dove soleva metter detta candela con discomodo della persona et doglia Insieme, simplacamente Ingenochiatasi dimando gratia a nostra signora che si degnasse farli gratia che non sentisse voglia nel metter tal candela a fine che con miglior animo come desiderava seguitasse questa sua divotione, Et cosi seguitando questa sua oratione ogni volta che vi poneva la candela, Ecco che a poco a poco In termine de puochi giorni rimase dritta et sana come se mai fosse stata gobba, dalla qual cosa avedutosi li vicini dimandorono come fusse cosi risanata La onde Intero il miracolo cominciorono molti a visitar detta Imagine con loro orationi,

Il second miracolo fu che passando ivi a caso uno a cavallo sopra un' cavallo fastidioso et essendo ivi vicino fu getato a terra dove apena gionta in terra fu colto da un paio de calzi nel petto da detto cavallo, et percio egli voltosi a detta Imagine nel medesimo tempo che hebbi i calci et dimandoso il suo aiutto, subito sbrigossi dal cavallo sano, senza alchuna offesa de detti calci,

Il terzo miracolo fu che ritrovandosi molto popolo à visitare detta imagine, Ecco che adormentatosi una carochiero sopra la carochia da la quale poco fa' erano smontate le patrone et fattosi Ivi vicino un strepito per il quale si spaventorono i cavalli, et percio messa in fuga havendone anche getato a terra il carochiero corsero dove era gran calca di persone presso detta Imagine et ivi ragirando con gran furia tra loro che tutti in bisbiglio non havendo altro rifugio ricorevano ala nostra signora per aiutto, detti cavalli con la carozza senza lesione alcuna delle persone transcorendo farono presi et tenuti a man salva sin che arrivato il carochiero vi monto sopra et governolli" BAM, P. 251 sup, 50r-51r.

18. BAM, P. 251 sup, 119v.

19. "Memoria come lanno 1590 adì 25. agosto fece miracolo quella Madona qual era in cappo la muraglia del Giardino di patri de la pasione di Milano. su la strata de ver Santo Pietro chiesato. era sul muro che guarda verso Porta Ticinese. Et il primo miracolo fu in sabato il giorno doppo Santo Bartolomeo qual primo miracolo fu che volendo uno per divotione basciare il

costato del signore che era in grembo alla Madonna come quando fu levato di croce: li resto al sudeto huomo la mano tinta di sangue che uscite dal costato del *signore. per* quanto subito fu ditto . . .

Et adì 30 ditto fu levata *con* bela arte Et fu portata in la Chiesa de la pasione alla terza capella da mane dir drita nel entrare in chiesa Et quando fu levata era una hora da notte la zobia venendo il venerdi Et la processione fu solum de li reverendi patri de la pasion *con* grande numero di populo *con* grande devotione. Laus Deo." BAM, Trotti 413, 144v. Modern transcription in Marcora, "Il diario di Giambattista Casale," 392.

20. Morigia, *Historia*, 3–16 and Serviliano Latuada, *Descrizione di Milano ornate con molti disegni in rame* . . . (Milano: Giuseppe Cairoli Mercante, 1737), 5 vols., III, 48–55.

21. Morigia, *Historia*, 17, and BAM, Trotti 413, 178r.

22. Morigia, *Historia*, 17–19. Also see Giuseppe Riccucci," L'attività della cappella musicale di S. Maria presso S. Celso e la condizione dei musici a Milano tra il XVI e il XVII secolo" in *Intorno a Monteverdi*, ed. Maria Caraci Vela and Rodobaldo Tibaldi (Lucca: L.I.M., 1999), 289–312.

23. Morigia, *Historia*, 39–41.

24. See Christine Getz, *Music in the Collective Experience in Sixteenth-Century Milan* (Aldershot: Ashgate, 2006), 243–248, as well as chapter four.

25. ASDM, Archivio spirituale X, Metropolitana LXXXII (Visite pastorali e documenti aggiunti), fasc. 20.

26. Carlo Marcora, "L'istitutzione della compagnia del Santo Rosario eretta da san Carlo," *Atti del Accademia di San Carlo* VI (1983), 111–117.

27. "Memoria come Nel 1584 adì 25 Marzo Illus*tris*simo Car*dinal*e Boromeo dete principio alla Co*mpa*gnia del Santissimo Rosario in Domo. Et ordino che la Madona del aboro [sic.] si chiamase la Madona del Santissimo Rosario Et volse che il ditto giorno se portase la ditta Madona in procesione. nella qua li era sua s*ignor*ia R*everendissi*ma & tutto il clero dil Domo. Et tanto populo che era uno stuporo. per dar principio a questa benedeta Et santa devotione del Santissimo Rosario . . . adì primo de aprile 1584 cioe otto giorno dopo ditta procesione io mi fece scrivere Et mio figliolo David in dita compagnia del santissimo rosario in Domo. per mia divotione perchè gia era per molti anni avanti scri'in ditta compagnia alla rosa insieme con mia muglier Catelina. David. Et angela miei figlioli. la qual chatelina Et angela si feceno scrive ancora nel rosario in Domo. ali 2 aprile lano ut supra" BAM, Trotti 413, 128v. Modern transcription in Marcora, "Il diario di Giambattista Casale," 363–364.

28. "AVE MARIA. Contempla qui anima divota, come essendo pervenuta la Vergine gloriosa alla età di anni tre, second il voto per loro fatto, fu presentata dalli parenti a Dio nel Tempio, dinanzi al Sacerdote. Et pervenuta alli gradi del Tempio, ch'erano quindici, con molta facilità per se stessa quelli ascese con grande ammiratione de circonstanti, iquali si maravigliavano della sapientissima & eloquentissima loquella sua, delle riverentie che faceva al sacro Tempio, all'altare, & al Sacerdote, che pareva che lungamente fosse stata in quello essercitata. Dove ben si verificava quel detto della Cantico Canticorum al 6.cap. Quae est ista, quae progreditur quasi aurora consurgens, pulchra et luna, electa ut Sol, terribilis ut castrorum acies ordinata? Quale è questa, la quale

camina come l'aurora, quando si leva la mattina, bella come la Luna, eletta come il sole, per lo splendore delle virtù et gratie, & terribile come una squadra ordinata di gente d'arme, per la repugnantia ad ogni vitio, & diabolica suggestione. Onde questo ascendere di quindici gradi, significa, che doveva ascendere sopra i nove ordini Angelici, e sei gradi de Santi. Non è da maravigliare, se Iddio nostro in ascendere quei gradi dette a Maria Vergine tanta gagliardezza, perche voleva dimostrare quanto mirabilmente doveva ascendere alla perfettione di tutte le virtù, & di ogni bene. Et che sia stata dotata di ogni virtù, & similmente specchio d'ogni santità, manifestamente appare a tutti." *Rosario della Gloriosa Vergine Maria. Con le stationi & Indulgetie delle Chiese di Roma per tutto l'anno.* Venezia: Giovanni Antonio Bertano, 1591. The front matter indicates that the volume was newly printed and corrected from an edition of 1571. A version dated 1587 exists as well.

29. "AVE MARIA, & c. *ora pro nobis pecatoris,* Virgo benignissima: Priega per noi peccatori, Vergine benignissima; la quale si come dopò li tre anni dal tuo glorioso nascimento secondo l'antico costume, et rito della legge fosti con solenne cerimonia presentata nel tempio con grandissima frequentia di popolo, che con maravigliosi sguardi ammirava in te rispendente un rarissimo lume d'honestà; un singolare simulacro de insite virtù, et gratie divine; una modestia verginale, et gravita nell'andare; nel spiegare concetti tuoi nelle divine lodi, una pia, ardente, et devotissima maniera d'orare; et finalmente una ammirabile humiltà, et religione nell'offrire al sommo Padre la vera adoratione, et precipuo honore; sic che come molta ragione pareva d'udirsi voci ribombanti; (Cant. 6) *Quae est ista, quae progreditur, quasi Aurora consurgens, pulchra ut Luna, electa ut sol, terribilis ut Castrorum acies ornata?* cosi noi, che di questa santa Presentatione celebriamo il giorno, mediante la tua intercessione, et prieghi, siamo fatti meritevole d'esser presentati nel tempio, che è CHRISTO nella celeste Gloria. Amen." Bartolomeo Scalvo, Le *Meditationi del Rosario della Gloriosissima Maria Vergine* (In Milano: appresso Pacifico Pontio, 1569), 6–7.

30. Morigia, *Historia.*

31. On the use of affective meditations, including those of Loyola, in Spain, see Elena Carrera, "The Emotions in Sixteenth-Century Spanish Spirituality," *Journal of Religious History* 31/3 (September 2007), 235–252.

32. See St. Ignatius of Loyola, *The Spiritual Exercises,* translated with commentary by George E. Ganss, S.J. (St. Louis: The Institute of Jesuit Sources, 1992).

33. Other potential Medieval influences include the *Sentenze* of Pietro Lombardo (c. 1150) and the fourteenth-century *De imitazione Christi* attributed to Jean Gerson. See Rogelio García Mateo, S.J., "Influsso medieval e rinascimentale nella formazione e nel contenuto degli Esercizi Ignaziani" in *Gli Esercizi Spirituali di sant' Ignazio. Linguistica-Storia-Spiritualità,* ed. Herbert Alphonsi, S.J. (Roma: Pomel S. a. S., 1998), 33–44, and Robert E. McNally, S.J., "The Council of Trent, the *Spiritual Exercizes* and the Catholic Reform," *Church History* 34/1 (March 1965), 41.

34. Sarah McNamer, "The Origins of the *Meditationes Vitae Christi,*" *Speculum* 84/4 (2009), 905–906. McNamer, 907–955, argues that Oxford, Bodleian Library MS Canonici Ital. 174, an early copy of the *Meditationes*

in the vernacular Italian rather than in Latin, contains the original layer of the text.

35. McNally, "The Council of Trent," 43–44.

36. Manuel Ruiz Jurado, "La portata pastorale-spirituale degli Esercizi Ignaziani per la spiritualità moderna e contemporanea" in *Gli Esercizi Spirituali di sant' Ignazio*, 49–52.

37. As seen, for example, in Dottore Ledesma della Compagnia di Giesù, *Modo per insegnar la Dottrina Christiana* (Roma: per gli heredi d'Antonio Blado stampatori cameriali, 1573), 9r-17v.

38. McNally, "The Council of Trent," 45.

39. Arcangelo Ballotino, *Pietosi affetti di compassione sopra li dolori della B.V. Maria* (In Bologna: per Bartolomeo Cochi, 1612), 115–117.

40. Ballotino, *Pietosi affetti*, 117–120.

41. St. Ignatius of Loyola, *The Spiritual Exercises*.

42. Bartolomeo Scalvo, *Le Meditationi del Rosario della Gloriosissima Maria Vergine* (Venezia: Domenico e Giovanni Battista della Guerra, 1583), 355. The text of the meditation itself is found on the facing page, 354.

43. See figures 5.7 and 5.8. These are discussed in greater depth in chapter five.

44. Ballotino, *Pietosi affetti*, 37–38.

45. Angelo Francesco Tinosi, *Statua di Maria Vergine fabbricata dall'humile servo di lei fra Angelo Tignosi, Servita, minimo Dottore di Sacra Theologia* (Milano: Agostino Tradate, 1605).

1. Venerating the Veil

1. "questa sacratissima vergine, si come tabernacolo di Dio, era la idea perpetua virginità, la forma dell'istessa honestà, la scuola d'ogni virtù." Morigia, *Historia*, 11.

2. Morigia, *Historia*, 13, and Serviliano Latuada, *Descrizione di Milano*, III, 48–50. Also see Ferdinando Reggiori, *Il santuario di Santa Maria presso San Celso e i suoi tesori* (Milano: Banco Popolare di Milano, 1968), 35–36. According to Urbino Monti, who was an eyewitness, Carlo Borromeo led four civic penitential processions from the Duomo to one of Milan's major churches during the plague of 1576. The last of the four reportedly culminated at Santa Maria presso San Celso, and this may explain why the Madonna of Miracles was credited, at least in part, with the eradication of the epidemic. The other churches involved included Sant'Ambrogio, Santa Maria della Scala, and San Nazaro. BAM, P. 248 sup, 104v.

3. Latuada and Reggiori describe it as a wall rather than a pilaster.

4. Morigia, *Historia*, 5–6, and Latuada, *Descrizione di Milano*, III, 48–49. The benefices are discussed in Milano, Archivio di Stato (hereafter ASM), *Patronati regi P.G.-1734*, facs. 3, which is a manuscript history of the ducal benefices to 1651 by Agostino Bassanini.

5. Morigia, *Historia*, 7–8, and Latuada, *Descrizione di Milano*, III. 53–54. Latuada claims that three hundred pilgrims were present during the miracle.

6. "al *Post-Communio* della detta Messa, vide l'Immagine viva della Beata Maria Virgine Maria con volto candido, e gran splendore co' bracchj aperti, e col Figliuolo Bambino su le braccia . . ." Latuada, *Descrizione di Milano,* III, 54.

7. Latuada, *Descrizione di Milano,* III, 53–54. Also documented, albeit less colorfully, in Morigia, *Historia,* 7–8.

8. Morigia, *Historia,* 7–8, and Latuada, *Descrizione di Milano,* III, 53–54.

9. "ci sono molti giorni ch'il numero de visitanti passa duecento mila persone, e moltissimi altri che passano il numero de cento mila; & tutte le prime Domeniche di Mese, e le feste d'essa gloriosa Madre la gran moltitudine del popolo, che ci concorre, pare un grosso fiume nel corrente dell'acqua; oltre che non c'è giorno che non passano le migliaia i visitanti questa lodatissima divotione." Morigia, *Historia,* 27–28.

10. Morigia, *Historia,* 5–14, and Latuada, *Descrizione di Milano,* III, 50–55. Latuada credits Filippo Maria Visconti with the founding of the Confraternity, claiming that he installed a company of twelve noblemen to supervise activities on the site, and, further, that Ludovico Maria augmented the size of the company to eighteen in 1486.

11. Reggiori, *Il santuario di Santa Maria presso San Celso,* 26.

12. Reggiori, *Il santuario di Santa Maria presso San Celso,* 27–28 and Nicole Riegel, *Santa Maria presso San Celso in Mailand* (Worms: Wernersche Verlagsgesellschaft, 1995). The latter is the most detailed single source on the exterior and interior work to 1565. It includes transcriptions of numerous archival documents relevant to the study of the construction of the church.

13. Paolo Morigia, *Calendario volgare* (In Milano: appresso Gio. Battista Bidelli, 1620).

14. Milano, Archivio Storico Diocesano (hereafter ASDM), *Archivio San Celso, Libri Maestri 1576–1581,* f. 31v, for example, details all of the expenses for the Assumption in the year 1576. Moreover, Giuseppe Riccucci, "L'attività della cappella musicale di S. Maria presso S. Celso," 297, reports payments made to musicians who participated in a procession from the Duomo to Santa Maria presso San Celso in 1613 and 1614.

15. ASDM, Archivio San Celso Amministrazione, Sedute, Registri 1592–1598, 125r. An order of 27 December 1598 to provide additional musicians for the feast day of the displaying of the veil.

16. ASDM, *Archivio San Celso, Libri Maestri, 1558–1576,* f. 223.

17. For a modern photograph of the altar, see Robert Kendrick, *The Sounds of Milan, 1585–1650* (Oxford and New York: Oxford University Press, 2002), figure 2.8.

18. On the history and theology of the Assumption, see Marina Warner, *Alone of All Her Sex: The Myth and the Cult of the Virgin Mary* (New York, Random House, 1976), 81–102.

19. Riegel, *Santa Maria presso San Celso,* 282–295 and Reggiori, *Il santuario,* 26–49.

20. Warner, *Alone of All Her Sex,* 238–254 and especially 245.

21. "non si deve credere fermamente che nel l'humana specie ci sia trovato in qualche tempo un'huomo, ò una donna, che con un sguardo solo uccidesse

quel mistico serpente della tentazione carnale . . . ecco la Vergine, la quale mutava le menti, e gli animi reguardanti, in casto, e sant'amore." Morigia, *Historia,* 10.

22. Morigia, *Historia,* 38.

23. "E la nostra Signora hà mostrato per esso molti miracoli, & hà fatto diverse gratie alle donne di parto, che non potendo partire, & havendo i dolori della morte, e subito mettendoli adosso questo santo velo, ad un tratto hanno partorito felicemente, senza sentire una minima passione." Morigia, *Historia,* 12.

24. Morigia, *Historia,* 29–31 and 38–40.

25. "hanno introdotti una bellissima divotione degna di lode, cioè, che ogni Sabbato la sera all'hora della Compieta s'habbi da Cantare la Salve Regina, con certi versetti e risponsori, con alquante orationi per venerar il Sabbato giorno dedicata da Santa chiesa alla gloriosa madre di Dio: il che all'hora deputata quivi si trova la Musica, e l'Organista, & i Sacerdoti parati, & dopò che hanno accesi molti cerei intorno alla balaustrata dell'Altare di N. Signora, la Musica comincia, e l'Organo risponde, ed hora l'Organo e la Musica unite, con tante dolcezza, e bellissima harmonia, che genera ne cuori de gli uditori una santa divotione verso la madre di Dio, & compontione di cuore, perche sembrano un choro angelico: Di modo che non ci vorebbe essere persona divota di quel santo luogo, che non vi si trovasse presente à sì dolce, e divota sinfonia, che non hà giusto impedimento, perche tutti questi sono iscusati; ma ben dico, che ci concorre molta nobiltà." Morigia, *Historia,* 17–18. Transcribed and translated with slight variation in Christine Getz, "Simon Boyleau and the Church of the 'Madonna of Miracles': Educating and Cultivating the Aristocratic Audience in Post-Tridentine Milan," *Journal of the Royal Music Association* 126/2 (2001), 148 and transcribed without translation in Kendrick, *The Sounds of Milan,* 383.

26. BAM, Trotti 413 numerous entries throughout and especially 150v and 151v. Modern transcription in Carlo Marcora, "Il diario di Giambattista Casale (1554–1598)," 207–437, but especially 399–400. On 174v Casale also mentions attending a mass of the Madonna on 11 June 1597 as the culmination of a procession of the Schools of Christian Doctrine, and on 178r he describes an altercation involving Count Stabile that took place outside the church on the feast of the Assumption in 1597.

27. Riccucci, "L'attività della cappella musicale di S. Maria presso S. Celso," 289–312; Christine Getz, "Simon Boyleau and the Church of the 'Madonna of Miracles'," 145–168; and Kendrick, *The Sounds of Milan,* 44–62.

28. "Essi tredici sacerdoti oltre la messa quotidiana che dicono caduno di loro in essa chiesa, Intervengono ogni giorno al cantare della Messa grande, et Vesperi, et anco cantano altre Messe votive, che per devoti si fanno celebrare, et tale elimosine provenienti da esse Messe votive si compartiscono tra di loro sacerdoti, et questa elimosina è oltra quella che per ordinario come di sopra se gli dà, Li Cantori, et organista Intervengono tutte le feste di commandimento alle Messe grandi, et alli vesperi, et l'organista In particolare anco Intervenire ogni sabbato alla messa grande," ASDM, Archivio San Celso Amministrazione, Sedute, Registri 1583–1591, 67r (new 135).

29. Archivio Sprituale, Sezione X, *Sant'Eufemia* VI (Visite pastorali e documenti aggiunti: S. Maria presso S. Celso), fasc. 3. The list is published in Christine Getz, *Music in the Collective Experience,* 236, and the singers in question are priests Paolo Fontana and Johannes.

30. ASDM, Archivio San Celso Amministrazione, Sedute, Registri 1583–1591, 45v (new 92) and 50r (101 new). One of the two, Don Francesco della Rosa, is further identified as a tenor.

31. ASDM, Archivio Sirituale, Sezione X, *Sant'Eufemia* VIII (Visite pastorali e documenti aggiunti: S. Maria presso S. Celso), fasc. 2.

32. ASDM, Archivio Sprituale, Sezione X, *Sant'Eufemia* VIII (Visite pastorali e documenti aggiunti: S. Maria presso S. Celso), fasc. 7, f. 26.

33. Isabella was the oldest of Carlo Borromeo's sisters. See Giovanni Pietro Guissano, *Vita di S. Carlo Borromeo prete cardinal del titolo di Santa Prassede arcivescovo di Milano* (Napoli: Tipografico arcivescovile, 1855), 14.

34. "Et a di 5 ziugno per una promessa fatta alla fabrica de paghar' la muxica a conto di *scudi* 40 l'*anno*: comenzando al *primo* no*vembre* a ragione de *scudi* 10 per quartero: p*er anni* 5 tanto q*ual* finirano al *primo* di novembre 1567 . . ." ASDM, Archivio San Celso, Libri Maestri, 1558–1576, 59v. Other documents from the period indicate that during this decade a scudo was worth approximately L5 s5.

35. See Getz, *Music in the Collective Experience,* 217, 226–227, especially notes 98 and 99, and 232.

36. ASDM, Archivio San Celso, Libri Maestri, 1558–1576, 65v, 71r, 73v, 91r, 101v, and 111r.

37. In December 1558, Martano was paid L16 s10 for the quarter, while in February 1559, his salary for the same amount of time was L21. By 1565, when Giovanni Antonio Brenna had assumed the post, the organist salary had risen to L25 per quarter. Archivio San Celso, Libri Maestri, 1558–1576, 10r, 11r, 13v, 18v, 92v, and 148v.

38. Kendrick, *The Sounds of Milan,* 49.

39. ASDM, Santa Maria presso San Celso: Chiesa 10 (Musica e musicisti 1606–1800), busta 1, f. 5. Dated to 1563 according to the coincidence of Sunday Mass and Vespers with the annual calendar. The singers listed include maestro di cappella Simon Boyleau, prete Paolo Fontana, prete Johannes, prete Cesare, Ferrando, and Manfredo.

40. ASDM, Santa Maria presso San Celso: Chiesa 10 (Musica e musicisti 1606–1800), busta 1, f. 3.

41. ASDM, Archivio San Celso, Libri Maestri, 1558–1576, 107r.

42. See Getz, "Simon Boyleau and the Church of the Madonna of 'Miracles,'" 154–155.

43. Simon Boyleau, *Modulationes in Magnificat ad omnes tropos . . . quatuor, quinque, ad sex vocibus distinctae* (Milano: Cesare Pontio, 1566). The dedication is transcribed in Getz, "Simon Boyleau and the Church of the 'Madonna of Miracles'," 167.

44. The most thorough overview of Boyleau's life and works is found in Lucia Marchi, *Simon Boyleau: studio biografico ed edizione critica dei Madrigali a quattro voci* (1546), Tesi di laurea, Università degli studi di Pavia, Scuola Paleografia e Filologia Musicale, 1995–1996.

45. St. Ignatius of Loyola, *The Spiritual Exercises,* 46 and 98–100.
46. St. Ignatius of Loyola, *The Spiritual Exercises,* 99.
47. St. Ignatius of Loyola, *The Spiritual Exercises,* 56–63.
48. On the teaching of rhetoric and Christian Doctrine see Paul F. Grendler, *Schooling in Renaissance Italy: Literacy and Learning, 1300–1600* (Baltimore and London: The Johns Hopkins University Press, 1989), 203–234 and 333–399. For information about the teaching of laude in the doctrine schools in Milan, see Giancarlo Rostirolla, "Laudi e canti spirituali nelle edizioni della prima 'controriforma' Milanese" in *Carlo Borromeo e l'opera della "grande riforma"* (Cinisello Balsamo (MI): Silvana Editoriale, 1997), 162–163.
49. ASDM, *Santa Maria presso San Celso, Libri giornalieri della cassa 1563–1569,* s.p. See Getz, *Music in the Collective Experience,* 213 and 225.
50. Renato and Rossella Frigerio, "Giovan Paolo Cima organist nella Madonna di S. Celso in Milano: documenti inediti dell'Archivio diocesano di Milano," *Il flauto dolce* XVI (April 1987), 32 and 36, and Kendrick, *The Sounds of Milan,* 49.
51. ASDM, Archivio San Celso, Libri Maestri, 1558–1576, 254 and 254a, as well as 293 and 293a.
52. Milano, Archivio di Stato (hereafter ASM), Notarile 16135, 15 November 1574.
53. ASDM, Archivio San Celso, Libri Maestri 1576–1581, 15 and 15a.
54. ASDM, Archivio San Celso, Libri Maestri 1576–1581, 44r.
55. Throughout ASDM, Archivio San Celso, Libri Maestri, 1558–1576, Libri Maestri 1576–1581, and Libri maestri 1581–1600, but summarized in Libri Maestri 1576–1581, 95. The particulars are also spelled out in a notarial instrument preserved in ASM, Culto p.a. 1093 (Culto, Chiese, Communi Milano, S. Maria presso S. Celso, P.G.), 14 February 1571, prepared by Nicolo Vinearca.
56. Throughout ASDM, Archivio San Celso, Libri Maestri, 1558–1576, including entries on 215a, 223, 231a, 239a, 240a, and 253a to name just a few. On Brenna as an organist, see Getz, *Music in the Collective Experience,* 233.
57. Frigerio and Frigerio, "Giovan Paolo Cima," 36.
58. See Kendrick, *The Sounds of Milan,* 51, footnote 172.
59. Archivio San Celso, Libri Maestri, 1558–1576, 256.
60. ASDM, Archivio Sirituale, Sezione X, *Sant'Eufemia* VIII (Visite pastorali e documenti aggiunti: S. Maria presso S. Celso), fasc. 2.
61. Kendrick, *The Sounds of Milan,* 49. The document in question is ASDM, Archivio San Celso Amministrazione, Sedute, Registri 1583–1591, 12v–13r (new 26–27). Entry of 4 July 1583.
62. See Federico Mompellio, "La capella del Duomo da Matthias Hermann di Vercore a Vincenzo Ruffo," *Storia di Milano* (Milano: Giovanni Treccani degli Alfieri, 1957), IX, 749–785. Also see Getz, *Music in the Collective Experience,* 90–93.
63. Throughout ASDM, Archivio San Celso, Libri Maestri, 1558–1576, Libri Maestri 1576–1581 and Libri maestri 1581–1600. On the organ, see Lorenzo Ghielmi, "Contributo per una storia degli organi del Santuario di Santa Maria dei Miracoli presso San Celso in Milano," *L'organo* 22 (1984), 3–22.

64. ASDM, Archivio San Celso Amministrazione, Sedute, Registri 1583–1591, 46v (new 94) 47v (new 96), and 98v (new 100). See Appendix A, documents 1.1, 1.2, and 1.3.

65. Basso Giovanni Paolo Candiano was given permission to sing only at Vespers for a remuneration of L50 per year so that he could be available to sing for "his excellency," presumably Milanese governor Don Carlo d'Aragona, while the salaries of singers Marcantonio Secco and Don Francesco della Rosa were raised to L150 in 1584 and 1586 respectively. ASDM, Archivio San Celso Amministrazione, Sedute, Registri 1583–1591, 30r (new 161) and 56v (new 114).

66. ASDM, Archivio San Celso Amministrazione, Sedute, Registri 1583–1591, 76v (153 new). Document first reported by Kendrick, *The Sounds of Milan*, 49. See especially page 432, note 149.

67. ASDM, Archivio San Celso Amministrazione, Sedute, Registri 1583–1591, 66v (new 134).

68. ASDM, Archivio San Celso Amministrazione, Sedute, Registri 1583–1591, 34v (new 70) and ASM, Notarile 18012 (Giulio Cesare Confalonieri q. Giuseppe 15/12/1584–03/09/1585), 6 May 1585. The latter is the contract itself, which was retroactive to January 1585. For more on Bariola and his compositions, see Kendrick, *The Sounds of Milan*, 50–51 and 245–251.

69. ASDM, Archivio San Celso Amministrazione, Sedute, Registri 1583–1591, 30r (new 161), 56v (new 114), and 101r (203 new).

70. Kendrick, *The Sounds of Milan*, 49–51, discusses a few of these instances.

71. "Proponendosi che sarebbe stato cosa decente perseverare nel far'cantare per l'avvenire ogni sabbato sera l'oration [Ave Maria crossed out] Salve Regina in questa chiesa, et havuto consideratione alla spesa ch'intorino à ciò s'è fatta per il passato, et fatta sopra di ciò matura consideratione.

Hanno ordinato che li signori Gio. Filippo Cavanesi et Carlo Brivio Provinciali della musica s'informino della spesa, che si fà nelle altre chiese di questa citta nelle quali si canta l'Ave Maria e Salve Regina, et insieme procurino ritrovare buoni musici et poi al predetto capitolo col loro parere rifferiscono, accio quanto prima, si puosi effettuare questa si pia divotione." ASDM, Archivio San Celso Amministrazione, Sedute, Registri 1592–1599, 22r. Document cited in Kendrick, *The Sounds of Milan*, 50, footnote 163.

72. See chapter 3.

73. ASDM, Archivio San Celso Amministrazione, Sedute, Registri 1592–1599, 23r.

74. ASDM, Archivio San Celso Amministrazione, Sedute, Registri 1592–1599, 56r-59r. See Appendix A, document 1.4.

75. ASDM, Archivio San Celso Amministrazione, Sedute, Registri 1592–1599, 56r-59r. See Appendix A, document 1.4.

76. See Frigerio and Frigerio, "Giovan Paolo Cima," 36, footnote 9. Also noted in Kendrick, *The Sounds of Milan*, 51.

77. Gaspare Costa, *Il primo libro de motetti et madrigali spirituali a cinque voci* (Venezia: Angelo Gardano, 1581), frontispiece and dedication. Costa is mentioned twice in the chapter registers of 1584. On 25 March 1584 he

received the equal of L236 of his salary in the form of a regal that had belonged to the Fabbrica and on 9 December of the same year it is noted that he had left abruptly and would be replaced by Ottavio Bariola. ASDM, Archivio San Celso Amministrazione, Sedute, Registri 1583–1591, 29r (new 59) and 34v (new 70). If his contract was structured similarly to those of Bariola, it likely was for three years, and there may have been several three-year contracts issued in succession.

78. Lothar Schmidt, "Beobachtungen zur Passionsthematik im intalianischen geistlichen Madrigal," *Schütz-Jahrbuch* 13 (1994), 70–77. Also see Kendrick, *The Sounds of Milan,* 139, for discussion of this spiritual madrigal.

79. Expenses of L61 s12 for the celebration of the "festa della Espettatione" in 1573 are reported in ASDM, Archivio San Celso, Libri Maestri, 1558–1576, 223, and the chapel of the Madonna del Parto itself is mentioned in ASDM, Archivio San Celso, Libri maestri, 1601–1615, 140–140a, at which time it was decorated with frescoes through the funding of the Serbelloni family. For more on the cult of the Madonna del Parto, see chapter 5.

80. The placement of the altar as described in Latuada, *Descrizione di Milano,* III, 61, coincides with the fourth central chapel detailed in Ferdinando Cassina, *Le fabbriche più cospicue a Milano* (Milano: Ferdinando Cassina e Domenico Pedrinelli, 1840), San Celso, introduction and XIX.

81. *Brevarium Ambrosianum Caroli S.R.E. Cardinalis Tit. S. Praxedis Archiepiscopi iussu editum & nunc recens recognitum.* (Milano: Pacifico Pontio, 1588).

82. See Howard Mayer Brown, "Clemens non Papa, the Virgin Mary, and Rhetoric," *Musicologia Humana: Studies in Honor of Warren and Ursula Kirkendale* (Firenze: Leo S. Olschki, 1994), 139–156.

83. Orazio Nantermi, *Partito del primo libro delli motetti a cinque voci . . . novamente ristampati* (Milano: Agostino Tradate, 1606). At least six of Nantermi's motets were printed in other Milanese collections between 1608 and 1620. He was dismissed by the deputies at Santa Maria presso San Celso in 1607.

84. ASDM, Archivio San Celso, Libri maestri 1581–1600, 300.

85. Riccucci, "L'attività della cappella musicale di S. Maria presso S. Celso," 297–298.

86. Riccucci, "L'attività della cappella musicale di S. Maria presso S. Celso," 302–303.

87. Kendrick, *The Sounds of Milan,* 54.

88. ASDM, Archivio Santa Maria presso San Celso 7, Chiesa Arredi Sacri, In Gernere. First reported in Frigerio and Frigerio, "Giovan Paolo Cima," 35. Also noted in Riccucci, "L'attività della cappella musicale di S. Maria presso S. Celso," 308, and Kendrick, *The Sounds of Milan,* 56.

89. Kendrick, *The Sounds of Milan,* 54 and 56.

90. Ulysse Chevalier, *Repertorium hymnologicum* (Louvain: Lefaver, 1892), 130. See entry 2211.

91. The panels, which sustained extensive damage from pollution and humidity, were restored in 1956 and are now housed in a Collegio near the church. Marco Rosci, *Il Cerano* (Milano: Electa, 2000), 117 and 293. Also see

Nancy Ward Nielson, "Cerano," Grove Art Online, http://www.oxfordarton
line.com.proxy.lib.uiowa.edu/subscriber/article/grove/art/T015547?q=Cerano
&search=quick&pos=1&_start=1#firsthit, accessed 10 January 2011.

92. Giovanni Paolo Cima, *Concerti Ecclesiastici a 1, 2, 3, 4, 5 e 8 voci.* (In
Milano: gl'heredi di Simon Tini e Filippo Lomazzo, 1610; reprinted in
Archivium Musicum 24, Firenze: Studio per edizioni scelte, 1986). A modern
edition is found in Giovanni Paolo Cima, *Concerti Ecclesiastici,* ed. by Rudolf
Hofstötter and Ingomar Rainer (Wein: Doblinger, 1998).

93. English translation of the text is "Blessed is the Virgin Mary, who bore
the Lord, who bore the Creator of the world, who brought forth him who made
her forever a Virgin. Alleluia." The entire concerto is transcribed in Cima,
Concerti Ecclesiastici, ed. Hofstötter and Rainer, 107–111.

2. The Art of Lamenting

1. "Stabat mater dolorosa iuxta crucem lacrimosa dum pendebat Filius."
Standard English metrical translation of the Stabat mater. The literal translation reads, "The sorrowful mother stood weeping beneath the cross where her
son was hanging." This chapter is a revised and expanded and version of a
paper that was given in Italian at the *XIV Convegno internazionale sulla
musica italiana nei secoli XVI–XVIII,* sponsored by A.M.I.S.-Como and the
Società italiana di musicologia in July 2007, and thereafter published in
*Barocco Padano 6: Atti del XIV Convegno internazionale sulla musica italiana
nei secoli XVI–XVIII,* ed. Alberto Colzani, Andrea Luppi, and Maurizio
Padoan (Como: A.M.I.S., 2010), 299–331, inclusive of examples and
appendices.

2. "Anima Christiana, pensa tu quanto fossero intensi li dolori, che nel
morire patì il Figliuolo di Dio Giesù, e Figliuolo di Maria; perche la forza del
dolore imita il grido: onde se Christo con voce alta gridò nel morire, fù perche
li dolori di lui erano intentissimi: pensa ancora quanto fossero penosi gli
affanni di Maria; che non potendo, per gran dolori, che le struggevano il cuore,
formar parola: replicava solo questi voci. Figliuol mio Giesù; Giesù Figliuol
mio, chi mi darà, ch'io possa morire con voi?" Arcangelo Ballotino, *Colloquio
affettuoso del pianto che fece Maria nella morte del suo dilettissimo Figliuolo
Giesù Christo* (In Bologna: per Bartolomeo Cochi, 1612.), 81.

3. See Jaroslav Pelikan, *Mary Through the Centuries: Her Place in the
History of Culture* (New Haven and London: Yale University Press, 1996),
125–133; Warner, *Alone of All Her Sex,* 206–217; Fr. Agostino M. Morini,
Origini del culto alla Addolorata. (Roma: Tipografia Poliglotta, 1893); Carol
M. Schuler, "The Seven Sorrows of the Virgin: Popular Culture and Cultic
Imagery in Pre-Reformation Europe" in *Simiolis: Netherlands Quarterly for
the History of Art* 21/1–2 (1992), 5–11; Arcangelo Ballotino, *L'origine et il
progresso del Sacro Ordine de' Servi di MARIA VERGINE* (In Vicenza:
Appresso Gio. Pietro Giovannini 1601); and Kurt Rathe, "Addolorata, devozi-
one alla." *Enciclopedia Cattolica* (Città del Vaticano: Ente per l'Enciclopedia
Cattolica e per il Libro Cattolico, 1953), I, 293–294.

4. *The Holy Bible: New Catholic Edition*, translated from the Latin Vulgate Douay and Confraternity editions (New York: Catholic Book Publishing Company, 1951), New Testament, 78.

5. Schuler, "The Seven Sorrows of the Virgin," 5–11.

6. Warner, *Alone of All Her Sex*, 218, and Rathe, "Addolorata," 293–294.

7. In some regions the feast of the Addolorata was assigned to Good Friday rather than Holy Saturday, the day to which it was assigned in Milan.

8. Determined through consultation of the *Officia propria festorum fratrum ord. Servorum B. Maria Virg.* (Mediolani: apud Pandulphum Malatesta, 1623); the *Officia Propria ordinis servorum beatae Maria Virginis.* (Roma: Hieronymi Mainardi, 1739; and the *Breviarium Romanum nuper impressum* (Venetijs, F.R.B., 1548).

9. ASDM, Archivo spirituale X, S. Sepolchro III (Visite pastorali e documenti aggiunti, S. Maria Beltrade 1369–1614), fasc. 11.

10. ASM, Fondo generale di Religione 640 (Milano, Confraternita, S. Maria Beltrade e S. Maria Addolorata, O.O.-V.V. and ASDM, Sezione X (Archivio spirituale), S. Sepolchro III (Visite pastorali e documenti aggiunti, S. Maria Beltrade 1369–1614), fasc. 11 and fasc. 15.

11. ASM, Fondo generale di Religione 635 (Milano, Confraternita, S. Maria Beltrade e S. Maria Addolorata, Fondazione), 6.

12. ASM, Fondo generale di Religione 640 (Milano, Confraternita, S. Maria Beltrade e S. Maria Addolorata, O.O.-V.V.) Nothing is known about the musicians or their salaries. An extant register of expenses of the fabbrica includes two payments of L22 s16 for the first Sunday of the month. The first is dated 1 September 1601 and is for "saldo delle di controaltanti." The second is for 1 September 1602 and designated as "saldo d'altanti ch'ha impestati." ASM, Fondo generale di Religione 635 (Milano, Confraternita, S. Maria Beltrade e S. Maria Addolorata, Fondazione), 3.

13. ASM, Fondo generale di Religione 635 (Milano, Confraternita, S. Maria Beltrade e S. Maria Addolorata, Fondazione), 2; and ASDM, Sezione X (Archivio spirituale), S. Sepolchro III (Visite pastorali e documenti aggiunti, S. Maria Beltrade 1369–1614), fasc. 11.

14. ASDM, Archivo spirituale X, S. Carlo XXIII (Visite pastorali e documenti aggiunti: Santa Maria dei Servi), fasc. 1.

15. See Fra Ubaldo M. Forconi, ed., "Chiesi e conventi dell'ordine dei Servi di Maria" in *Quaderno di notizie* 22 (Viareggio, 1978) 172; Davide Maria Montagna, O.S.M., *Santa Maria dei Servi a Milano dal trecento al cinquecento* (Milano: Conventi dei Servi in San Carlo, 1997), 14; and Mario Caciagli, Jaqueline Ceresoli, Pantaleo di Marzo, *Milano, le Chiese scomparse*, 3 vols, (Milano: Civica Biblioteca d'Arte, 1998), II, 4–5. The other two Servite churches were San Dionigio and Santa Maria del Paradiso presso Porta Vigentina.

16. Morigia, Paolo, *Santuario della città, e diocesi di Milano* (In Milano: ad instanza di Antonio degli Antonij, 1603), s.p., and Conte Galeazzo Gualdo Priorato, *Relatione della città, e stato di Milano* (Milano: Ludovico Monza, 1666), 49–50.

17. Roma, Archivio Generale o.s.m., *Fondo Negotia Religionis a saeculo XVII*, 174, ff. 97–98. Copies of this map are published in Montagna, *Santa Maria dei Servi a Milano*, 82, and in Caciagli, Ceresoli, and di Marzo, *Milano, le Chiese scomparse*, II, 6.

18. Milano, Raccolta Bertarelli, Triv 6–7. Odeardus Ritius Delin, *Apparato fatto in Milano nella Chiesa di Nostra Signora del Sacro Ordine dc suoi Servi per l'essequie del Reverendissimo Padre Maestro* GIROLAMO MARIA PURICELLI, *Milanese, Generale del medesimo Ordine, morto in Bologna alli 29 Ottobre 1658*.

19. Some altars may have been shared by two different saints or may have been known by different names at different times.

20. Montagna, O.S.M., *Santa Maria dei Servi*, 75–81.

21. Ermes Maria Ronchi, ed. *Santa Maria dei Servi tra Medioevo e Rinascimento: Arte superstite di una chiesa scomparsa nel cuore di Milano* (Milano: Editoriale Giorgio Mondadori, 1997).

22. ASM, Fondo generale di Religione 1561 (Milano, Conventi, Santa Maria dei Servi OO. VV., Busta Cappelle).

23. BAM, P. 250 sup, 5v–6v.

24. "Siamo giunti alla Chiesa de' Padri Serviti detta S. Maria, ed è quella che si tiene contigua il Palazzo Serbelloni . . . al lungo della publica strada, in una sola Nave con soffitta di Legno dipinto dal Fiammenghino, in cui essigiò una Vergine frà commitiva di volante spiriti seminando abiti neri, divotione, ed insegna particolare di questa Religione. Veggonsi dieci Cappelle metà per lato, e due nel Frontispizio tenendosi in mezzo il Maggior'Altare; Gio. Paolo Lomazzo dipinse la Tavola del Cristo all'Orto, ed in tal Cappella miransi in più lastre di marmo memorie di Casa Cossellina, mà in particolare di Giuliano persona erudita, e Poeta leggiadro de' suoi tempo molto amico dell'accennato Pittore, come ne danno chiara notizia i suoi scritti stampati. La Cappella, che siegue viene dedicata à S. Filippo Benizzi Servita, e santificato da Clemente X. e restò sua Tavola, in cui trovasi egli effigiato, colorita dal Famoso Daniele Crespi; il Quadro dell'Adorazione de' Magi nella Cappella accanto alla Porta, che apre il passo al Monsitero, dicesi essere da Bernardino Lovini, ed il Fiammenghino dipinse l'ultima Cappella verso il limitare della Chiesa. La Tavola della Vergine Assunta è di antico pennello di molto grido. Invitovi poi un'altro giorno, ad ossequiare il Sacro Corpo di B. Angelo Porro Milanese di questa Religione, che stassi incorrotto, e palpabile entro nobile Arca, tuttoche sia più d'un secolo, e mezzo, che si ritrovi senza spirito. Nel 1290. fù questa Chiesa con Monastero consegnata a' Padri Serviti, che ne' suoi primi anni fù Palazzo con Chiesa contigua della Nobile Famiglia Mozzanica, e veggonsi ancora nel Refettorio insegne di tal Casato, e nel Coro mirasi di lui ritratto di basso rilievo in lastra di marmo. Comoda Abitazione godono questi Padri, benche sia posta trà Cittadinesche strettezze, non mancando Cortili con Portici à Colonne, dipinti dal Fiammenghino, rappresentando l'Istoria di questa Religione sino da'suoi principij." Carlo Torre, *Il ritratto di Milano divisi in tre libri colorati da Carlo Torre*, 3 vols. (Milano: Federico Agnelli, 1674), III, 354.

25. See Ronchi, ed., *Santa Maria dei Servi*.

26. Serviliano Latuada, *Descrizione di Milano*, V, 163–166.

27. Carlo Bianconi, *Nuova guida di Milano per gli amanti delle belle arti* (Milano: Stamperia Sirtori, 1787; reprinted in facsimile Milano: Monte di Credito-Banca del Monte di Milano, 1979), 68–69.

28. Roma, Archivio Generale o.s.m, *Fondo Negotia Religionis* a saeculo XVII, 174, f. 96. Letter from the Prior at Milan to Luca Ferrarij, Prior of Prato, dated 28 September 1594.

29. "fratelli e sorelle di questa scuola." ASM, *Fondo generale di Religione* 679 (Milano, Confraternita, S. Maria dei Servi, Addolorata, Fondazione).

30. ASM, *Fondo generale di Religione* 679 (Milano, Confraternita, S. Maria dei Servi, Addolorata, Fondazione).

31. Roma, Archivio Generale o.s.m, *Fondo Negotia Religionis* a saeculo XVII, 174, f. 96.

32. ASM, *Fondo generale di Religione* 679 (Milano, Confraternita, S. Maria dei Servi, Addolorata, Fondazione, Ammistrazione d'Archivio).

33. ASDM, Archivio spirituale X, San Carlo XXIII (Visite pastorali e documenti aggiunti: Santa Maria dei Servi), fasc. 3, f. 5.

34. Ermes Maria Ronchi, ed., *Santa Maria dei Servi tra Medioevo e Rinascimento*, 18.

35. "Un' altra divotione s'hà da notare in questo luogo, che devono essercitare i servi di Maria, cio è fare memorie spesse volte delle sette Festività di lei, Concettione, Natività, Presentatione al tempio, Annuntiatione, Visitatione à S. Elisabetta, Purificatione, Assuntione al Cielo, con recitare divotamente sette Ave Maria, essercitandosi nella contemplatione de' misteri di dette solemnità." Ignazio Carnago, *Città di refugio a' mortali* (In Milano. appresso Lodovico Monza, alla Piazza de'Mercanti, 1655), 268.

36. ASDM, *San Carlo* XXIII (Visite pastorali e documenti aggiunti: Santa Maria dei Servi), fasc. 2, f. 5. See Appendix A, document 2.1.

37. Compiled through consultation of the *Officium Beatae Mariae Virg. In Sabbato à Fratribus Ordinis Servorum* (Romae: apud Gugliuelmum Facciottum, 1606); *Officia propria festorum fratrum ord. Servorum B. Maria Virg.* (Mediolani: apud Pandulphum Malatesta, 1623); *Officia Propria ordinis servorum; Breviarium Romanum nuper impressum* of 1548; and *Ordo officii divini recitandi iuxta ritum Sanctae Romanae Ecclesiae* (Roma: In Aedibus Populi Romani, 1584).

38. ASM, *Fondo generale di Religione* 679 (Milano, Confraternita, S. Maria dei Servi, Addolorata, Fondazione).

39. ASM, *Fondo generale di Religione* 679 (Milano, Confraternita, S. Maria dei Servi, Addolorata, Fondazione).

40. Archivio della Veneranda Fabbrica del Duomo di Milano, Mandati 1598, 2 April 1598. At least one of the seven singers on this list was employed at Santa Maria presso San Celso, but the evidence does not indicate that all of them were.

41. ASM, *Fondo generale di Religione* 679 (Milano, Confraternita, S. Maria dei Servi, Addolorata, Fondazione, Amministrazione d'Archivio).

42. ASM, *Fondo generale di Religione* 679 (Milano, Confraternita, S. Maria dei Servi, Addolorata, Fondazione, Amministrazione d'Archivio. See Appendix A, document 2.2).

43. Giovanni Battista Ala, *Secondo libro de' concerti ecclesiastici a una, due, tre, e quattro voci . . . opus 3.* (Milano: Filippo Lomazzo, 1621). Formerly housed in Vercelli, Biblioteca Capitolare, but now lost.

44. Ala, *Secondo libro,* frontispiece. Although this volume is now lost, Mariangela Donà catalogued it in *La stampa musicale a Milano fino all'anno 1700* (Firenze: Leo S. Olschki, 1961), and claims in "Ala, Giovanni Battista," *Grove Music Online* (http://www.oxfordmusiconline.com.proxy.uiowa.edu/subscriber/article/grove/music/00387; accessed 5 January 2009), that it indicates that Ala was at Santa Maria dei Servi.

45. Filippo Lomazzo, ed. *Flores praestantissimorum viorum* (Mediolani: Filippi Lomatii, 1626), tavola. CAT in Cesena, Biblioteca Malatestiana and B at Rochester, Sibley Library of the Eastman School. The print contains sacred concerti for one to four voices by Milan's foremost ecclesiastical musicians and is discussed further in chapter 4.

46. Filippo Picinelli, *Ateneo dei letterati milanesi* (Milano: Francesco Vigone, 1670), 268–269.

47. Giovanni Battista Ala: *Il primo libro di concerti ecclesiastici a una, due, tre, e quattro voci col partitura per l'organo. Di Gio: Battista Ala da Monza. Organista nella Collegiata di Decio. Novellamente posto in luce e dedicato al Virtuoso Signor Giovanni Battista Casato de Marsili* (Milano: Appresso Filippo Lomazzo, 1618), frontispiece. Vercelli, Biblioteca Capitolare, no. 51.

48. Picinelli, *Ateneo,* 268–269.

49. Picinelli, *Ateneo,* 268–269.

50. Donà, "Ala," *Grove Music Online.*

51. *Pratum musicum variis cantionum sacrarem flosculis consitum, 1–4 vv, bc quarum aliae decerptae ex libro secondo sacrarum cantionum I. B. Ala da Monza*=RISM 16342 (Antwerp: Petrus Phalèsé, 1634). I am grateful to Robert Kendrick for sharing his photocopy of this collection with me.

52. See Warner, *Alone of All Her Sex,* 121–133 and 206–223; and Pelikan, *Mary Through the Centuries,* 113–136.

53. Pamela Jones, *Federico Borromeo and the Ambrosiana* (Cambridge, UK: Cambridge University Press, 1993), 164–167.

54. Ronchi, ed., *Santa Maria dei Servi.*

55. Warner, *Alone of All Her Sex,* 210.

56. Angelo Francesco Tignosi, *Statua di Maria Vergine,* 260–264, and Archangelo Ballotino. *Pietosi affetti di compassione,* 319 and 249–256.

57. Anonymous Lombard, *Madonna and Child Enthroned between Saints Vito and Modesto* (second half of sixteenth century). Milano, San Carlo al Corso.

58. "Usa la santa chiesa, quando rappresenta il martirio d'un Santo, ò Santa, dipingere la sua effigie, e porgli in mano l'istromento del suo martirio . . . la vostra madre, ò Christo, sempre si dipinge con voi suo Figliuolo, hora bambino in braccio vivo, hora stando alla vostra Croce moriente, hora nel grembo morto, per segno, che voi sete stato il coltello, e la spada del suo martirio . . ." Ballotino. *Pietosi affetti di compassione,* 37–38.

59. Ballotino. *Pietosi affetti di compassione,* 37–38.

60. On the schools of Christian Doctrine see Giambattista Castiglione, *Istoria delle scuole della dottrina cristiana fondata a Milano* (Milano: Cesare Orena nella Stamperia Malatesta, 1800); Paul F. Grendler, *Schooling in Renaissance Italy,* 333–362; Miriam Turrini, "'Riformare il mondo a vera vita cristiana': le scuole de catechismo nell'Italia del Cinquecento," *Annali dell'Istituto storico italo-germanico in Trento* VII (1981), 419–447; and Angelo Bianchi, "Le scuole della dottrina cristiana: linguaggio e strumento per una azione educative 'di massa'" in *Carlo Borromeo e l'opera della «grande riforma,"* ed. by Franco Buzzi and Danilo Zardin (Milano: Silvana Editoriale, 1997), 145–158.

61. *Lodi e canzoni spirituali per cantar insieme con la Dottrina Chistiana.* (In Milano: Pacifico Pontio, 1576).

62. *Lodi devote per cantarsi nelle scuole della Dottrina Christiana raccolta nuovamente.* (In Milano: Pacifico Pontio, 1586).

63. *Lodi devote per cantarsi nelle scuole della Dottrina Christiana,* s.p.

64. Fra Serafino Razzi, *Libro primo delle laudi spirituali* (Venezia: ad instantia de' Giunti di Firenze, 1563; reprinted in facsimile in Bologna: Forni Editore, 1969).

65. *Lodi e canzoni spirituali,* 22r–26v. The melody was used for four songs in this volume.

66. See, for example, Ballotino, *Pietosi affetti di compassione,* 321–334.

67. St. Ignatius of Loyola, *The Spiritual Exercises,* 9–12.

68. "questo mio cuore con infinite punture di dolore è percosso, e trafitto: se volete sepolchro dentro d'un horto chiuso, e serrato; questo mio cuore è l'orto vostro, da voi piantato, chiuso, e serrato colle vostre mani, sì che l'invidioso serpente non vi è mai potuto entrare, e spargerui il suo veleno: se volete esser rinvolto in bianco lenzuolo; eccovi il mio cuore candido per la verginale integrità, e bianco per l'innocente purità: se volete esser'onto di mirra, & aloè, misture amare; eccovi il mio cuore, dove l'amaritudine della mirra sono le pene, & angustie mie . . ." Arcangelo Ballotino, *Colloquio affettuoso del pianto che fece Maria,* 103.

69. St. Ignatius of Loyola, *The Spiritual Exercises,* 42–43.

70. "O Mary, why do cry before the temple? Why did they cause you to sorrow? They crucified my love and murdered him who gave me life. Dry your falling tears and forgive the faithless Jews. He lives and lives eternally. O my life, o my soul, my heart will rejoice when you come to tell me that you will kiss and delight me eternally."

71. St. Ignatius of Loyola, *The Spiritual Exercises,* 46.

72. St. Ignatius of Loyola, *The Spiritual Exercises,* 100.

73. "*Stabat,* ò Dio datemi parole, ch'io possa raccontare le gran prodezze, e le forze singolari di Maria, con questa parola *Stabat;* horsù udite, vi prego, divotamente: Se parliamo quanto al senso literale, *Stabat,* stava in piedi perche la morte della Croce era stimata obbrobriosissima; ne si potevano piangere li crocefissi morti stando à sedere, come si facevano l'altre cose honorate . . ." Ballotino, *Pietosi affetti di compassione,* 117–118.

74. "Be consoled, oh Mother. Oh my beloved son, oh sweet Jesus. He has risen in glory. Rejoice. Oh my Mother. Oh my son, my heart, they wounded you. Now you see your first born triumphant. Oh joy, oh real gladness."

75. Marina Toffetti, *Gli Aredemanio e la musica in Santa Maria della Scala* (Lucca: LIM Editrice, 2004), 69–72, 206, and 241–243. The latter pages contain a transcription of Ardemanio's setting.

76. "In my bed by night I sought him whom my soul loveth: I sought him and found him not. I will rise and will go about the city: in the streets and broad ways I will seek him whom my soul loveth." *The Holy Bible,* Old Testament, 690.

77. Ballotino, *Colloqui affetuosi del pianto che fece Maria,* 142–143 and 272–273.

78. *Flores praestanissimorum viorum.* The collection also contains several sonate and canzone for organ.

3. Singing before a Madonna on the Pilaster

1. "La Devotione dell'Ave Maria, qual si canta ogni sera nella Chiesa Maggiore del Duomo di Milano, hebbe principio circa l'anno 1495-, et fù un Heremita forastiero, il quale dal Popolo era chiamato, Missus à Deo. Trovasi quest'Heremita la sera al Tardi nella Piazza del Duomo, et publicamente predicando, esortava à vivere Christianamente, con lasciare li peccati, et servare li Divini prefetti, et come sentiva la Campana dell'Ave Maria, invitava l'Audienti ad'entrare seco in Duomo à fare oratione, et dire l'Ave Maria: Esortà in particolare alcuni à voler convenirsi insieme, et far cantare ogni sera in Duomo l'Ave Maria, con qualche laude in honore della Gloriosa sempre Vergine Maria, ringratiandola della ricevuti benifitij, et supplicandola ad impetiare dal suo diletto figliolo misericordia et aggiunto *per* avenire. À quest'esortazione si unirono alcuni Gentilhuomini, e Mercanti, sotto il nome del Santiss*i*mo Crucifisso, diedero principio à fare cantare l'Ave Maria al Terzo Pilone, entrando nel Duomo, à mano sinistra. Il quale Pilone, verrà ad'esser il sesto, quando la chiesa sarà finità, havendogli, *per* questo effetto, posta un'immagine dipinta della Gloriosa Vergine; di poi vi fecero fare una statua di Marmo dell'istessa Gloriosa Vergine, et in *detto* luogo Iddio *per* li meriti di essa Glorios*a* Vergin*e* dimostrò molti Miracoli, per il che era tanto il concorso del Popolo à quella Divotione . . ." ASDM, Archivio spirituale X, Metropolitana LXXXII (Visite pastorali e documenti aggiunti), fasc. 20. For more on the early documentation of the Society, see Christine Getz, *Music in the Collective Experience in Sixteenth-Century Milan* (Aldershot: Ashgate, 2006), 243–246.

2. Giovanni Battista Sannazaro, "Altari" in *Il Duomo di Milano: Dizionario storico artistic e religioso* (Milano: NED, 1986), 21.

3. "Ordinò inoltre si facessero altari per tutte le contrade, affine tutte le genti vedessero almeno (se non potevano udire) il santissimo sacrificio della Messa, volse che le campane del Duomo, delle parochie & de monasteri tocassero certi segni con l'Ave Maria sette volte il giorno: acciò che à somiglianza

delle sett'hore canoniche, sette volte le genti tutti insieme, o nelle case, o alle finestre si ponessero in oratione dicendo l'Ave Marie, le Litanie, over Salmi penetentiali, o corone, over altri pietosi prieghi: e che'l popolo dalle dette finestre, balconi, o porte rispondesse à certi deputati di spatio in spatio d'ogni contrada, alle litanie, o Salmi, over ordinationi, chi in parole (altamente però) chi in canto, e chi in contraponto sonoro, e musicale compassiono, e devote, cantandosi, e rispondendosi da l'una, e l'atra parte à vicenda, e choro à choro d'esse contrade da gli huomini, donne, fanciulli, e fanciulle, grand'e piccolo, giovani, e vecchi: à tal che la città, parve la gran chiesa di Paradiso . . ." Gaspare Bugati, *L'aggiunta dell'Historia universale, et delle cose di Milano*. (In Milano: per Francesco, & herede di Simon Tini, 1587), 156.

4. "Di poi l'anno-1578-in essa il *Beato* Carlo Borromeo Card*inal*e del Titolo di S*an*ta Prassede, all'hora nostro vigilantis*s*imo Arcivescovo, transportò *dett*a Divotione all'altare dov'era la Madonna del Arbore qual all'presente è di S*an*ta Tecla, et ivi alcuni volte esso B*eat*o Carlo interveniva à *dett*a Divotione, all'Altare Mag*gio*re di *dett*a Chiesa per più decoro et Commodità, stando che li Hostarij erano soliti Doppo la liberatione della Città della pros*s*ima passata Peste dell'anno 1577, ogni sera dire la lettanie con alcune oratione al *det*to Altare Maggiore per ringratiare N*o*stro S*igno*re di tanto beneficio per *dett*a liberatione, pregarlo ad haverci misericordia, et preservarei p*er* l'avenire; per ciò ordinò, che al suono dell'Ave Maria, si trovassero Avanti à *dett*o Altare M*aggio*re, et detta prima la salutatione Angelica, secondo il costume, mentre si sona susseguentiam*ent*e dicessero le *dett*e litanie et ordinationi solite, et subito si cantasse l'Ave Maria, e che sempre v'intervenisse uno de S*igno*ri Canonici Ord*inar*ij, à dire tutte le *dett*e Orationi, e così si è sempre perseverato, accendovi li Cerei avanti la prima Balustrata del Choro, mentre si dice la *dett*a Oratione, et Ave Maria." ASDM, Archivio spirituale X, Metropolitana LXXXII (Visite pastorali e documenti aggiunti), fasc. 20.

5. Urbano Monti, BAM, P. 250 sup, 91v.

6. Milano, Archivio dei Luoghi Pii Elimosinieri (hereafter ALPM) 289/1, all. 12, q. 9: 11 gen. 1585.

7. BAM, Trotti 413, 169r.

8. ASDM, Archivio spirituale X, Metropolitana XXXIII (Visite pastorali e documenti aggiunti), fasc. 28.

9. "Miglorandosi la musica non è dubio che multiplicarà l'audienza, et conseguent*emen*te la elimosina . . . ALPM 289/9 (Ave Maria: Uffici A-Z, Musici, 1605–1629), s.d.

10. ASDM, Archivio spirituale X, Metropolitana LXXX (Visite pastorali e documenti aggiunti), fasc. 24.

11. Daniela Bellettati, "Ave Maria in Duomo," *Milano: Radici e luoghi della carità*, ed. by Lucia Aiello, Marco Bascapè, and Sergio Rebora (Torino, London, Venezia, New York: Umberto Allemandi & C., 2008), 48

12. ASDM, Archivio spirituale X, Metropolitana XLVI (Visite pastorali e documenti aggiunti), fasc. 28.

13. See Blake Wilson, *Music and Merchants: The Laudesi Companies of Republican Florence* (Oxford: Clarendon Press, 1992), 1–36.

14. "M. Chi ha fatta l'Ave Maria? D. L'Angelo Gabriello, quando venne a salutare la Madonna, ets'aggiongono alcune parole di S. Elizabetta, et della chiesa. M. Con chi parla nell'Ave Maria? D. Con la Madonna. M. Chi è la Madonna? D. E madre di Dio, Vergine, piena di gratia, et d'ogni virtù, Regina del Cielo, & della Terra, & Avvocata nostra. M. Dove è la Madonna? D. E in cielo . . . [Intervening questions make distinction between Madonna and images of her.] M. Perche donque chi amiamo la Madonna della Pietà, del Remedio, della consolatione, è d'altri nomi? D. E chiamata per tanti nomi per li molti & diversi beneficij, che ci fa come madre di Dio, madre di misericordia, & per tanto appresso lui. M. Che si dice nell'Ave Maria? D. La salutiamo, et lodiamo, raccomandandoci a lei." Diego Ledesma, *Giesu Maria. Dottrina Cristiana, a modo di dialogo del maestro, et Discepolo, per insegnare alli Fanciulli* (In Milano: per Pacifico Pontio, 1576), s.p.

15. "I Cieli rispondono, gli Angeli giubilano, il Mondo essulta, & i demonii tremano, quando io dico Ave Maria; cosi dice San Bernardo." Morigia, *Historia*, 39.

16. ASDM, Archivio spirituale X, Metropolitana XXXIII (Visite pastorali e documenti aggiunti), fasc. 26; and Archivio spirituale X, Metropolitana LXXX (Visite pastorali e documenti aggiunti), fasc. 24.

17. "Provegga il Priore, che le cose della Scola, massime della detta devotione dell'Ave Maria passino secondo il suo dritto, & che li Cantori si trovino à l'hora debita del suonare dell'Ave Maria su'l letorino, dove sono soliti cantare le laudi, acciò non habbiano occasione di correre per esser à tempo di cantare, dove non possono poi esser atti à servire al bisogno, nè il Maestro di Capella può sapere à quante voci habbia d'apparecchiare, se prima non vede presenti li Cantori; avertendo anco, che detti Cantori stiano ivi con modestia, & devotione, et che il ditto Maestro di Cappella si trovi sempre prima degl'altri per apparechiare li libri.

Deputi ancora ditto Priore alcuno delli Servitori, ò altro chi più li piace, che tenga nota sopra un quinternetto delli giorni, che detti Cantori mancaranno di convenire, per ritenerli poi quella parte nel farli il pagamento, & per poter ancor vedere se li mancamenti continuassero in maniera tale, che fosse bisogno mettere altro in suo loco secondo, che al Capitolo parerà.

Habbi parimente cura, che li Servitori si trovino ogni sera à portar li cerei avanti l'altare Maggiore al luoco solito, & che al primo tocco dell'Ave Maria siano tutti accesi, quali doppò finita detta Ave Maria, riportino à governarli, tenendone buon conto, & cosi de la cera, che cola da essi, come anco delli libri di musica, & che mentre la musica canta, vadino al solito con la bacilletta per la Chiesa raccogliendo elimosine . . ." ASDM, Archivio spirituale X, Metropolitana XXXIII (Visite pastorali e documenti aggiunti), fasc. 26.

18. ASDM, Archivio spirituale X, Metropolitana LXXX (Visite pastorali e documenti aggiunti), fasc. 24. Also see Getz, *Music in the Collective Experience*, 245 and 287, Document 16.

19. ALPM 289/8 (Ave Maria: Uffici A-Z, Musici, 1605–1629).

20. Archivio della Veneranda Fabbrica del Duomo (hereafter AVFDM), Mandati 26 (luglio–decembre 1605), Mandati 35 (gennaio–giugno 1610), and Mandati 36 (luglio–decembre 1610).

21. AVFDM, A.S. 421 (Cantanti. Oggetti varii, Spese 1589–1802), 2 (Richeste di musici della Cappella del Duomo avanzate da Terzi, 1628–1787). These include Giovanni Blancino, basso, who sang for the Scuola from 1618–1623, and Hieronymo Vimercate, tenor, who sang for the Society from 1616–1619.

22. See the discussion in chapter 1.

23. *Concerti de diversi eccell. auttori, a due, tre, et quattro voci raccolti dal R.D. Francesco Lucino musico nella Chiesa Metropol. di Milano. Con la partitura per l'organo* (Milano: eredi di S. Tini e F. Lomazzo, 1608).

24. See Robert Kendrick, *The Sounds of Milan, 1585–1650* (Oxford and New York: Oxford University Press, 2002), 234–244.

25. ALPM 289/9 (Ave Maria: Uffici A-Z, Musici, 1605–1629), s.d., but with references to singers from the first decade of the century. See Appendix A, document 3.1.

26. Many of these appear to have been intended for double choirs. See Claudio Sartori, *La cappella musicale del Duomo di Milano: Catalogo delle musiche dell'archivio* (Milano: Instituto Editoriale Italiano per la Veneranda Fabbrica del Duomo di Milano, 1967), 54.

27. Compère's *Ave Maria* is on folios 187v-188r, and its potential role in the Ave services of the sixteenth century is discussed in Getz, *Music in the Collective Experience,* 247–248. For a facsimile edition of the third choirbook, see *Milan, Archivio della Veneranda Fabbrica del Duomo, Sezione Musicale, Librone 3* (olim 2267) [Renaissance Music in Facsimile 12 c], introduction by Howard Mayer Brown (New York and London: Garland Publishing, Inc., 1987).

28. The former is copied on folios 118v-119r, while the latter is located on folios 127v-128r. Photographic reproductions of both are found in Angelo Ciceri e Luciano Migliavacca, eds., *Liber capelle ecclesie maioris: Quarto codice di Gaffurio* in *Archivium Musices Metropolitanum Mediolanense 16* (Milano: La Musica Moderna, S.p.A. per La Veneranda Fabbrica del Duomo di Milano, 1968), 236, 237, and 254–255. Lynn Halpern Ward, "The *Motetti Missales* Repertory Reconsidered," *Journal of the American Musicological Society* XXXIX/3 (Fall 1986), 502, assigns the anonymous *Ave Maria spiritus sancti* to a motet cycle B.V.M on the basis of its text, position in the source, cleffing, system, and final.

29. Ludwig Finscher, *Loyset Compère (c. 1450–1518): Life and Works* [Musicological Studies and Documents 12], general ed. Armen Carapetyan (Rome: American Institute of Musicology, 1964), 44 and 161–162.

30. See Jeffrey Dean, "The Evolution of a Canon at the Papal Chapel: The Importance of Old Music in the Fifteenth and Sixteenth Centuries" in *Papal Music and Musicians in Late Medieval and Renaissance Rome,* ed. Richard Sherr (Oxford: Clarendon Press, 1998), 151–153.

31. Josquin des Prez, *Motets on non-biblical texts* 3 [New Josquin Edition 23.6], ed. Willem Elders (Utrecht: Koningklijke Vereniging voor Nederlandse Muziekgeschiedenis, 2006), Critical Commentary, 54–77.

32. Joshua Rifkin, "Munich, Milan, and a Marian Motet: Dating Josquin's *Ave Maria . . . virgo serena," Journal of the American Musicological Society* 56/1 (Summer 2003), 239–350.

33. David Fallows, *Josquin* (Brepols: Centre d'Études Supérieures de la Renaissance, 2009), 60–65.

34. Giovanni Pierluigi da Palestrina, *Liber II. Motectorum quatuor vocum. Nuper recognitus.* (Mediolani: heredes di Francesco e Simone Tini, 1587). AVFDM, Busta 1, no. 3.

35. ALPM, 289/8 (Ave Maria: Uffici A-Z, Archivio). See Appendix A, document 3.2.

36. Jennifer Thomas, ed. Motet Database on line, http://www.arts.ufl.edu/ motet/results.asp, accessed 1 November 2011. Also see Charles Hamm and Herbert Kellman, eds., *Census-catalogue of manuscript sources of polyphonic music, 1400–1550* (Neuhausen and Stuttgart: American Institute of Musicology, 1986), IV, 423, and Janez Höfler and Ivan Klemenčič, *Glasbeni rokopisi in tiski na Slovenskem do leta 1800* (Ljubljana: Narodna in univerzitetna knjižnica,1967), 23.

37. " . . . li Cantori si trovino à l'hora debita del suonar dell'Ave Maria su'l letorino, dove sono soliti cantare le laudi." ASDM, Archivio spirituale X, Metropolitana XXXIII (Visite pastorali e documenti aggiunti), fasc. 26.

38. On the *cantasi come* tradition and its sources in sixteenth-century Florence, see Blake Wilson, *Singing Poetry in Renaissance Florence: The Cantasi Come Tradition (1375–1550) with CD-ROM* [Italian Medieval and Renaissance Studies 9] (Firenze: Leo S. Olschki, 2009), 145–187, as well as Patrick Macey, *Bonfire Songs: Savonarola's Musical Legacy* (Oxford: Clarendon Press, 1998), 31–58 and 112–113; and Patrick Macey, ed., *Savonarolan laude, motets, and anthems* in *Recent Researches of the Renaissance* 116 (Madison: A-R Editions, 1999).

39. *Lodi e canzoni spirituali per cantar insieme con la Dottrina* and *Lodi devote per cantarsi nelle scuole*.

40. For further information on the content of these collections, see Giancarlo Rostirolla, "Laudi e canti spirituali," 159–176, and Getz, *Music in the Collective Experience,* 248–256. Appended to the 1586 edition are some lauda tunes in manuscript.

41. *Lode e Canzoni spirituali accomodate a tutte le feste . . . Per cantar insieme con la dottrina cristiana* (Torino: eredi Bevilacqua, 1579).

42. *Lodi devote per uso della Dottrina Cristiana* (Como: Girolamo Frova, 1596).

43. AVFDM, Musica, Busta 1, no. 2; Busta 1, no. 4; Busta 2, no. 3; Busta 4, no. 3; Busta 4, no. 8; and Busta 5, no. 2.

44. Bellettati, "Ave Maria in Duomo," 48.

45. Bellettati, "Ave Maria in Duomo," 48.

46. ALPM 289/8 (Ave Maria: Uffici A-Z, Musici). See Appendix A, document 3.3.

47. ALPM 289/8 (Ave Maria: Uffici A-Z, Musici). See Appendix B.

48. ALPM 289/7 (Ave Maria L.P. Ammistrazione, Capitolo, Deputati, Regi Assistenti): Ordinazioni capitolari.

4. Invoking the Mulier Fortis

1. On the Mulier fortis, see Jaroslav Pelikan, *Mary through the Centuries,* 26–27, 42–45 and 81–85; and Marina Warner: *Alone of All Her Sex,* 244–245.

2. "Messer Alano della valle Coloata in Bretagna appresso alla città di Dinamio, andando à combattere contra li Heretici Albigensi nelle parti di Tolosa, sotto il vessillo del magnifico Conte Simone da Monteforte, nel tempo, che San Domenico predicava . . . & indotto il Conte a dir il Rosario ogni giorno, infatigabilmente inginocchioni diceva questo Rosario, meditando la incarnatione, passione, & glorificatione di Iesu Christo. Combattendo costui con pochi compagni contra una gran moltitudine di Heretici; et essendo da loro circondato, che non poteva fuggire la morte; la gloriosa Vergine Maria gli apparse e gitto 150. pietre contra quelli Hertici e tutti li gittò a terra: e lui fu liberato con suoi compagni." *Miracoli della sacratissima Vergine Maria Seguiti ai benefitio di quelli che sono stati devoti della compagna del santissimo Rosario* (In Venetia, appresso Bernardo Giunti, 1587), f. 8v. The Messer Alain in question is no doubt Alain de la Roche (=Alanus de Rupe), who has long been associated with the founding of the first Confraternity of the Rosary.

3. "Memoria come adì 7 d'ottobre. La soma et innefabile providenza d'Iddio nostro signore doppo tante sciagure, Et travagli che per li peccati nostri ha permesso ne la christianitade, hoggi ha voluto mosso dalla sua immensa bonta, Et clementia. visitare, Et favorire la sua chiesa santa. con la maravigliosa. Et inaudita vitoria che ha riportato il serenissimo signor don gioanne d'austria contra la superbia Et tirania del turcho, nemico del nome christiano, nel golfo di lepanto . . ." BAM, Trotti 413, 35r. Modern transcription in Marcora, "Il diario di Giambattista Casale," 257.

4. Francesco Fontana, *Rosario della Gloriosa Vergine Raccolta dal R.F.P. Francesco Fontana Comasco* (Como: appresso G. Trova, 1587), ff. 3r-4r. Perhaps the most famous company was that organized by Jacob Sprenger of Cologne in 1475, the year of the death of Alain de la Roche.

5. *Brevi, bolle et indulgenze concesse da diversi Pontenfici, et altri Prelati di Santa Chiesa alli divoti christiani della Compagnia del Santissimo Rosario, Già raccolte da Giuseppe Stefano Valentino: & hora ultimamente di numero accresciute, e con sommarij dichiarate* (In Venetia, Appresso Bernardo Giunti, 1587), 11–13.

6. *Brevi,* 6 and 32–33.

7. Some instances of elite companies have been reported in Spain. See Lorenzo Calendaria, *The Rosary Cantoral: Ritual and Social Design in a Chantbook from Early Renaissance Toledo* (Rochester: University of Rochester Press, 2007), 33–38 and 116–127.

8. Fontana, *Rosario della Gloriosa Vergine,* 10r-22v, and *Brevi.* Also see ASDM, Archivio spirituale X, Metropolitana XLVI (Visite pastorali e documenti aggiunti), fasc. 28.

9. BAM, P. 24 inf, I, 167. Document first reported by Carlo Marcora, "L'istituzione della compagnia del Santo Rosario," 111–112 and 114. Also see passing reference in Maria Luisa Gatti Perer, "Per la definizione dell'iconografia

della Vergine del Rosario" in *Carlo Borromeo e l'opera della "Grande Riforma,"* ed. by Franco Buzzi and Danilo Zardin (Milano: Silvano Editoriale, 1997), 186.

10. BAM, P. 24 inf, I, 167. "et in ogni caso io non impedisco le due Compagnie del Rosario ch'essi padri hanno qui cioè alla Rosa et a S. Eustorgio, Chiese ne anco così a proposito per questo effetto, quella perchè non v'ha convento et vi stanno solamente due, o tre frati, et serve propriamente alla predica, questa per lontananza et scomodità, essendo così fuori di mano che le genti non la possino tuttavia frequentare, come V.S. sà . . ." First cited in Carlo Marcora, "L'istituzione della compagnia del Santo Rosario," 111.

11. BAM, Trotti 413 (Diario Giambattista Casale), 128v. Modern transcription in Carlo Marcora, "Il diario di Giambattista Casale," 117.

12. ASDM, Archivio spirituale X, Miscellanea Citta IX (Visite pastorali e documenti aggiunti), fasc. 19. The supplication is from September of an unspecified year, but since Carlo Borromeo died on 3 November 1584, it dates from 1584 or before.

13. Maria Cecilia Visentin, *La pieta mariana nella Milano del Rinascimento* (Milano: NED, 1995), 66 and 104–105.

14. ASM, Fondo generale di Religione 557 (Milano, Confraternita, S. Eustorgio, Rosario, Legati Clerici-Antonio), 14 February 1568.

15. Serviliano Latuada, *Descrizione di Milano,* III, 199–200.

16. "robbe vedute alla tromba." ASM, *Fondo generale di Religione* 560 (Milano, Confraternita, S. Eustorgio, Rosario, O.O.-V.V.) L H. I Cassetto III, Cartella K, fol. 1. Note e Ricevuti dall'anno 1604. The busta actually contains receipts from 1603–1662.

17. Cabiago is identified as the current organist at Sant'Eustorgio in the table of contents of the *Flores praestanissimorum viorum.* The volume contains a two-voice reduction of one of his four-voice canzone.

18. BAM, Trotti 413 (Diario Giambattista Casale), 96r. Modern transcription in Carlo Marcora, "Il diario di Giambattista Casale," 324.

19. ASM, *Fondo generale di Religione* 678 (Milano, Confraternità, S. Maria della Rosa, Rosario, OO. VV.)

20. ASM, *Fondo generale di Religione* 678 (Milano, Confraternità, S. Maria della Rosa, Rosario, OO. VV.)

21. BAM, P. 24 inf., II, fol.475r-v. " . . . quelli della Rosa suddetti l'anno passato hebbe così grossa elemosina in quella Chiesa di si deliberarono voltarla al Convento delle grazie per la maggior parte." Document first reported in Marcora, "L'istituzione della compagnia del Santo Rosario," 114–115.

22. BAM, P. 24 inf., II, fol.475r-v. "Occorre di nuovo che la Compagnia del Rosario nella chiesa della Rosa anche una licenza havuta dal Magistrato andavo circando per Milano bussola senza licenza ma anzi haendoglila ma io ixpressamente negate . . ." Document first reported in Marcora, "L'istituzione della compagnia del Santo Rosario," 114–115.

23. ASM, *Fondo generale di Religione* 678 (Milano, Confraternità, S. Maria della Rosa, Rosario, OO. VV.)

24. ASM, *Notarile* 14835 (Giovanni Battista Ghiringhelli q. Simone 18/09/1584–28/07/1587) 11 February 1585.

25. ASDM, Archivio spirituale X, Metropolitana XXXIII (Visite pastorali e documenti aggiunti), fasc. 33.

26. ASDM, Archivio spirituale X, Metropolitana LXXX (Visite pastorali e documenti aggiunti), fasc. 24. Filippo Ghisolfo was active as a printer in Milan between approximately 1631 and 1669.

27. Gatti Perer, "Per la definizione dell'iconografia della Vergine del Rosario," 188.

28. "Memoria come la prima volta che ando in Domo il detto Cardinale dopo la sua Venuta dise mesa abasa nel scurolo del Domo dopo entro in coro Et ivi stete alla predica Et alla messa grande Et dopo il mangiare vene in Domo Et ivi stete al vespero Et alla compieta. Et subito si porta la Madona del rosario del Domo Et lui la comagno in procesione Con il confalone de la madona perchè quel giorno non si porta la madona de relevo dita de larbore." BAM, Trotti 413, 168v. Modern transcription in Marcora, "Il diario di Giambattista Casale," 420.

29. "Memoria come adì 13 dopo la sua entrata, che fu il giorno della Natività de la Madona, qual è la festa in Domo, il detto Cardinale cantò la prima Mesa grande. che cantasse in Milano . . . et tante furno le ceremonie fatte a questa Mesa. quante se posano fare. et il simile si fece dopo il mangiare il Vespero. et all Compieta. et subito si fece la procesione de la Madona del Rosario deta d l'Arboro. propria de relevo nel suo tabernacolo, et li era il Cardinale stesso. Con tutto il Semenario. et tutto il clero. solo del Domo. alla detta Messa. Vespero. et procesione li era una infinità di populo. et al sonare de l'Ave Maria fu fatto compimento a ogni cosa." BAM, Trotti 413, 169r. Modern transcription in Marcora, ""Il diario di Giambattista Casale," 421.

30. Comparing, for example, ASDM, Archivio spirituale X, Metropolitana XXXIII (Visite pastorali e documenti aggiunti), fasc. 33, which contains the original printed letter issued in 1584 with ASDM, Archivio spirituale X, Metropolitana XXXIII (Visite pastorali e documenti aggiunti), fasc. 24, a copy printed around 1630 by Filippo Ghisolfo containing identical text.

31. Noted, for example, in the *Brevi* and ASDM, Archivio spirituale X, Metropolitana XLVI (Visite pastorali e documenti aggiunti), fasc. 28. The latter is a Breve of Paul V printed for the Chiesa Metropolitana on 13 August 1612

32. ASDM, Archivio spirituale X, Miscellanea Citta XI (Visite pastorali e documenti aggiunti), fasc. 29. The draft of a notary document drawn up by Giovanni Battista de Nobilis for the erection of a Confraternity of the Rosary dated 24 September 1595.

33. ASDM, Archivio spirituale X, S. Lorenzo IX (Visite pastorali e documenti aggiunti), fasc. 4. A memoriale dated 21 August 1627 that indicates that some concerns had been raised about the existence of a company of the Rosary at San Lorenzo by the nearby chapter at Sant'Eustorgio.

34. ASDM, Archivio spirituale X, S. Lorenzo IX (Visite pastorali e documenti aggiunti), fasc. 4. See Appendix A, document 4.1.

35. ASDM, Archivio spirituale, Sezione XIII (Ospedali-Collegi-Confraternitè enti vari), vol. 62, fasc. 12.

36. Caciagli, Ceresoli, and di Marzo, *Milano, le Chiese scomparse*, I, 244–245.

37. Caciagli, Ceresoli, and di Marzo, *Milano: le Chiese scomparse*, I, 244–246; Giulio Ferrario, *Memorie per servire alla storia dell'Architettura Milanese dalla decadenza dell'Impero Romano fino ai nostri giorni* (Milano: Tipografia Bernardoni, 1843), 401; Latuada, *Descrizione di Milano*, IV, 132–133; and Carlo Bianconi, *Nuova guida di Milano*, 265–266. Ferrario and Latuada attribute the design to Donato Bramante, while Bianconi argues for Vincenzo Seregni. Moreover, Latuada claims that construction was completed in 1493, but Ferrario states that it continued until 1495. Caciagli, Ceresoli, and Di Marzo, who have conducted extensive research on the edifice, argue for a completion date of 1495.

38. Morigia, *Santuario della città*, s.p.

39. BAM, Trotti 413, 134r, 140v, 143r, 152v, 157v, 166v, 170r, and 176r. Also see Gatti Perer, "Per la definizione dell' iconografia della Vergine del Rosario," 186.

40. Milano, Archivio Storico Civico e Biblioteca Trivulziana, Raccolta Bianconi V.24–25. On the location of the cappella of the Rosary, see Latuada, *Descrizione di Milano*, IV, 137, and Bianconi, *Nuova guida di Milano*, 265–266.

41. See Francesco Riva, *Duecento anni di musica in Santa Maria della Rosa* (1588–1798) (Tesi di laurea, Università degli Studi di Milano, 2007), 14.

42. ASM, Notarile 14363 (Francesco Tessera q. Bartolomeo 17/10/1587–10/02/1589), 3 Junij 1588. See Appendix A, document 4.2 Photographed and transcribed with several minor, yet significant differences in Riva, *Duecento anni di musica*, 64–69. Casale reports that construction on the organ was begun on 8 August 1588. BAM, Trotti 413, 140v.

43. "La chiesa è bella quadrata tutta dipinta d'alto e basso da Giovanni Battista e Marco Fiamenghi. Alla parte dell'Organo nella facciata è dipinta la battaglia navale contro il Turco data dalla Lega Cattolica il giorno di S. Guistiziana nel 1572. con la vittoria de Christiani. L'ante dell'Organo sono di mano di Gratio Cosselle Bresciano, vi sono pitture d'Ambrosio Figino, di Camillo Proccacino, e due statue sopra la porta d'Annibale Fontana." Priorato, *Relatione della città*, 80.

44. "Di rimpetto all'Altare maggiore si vede un bellissimo Organo di considerabile grandezza, sostenuto da alcune colonne di pietra viva, sopra delle quali poggiano le ringhiere di legno dorato, ed è rinserrato dalle regge, nelle quali vennero dipinte da una parte li trionfi di Davide, e dall'altra quello di Giuditta, dal poc'anzi mentovato Cossali Bresciano. . . . tutta, come scrivemmo, vestivano questa Chiesa, sono le opere de' fratelli Fiammenghini, li quali sopra il muro laterale all'Organo rappresentarono al vivo la Vittoria navale ottenuta dalle Armi Cattoliche contra de' Turchi vicino al Golfo di Lepanto sotto il Pontificato di San Pio V.; Ed in vero sono così al vivo effigiate Navi, Cocche, e Galee, assalti, prede, incendj, uccisioni, naufragj, che non se ne scostare per molto tempo l'occhio ammiratore di una si ben'espressa vittoria." Latuada, *Descrizione di Milano*, IV, 138.

45. ASM, *Fondo generale di Religione 678* (Milano, Confraternità, S. Maria della Rosa, Rosario, OO. VV.) and Morigia, *Santuario della città*, s.p.

46. ASM, *Notarile* 14838 (Giovanni Battista Ghiringhelli q. Simone 23/05/1594–16/05/1598), 1 July 1597.

47. BAM, Trotti 413,145v.

48. BAM, Trotti 413, 181v.

49. Agostino Soderini, *Canzoni à 4 & 8 voci, di Agostino Soderini Organista nella Chiesa di N. S. della Rosa in Milano. Libro primo. Opera Seconda.* (In Milano: per l'herede di Simon Tini e Filippo Lomazzo,1608). Copy preserved in Bologna, Civico Museo Bibliografico Musicale and referenced in Mariangela Donà, *La stampa musicale a Milano fino all'anno 1700* (Firenze: Leo S. Olschki, 1961), 103. A modern edition is found in Agostino Soderini, *Canzoni à 4. & 8. voci . . . libro primo (Milan, 1608)* in *Italian Instrumental Music of the Sixteenth and Early Seventeenth Centuries* 19, ed. by James Ladewig. (New York and London: Garland, 1992).

50. On the canzona-motet in Milan, see Giuseppe Vecchi, "La canzone strumentale e la canzone-motetto a Milano nella prima metà del seicento" in *La musica sacra in Lombardia nella prima metà del Seicento,* ed. by Alberto Colzani, Andrea Luppi, and Maurizio Padoan (Como: A.M.I.S. Como, 1987), 81–97.

51. *En dilectus meus* (Song 2: 10–12) and *Egredimini filiae Sion* (Song 2:5–6 and Song 8:6). These two works are briefly discussed in Robert Kendrick, *The Sounds of Milan,* 222–223. Also see Gaetano Gaspari, *Bologna. Conservatorio di musica "G.B. Martini." Biblioteca. Catalogo della biblioteca del Liceo musicale di Bologna,* 3 vols. (Bologna: Libreria Romagnoli dell'Acqua, 1890), III, 257.

52. Soderini, *Canzoni à 4,* ed. Ladewig, xi. Also see Mariangela Donà, "Soderini, Agostino." *Grove Music Online. Oxford Music Online.* http://www.oxfordmusiconline.com.proxy.lib.uiowa.edu/subscriber/article/grove/music/26086; accessed 4 July 2008.

53. Modern edition in Soderini, *Canzoni à 4 & 8 voci,* ed. James Ladewig, 222–241.

54. "Salve virgo et mater, Ave hera et domina super omnes mulieres castitor et pulchrior, O faemina super faeminas benedicta, tu arca Dei concepisti filium, mundi peperisti creatorem, per te choros ducunt Angeli, quam celebrant Archangeli, et nos cantemus et dicamus Alleluia."

55. Soderini, *Canzoni à 4 & 8 voci,* ed. James Ladewig, xiii.

56. Andrea Cima, *Il secondo libro delli concerti, a due, trè, & quattro voci* (Milano: appresso Filippo Lomazzo, 1627), frontispiece.

57. "memoriale de miei spirituali pensieri." Cima, *Il secondo libro delli concerti,* dedication.

58. Robert Kendrick, *Celestial Sirens: Nuns and their Music in Early Modern Milan* (Oxford: Clarendon Press, 1996), 136, 143, and 251.

59. This concerto is discussed at length in Kendrick, *Celestial Sirens,* 251–254.

60. Warner, *Alone of All Her Sex,* 248 and 255–268. On the use of some of these representations in specific music and art, see Christine Getz, "L'altare mariano nella Milano della Controriforma e *La donna vestita di sole* (1602)," *Barocco padano* 3, ed. by Alberto Colzani, Andrea Luppi, and Maurizio

Padoan (Como: A.M.I.S. Como, 2004), 83–101; Bonnie Blackburn, "The Virgin in the Sun: Music and Image for a Prayer Attributed to Sixtus IV," *Journal of the Royal Music Association* 124/2 (1999), 157–195; and Maria Luisa Gatti Perer, "Per la definizione dell'iconografia della Vergine del Rosario," 185–216. For an example of a discussion from the era, see Arcangelo Ballotino, *Pietosi affetti di compassione sopra li dolori della B.V. Maria* (In Bologna: per Bartolomeo Cochi, 1612), 319.

61. Prospero Rossetti florentini ordinis servorum, *In cantica canticorum salamonis prophetae commentariorum libri duo* (Venetiis: apud Franciscum de Franciscis senesem, 1594), 490–491.

62. Kendrick, *The Sounds of Milan,* 84.

63. Paolo Morigia, *Calendario volgare* (Milano: appresso Gio. Battista Bidelli, 1620), s.p. Braidense BB.VI.63/1. Exactly when the procession for the victory over the Turks at Lepanto was separated from the feast of the Rosary is unclear, but during the year in which the *Calendario* was published a Roman feast in honor of the victory over the Turks at Prague was introduced and celebrated on the second Sunday in November.

64. On the role of the Song of Songs in forging the Marian *historia,* see Rachel Fulton, '"Quae est iste quae ascendit sicut aurora consurgens?: The Song of Songs as the Historia for the Office of the Assumption," *Medieval Studies* 60 (1998), 55–122; and Rachel Fulton, "Mimetic Devotion, Marian Exegesis, and the Historical Sense of the Song of Songs," *Viator: Medieval and Renaissance Studies* 27 (1996), 85–116. Also see Ann E. Matter, *Solomon's Divine Arts* (Cleveland: Pilgrim Press, 1991). On the historia of the Assumption in Medieval polyphony, see David J. Rothenberg, *The Flower of Paradise: Marian Devotion and Secular Song in Medieval and Renaissance Music* (Oxford and New York: Oxford University Press 2011), 24–57.

65. *Commentarii Michaelis Ghislerii Romani ex clericis regularibus, quos Theatinos nuncupant in Canticum Canticorum Salomonis* (Venetiis: apud Bernardum Iuntam e Io. Baptista Ciottum & Socios, 1613). The four editions date from 1609, 1613, 1616, and 1617, 1620, and were printed in Venice (1609, 1613, and 1617), Antwerp (1616), and Lyon (1620).

66. *Commentarii Michaelis Ghislerii,* 87–90.

67. *Commentarii Michaelis Ghislerii,* 132–133.

68. *Commentarii Michaelis Ghislerii,* 535–536.

69. Rossetti, *In cantica canticorum salomonis prophetae,* 33.

70. Several of his works appeared in Giovanni Paolo Cima's *Concerti ecclesiastici* of 1610 and his own first book of concerted motets, which was published by Filippo Lomazzo of Milan in 1614, identifies him as the organist at Santa Maria del Carmine. There is no archival evidence to support the often-made claim that he was employed at the Duomo that same year.

71. R.M. Gaspare Ancarano da Bassano, *Novo Rosario della Gloriosissima Vergine Maria* (In Venetia: appresso Bernardo Giunti, 1588).

72. Ancarano da Bassano, *Novo Rosario,* 44r.

73. Bartolomeo Scalvo, *Rosariae preces ad gloriosam Dei genetricem Mariam Virginem* (Milano: Pacifico Pontio, 1569).

74. Bartolomeo Scalvo, *Le meditazioni del Rosario della Gloriosa Maria Vergine* (Milano: Pacifico Pontio, 1569).

75. Bartolomeo Scalvo, *Le meditazioni del Rosario della Gloriosa Maria Vergine* (Venezia: Domenico e Giovanni Battista della Guerra, 1583).

76. Gatti Perer, "Per la definizione dell'iconografia della Vergine del Rosario," 196–199.

77. For a summary of these, see Pamela Jones, *Federico Borromeo and the Ambrosiana* (Cambridge, UK: Cambridge University Press, 1993), 64–72.

78. MARIA, Madre santissima, con ogni prestezza, et velocità incaminata verso la città di Gierusalem per farti incontro al tuo dolcissimo figliuolo, tutta lagrimosa, et addolorata non solamente per le passate afflitioni, et dolori di quel pretiosissimo corpo; ma anchora et molto piu ramaricata per li furturi stratij; anzi per la istessa istante morte da tutta prenuntiata; Aime quanti erano li gemiti nella via mandati al cielo? quante le lagrime? quanti li singolti, et li sospiri? quanto avanti gli occhi con cosi miseranda meditatione proponendosi il tuo amabilissimo figliolo, mostravi il sembiante di donna quasi fuori si se stessa uscita? Deh quanto fu miserabile quel cruccio, quel sbattimento delle mani tue santissime; quando arrivata alla città dalla numerosa turba del popolo ti vedesti rinchiusa la via di approssimarti al tuo amantissimo figliuolo; E come finalmente fu incomparabile, & estremo quel dolore, che à guisa di pungentissimo cotello ti trafisse l'anima, e il cuore, veduto quel tormentatissimo corpo sotto il peso di cosi ponderosa croce in diversi modi da quelli cani violentato alla salita del Monte; quel GIESV figliuolo di Dio cosi deformato, et stratiato con grandissima compassione etiandio delli falsi istessi, et delle fiere esser cosi ignominiosamente, come Angello semplicissimo, condotto all'estremo supplicio della croce; appresso il quale, Ò MARIA, Madre santissima, intercede per noi peccatori. Amen. Scalvo, *Le meditationi del Rosario,* 1569, 97–98.

79. Rejoice daughters of Zion, rejoice virgins of Jerusalem, be glad you faithful people and congratulate the glorious victor Mary, queen of the strengthening Rosary. Bring roses and lilies from the valleys of Zion; celebrate the festive day in psaltery and song; magnify her name in an extolling voice. All glorify the conqueror Mary, destroyer of the head of the hydra and the dragon. Rejoice and exult in this her victory.

80. Scalvo, *Le meditationi del Rosario,* 1569, 164.

81. Elizabeth heard Mary's voice, and upon hearing her salutation, the infant in her womb rejoiced, and she was filled with the Holy Spirit and cried aloud and said "Blessed art thou among women, and blessed is the fruit of thy womb." Alleluia. (Luke 1:41–42)

82. Kendrick, *Celestial Sirens,* 251.

83. Kendrick, *Celestial Sirens,* 251 and 254.

84. *Flores praestanissimorum viorum,* dedication.

85. Katarzyna Grochowska, "From Milan to Gdańsk: The Story of a Dedication," *Polish Music Journal* 5/1 (Summer 2002), http://www.usc.edu/dept/polish_music/PMJ/Issue5.1.02/grochowska.html/, accessed 7 July 2008.

86. " . . . slilicet Excellentissimorum Hominum hac in arte flores à me collectos." *Flores praestanissimorum viorum,* dedication.

87. See Candelaria, *The Rosary Cantoral,* 39–51.

88. Giovanni Francesco Anerio, *Ghirlanda Di Sacre Rose Musicalmente Contesta, & Concertata. A cinque voci.* (In Roma: Per Luca Antonio Soldi, 1619), 3.

89. Daniele V. Filippi, "Giovanni Francesco Anerio: *Selva armonica (Rome, 1617) Edited by Daniele V. Filippi,"* Embellishments: A Newletter about Recent Researches 29 (Summer 2006), 1. Also see Giovanni Francesco Anerio, *Selva armonica* (Rome, 1617) in *Recent Researches in Music of the Baroque Era* 141, ed. by Daniele V. Filippi (Madison: A-R Editions, 2006), ix–xx.

90. Tignosi, *Statua di Maria Vergine,* dedication. The volume was dedicated to Marguerite of Austria on the event of the birth of her firstborn son.

91. See Roberta J.M. Olson, *The Florentine Tondo* (Oxford, UK: Oxford University Press, 2000) 23–29 and 83–104; and Roberta J.M. Olson, "The Rosary and its Iconography," *Arte Cristiana* 86/787 (August 1998), 263–276, and 86/788 (October 1998), 334–342.

92. Gatti Perer, "Per la definizione dell'iconografia della Vergine del Rosario."

5. Clothed in the Sun and Standing on the Moon

1. "Una certa Giudea molto faticando nel partorire, e non facendo altro che piangere, non aspettava più altro, se non dover tosto render lo spirito, havendola fatta spacciata l'allevatrice, e tuttavia crescendo maggiormente il dolore, e l'angustia, quando infra tanti dolori d'anima, e di corpo, fu veduta una gran luce venir di sopra, & insieme undita una voce, che da essa luce usciva, la qual disse. Invoca il nome di Maria, e sarai salva: . . . la donna tutta nel cuor' fedele, e piena di confidanza nel Sig. a gran voce invocò il nome di Maria, e subito partorì felicemente un figliuolo . . ." R.P. Don Silvano Razzi Monaco Camaldolense, *Dei miracoli della Gloriosa Vergine Maria Nostra Signora.* (In Trevigli: appresso Angelo Reghettini, 1612), 133–134.

2. Margaret L. King, *Women of the Renaissance* (Chicago: University of Chicago Press, 1991), 2.

3. King, 2–4.

4. BAM, Trotti 413, 1v–6v. Also see Carlo Marcora, "Il diario di Giambattista Casale (1554–1598)," 212–218.

5. According to Casale, David's wife Vittoria could not continue nursing because she had been exorcised of witchcraft by a brother at Sant'Ambrogio. BAM, Trotti 413, 171v. Also see Marcora, "Il diario di Giambattista Casale," 425.

6. Christiane Klapisch-Zuber, *Women, Family, and Renaissance Italy,* translated by Lydia G. Cochrane (Chicago and London: The University of Chicago Press, 1985), 132–144.

7. On lactation practices and infant mortality, see King, 4–19.

8. Marina Warner, *Alone of All Her Sex,* 177–191. Also see Maria Cecilia Vesentin, "La Madonna del Parto nella pieta popolare," in *La Madonna*

nell'attesa del parto: Capolavori dal patrimonio italiano del '300 e '400, ed. Maria Alessandra Molta (Milano: Libri Scheiwiller, 2000), 39.

9. Renzo Manetti, *Le Madonne del Parto: Icone templari* (Firenze: Edizione Polistampa, 2005), 10–11, and Ermes Ronchi, "Iconografia della Madonna del Parto" in *La Madonna nell'attesa del parto*, 27–28.

10. Gianfranco Ravasi, "Maria, incinta di Gesù" in *La Madonna nell'attesa del parto*, 13.

11. Ravasi, 12–14 and Manetti, 11–21.

12. Other variations in the iconography are discussed in Ronchi, 27.

13. See both Manetti and Molta, ed., for examples.

14. Latuada, *Descrizione di Milano*, V, 165.

15. Ronchi, 65–66.

16. ASDM, Archivio San Celso, Libri Maestri, 1558–1576, 116v.

17. ASDM, Archivio San Celso, Libri Maestri, 1558–1576, folio 223, records L61 s12 in elimosine distributed to 14 above the L13 s4 paid to the sacerdotes for services in honor of the Espettatione held on the third Sunday and its octave.

18. "Avvi altra Cappella dedicata alla Beata Vergine del Parto rappresentava come seduta in istatoa colorita, e coperta di vetri, è tenuta di mezzo da due Tavole, quella alla destra rappresenta Sant'Anna con la sua Santissima Figlia ancora fanciulla, pittura di Federigo Panza; come pure quella di San Carlo, che porta il Sacro Chiodo in processione a questa chiesa (la qual cosa avvenne nell'anno 1576, in tempo di peste, e ne ottenne per l'inercessione di Nostra Signora la liberazione)." Latuada, *Descrizione di Milano*, III, 61.

19. Carlo Torre, *Il ritratto di Milano*, 78.

20. See Nicole Riegel, *Santa Maria presso San Celso*, 50–51.

21. Maria Cecilia Visentin, "La Madonna del Parto nella pieta popolare" in *La Madonna nell'attesa del parto*, 39.

22. Caciagli, Ceresoli, and di Marzo, *Milano, le Chiese scomparse*, I, 188.

23. Morigia, *Santuario della città*, s.p.; Paolo Morigia, *Il Duomo di Milano descritto da R. P. F. Paolo Morigi* (Milano: Giovanni Battista Bidelli, 1642), 83; and Priorato, *Relatione della città*, 14.

24. "è ancora una divota effigie di Nostra Signora detta volgarmente del Parto . . . Avanti all'Immagine della Madonna del Parto v'era prima un Altare sotto l'invocazione di Santa Maria ed Elisabetta, e v'erano instituite alcune Messe quotidiane, ed altri legati, che poi, fatto demolire l'Altare, furono per ordine di San Carlo, così le rendete, come i pesi transferiti all'Altare di Sant'Agnese, non molto da questo discosto . . ." Latuada, *Descrizione di Milano*, I, 107–108.

25. ASM, *Fondo generale di Religione* 151 (Milano, Capitolo Maggiore del Duomo Cassetto 24), Carteggio K, no. 18, and ASDM, Archivio spirituale X (Visita patorali e documenti aggiunti), Metropolitana XXVI, fasc. 6. Also see the brief discussion in Enrico Cattaneo, *Maria Santissima nella Storia della spiritualità Milanese [Archivio ambrosiano]* (Milano: Scuola tipografica di San Benedetto Abbazia di Viboldone, 1955), 104.

26. ASDM, Archivio spirituale X (Visite pastorali e documenti aggiunti), Metropolitana XXVI, fasc. 22 and 35.

27. Cattaneo, 104, bases this claim on a register entry reported in the *Annali Fabbrica Duomo,* IV, 62. The entry itself is found in AVFDM, Registro 747 (Vacchette 1565–1566), 88r, and reads "Al Capitolo de spexe diverse cont. a messer Jo. Petro Sormano pictore per la pictura de due Arme di Papa Pio quinto poste ne la prefata giesia et per la picture di la tavola de la Madonna del Parto per vn' scritto. L7 d 7."

28. "Usa la santa chiesa, quando rappresenta il martirio d'un Santo, ò Santa, dipingere la sua effigie, e porgli in mano l'istromento del suo martirio . . . la vostra madre, ò Christo, sempre si dipinge con voi suo Figliuolo, hora bambino in braccio vivo, hora stando alla vostra Croce moriente, hora nel grembo morto, per segno, che voi sete stato il coltello, e la spada del suo martirio . . ." Ballotino. *Pietosi affetti di compassione,* 37–38.

29. Marina Warner, *Alone of All Her Sex,* 192–205.

30. See, for example, Castore Durante, *Del parto della Vergine libri tre di M. Castore Durante da Gualdo ad imitatione del Sanazaro con gli argomenti di M. Ieronimo Pallantieri* (In Roma: appresso Gio. Battista de Cavalleri, 1573); *Il parto della Vergine del Sannazaro. Tradotto in ottava rima dal Signor Gio. Vincenzo Plantamuro Canonico d'Altamura. Diviso in tre Libri. Con gli Argomenti à ciascun Libro* (In Viterbo: Appresso Pietro, & Agostino Discepoli. Con licenza de' superiori. 1617); and Giovanni Gioliti de Ferrari, *Del parto della Vergine del Sanazaro. Libre tre. Tradotti in versi Toscani da Giovanni Giolito de' Ferrari al Ser. Signor Don Vincenzo Gonzaga, Duca di Mantova, e di Monferrato, & c.* (In Venetia, appresso i Gioliti, 1587).

31. Durante, *Del parto della Vergine,* 46.

32. Durante, *Del parto della Vergine,* 49.

33. See, for example, Ballotino, *Pietosi affetti di compassione;* Tignosi, *Statua di Maria Vergine;* and Ballotino, *Colloqui affettuoso del pianto che fece Maria.*

34. See King, *Women of the Renaissance,* 1–24.

35. Ferrari, *Del parto della Vergine del Sanazaro,* s.p.

36. *Officia Propria ordinis servorum,* 1739.

37. For some of the variations that have been identified by scholars see Pietro Borella, *Il rito ambrosiano* (Brescia: Morcelliana, 1964), 112–116.

38. AVFDM, Musica, Busta 2, No. 4-Regio, *Missarum ac sacrarum cantionum.* On Benedetto Regio-Re and Caterina Assandra see Robert L. Kendrick, "Assandra, Caterina," *Grove Music Online,* http://www.oxfordmusiconline .com.proxy.lib.uiowa.edu/subscriber/article/grove/music/01427?q=Assandra% 2C+Caterina&search=quick&pos=1&_start=1#firsthit. Accessed 10 March 2010. Benedetto Regio was a German exile who served as maestro di cappella at Santa Maria Assunta e San Stefano Protomartire during the first decade of the seventeenth century. At the time of the publication of the *Missarum ac sacrarum cantionum,* he was Assandra's music teacher. An accomplished composer in her own right, Assandra took vows in a rural Benedictine convent in 1609.

39. ASDM, Archivio San Celso 7, Chiesa (Santa Maria presso San Celso), Arredi Sacri, In Genere, 21 decembre 1607. First cited in Frigerio, "Giovan Paolo Cima," 33. AVFDM, Busta 2, No. 4.

40. Ballotino, *Colloqui affetuoso del pianto che fece Maria, 66–69,* and *Ballotino, Pietosi affetti di compassione, 128–142* and elsewhere.

41. Claudio Sartori, *La cappella musicale del Duomo di Milano: Catalogo delle musiche dell'archivio* (Milano: Istituto Ediotoriale Italiano a cura della Veneranda Fabbrica del Duomo, 1957), 30–31.

42. Giovanni Giacomo Gastoldi, *Missarum quatuor vocibus* (Venetijs: Ricciardum Amadinum, 1602). Milano, Biblioteca del Conservatorio Giuseppe Verdi S.B. 72–73. Copies of a 1611 reprint are housed in Piacenza, Archivio del Duomo, Stampati n. 20, Fascia 9, fila 3, cassetta 7, ATB only, and Bologna, Civico Museo Bibliografico Musicale. Additionally, a modern edition of the *Missa Ne timeas Maria* prepared from the 1602 copy in Milano, Biblioteca del Conservatorio is found in Giovanni Giacomo Gastoldi, *Missa "Ne timeas Maria" e Antifone Mariane,* ed. Giovanni Acciai (Milano: Savini Zerboni, 1984).

43. See Mary Lewis, *Antonio Gardano: Venetian Music Printer 1538–1569,* 3 vols. (New York and London: Garland, 1988), I, 417–418.

44. AVFDM, A.D. Librone 23.

45. "Mary arose and went with haste into the hills, to a town of Juda. And Mary entered into the house of Zachary and saluted Elizabeth. And when Elizabeth heard the greeting of Mary, the babe in her womb leapt, and, filled with the Holy Spirit, she exclaimed 'Alleluia. Blessed art thou among women and blessed is the fruit of thy womb. And when the sound of your greeting came to my ears, the babe in my womb rejoiced. Alleluia.'"

At the Magnificat in First Vespers. "Blessed is Mary who has believed that which was promised by the Lord shall be accomplished in her."

At the Magnificat in Second Vespers. "All generations shall call me blessed because he regarded the lowliness of his handmaiden. Alleluia." The text is a paraphrase of Luke 1: 39–45, and 48.

46. On the *desco di parto,* or confinement-period presentation plate in Renaissance visual culture, see Adrian W.B. Randolph, "Gendering the Period Eye: *Deschi da parto* and Renaissance Visual Culture," *Art History* 27/4 (September 2004), 538–562.

47. Orfeo Vecchi, *La donna vestita di sole* (Milano: erede di Simone Tini e Giovanni Francesco Besozzi, 1602), dedication. Rochester, Sibley Music Library of the Eastman School of Music, PM 1419. The collection is transcribed in Orfeo Vecchi, *Donna Vestita di Sole, Coronata di Stelle, Calcante la Luna,* research and notes by Dolores Mather-Pike and edited by Kent Carlson (Frankfurt am Main: Garri Editions, c. 2006). The research notes are somewhat dated, and seem to be based on Dolores Mather-Pike, *La donna vestita di sole: A Collection of Sacred Madrigals by Orfeo Vecchi* (D.M.A. thesis, Eastman School of Music, 1961).

48. "And a great sign appeared in heaven: a woman clothed with the sun, and the moon was under her feet, and upon her head a crown of twelve stars." *The Holy Bible,* New Testament, 334.

49. On the doctrine of the Immaculate Conception and the interpretation of Revelation 12:1, see Marina Warner, *Alone of All Her Sex,* 236–254 and 261–269, and Anne Walters Robertson, "The Savior, the Woman, and the Head of the Dragon in the Caput Masses and Motet," *Journal of the American Musicological Society* 59/3 (Autumn 2006), 557–562.

50. The program of this collection is discussed in Marco Giuliani, "'Musica spirituale de eccellentissimi autori' (1586): un itinerario devote collettivo nel mondo del madriale," *Rivista italiana di musicologia* XXXVII/2 (2002), 219–248.

51. Giovanni Francesco Anerio, *Ghirlanda di sacre rose* (In Roma: per Luca Antonio Soldi, 1619). Roma, Biblioteca Casantense Mus.111.3.

52. I discussed this program and its relationship to a number of Milanese devotional practices at length in Christine Getz, "L'altare mariano nella Milano della Controriforma e *La donna vestita di sole (1602),*" *Barocco padano 3: Atti dell'XI Convegno internazionale sulla musica italiana nei secoli XVII–XVIII* (Como: Antiquae Musicae Italicae Studiosi, 2004) 83–101.

53. Vecchi, *La donna vestita di sole,* dedication. ASM, *Popolazione* p.a. 107 (Registri mortuari 1602–1604), 1 febbraio 1602 and 13 marzo 1602 report that Hippolita died in childbirth from post-partum complications and further than her infant son Giovanni Battista died approximately one month later from a seizure. According to Fausto Bagatti-Valsecchi, Felice Calvi, Luigi Agostino Casati, Damiano Muoni, e Leopoldo Pullé, *Famiglie notabili milanesi* (Milano: Antonio Vallardi editore, 1875), II, tavola 6, Hippolita had at least one other son named Carlo, as well as two daughters named Paola and Barbara.

54. Vecchi, *La donna vestita di sole,* frontispiece.

55. Bartolomeo Scalvo, *Le meditationi del Rosario,* 1583, frontispiece.

56. Durante, *Del parto della Vergine,* 59.

57. *Miracoli della Sacratissima Vergine Maria,* 18r–20r.

58. Razzi, *Dei miracoli della Gloriosa Vergine Maria,* 118–119, 133–134, 221–222, 257–259.

59. Ballottino, *Pietosi affetti,* 115–145.

60. Stefano Limido, *I Regii Concenti Spirituali . . . libro primo a 5. e 6. voci* (Milano: Agostino Tradate, 1605), dedication.

61. Madrid, Biblioteca Nacional R 14441–14445. Only five of the six partbooks survive.

62. María Cruz de Carlos Varona, "Entre el reisgo y la necesidad; embarazo, almubramiento y culto a la Virgen en los espacios femeninos del Alcázar de Madrid (siglo XVII)," *Arenal* 13/2 (julio–diciembre 2006), 263–290, but especially 276–283. According to Ignazio Carnago, *Città di refugio a' mortali,* 279, the Novena, Avventino, or Festa dell'O, which commemorated the nine months in which the Virgin was pregnant, was established by St. Idelfonso and instituted in Spain around 660 by Martin I during the tenth Council of Tolentano.

63. María Jesús Pérez Martín, *Margarita de Austria, Reina de España* (Madrid: Espasa-Calpe, S.A., 1961), 96–97.

64. "Margherita d'Austria moglie di Filippo Terzo Rè di Spagna era divota de' principali misteri, che concernono la vita di Maria, che sono nove. Concettione, Immaculata di Maria, Natività, Presentatione, Sposalitio,

Annutiatione, Visitatione, Parto, Purificatione, & Assuntione; però quando s'avvincinava à suoi parti faceva dire nove Messe, una dopo l'altra ad honorare de' soddetti principali misteri della vita, e morte della B. Vergine, assistendovi ella stessa divotamente. Nel giorno poi dell'Annuntiatione ella stessa serviva con le proprie mani nove povere donne ad honore de' soddetti misteri in memoria de' quali si ponno dire nove Ave Maria . . ." Carnago, *Città di refugio a' mortali*, 275.

65. Madrid, Museo del Prado.

66. Magdalena S. Sánchez, *The Empress, the Queen, and the Nun: Women and Power at the Court of Philip III of Spain* (Baltimore and London: The Johns Hopkins Press, 1998), 152–153 and figure 3.

67. Vienna, Kunsthistorisches Museum.

68. Cruz, "Entre el reisgo y la necesidad," 278–279.

69. Cruz, "Entre el reisgo y la necesidad," 269–271. I wish to thank the author for sharing her full transcription of AGP, Real Capilla, Caja 78, exp. 1 with me.

70. See Miguel Quyerol Galvadà, ed, *Cancionero musical de la Casa de Medinaceli in Monumentos de la música española* 8–9 (Barcelona: Consejo Superior de Investigaciones Científicas, Instituto Español de Musicología, 1949–1950), VIII, 19.

71. ASM, Dispacci Reali 48–49 (1607–1609: Filippo III), 13 Novembre 1508.

72. A modern edition of the text is published in Elio Durante and Anna Martellotti, *Don Angelo Grillo O.S.B. alias Livio Celiano. Poeta per musica del secolo decimosesto* (Firenze: Studio per Edizioni Scelte, 1989), 368–370. The text was also set by Leone Leoni. See Durante and Martellotti, *Don Angelo Grillo*, 479.

Epilogue

1. Caciagli, Ceresoli, and di Marzo, *Le chiese scomparse*, II, 224–228; and, Latuada, *Descrizione di Milano*, V, 12–13.

2. Latuada, V, 14–15.

3. ASDM, Archivio Spirituali Sexione X (Visite pastorali e documenti aggiunti), Santa Maria Segreta I, fasc, 5.

4. Latuada, V, 14.

5. Paola Curatolo, "Notabili a Milano tra cinque e seicento: le confraternite nella parrocchia di S. Maria Segreta," *Archivio Storico Lombardo*, Series 11, Vol. 8 (1991), 59–66. The latter part of this study is concerned with confraternity finances and membership.

6. ASDM, Archivio spirituale, Sezione X (Visita pastorali e documenti aggiunti), Miscellanea Città XX (1682–1689), s.n.

7. Curatolo, "Notabili a Milano tra cinque e seicento," 66–72. Corroborative documentation is also found in ASM, Fondo generale di Religione 1518 (Milano-Conventi-Santa Maria Segreta-Somaschi-Fondazione) and ASDM, Archivio spirituale, Sezione X (Visita pastorali e documenti aggiunti), Miscellanea Città XIV (1682–1689), fasc. 13.

8. ASDM, Archivio spirituale, Sexione X (Visite pastorali e documenti aggiunti), Santa Maria Segreta I, fasc, 5.

9. Curatolo, "Notabili a Milano tra cinque e seicento," 67 and 69. Giambattista Casale also mentions the procession, noting that the Christian Doctrine Schools were also present. Marcora, "Il diario di Giambattista Casale," 353.

10. ASM, Fondo generale di Religione 1824 (Milano-Conventi-S. Maria Segreta-Somaschi-Culto), s.n. *Libro della Cura di S. Nazaro Pietra Santa e Santa Maria Segreta dal 1570 al 1580,* 10 August 1577 and 1 August 1578.

11. ASM, Fondo generale di Religione 1824 (Milano-Conventi-S. Maria Segreta-Somaschi-Culto), s.n., *Libro della Cura di S. Nazaro Pietra Santa e Santa Maria Segreta dal 1570 al 1580,1586–1588.*

12. ASM, Fondo generale di Religione 1824 (Milano-Conventi-S. Maria Segreta-Somaschi-Culto), s.n. *Libro della Cura di S. Nazaro Pietra Santa e Santa Maria Segreta dal 1570 al 1580,* 1580.

13. ASM, Fondo generale di Religione 1824 (Milano-Conventi-S. Maria Segreta-Somaschi-Culto), s.n., *Libro della Cura di S. Nazaro Pietra Santa e Santa Maria Segreta dal 1570 al 1580,* 1586–1588.

14. Kendrick, *The Sounds of Milan,* 383, contains a transcription of ASM, Fondo di Religione 1824 (Milano-Conventi-S. Maria Segreta-Somaschi-Culto), s.n., 22 January 1593.

15. Giuseppe Gallo, *Sacri operis musici alternis modulis concinendi liber primus* (Milano: Francesco et Simone Tini, 1598). Cantus II housed in Zurich, Zentralbibliothek, Musikabteilung Musik, Magazin (Mus Jac D 74) and Altus I housed in München, Bayerische Staatsbibliothek, Musiksammlung 4 Mus. Pr. 23. St. Michael's, Tenbury, also reportedly owns a partial copy.

16. Facsimile reproduction in Adam Sutkowski and Alina Osostowicz-Sutkowska, eds., *The Pelplin Tablature (Tabulatura organowa cystersów z Pelplina),* 7 vols., in *Antiquitates musicae in Polonia* (Warszawa: Polish Scientific Publishers, 1963–70), VI, 142–143.

17. Kendrick, *The Sounds of Milan,* 197–199.

18. Lomazzo, ed., *Flores prestantissimorum viorum.*

Bibliography

Ala, Giovanni Battista, *Il primo libro di concerti ecclesiastici a una, due, tre, e quattro voci col partitura per l'organo.* Milano: Appresso Filippo Lomazzo, 1618. Vercelli, Biblioteca Capitolare, no. 51.

Alphonsi, S.J., Herbert, ed. *Gli Esercizi Spirituali di sant' Ignazio. Linguistica-Storia-Spritualità.* Roma: Pomel S. a. S., 1998.

Ancarano da Bassano, R.M. Gaspare. *Novo Rosario della Gloriosissima Vergine Maria.* In Venezia: Appresso Bernardo Giunti, 1588. Milano, Biblioteca Nazionale Braidense XX.9.2/3.

Anerio, Giovanni Francesco. *Ghirlanda di Sacre Rose Musicalmente Contesta, & Concertata. A cinque voci.* In Roma: Per Luca Antonio Soldi, 1619. Roma, Biblioteca Casantense Mus.111.3.

Anerio, Giovanni Francesco. *Selva armonica* (Rome, 1617) in *Recent Researches in Music of the Baroque Era* 141, ed. by Daniele V. Filippi. Madison: A-R Editions, 2006.

Bagatti-Valsecchi, Fausto and Felice Calvi, Luigi Agostino Casati, Damiano Muoni, and Leopoldo Pullé, *Famiglie notabili milanesi.* Milano: Antonio Vallardi editore, 1875.

Ballotino, Archangelo. *Colloquio affettuoso del pianto che fece Maria nella morte del suo dilettissimo Figliuolo Giesù Christo.* In Bologna: per Bartolomeo Cochi, 1612. Roma, Marianum bibMAR FAS p1612 2.

———. *L'origine et il progresso del Sacro Ordine de' Servi di MARIA VERGINE.* In Vicenza: Appresso Gio. Pietro Giovannini 1601. Roma, Marianum Servitana II 001 int. 1.

———. *Pietosi affetti di compassione sopra li dolori della B.V. Maria.* In Bologna: per Bartolomeo Cochi, 1612. Roma, Marianum, bibMAR FAS p1612 1.

Barrella, P.G.M., S.J. *Mater Dolorosa nell'ascetica, nella poesia, nell'arte.* Napoli: Tipocrafia Commerciale, 1929.

Bellettati, Daniela. "Ave Maria in Duomo," *Milano: Radici e luoghi della carità,* ed. by Lucia Aiello, Marco Bascapè, e Sergio Rebora. Torino, Londra, Venezia, New York: Umberto Allemandi & C., 2008, 47–48.

Bianchi, Angelo. "Le scuole della dottrina cristiana: linguaggio e strumento per una azione educative 'di massa'" in *Carlo Borromeo e l'opera della "grande riforma,"* ed. by Franco Buzzi and Danilo Zardin. Milano: Silvana Editoriale, 1997, 145–158.

Bianconi, Carlo. *Nuova guida di Milano per gli amanti delle belle arti.* Milano: Stamperia Sirtori, 1787; reprinted in facsimile Milano: Monte di Credito-Banca del Monte di Milano, 1979. Milano, Biblioteca Trivulziana ed. Archivio Storico Civico Cons. ST. Milanese Guide 69.

Bireley, Robert. *The Refashioning of Catholicism, 1450–1700*. Washington, D.C.: The Catholic University of America Press, 1999.

Blackburn, Bonnie. "The Virgin in the Sun: Music and Image for a Prayer Attributed to Sixtus IV," *Journal of the Royal Music Association* 124/2 (1999):157–195.

Bonani, Gian Paolo and Serena Baldassare Bonani. *Maria lactans*. Roma: Marianum, 1995.

Boyleau, Simon. *Modulationes in Magnificat ad omnes tropos . . . quatuor, quinque, ad sex vocibus distinctae*. Milano: Cesare Pontio, 1566. London, British Museum Music k3m2.

Brevi, bolle et indulgenze concesse da diversi Pontenfici, et altri Prelati di Santa Chiesa alli divoti christiani della Compagnia del Santissimo Rosario, Già raccolte da Gioseppe Stefano Valentino & hora ultimamente di numero accresciute, e con sommarij dichiarate. In Venetia, Appresso Bernardo Giunti, 1587. Milano, Biblioteca Nazionale Braidense XX.9.2/3.

Breviarium Ambrosianum Caroli S.R.E. Cardinalis Tit. S. Praxedis Archiepiscopi iussu editum & nunc recens recognitum. Milano: Pacifico Pontio, 1588. Milano, Pontificio Istituto Ambrosiano di Musica Sacra MA IV 1/11 and 2/1.

Breviarium Romanum nuper impressum. Venetijs, F.R.B., 1548. Milano, Biblioteca Nazionale Braidense H. XV. 170.

Brown, Howard Mayer. "Clemens non Papa, the Virgin Mary, and Rhetoric," in *Musicologia Humana: Studies in Honor of Warren and Ursula Kirkendale*, ed. by Siegfried Gmeinweiser, David Hiley, and Jörg Riedlbauer. Firenze: Leo S. Olschki, 1994, 139–156.

Bugati, Gaspare. *L'aggiunti dell'Historia universale et delle cose di Milano . . . dall 1566 fin'al 1581*. Milano: Francesco ed heredi Simone Tini, 1587. Milano, Biblioteca Nazionale Braidense 8.09.F. 0018.

Caciagli, Mario, Jaqueline Ceresoli, and Pantaleo di Marzo, *Milano, le Chiese scomparse*, 3 vols. Milano: Civica Biblioteca d'Arte, 1998.

Calendaria, Lorenzo. *The Rosary Cantoral: Ritual and Social Design in a Chantbook from Early Renaissance Toledo*. Rochester: University of Rochester Press, 2007.

Cancionero musical de la Casa de Medinaceli in *Monumentos de la música española* 8–9, ed. Miguel Quyerol Galvadà, Barcelona: Consejo Superior de Investigaciones Científicas, Instituto Español de Musicología, 1949–1950.

Carnago, Ignazio. *Città di refugio a' mortali*. In Milano:appresso Lodovico Monza, alla Piazzade'Mercanti, 1655. Torino, Biblioteca dei Frati minori Cappuccini D VI I.

Carrera, Elena. "The Emotions in Sixteenth-Century Spanish Spirituality," *Journal of Religious History* 31/3 (September 2007), 235–252.

Cassina, Ferdinando, *Le fabbriche più cospicue a Milano*. Milano: Ferdinando Cassina e Domenico Pedrinelli, 1840. Milano, Biblioteca d'Arte ATL.0.22, I.

Castiglione, Giambattista. *Istoria delle scuole della dottrina cristiana fondata a Milano.* Milano: Cesare Orena nella Stamperia Malatesta, 1800.

Cattaneo, Enrico. *Maria Santissima nella Storia della spiritualità Milanese* [*Archivio ambrosiano*] Milano: Scuola tipografica di San Benedetto Abbazia di Viboldone, 1955.

Chevalier, Ulysse. *Repertorium hymnologicum.* Louvain: Lefaver, 1892.

Cima, Andrea. *Il secondo libro delli concerti, a due, trè, & quattro, voci.* Milano: appresso Filippo Lomazzo, 1627. Milano, Biblioteca Nazionale Braidense Musica B.4 and Rochester, Sibley Library of the Eastman School Rare M1490.C573.

Cima, Giovanni Paolo. *Concerti Ecclesiastici a 1, 2, 3, 4, 5 e 8 voci.* In Milano: gl'heredi di Simon Tini e Filippo Lomazzo, 1610; reprinted in Archivium Musicum 24, Firenze: Studio per edizioni scelte, 1986.

———. *Concerti Ecclesiastici,* ed. by Rudolf Hofstötter and Ingomar Rainer. Wein: Doblinger, 1998.

Costa, Gaspare. *Il primo libro de motetti et madrigali spirituali a cinque voci.* Venezia: Angelo Gardano, 1581. Kassel: Universitätsbibliothek 115/01.

Cruz de Carlos Varona, María. "Entre el reisgo y la necesidad; embarazo, almubramiento y culto a la Virgen en los espacios femeninos del Alcázar de Madrid (siglo XVII)," *Arenal* 13/2 (July-December 2006): 263–290.

Curatolo, Paola. "Notabili a Milano tra cinque e seicento: le confraternite nella parrocchia di S. Maria Segreta, *Archivio Storico Lombardo,* Series 11, Vol. 8 (1991): 59–103.

Dean, Jeffrey. "The Evolution of a Canon at the Papal Chapel: The Importance of Old Music in the Fifteenth and Sixteenth Centuries" in *Papal Music and Musicians in Late Medieval and Renaissance Rome,* ed. Richard Sherr. Oxford: Clarendon Press, 1998, 138–166.

Dei miracoli della Gloriosa Vergine Maria Nostra Signora. Tratti da diversi Catholici, & approvati Auttori dal R.P. Don Silvano Razzi Monaco Camaldolense. E novamente con aggiunta ristampati, & ricorretti. In Trevigli: Appresso Angelo Reghettini, 1612. Roma, Biblioteca Nazionale Centrale Vittorio Emmanuele 14. 32A. 11.

De Ferrari, Giovanni Giolito. *Del parto della Vergine del Sanazaro. Libre tre. Tradotti in versi Toscani da Giovanni Giolito de' Ferrari al. Ser. Signor Don Vincenzo Gonzaga, Duca di Mantova, e di Monferrato, & c.* In Venetia: appresso I Gioliti, 1587. Milano, Biblioteca Nazionale Braidense 25.13.0.19.

Des Prez, Josquin. *Motets on non-biblical texts 3* [*New Josquin Edition* 23.6], ed. Willem Elders. Utrecht: Koningklijke Vereniging voor Nederlandse Muziekgeschiedenis, 2006.

Dini, Vittoria and Laura Sonni, *La Madonna del Parto: Immaginario e realtà nella cultura agropastorale.* Roma: Editrice Ianua, 1980.

Donà, Mariangela. "Ala, Giovanni Battista," *Grove Music Online,* http://www.oxfordmusiconline.com.proxy.uiowa.edu/subscriber/article/grove/music/00387, accessed 5 January 2009.

———. "Soderini, Agostino," *Grove Music Online. Oxford Music Online.*
http://www.oxfordmusiconline.com.proxy.lib.uiowa.edu/subscriber/
article/grove/music/26086, accessed 4 July 2008.

———. *La stampa musicale a Milano fino all'anno 1700.* Firenze: Leo S.
Olschki, 1961.

Durante, Castore. *Del parto della Vergine libri tre di M. Castore Durante da
Gualdo ad imitatione del Sanazaro con gli argomenti di M. Ieronimo
Pallantieri.* In Roma: appresso Gio. Battista de Cavalleri, 1573. Roma,
Biblioteca Nazionale Centrale Vittorio Emmanuele 71.7.A.1

Durante, Elio and Anna Martellotti. *Don Angelo Grillo O.S.B. alias Livio
Celiano. Poeta per musica del secolo decimosesto.* Firenze: Studio per
Edizioni Scelte, 1989.

Fallows, David. *Josquin.* Brepols: Centre d'Études Supérieures de la
Renaissance, 2009.

Ferrario, Giulio. *Memorie per servire alla storia dell'Architettura Milanese
dalla decadenza dell'Impero Romano fino ai nostri giorni.* Milano:
Tipografia Bernardoni, 1843.

Filippi, Daniele V. "Giovanni Francesco Anerio: *Selva armonica (Rome,
1617) Edited by Daniele V. Filippi," Embellishments: A Newletter about
Recent Researches* 29 (Summer 2006): 1.

Finscher, Ludwig. *Loyset Compère (c. 1450–1518): Life and Works* in
Musicological Studies and Documents 12, general ed. Armen
Carapetyan. Rome: American Institute of Musicology, 1964.

Fontana, Francesco. *Rosario della Gloriosa Vergine Raccolta dal R.F.P.
Francesco Fontana Comasco.* Como: appresso G. Trova, 1587. Milano,
Biblioteca Nazionale Braidense, Gerli 2321.

Flores praestantissimorum viorum. Mediolani: Filippi Lomatii, 1626. Cesena,
Biblioteca Malatestiana and Rochester, Sibley Library of the Eastman
School Rare M1490.F634.

Forconi, Fra Ubaldo M, ed. "Milano-S. Dionisio, S. Maria dei Servi in San
Carlo," in *Chiesi e Conventi dell'ordine dei Servi di Maria: Quaderno
di notizie* 22 (Viareggio, 1978):172–187.

Frigerio, Renato e Rossella Frigerio. "Giovan Paolo Cima organist nella
Madonna di S. Celso in Milano: documenti inediti dell'Archivio diocesano di Milano," *Il flauto dolce* XVI (April 1987): 32–37.

Fromson, Michelle. "A Conjunction of Rhetoric and Music: Structural
Modeling in the Italian Counter-Reformation Motet," *Journal of the
Royal Music Association* 117/2 (1992): 208–246.

Fulton, Rachel. "Mimetic Devotion, Marian Exegesis, and the Historical
Sense of the Song of Songs," *Viator: Medieval and Renaissance Studies*
27 (1996): 85–116.

———. "'Quae est iste quae ascendit sicut aurora consurgens?: The Song
of Songs as the Historia for the Office of the Assumption," *Medieval
Studies* 60 (1998):55–122.

Gaspari, Gaetano. *Bologna. Conservatorio di musica "G.B. Martini."
Biblioteca. Catalogo della biblioteca del Liceo musicale di Bologna,*
3 vols. Bologna: Libreria Romagnoli dell'Acqua, 1890.

Gasser, Nolan Ira. *The Marian Motet Cycles of the Gaffurius Codices: A Musical and Liturgico-Devotional Study.* Ph.D. dissertation, Stanford University, 2001.

Gastoldi, Giovanni Giacomo. *Missa "Ne timeas Maria" e Antifone Mariane,* ed. Giovanni Acciai. Milano: Savini Zerboni, 1984.

———. *Missarum quatuor vocibus.* Venetijs: Ricciardum Amadinum, 1602. Milano, Biblioteca del Conservatorio Giuseppe Verdi S.B. 72–73.

Gatti Perer, Maria Luisa. "Per la definizione dell'iconografia della Vergine del Rosario" in *Carlo Borromeo e l'opera della "Grande Riforma,"* ed. by Franco Buzzi and Danilo Zardin. Milano: Silvano Editoriale, 1997, 185–216.

Getz, Christine. "L'altare mariano nella Milano della Controriforma e *La donna vestita di sole* "(1602), *Barocco padano* 3, ed. by Alberto Colzani, Andrea Luppi, and Maurizio Padoan (Como: A.M.I.S. Como, 2004):83–101.

———. *Music in the Collective Experience in Sixteenth-Century Milan.* Aldershot, UK: Ashgate, 2006.

———. "Simon Boyleau and the Church of the 'Madonna of Miracles': Educating and Cultivating the Aristocratic Audience in Post-Tridentine Milan," *Journal of the Royal Music Association* 126/2 (2001): 145–168.

Ghielmi, Lorenzo. "Contributo per una storia degli organi del Santuario di Santa Maria dei Miracoli presso San Celso in Milano," *L'organo* 22 (1984):3–22.

Ghislerii Romani ex clericis regularibus, quos Theatinos nuncupant, Michaelis. *Commentarii in Canticum Canticorum Salomonis.* Venetiis: apud Bernardum Iuntam e Io. Baptista Ciottum & Socios, 1613. Roma, Biblioteca Nazionale Vittorio Emanuele 8.26.I.16.

Giuliani, Marco. "'Musica spirituale de eccellentissimi autori' (1586): un itinerario devoto colletivo nel mondo del madrigale," *Rivista italiana di musicologia* 37/2 (2002):219–248."

Giussani, Giovanni Petro. *Vita di S. Carlo Borromeo prete cardinale del titolo di Santa Prassede arcivescovo di Milano.* Napoli: Tipografico arcivescovile, 1855.

Glixon, Jonathan Emmanuel. *Honoring God and the City: Music at the Venetian Confraternities, 1260–1807.* Oxford and New York: Oxford University Press, 2003.

Grendler, Paul F. *Schooling in Renaissance Italy: Literacy and Learning, 1300–1600.* Baltimore and London: The Johns Hopkins University Press, 1989.

Grochowska, Katarzyna "From Milan to Gdańsk: The Story of a Dedication," *Polish Music Journal* 5/1 (Summer 2002), http://www.usc.edu/dept/polish_music/PMJ/Issue5.1.02/grochowska.html/, accessed 7 July 2008.

Hamm, Charles, and Herbert Kellman, eds., *Census-Catalogue of Manuscript Sources of Polyphonic Music, 1400–1550,* 5 vols. Neuhausen and Stuttgart: American Institute of Musicology, 1986, IV.

Höfler, Janez, and Ivan Klemenčič. *Glasbeni rokopisi in tiski na Slovenskem do leta 1800* Ljubljana: Narodna in univerzitetna knjižnica, 1967.

The Holy Bible: New Catholic Edition, translated from the Latin Vulgate Douay and Confraternity editions. New York: Catholic Book Publishing Company, 1951.

Jedin, Hubert. *Carlo Borromeo.* Rome: Isitituto della enciclopedia italiana 1971.

Jones, Pamela. *Federico Borromeo and the Ambrosiana.* Cambridge: Cambridge University Press, 1993.

Kendrick, Robert L. "Assandra, Caterina," *Grove Music Online,* http://www .oxfordmusiconline.com.proxy.lib.uiowa.edu/subscriber/article/grove/ music/01427?q=Assandra%2C+Caterina&search=quick&pos=1&_ start=1#firsthit, accessed 10 March 2010.

———. *Celestial Sirens: Nuns and their Music in Early Modern Milan.* Oxford: Clarendon Press, 1996.

———. *The Sounds of Milan, 1585–1650.* Oxford and New York: Oxford University Press, 2002.

King, Margaret L. *Women of the Renaissance.* Chicago: University of Chicago Press, 1991.

Klapisch-Zuber, Christiane. *Women, Family, and Renaissance Italy,* translated by Lydia G. Cochrane. Chicago and London: The University of Chicago Press, 1985.

Latuada, Serviliano. *Descrizione di Milano ornate con molti disegni in rame,* 5 vols. Milano: Giuseppe Cairoli Mercante, 1737. Milano, Biblioteca Nazionale Braidense Rari. R. 40/1–5 and FF.VIII.60.

Ledesma, Diego. *Giesu Maria. Dottrina Cristiana, a modo di dialogo del maestro, et Discepolo, per insegnare alli Fanciulli.* In Milano: per Pacifico Pontio, 1576. Milano, Biblioteca Nazionale Braidense B 39/1.

Ledesma della Compagnia di Giesù, Dottore. *Modo per insegnar la Dottrina Christiana.* Roma: per gli heredi d'Antonio Blado stampatori cameriali, 1573. Milano, Biblioteca Nazionale Braidense B 39/3.

Lewis, Mary. *Antonio Gardano: Venetian Music Printer 1538–1569,* 3 vols. New York and London: Garland, 1988.

Liber capelle ecclesie maioris: Quarto codice di Gaffurio in *Archivium Musices Metropolitanum Mediolanense* 16, ed. by Angelo Ciceri e Luciano Migliavacca. Milano: La Musica Moderna, S.p.A. per La Veneranda Fabbrica del Duomo di Milano, 1968.

Limido, Stefano. *I Regii Concenti Spirituali . . . libro primo a 5. e 6. Voci.* Milano: Agostino Tradate, 1605. Madrid, Biblioteca Nacional R 14441–14445.

Lode e canzoni spirituali accomodate a tutte le feste . . . Per cantar insieme con la dottrina Cristiana. Torino: eredi Bevilacqua, 1579. Milano, Biblioteca Nazionale Braidense Musica B 0030.

Lodi devote per cantarsi nelle scuole della Dottrina Christiana raccolta nuovamente. In Milano: Pacifico Pontio, 1586. Milano, Biblioteca Nazionale Braidense ZY.II.III.

Lodi devote per uso della Dottrina Cristiana (Como: Girolamo Frova, 1596), Milano, Biblioteca Nazionale Braidense Musica B.29.2.

Lodi e canzoni spirituali per cantar insieme con la Dottrina Chistiana. In Milano: Pacifico Pontio, 1576. Milano, Biblioteca Nazionale Braidense Musica B 39/3.

Lucino, Francesco. *Concerti de diversi eccell. auttori, a due, tre, et quattro voci . . . Con la partitura per l'organo.* Milano: eredi di S. Tini e F. Lomazzo, 1608. Piacenza, Biblioteca e Archivio Capitolare.

Macey, Patrick. *Bonfire Songs: Savonarola's Musical Legacy.* Oxford: Clarendon Press, 1998.

———, ed. *Savonarolan laude, motets, and anthems* in *Recent Researches of the Renaissance* 116. Madison: A-R Editions, 1999.

Marchi, Lucia. *Simon Boyleau: studio biografico ed edizione critica dei Madrigali a Quattro voci* (1546), Tesi di laurea, Università degli studi di Pavia, Scuola Paleografia e Filologia Musicale, 1995–1996.

Marcora, Carlo. "Il diario di Giambattista Casale (1554–1598)," *Memorie storiche della diocese di Milano* XII (Milano 1965): 209–437.

———. "L'istitutzione della compagnia del Santo Rosario eretta da san Carlo," *Atti del Accademia di San Carlo* VI (1983), 111–117.

Manetti, Renzo. *Le Madonne del Parto:Icone templari.* Firenze: Edizione Polistampa, 2005.

Martín, María Jesús Pérez. *Margarita de Austria.* Madrid: Espasa-Calpe S. A., 1961.

Maselli, Domenico. "I concilii provinciali nella prassi di S. Carlo e i loro rapporti con il Concilio di Trento," *Studia borromaica* 7 (1993): 71–81.

Mather-Pike, Dolores. *La donna vestita di sole: A collection of sacred madrigals by Orfeo Vecchi.* D.M.A. thesis, Eastman School of Music, 1961.

Matter, Ann E. *Solomon's Divine Arts.* Cleveland: Pilgrim Press, 1991.

McNally, S.J., Robert E. "The Council of Trent, the *Spiritual Exercizes* and the Catholic Reform," *Church History* 34/1 (March 1965):36–49.

McNamer, Sarah. "The Origins of the *Meditationes Vitae Christi,*" *Speculum* 84/4 (2009): 905–955.

Milan, Archivio della Veneranda Fabbrica del Duomo, Sezione Musicale, Librone 3 (olim 2267) in *Renaissance Music in Facsimile* 12 c, introduction by Howard Mayer Brown. New York and London: Garland Publishing, Inc., 1987.

Miracoli della sacratissima Vergine Maria Seguiti ai benefitio di quelli che sono stati devote della compagna del santissimo Rosario.(In Venetia: appresso Bernardo Giunti, 1587), f. 8v. Milano, Biblioteca Nazionale Braidense XX.9.2/2.

Molta, Maria Alessandra, ed. *La Madonna nell'attesa del parto: Capolavori dal patrimonio italiano del '300 e '400.* Milano: Libri Scheiwiller, 2000.

Mompellio, Federico. "La capella del Duomo da Matthias Hermann di Vercore a Vincenzo Ruffo," in *Storia di Milano.* Milano: Giovanni Treccani degli Alfieri, 1957, IX, 749–785.

Montagna, Davide Maria, O.S.M., *Santa Maria dei Servi a Milano dal trecento al cinquecento*. Milano: Conventi dei Servi in San Carlo, 1997.

Monti, Urbano. *Delle cose più notabili successe alla città di Milano*. Milano, Biblioteca Ambrosiana P. 248–251 bis.

Morigia, Paolo. *Calendario volgare*. In Milano: appresso Gio. Battista Bidelli, 1620. Milano, Biblioteca Nazionale Braidense BB.VI.63.

———. *Il Duomo di Milano descritto da R. P. F. Paolo Morigi*. Milano: Giovanni Battista Bidelli, 1642. Milano, Biblioteca Nazionale Braidense II.I.50.

———. *Historia dove si narra l'origine della famosa divotione della Chiesa della Madonna, posta vicina à quella di S. Celso di Milano*. Milano: Pacifico Pontio, 1594. Milano, Biblioteca Nazionale Braidense II.I.74

———. *Santuario della città, e diocesi di Milano*. In Milano: ad instanza di Antonio degli Antonij, 1603. Milano, Biblioteca Nazionale Braidense II.I.69/1.

Morini, Fr. Agostino M. *Origini del culto alla Addololorata*. Roma: Tipografia Poliglotta, 1893.

Muir, Edward. "The Virgin on the Street Corner: The Place of the Sacred in Italian Cities" in *Religion and Culture in Renaissance and Reformation*, ed. Steven Ozment (Kirksville: Sixteenth Century Journal Publishers, 1989), 25–40.

Nantermi, Orazio. *Partito del primo libro delli motetti a cinque voci . . . novamente ristampati* (Milano: Agostino Tradate, 1606). Bologna, Civico Museo Bibliografico Musicale BB.28 (Microfilm 1641).

Nielson, Nancy Ward. "Cerano," Grove Art Online. http://www.oxfordartonline.com.proxy.lib.uiowa.edu/subscriber/article/grove/art/T015547?q=Cerano&search=quick&pos=1&_start=1#firsthit, accessed 10 January 2011.

Olson, Roberta J.M. *The Florentine Tondo*. Oxford: Oxford University Press, 2000.

———. "The Rosary and its Iconography," *Arte Cristiana* 86/787 (August 1998): 263–276, and 86/788 (October 1998): 334–342.

Officia propria festorum fratrum ord. Servorum B. Maria Virg. Mediolani: apud Pandulphum Malatesta, 1623. Roma, Marianum bibMAR FAS p1623 O43.

Officia propria ordinis servorum beatae Maria Virginis. Roma: Hieronymi Mainardi, 1739. Milano, San Carlo al Corso, Biblioteca dei Servi A I 299.

Officium Beatae Mariae Virg. In Sabbato à Fratribus Ordinis Servorum. Romae: apud Gugliuelmum Facciottum, 1606. Roma, Marianum, Servitana II 001 int. 2.

Ordo officii divini recitandi iuxta ritum Sanctae Romanae Ecclesiae. Roma: In Aedibus Populi Romani, 1584. Milano, Biblioteca Nazionale Braidense H.VIII.343.

Palestrina, Giovanni Pierluigi da. *Liber II. Motectorum quatuor vocum. Nuper recognitus.* Mediolani: heredes di Francesco e Simone Tini, 1587.

Milano, Archivio della Veneranda Fabbrica del Duomo, Musica Busta 1, no. 3.

Pelikan, Jaroslav. *Mary Through the Centuries: Her Place in the History of Culture.* New Haven and London: Yale University Press, 1996.

Picinelli, Filippo. *Ateneo dei letterati milanesi.* Milano: Francesco Vigone, 1670. Milano, Biblioteca Nazionale Braidense Cons. MI 353 A2.

Plantamuro, Vincenzo. *Il parto della Vergine del Sannazaro. Tradotto in ottava rima dal Signor Gio. Vincenzo Plantamuro Canonico d'Altamura. Diviso in tre Libri. Con gli Argomenti à ciascun Libro.* In Viterbo: Appresso Pietro, & Agostino Discepoli. Con licenza de' superiori. 1617. Roma, Biblioteca Nazionale Centrale Vittorio Emmanuele 6. 21.D. 20.

Powers, Katherine. *The Spiritual Madrigal in Counter-Reformation Italy: Definition, Use, and Style.* Ph.D. dissertation, University of California-Santa Barbara, 1997.

Pratum musicum variis cantionum sacrarem flosculis consitum, 1–4 vv, bc quarum aliae decerptae ex libro secondo sacrarum cantionum I. B. Ala da Monza. Antwerp: Petrus Phalèsé, 1634. Gaesdonk, Collegium Augustinianum.

Priorato, Conte Galeazzo Gualdo. *Relatione della città, e stato di Milano.* Milano: Ludovico Monza, 1666. Milano, Biblioteca Nazionale Braidense II.III.3.

Randolph, Adrian W. B. "Gendering the Period Eye: *Deschi da parto* and Renaissance Visual Culture," *Art History* 27/4 (September 2004): 538–562.

Rathe, Kurt. "Addolorata, devozione alla." *Enciclopedia Cattolica.* Città del Vaticano: Ente per l'Enciclopedia Cattolica e per il Libro Cattolico, 1953, I, 293–294.

Razzi, Fra Serafino. *Libro primo delle laudi spirituali.* Venezia: ad instantia de' Giunti di Firenze, 1563; reprinted in facsimile in Bologna: Forni Editore, 1969.

Razzi Monaco Camaldolense, P.D. Silvano, *Dei miracoli della Gloriosa Vergine Maria Nostra Signora.* In Trevigli: appresso Angelo Reghettini, 1612. Roma, Biblioteca Nazionale Centrale Vittorio Emmanuele 14.32A.11.

———. *Vita della Gloriosa Vergine Maria. Nuovamente ristampata & con diligenza corretta,& di figure adornata. Con licenza de' Superiori.* In Venetia: appresso Domenico Imberti, 1614. Roma, Biblioteca Nazionale Centrale Vittorio Emmanuele 14.32A.11.

Reggiori, Ferdinando. *Il santuario di Santa Maria presso San Celso e i suoi tesori.* Milano: Banco Popolare di Milano, 1968.

Regio, Benedetto. *Missarum ac sacrarum cantionum quinque, & octo vocibus concinendarum liber primus.* Mediolani: Apud haer. Simonis Tini, & Philippum Lomatium, 1607. Milano, Archivio della Veneranda Fabbrica del Duomo, Musica, Busta 2, No. 4.

Riccucci, Giuseppe. "L'attività della cappella musicale di S. Maria presso S. Celso e la condizione dei musici a Milano tra il XVI e il XVII secolo" in *Intorno a Monteverdi*, ed. by Maria Caraci Vela e Rodobaldo Tibaldi. Lucca: L.I.M., 1999, 289–312.

Riegel, Nicole. *Santa Maria presso San Celso in Mailand*. Worms: Wernersche Verlagsgesellschaft, 1995.

Rifkin, Joshua. "Munich, Milan, and a Marian Motet: Dating Josquin's Ave Maria . . . virgo serena," *Journal of the American Musicological Society* 56/1 (Summer 2003), 239–350.

Rigo, Vera Franci. "La donna dei dolori tra poesia e musica," *Città di vita* 52/5 (September 1997): 451–460.

Riva, Francesco. *Duecento anni di musica in Santa Maria della Rosa (1588–1798)*. Tesì di laurea, Università degli Studi di Milano, 2007.

Robertson, Ann Walters. "The Savior, the Woman, and the Head of the Dragon in the Caput Masses and Motet," *Journal of the American Musicological Society* 59/3 (Autumn 2006): 537–630.

Ronchi, Ermes Maria, ed. *Santa Maria dei Servi tra Medioevo e Rinascimento: Arte superstite di una chiesa scomparsa nel cuore di Milano*. Milano: Editoriale Giorgio Mondadori, 1997.

Rosario della Gloriosa Vergine Maria. Con le stationi &Indulgetie delle Chiese di Roma per tutto l'anno. Venezia: Giovanni Antonio Bertano, 1591. Milano, Biblioteca Ambrosiana L.P. 2177.

Rosci, Marco. *Il Cerano*. Milano: Electa, 2000.

Rossetti florentini ordinis servorum, Prospero. *In cantica canticorum salomonis prophetae commentariorum libri duo*. Venetiis, apud Franciscum de Franciscis senesem, 1594. Roma, Biblioteca Nazionale Centrale Vittorio Emanuele 8.30.L.18.

Rostirolla, Giancarlo. "Laudi e canti spirituali nelle edizioni della prima 'controriforma' Milanese" in *Carlo Borromeo e l'opera della "grande riforma,"* ed. by Franco Buzzi and Danilo Zardin. Cinisello Balsamo (MI): Silvana Editoriale, 1997, 159–176.

Rothenberg, David J. *Marian Devotion and Secular Song in Medieval and Renaissance Music*. Oxford and New York: Oxford University Press, 2011.

———. "The Marian Symbolism of Spring, ca. 1200–ca. 1500: Two Case Studies," *Journal of the American Musicological Society* 59/2 (Summer 2006):319–398.

Sánchez, Magdalena S. *The Empress, the Queen, and the Nun: Women and Power at the Court of Philip III of Spain*. Baltimore and London: The Johns Hopkins University Press, 1998.

Sannazaro, Giovanni Battista. "Altari" in *Il Duomo di Milano: Dizionario storico artistic e Religioso*. Milano: NED, 1986, 14–24.

Sartori, Claudio. *La cappella musicale del Duomo di Milano: Catalogo delle musiche dell'archivio* Milano: Instituto Editoriale Italiano per la Veneranda Fabbrica del Duomo di Milano, 1967.

Scalvo, Bartolomeo. *Le Meditationi del Rosario della Gloriosissima Maria Vergine*. In Milano: appresso Pacifico Pontio, 1569. Milano, Biblioteca Nazionale Braidense H. IV.21.

————. *Le Meditationi del Rosario della Gloriosissima Maria Vergine.* Venezia: Domenico e Giovanni Battista della Guerra, 1583. Milano, Biblioteca Nazionale Braidense Gerli 2313.

————. *Rosariae preces ad gloriosam Dei genetricem Mariam Virginem.* Milano: Pacifico Pontio, 1569. Milano, Biblioteca Nazionale Braidense E.III.145.

St. Ignatius of Loyola, *The Spiritual Exercises,* translated with commentary by George E. Ganss, S.J. St. Louis: The Institute of Jesuit Sources, 1992.

Schmidt, Lothar. "Beobachtungen zur Passionsthematik im intalianischen geistlichen Madrigal," *Schütz-Jahrbuch* 13 (1994), 67–84.

Schuler, Carol M. "The Seven Sorrows of the Virgin: Popular Culture and Cultic Imagery in Pre-Reformation Europe," *Simiolis: Netherlands Quarterly for the History of Art* 21/1–2 (1992): 5–28.

Sella, Domenico. *Lo stato di Milano in età spagnola.* Torino: UTET Libreria, 1987.

Serrera, J.M. "La mechanica del retrado de corte" in *Alonso Sánchez Coello y el retrado en la corte de Felipe II,* ed. by Santiago Saavedra. Madrid: Museo del Prado, 1990.

Soderini, Agostino. *Canzoni à 4. & 8. voci . . . libro primo (Milan, 1608)* in *Italian Instrumental Music of the Sixteenth and Early Seventeenth Centuries* 19, ed. by James Ladewig. New York and London: Garland, 1992.

Sutkowski, Adam, and Alina Osostowicz-Sutkowska, eds. *The Pelplin Tablature (Tabulatura organowa cystersów z Pelplina),* in *Antiquitates musicae in Polonia,* 7 vols. Warszawa: Polish Scientific Publishers, 1963–70, VI, 142–143.

Thomas, Jennifer, ed. Motet Database online, http://www.arts.ufl.edu/motet/results.asp, accessed 1 November 2011.

Tignosi, Angelo Francesco. *Statua di Maria Vergine fabbricata dall'humile servo di lei fra Angelo Tignosi, Servita, minimo Dottore di Sacra Theologia.* Milano: Agostino Tradate, 1605. Roma, Marianum MAR FAS p1605 T55.

Toffetti, Marina. *Gli Aredemanio e la musica in Santa Maria della Scala.* Lucca: LIM Editrice, 2004.

Tomaro, John B. "San Carlo Borromeo and the Implementation of the Council of Trent" in *San Carlo Borromeo: Catholic Reform and Ecclesiastical Politics in the Second Half of the Sixteenth Century,* ed. John M. Headley and John B. Tomaro. London and Toronto: Associated University Presses, 1988, 67–84.

Torre, Carlo. *Il ritratto di Milano divisi in tre libri colorati da Carlo Torre,* 3 vols. Milano: Federico Agnelli, 1674. Milano, Biblioteca Nazionale Braidense II. III. 36.

Turrini, Miriam. "'Riformare il mondo a vera vita cristiana': le scuole de catechismo nell'Italia del Cinquecento," *Annali dell'Istituto storico italo-germanico in Trento* VII (1981), 419–447.

Vecchi, Giuseppe. "La canzone strumentale e la canzone-motetto a Milano nella prima metà del seicento" in *La musica sacra in Lombardia nella prima metà del Seicento,* ed. Alberto Colzani, Andrea Luppi, and Maurizio Padoan (Como: A.M.I.S. Como, 1987), 81–97.

Vecchi, Orfeo. *Donna Vestita di Sole, Coronata di Stelle, Calcante la Luna,* research and notes by Dolores Mather-Pike and edited by Kent Carlson. Frankfurt am Main: Garri Editions, c. 2006.

Vecchi, Orfeo. *La donna vestita di sole.* Milano: erede di Simone Tini e Giovanni Francesco Besozzi, 1602. Rochester, Sibley Music Library of the Eastman School of Music PM 1419.

Villa, Giovanni Battista. *Le sette chiese o' siano basiliche stationali della città di Milano, seconda Roma.* In Milano: Carlo Antonio Malatesta, 1627. Milano, Biblioteca Nazionale Braidense II.I. 46.

Visentin, Maria Cecilia. *La pieta mariana nella Milano del Rinascimento.* Milano: NED, 1995.

Ward, Lynn Halpern. "The *Motetti Missales* Repertory Reconsidered," *Journal of the American Musicological Society* XXXIX/3 (Fall 1986):491–523.

Warner, Marina. *Alone of All Her Sex.* New York: Alfred A. Knopf, 1976.

Wilson, Blake. *Music and Merchants: The Laudesi Companies of Republican Florence.* Oxford: Clarendon Press, 1992.

———. *Singing Poetry in Renaissance Florence: The* Cantasi Come *Tradition (1375–1550) with* CD-ROM *[Italian Medieval and Renaissance Studies 9].* Firenze: Leo S. Olschki, 2009.

Index

Page locators in *italics* refer to examples, figures, and tables.

Aggazzari, Agostino, 80
Aggiunta (Lucino), 66
Ala, Giovanni Battista, 57–58;
  Consolare, o mater, 63–64,
  65–67, 239–244; *In lectulo
  meo,* 58, 67, 245–248;
  Magnificat, 67–68; *O Maria
  quid ploras,* 63–64, 234–238;
  *Secondo libro de' concerti
  ecclesiastici,* 57, 58, 63, 67,
  176, 234–248
Alain del la Roche, 82–84, 105
Albanese, Tullio, 27
Alessi, Galeazzo, 20
Alexander V, 84
Ambrose, St., 17, 96
Ambrosian Breviary of 1582, 36,
  118, 125–126, 145
Ambrosian rites, 36, 48, 118, *121,*
  122, 125–126
Anerio, Giovanni Francesco, 80,
  105, 125, 128
"Angelo Custode" (Taurini), 144
Angilberto, Archbishop, 144
Annunciation (de la Cruz), 139
Annunciation, feast of, 20–21, 30,
  36, 40, 118, 122–123, 125,
  135, 145, 148
Anselm of Canterbury, 22, 24, 47
Arconata, Paola Maria, *95,* 105
Ardemanio, Giulio Cesare, 66
Arnone, Guglielmo, 80
Arrigoni, Ferdinando, 21
Assandra, Caterina, 120
Assumption, feast of, 20, 22, 25, 39,
  96, 146; *Beata es, virgo Maria,
  Dei genitrix, 38; Beata es Virgo
  Maria* (Cima), *43–44, 45;
  Virgo prudentissima, 36–37*

Assumption, visual elements, 58–59
Ave Maria: as appeal, 24; poly-
  phonic, 77; texts, 35–36, *36*
Ave Maria (Compère), 77–78
Ave Maria (Palestrina), 78
Ave Maria . . . virgo serena
  (Josquin), 77–78
Ave Maria gratia plena, 79
Ave Maria in Duomo, cult of:
  Borromeo and, 8–9, 70; pay
  records, 72–73, 76, 80–81,
  165–171; Santa Maria del
  Pilone (Madonna on the
  Pilaster), 8, 69, 87; second
  transfer of, 81; settings, 77–79;
  Vespers, 8–9, 32, 33–34,
  69–72, 95, 118. *See also*
  Society of the Ave Maria in
  Duomo
Ave Maria spiritus sancti, 77
Ave maris stella, 116
Ave santissima Maria (Costa),
  35–36, *36*
Ave virgo gratiosa (Regio), 40,
  42–43, 94, *216–233*
Avogadro, Felice, 55

Bagarotto, Giovanni Battista, 144,
  145–146
Ballotino, Arcangelo, 13–14, 46, 59;
  *Colloqui affettuosi del pianto
  che fece Maria,* 64; *Pietosi
  affetti di compassione sopra li
  dolori della B.V. Maria,* 13–14,
  15, 65–66, 135
Barbiana, Hippolita Borromea
  Sanseverino (Countess of
  Belgioioso), 128–129, 133
Bariola, Ottaviano, 32, 35

Beata es Virgo Maria (Cima), 43–44, 45
Belloni, Giuseppe, 40
Benedictines, 18, 27
Bernard of Clairvaux, 23, 24, 47, 59, 74
Bernardino of Siena, 110
Bianconi, Carlo, 51
Bidelli, Giovanni Battista, 19
Borromeo, Carlo, 27, 112; Ambrosian rite and, 122; assassination attempt on, 4; Ave Maria at Vespers in Duomo, 8–9, 70; concerto in honor of, 96; Confraternity of the Rosary and, 81–90; devotional processions, 1–2, 70–72; education of, 13; music dedicated to, 29; pastoral letter, 87, 88; Santa Maria Segreta and, 144, 145
Borromeo, Federico, 2, 25, 69, 72; Confraternity of the Rosary, 87–88
Boyleau, Simon, 27–31; *Magnificat 8 toni*, 29, 186–207; *Modulationes in Magnificat ad omnes tropos*, 29–30
Le braccia aperse (Grillo), 135, 138, 139, 290–293
Bracco, Gabriel, 146
Brenna, Giovanni Antonio, 31

Cabezón, Antonio de, 139
Cabiago, Jacopo Filippo, 86
Caimo, Giuseppe, 129
Calendario volgare (Morigia), 19, 96
Candiano, Giovanni Paolo, 31
Canticum Canticorum, 67
Cantuum quinque vocum (Werrecore), 118
Canzoni à 4 & 8 voci (Sodarini), 93–95
Carnago, Ignazio, 138
Casale, Giambattista, 2, 3–4, 15, 83; on Confraternity of Rosary, 8–9, 88; on Madonna of the

Passione, 6; wives and childbirth, 108–109
Cassina, Ferdinando, 23
Castellino de Castello, P., 3
Castello, Alberto da, 10–11, 14, 15, 100
Celsus, St., 17–18
Certosa di Pavia, 19
Chiesa degli Apostoli (San Nazaro), 17
Christian Doctrine Schools, 2, 3–4, 30, 59, 61; for girls, 70; laude, 79–80
Christian League, 83
Cima, (Giovanni) Andrea, 43; *Audi dulcis amica me, nigra sum sed Formosa*, 98; *Gaudete filiae sion*, 95–96, 97, 100, 103, 249–258; *Il secondo libro delli concerti*, 95–98, 97, 177–178; *Indica mihi*, 98; *O Domina nostra Sanctissima Maria*, 95; *O Quam humilis*, 95; *Quam pulchra es*, 98; *Vocem Mariae*, 95, 102, 104, 106–107, 259–268.
Cima, Giovanni Paolo, 35, 39–40; *Assumpta es Maria*, 43; *Beata es Virgo Maria*, 43–44, 45; *Concerti ecclesiastici a una, due, tre, e quattro voci*, 40, 41, 43, 172–175
Città di refugio a' mortali (Cornago), 54
Colin, Pierre, 125
Collegiate Church in Desio, 57
Colloqui affettuosi del pianto che fece Maria (Ballotino), 64
colloquy format, 11, 14, 46, 59, 63–64
Compagnia dell'Abito (Santa Maria del Carmine), 143
Company of the Sacred Cross, 2, 3, 72
Compère, Loyset, 77–78
Concerti di eccellentissimi autori (Lucino), 76

Concerti ecclesiastici a una, due, tre, e quattro voci (Cima), 40, 41, 43, *172–175*
concerto, small sacred, 13, 63–64, 76–77, 147. *See also individual collections*
Confraternities of the Seven Sorrows, 47
Confraternity of the Madonna Addolorata at Santa Maria Beltrade, 48
Confraternity of the Madonna Addolorata at Santa Maria dei Servi, 48, 51–58, 68; liturgical program, 54–55; membership, 51, 53–54; *Ordinationes,* 53
Confraternity of the Most Blessed Sacrament, 2
Confraternity of the Rosary, 2, 4, 32, 71; devotional processions, 9, 71, 84, 87–89, 91, 96; Dominicans and, 83–85, 89–90; in Duomo, 8–9, 81, 87–90; history of in Milan, 83–90; indulgences, 73; music as mediation, 15; San Lorenzo Maggiore, 89–90; Santa Maria della Rosa, 9, 84, 86–87, 89, 90–93; Santa Maria della Rosa, music at, 93–98, *97, 103;* Sant'Eustorgio, 84–86, 89–90; women's roles, 105, 107
Congregation of Sacred Rites and Rituals, 90
Congregatione di SS. Giacomo e Filippo, 3
Consolare, o mater (Ala), 63–64, 65–67, *239–244*
Cornago, Ignazio, 54
Corona Isabella, Suor, 27
Corpus Christi, feast of, 146, 147
Corso Vittorio Emmanuele, 3
Cossali, Graziano, 91–92
Costa, Gaspare, 34–35; *Ave santissima Maria,* 35–36, *36; O sacro santo aventuroso chiodo,* 35; *Primo libro de motetti et*

madrigal spirituali a cinque voci, 35–37, *36; Virgo prudentissima,* 36–37, 94, *208–215*
Coudemburghe, Jan van, 47
Council of Trent, 2, 83
Counter-Reformation, 109, 110, 142
Crespi, Daniele, 51
Crespi, Giovanni Battista (il Cerano), 19, 40–41
Crucifixion, 47, 122, 135, 138; meditations on, 14, 61; musical settings of, 61, 64, 122–123; visual representations of, 58, 59
Curatolo, Paola, 144, 145
Curiano, Angelo, 111
Czirenberg, Constantine, 104–105

de la Cruz, Juan Pantoja, 138–139
De partu virginis (Sannazaro), 115
Dei miracoli della Gloriosa Vergine Maria (Razzi), 133
"Del parto" (Vecchi), 129, *131,* 131–133, *132, 134–135*
Del parto della Vergine del Sanazaro, 119
Del parto della Virgine (Durante), 115–116, *117,* 133, *137*
dell' Aqua, Catelina, 3–4
desco di parto, 107, 128, 139
devotional processions, 39, 145–146; Confraternity of the Rosary, 9, 71, 84, 87–89, 91, 96; Madonna Addolorata, 54, 59; Sacred Nail, 1, 2, 4, 35, 48, 111
Dodecachordon (Glareanus), 77–78
Dominicans, 8, 23, 81, 128; Confraternity of the Rosary and, 83–85, 89–90; of Santa Maria delle Grazie, 90
Donà, Mariangela, 57
La donna vestita di sole (Vecchi), 128–133, *130, 131, 132, 134–135, 139–140, 183–184*
Douai, 82, 83–84

double-choir repertoire, 40, 43, 78, 147

Duomo: altar of Quattro Marie, 80; archives, 77–78, 80; Confraternity of the Rosary, 8–9, 81, 87–90; documentation, 155–158; Librone 23, 125–128, *126, 270–287;* Madonna del Parto, 110, 112, *114;* Madonna dell'Albore, 71, 81, 87; Madonna of the Rosary, 72, 88, 98–104, *103, 105;* maestro di cappella, 27; "missionary from God," 69–70; Santa Maria della Neve, 143; Vespers of the Expectatio Partus, 118; Visitation, feast of, 123, 125–127

Durante, Castore, 115–116, *117, 133, 137*

Egyptian art and mythology, 110
Expectatio Partus, feast of, 138
Expectatio Partus, Vespers of, 118, *120, 122*

female patrons, 95, 105, 107, 120
Fiamminghini brothers, 91, 92
Flemish churches, 47
Flores praestantissimorum viorum (Lomazzo), 57, 67–68, 104–105, 107, 147, *179–182*
Fontana, Annibale, 20
Francis of Assisi, 47
Franciscans, 109–110
Frissone, Lorenzo, 147

Gabussi, Giulio Cesare, 76, 78
Gallo, Giuseppe, 146, 147
Gardano, Angelo, 128
Gastoldi, Giovanni Giacomo, 125
Gaudete filiae sion (Cima), 95–96, *97, 100, 103, 249–258*
Ghirlanda Di Sacre Rose Musicalmente Contesta, & Concertata (Anerio), 105, 128
Ghisleri, Michele, 96, 98

Ghisolfi, Filippo, 87, *88*
Giunti, Bernardo, 82, 99, 133
"Giunto che fù quel giorno" (laude), 61, *62–63, 64*
Glareanus, 77–78
Grillo, Angelo, 135, 138, 139
Guerra, Domenico della, 11
Guerra, Giovanni della, 11

Hapsburg dynasty, 2–3
Historia (Morigia), 4, 17, 18–20, 22–23, 35
Humiliati, 144

I Regii Concenti Spirituali (Limido), 135, 139–140, *141, 185*
Ignatius of Loyola, 12–13, 14, 38; meditations promoted by, 58, 61, 99; repetition, view of, 29–30, 65–66, 94, 102–103
imagination, 12, 30, 44, 61, 63
Immaculate Conception, 22–23, 40, 95, 128
In lectulo meo (Ala), 58, 67, 245–248indulgences, 73, 84
infant mortality rates, 108–109

Jerome, St., 22
Jesuits, 12
Josquin des Pres, 77–78
Julius II, 48

Landolfo, Archbishop, 18
Lasso, Orlando, 147
Lattuada, Giacopina, 18
Latuada, Serviliano, 18, 51, 85, 91–92; on Madonna del Parto, 111, 112; on Santa Maria Segreta, 144
laude, 59, 61, *62–63,* 79–80
laudesi companies (Florence), 73
Le braccia aperse (Limido), 139–140, *141, 185, 290–296*
Ledesma, Diego, 74
Leonardo, 111
Lepanto, victory at, 83, 84, 91, 92, 96

Libro octo missarum, quarum priores, quae numero sex sunt, quatuor vocum concentu compositae sunt (Moderne), 125

Librone 23 (Anonymous), 125–128, *126, 270–287;* Ad Magnificat. In Primis Vesperis. Beata es Maria, *270–285;* Ad Magnificat. In Secundis Vesperis. Beatem me, *286–287*

Limido, Stefano: *I Regii Concenti Spirituali,* 135, 139–140, *141, 185; Le braccia aperse,* 139–140, *141, 185, 290–296*

Litany of the Virgin, 35

Ljubljana, N 207, 79

Lodi e canzoni spirituali (Pontio), 61

Lomazzo, Filippo, 57, 67–68, 104–105, 107, 147, *179–182*

Lomazzo, Giovanni Paolo, 40

Lovino, Bernardino, 51, 111, 144

Lucino, Francesco, 43, 66, 76

Ludolf of Saxony, 12

Madonna Addolorata (Virgin of Sorrows), 9, 15, 46, 48, 112, 135; meditating, 58–68; meditation books, 15, 47–48, 58, 61; processions, 59

Madonna Addolorata at Santa Maria Beltrade, 48

Madonna Addolorata at Santa Maria dei Servi, cult of, 15, 46, 48–68, 51–58; Santa Maria dei Servi; history of cult, 47–48; visual elements, 47, 50–51, 58–59. *See also* Santa Maria dei Servi

Madonna Annunziata, image of, 145

Madonna del Parto (Madonna of Childbirth), cult of, 9, 10, 36, 40, 107, 108–142; history of cult, 109–110; Maria Platytera, 110; meditating in private spaces, 128–142; meditating

in public spaces, 112–127; meditation books, 14–15, 112, 115–118; shrines for in Milan, 110–112, *113, 114*

Madonna del Pilone (the Madonna on the Pilaster), 8, 69, 87

Madonna della Passione, 143

Madonna della Scala (Santa Maria della Scala), 111–112

Madonna dell'Albore (Duomo), 71, 81, 87

Madonna of Miracles at Santa Maria presso San Celso, cult of, 6–9, 15, 17–45, 69, 94, 148; devotions of the 1560s and 1570s, 25–31; history of cult, 17–19; theology of, 19–25

Madonna of San Lorenzo, 5–6

Madonna of the Passione, 6, 7

Madonna of the Rosary (Duomo), 72, 88, 98–104, *103,* 135

Madonna with Child Enthroned (Santa Maria dei Servi), 52, 59, *60,* 111

Madonnas, street-corner, 4–7, 142, 148

madrigal, influence of, 29

madrigals, spiritual, 35, 38, 44, 105, 128–129, 142; "Del parto" (Vecchi), 129, *131, 131–133, 132, 134–135*

Magnificat, 28–30, 126; in Librone 23 (Anonymous), *285–289*

Magnificat (Ala), 67–68

Magnificat 8 toni (Boyleau), 29, *186–207*

Manni, Agostino, 105

Marguerite of Austria, 135, 138–139

Maria Eugenia, princess, 139

Maria Platytera, 110

Matins, 125–127, 139

meditation: affective, 12–13; colloquy format, 11, 14, 46, 59, 63–64; contemplation as composition, 30, 38; on Crucifixion, 14, 61; second

person, use of, 99, 120, 122; senses and, 30, 63, 100; structure of concerti based on, 63–64; transcendence, 64, 66–68, 104
meditation books, 9–12, 44; internalization, practice of, 30, 61, 68, 140; Latin quotations in, 13, 14, 15, 116; Madonna Addolorata, 15, 47–48, 58, 61, 65, 148; Madonna del Parto, 14–15, 112, 115–118, 148; *Le Meditationi del Rosario della Gloriosissima Maria Vergine*, 11, 14, *16*; mythological tropes, 99–100, 110, 115–116; *Pietosi affetti di compassione sopra li dolori della B.V. Maria,* 13–14, 15, 65–66, 135; rhetorical devices, 12, 13–15; *Rosario della Gloriosa Vergine Maria,* 10–11, 14, 15; on Rosary, 98–104, 148; *Spiritual Exercises* (Ignatius of Loyola), 12–13; in vernacular, 10–12, 30, 98–110, 115, 116, 129, 135, 142; visual elements, 14–15, *16*
Meditationes Vitae Christi (Ludolf of Saxony), 12
Le Meditationi del Rosario della Gloriosissima Maria Vergine (Scalvo), 11, 14, *16, 136*
mendicant preachers, 109–110
merchants and tradesmen, 3, 73
Milan: churches, location of, *7;* devotion to Virgin, 4; ecclesiastical reforms, 2; number of churches, 4–5; plague of 1485, 17, 18; plague of 1576, 1–2, 4, 17, 70, 87, 111; plague of 1577, 71; plague of 1630, 57
Milan choirbooks, 77–78, 118, 125
Milanese nobility, 2–3; benefices, 7, 18, 25–26; ducal chaplains sustained by, 18–19, 26–28, 31; at "Salve" service, 25

Milanese style, 78
Minims, 135
miracles: cultic images and, 5–6; Madonna Annunziata, 145; Madonna of San Lorenzo, 5–6; Rosary and, 82–83. *See also* Madonna of Miracles at Santa Maria presso San Celso, cult of
Miracoli della sacratissima Vergine [Maria . . . del santissimo Rosario] (Giunti), 82–83, 133
Missa Beatus vir (Colini), 125
Missa Christus Resurgens (Colini), 125
Missa Ne timeas Mariae (Gastoldi), 125
Missa Papae Marcelli (Anerio), 125
Missa Pape Marcelli (Palestrina), 125
Missarum ac sacrarum cantionem quinque & octo vocibus conconcinendatum (Regio), 40–41, 42–43
Missarum ac sacrarum cantionum quinque et octo vocibus concinendarum. Liber primus (Tini and Lomazzo), 118, 120
Moderne, Jacques, 125
Modulationes in Magnificat ad omnes tropos (Boyleau), 29–30
Molinaro, Simone, 40
Monte, Angelo, 2–3
Monte, Giovanni Battista, 6
Monte, Urbano, 2–3, 4, 5, 15, 49, 72
Morigia, Paolo, 12, 17, 143; *Calendario volgare,* 19, 96; *Historia,* 4, 17, 18–20, 22–23, 35
Mortaro (organist), 27
Most Holy Crucifix, confraternity, 70
motets, 13; *Ave santissima Maria* (Costa), 35–36, *36; Canzoni à 4 & 8 voci,* 93–95; eight-voice, 40; *Primo libro de motetti et madrigal spirituali a cinque voci,* 35–37, *36; Primo*

libro di motetti a cinque voci (Nantermi), 35, 38; Santa Maria presso San Celso, 28–29; seventeenth-century concerted, 38; three-part rhetorical structure, 36, 43, 94

Motetti a due e tre voci . . . opera seconda (Assandra), 120

motherhood: infant mortality rates, 108–109; nursing, 108–109; rates of childbirth, 108–109; social education, 109–110. *See also* Madonna del Parto (Madonna of Childbirth), cult of

Musica spirituale di ecellentissimi autori (Gardano), 128

mythological tropes, 99–100, 110, 115–116

Nacimiento de la Virgen (de la Cruz), 138–139

Nantermi, Filiberto, 31, 32, 35, 39

Nantermi, Orazio, 30–31, 39, 43; *Ave mundi spes Maria,* 38; *Beata es, virgo Maria, Dei genitrix,* 38; *Primo libro di motetti a cinque voci,* 35, 38; *Quae est ista, quae processit,* 38

narrative, 38, 64–65, 99, 102, 126–127

Nativity, feast of, 89, 118, 135, 139, 145, 146

Nazaremus, St. (San Nazaro), 17–18, 20

Niguarda, Margarita, 3

Novo Rosario della Gloriosissima Vergine Maria, 99

O Maria quid ploras (Ala), 63–64, 234–238

"O quam pulchra es amica mea" (Frissone), 147

O sacro santo aventuroso chiodo (Costa), 35

Olelkowicz, Jerzy (Duke of Slutsk), 35

organists: Santa Maria presso San Celso, 26, 27, 31, 34, 34–35, 39–40; Santa Maria Segreta, 146

organs, 15, 24–25, 32; Santa Maria della Rosa, 90–91, 159–164

Palazzo Serbelloni, 49, 50

Palestrina, Giovanni Pierluigi da, 78, 80, 125

Panza, Federico, 111

Passion, 58, 68

"Pastoralis officii" (Paul III), 12

Pater Noster, 77

Paul III, 12

pay records: Ave Maria in Duomo, 72–73, 76, 80–81, *165–171;* Santa Maria presso San Celso, 27–28, 31–32, 39

Pelplin tablature, 147

Perer, Maria Luisa Gatti, 100, 107

Phalèsé, Petrus, 58

Philip II, 139

Philip III, 135, 138

Philip the Fair, 47

Piazza of the Largo di San Lorenzo, 5

Picinelli, Filippo, 57

Pietosi affetti di compassione sopra li dolori della B.V. Maria (Ballotino), 13–14, 15, 65–66, 135

pilgrims, 7, 18

Pisani, Nicola, 80

plainchant, 26, 29, 47, 127

polyphony: double-choir repertoire, 40, 43, 78, 147; Duomo, 76, 123, 125; eight-voice, 40, 77, 80, 93–95, 123, 147; five-voice, 29, 38, 40, 77, 80, 105, 135, 139, 147; four-voice, 29, 40, 43, 67, 76–79, 101–102, 122–123, 125–128, 126; Madonna del Parto, 123–125; at Santa Maria dei Servi, 55, 57

Pontio, Pacifico, 11, 59, 61, 79, 100

Porra, Giovanni Pietro, 18

Porro, Angelo, 49, 51, 54
Pratum musicum (Phalèsé), 58
Presentation in the Temple, meditations on, 10–11, 13
Primo libro de motetti et madrigal spirituali a cinque voci (Costa), 35–37, 36
Primo libro delle laudi spirituali (Razzi), 61
Primo libro di motetti a cinque voci (Nantermi), 35, 38
Priorato, Galeazzo Gualdo, 91

"Qualis est dilectus" (Frissone), 147
Quam dulces et misterijs pleni sunt tui partus (Regio), 118, 120, 122–125, *123, 124,* 127, 128, *260–269*

Radesca, Ernesto, 40
Ravasi, Gianfranco, 110
Razzi, Serafino, 61
Razzi, Silvano, 108, 133
record-keeping, 2
Regensburg, Bertold von, 109–110
Reggio, Hosta da, 129
Regio, Benedetto, 40–41, 80; *Ave virgo gratiosa,* 40, *42–43,* 94, *209–216; Quam dulces et misterijs pleni sunt tui partus,* 118, 120, 122–125, *123, 124,* 127, 128, *260–269*
repetition, 12, 13–14, 41; in Madonna Addolorata works, 65–67; in *Modulationes,* 29–30; musical motives, 66–67; staggered entrances, 94
rhetorical devices: meditation books, 12, 13–15; musical composition, 14, 29–30, 37–38; three-part structure, 36, 43, 94
Riccucci, Giuseppe, 39
Rosario della Gloriosa Vergine Maria. Con le stationi & Indulgetie delle Chiese di Roma per tutto l'anno (Castello), 10–11, 14, 15

Rosario preces ad gloriosam Dei genetricem Mariam Virginem (Scalvo), 100–101, 102
Rosary, 82, 133; fifteen mysteries of, 13, 82, 84, 98–99, 100; indulgences and, 84; joyful mysteries, 99, 128, 135; meditation books on, 98–104; other collections, 104–105, 107; visual depictions of, 15
Rosary of the Addolorata, 47
Rosino, Alberto, 31
Rossino, Cesare, 55
Rovere, Giovanni Mauro della (il Fiamminghino), 49–50
Ruffo, Vincenzo, 27

Sacri operis musici alternis modulis concinendi liber primus (Gallo), 147
Salve Regina, 90; at Santa Maria presso San Celso, 24–25, 33–34
Salve sancta parens matris, 116
Salve virgo et mater (Sodarini), 93–94
San Babila, 3, 72
San Carlo, painting of, 111
San Carlo al Corso, 48, 49, 51
San Celso, monastery of, 27
San Fedele, 4, 112, *113*
San Francesco di Paola, 135
San Lorenzo Maggiore, 5–6, 7, 89–90, *158–159*
San Nazaro, 17, 32
San Protasio in Campo (also al Castello or al Porto Giovio), 7, 85, 89, 140
San Sepolchro, 148
Sanchez, Magdalena S., 139
Sancta Maria ora pro nobis (Cabezón), 139
Sannazaro, Jacopo, 115
Santa Maria Annunziata, cult of, 144–146
Santa Maria Beltrade, 7, 48
Santa Maria dei Monti, 105

Santa Maria dei Servi, 3, 7, 9,
48–51, *50*; altars, 49; chapels,
50–51, *52–53*; documentation,
153–155; Madonna with Child
Enthroned, *52, 59, 60*, 111;
musicians, 55, 57; shrine to
Madonna del Parto, 110–111;
Vespers BVM, 55, *56*; Vespers
of the Madonna Addolorata,
48, 54–55, *56*; visual images,
58–59. *See also* Madonna
Addolorata at Santa Maria dei
Servi, cult of
Santa Maria del Carmine, 143
Santa Maria della Neve (Duomo),
143
Santa Maria della Passione, 143;
Madonna of the Passione, 6, 7
Santa Maria della Pissina, cult of,
144–145, 148
Santa Maria della Rosa, 4, 7, 9,
148; Confraternity of the
Rosary, 9, 84, 86–87, 89,
90–93; construction of, 90–93,
92; feasts, 96; frescoes, 91–92;
music for Confraternity of the
Rosary, 93–98, *97, 103*; organ,
159–164
Santa Maria della Scala, 7, 10, 66,
129, 148; shrine to Madonna
del Parto, 110, 111–112
Santa Maria dell'Annunciazione
alla Vecchiabbia, 27
Santa Maria delle Grazie, 86, 90, 95
Santa Maria presso San Celso,
6–8, 9, 69, 148; Annunciation,
feast of, 20–21, 22, 36; benefices, 7, 18, 25–26; calendar
of 1612, 39, 43; chaplains,
18–19, 26–28, 31; construction
projects, 19, 25, 32; devotions
after 1600, 38–44; devotions of
the 1580s and 1590s, 31–38;
documents, 149–152; feasts,
19–20; High Masses, 25, 27,
28, 39; interior, 20–22, *21, 23*,
37, 40–41; maestros di cap-

pella, 27–31, 39–40; organists,
26, 27, 31, 34, 34–35, 39–40;
pay records, 27–28, 31–32, 39;
polyphonic tradition, 25; Porta
Ludovico, 19; "Salve" service,
24–25, 33–34, 39; shrine to
Madonna del Parto, 110–111;
singers, 26–31, 34; singers,
complaints about, 32–33;
Vespers of the Expectatio
Partus, 118; Vespers ser-
vices, 25, 27, 28, 33. *See also*
Madonna of Miracles at Santa
Maria presso San Celso, cult of
Santa Maria Segreta, 7, 143–148;
destruction of, 144, 148; mus-
ical prominence, 147–148
Santa Tecla, 71
Sant'Alessio, feast of, 146
Sant'Ambrogio, 148
Sant'Ambrogio, chapel of, 145
Sant'Eustorgio, 7, 84–86, 89–90,
159
Santissimo Sacramento confrater-
nity, 145, 146
Sartori, Claudio, 125
Savonarola, Girolamo, 69
Scaletta, Orazio, 40
Scalvo, Bartolomeo: *Le Meditationi*
del Rosario della Gloriosissima
Maria Vergine, 11, 14, *16*,
136; Rosario preces ad glorio-
sam Dei genetricem Mariam
Virginem, 100–101, *102*
School of the Sacred Cross (Society
of the Ave Maria), 75
Scuola di SS. Cosmo e Damiano, 4
Secondo libro de' concerti ecclesias-
tici (Ala), 57, 58, 63, 67, *176*,
240–245
Il secondo libro delli concerti
(Cima), 95–98, *97, 177–178*
Selva armonica (Anerio), 105
Serono, Matteo Retondo de, 112
Servites, 3, 9, 47–48
Sforza, Ludovico Maria, 7, 19,
25–26

Sforza chapel, 78
singers: Ave Maria in Duomo, 32,
72–73, 75, *165–171;* remu-
neration, 27–28, 31–32, 39, 72,
80–81; role-playing, 59; Santa
Maria presso San Celso, 26–33,
34; virtuoso, 43–44
Society of Jesus, 12
Society of the Ave Maria in Duomo,
9, 10, 15, 69–81; School of
the Sacred Cross, 75; spiri-
tual program, 73–74. *See also*
Ave Maria in Duomo, cult of;
Duomo
Society of the Most Holy Name of
God, 86–87, 90
Socratic dialogue, 74
Sodarini, Agostino, 93
soliloquy format, 64, 65
Somaschi, 144, 147
Song of Songs, 10–11, 20, 58, 147;
commentaries on, 96–98; in
Il secondo libro delli concerti,
96, 98
Sormani, Jacopo, 112, *114*
Spain, 85, 138–139
Speciano, Cesare, 84
Spiritual Exercises (Ignatius of
Loyola), 12–13, 14, 29–30, 38,
61, 63
St. Nicholas church, Ljubljana, 79
*Stabat iuxta Crucem Iesu Mater
eius,* 14
Statua di Maria Vergine (Tignosi),
107

Taglia, Pietro, 30
Taurini, Jacopo, 144
Tignosi, Angelo, 107
Tinosi, Angelo Francesco, 15
Todi, Jacopo da, 46, 47
Torino, Madonna del Pilone cult, 69
Torre, Carlo, 49–51, *111*
transcendence, 64, 66–68, 104
Tudor, Mary, 139

Una es. O Maria, 95
"Una ex o Maria" (Frissone), 147
Urban IV, 73
Urbano, Cesare, 3
Urbano, Giovanni Battista, 3

Valvasore, Cristoforo, 91, 159–164
Vecchi, Orfeo, 40; *La donna ves-
tita di sole,* 128–133, *130,
131, 132, 134–135, 139–140,
183–184*
"Veni in hortum meum" (Gallo),
147
Vespers: Ave Maria in Duomo, 8–9,
32, 33–34, 95, 118; devotion
to Madonna of Miracles, 8;
at Santa Maria dei Servi, 48,
54–55, *56;* at Santa Maria
presso San Celso, 25, 27,
28, 33
Vespers BVM, 55, 56
Vespers for the Visitation, 125, *126*
Vespers of the Madonna
Addolorata, 48, 55, *56*
Vespers of the Purification, 55
Vespers of the Seven Sorrows, 47
Viadana, Ludovico, 40
Virgin Mary: Annunciation, 20–21,
22; attributes of, 23–24, 41,
43–44, 95, 128; biography of,
63, 67–68, 93, 100, 147; as
bride of Christ, 58, 67, 115;
cultic images, 4–7; Immaculate
Conception, 22–23; as intercessor, 10, 11, 23–24, 35, 36, 41,
46–47, 67, 82; as martyr, 59,
61, 62–63; as Mulier Fortis,
82, 91, 93–96, 147; Our Lady
of Hope, 138; sanctioned
biography of, 63; as second
Eve, 20, 22, 59; seven feasts
of, 54; seven sorrows, 47, 59,
63; sorrow of, 46, 49; translation of, 20, 49; veil of, 24;
visual depictions of, 14–15,
16. See also Assumption, feast

of, Annunciation, feast of;
Nativity, feast of; Visitation,
feast of
Virgins of St. Ursula, 54–55
Virgo prudentissima (Costa), 36–37,
94, 208–215 Visconti, Filippo
Maria, 18, 19, 25–26
Visconti, Gaspare, 2
Visentin, Maria Cecilia, 85
Visitation, 30, 122–123, 125, 135
Visitation, feast of, 15, 38, 43, 95,
96, 102, 112; at Duomo, 123,
125–127
visual elements: Assumption,
58–59; in cult of Madonna
Addolorata, 47, 50–51, 58–59;
frescoes, 49, 52, 85, 91–93,

111–112; iconography, 20,
68, 85, 100, 107, 110, 112;
Madonna and Child, 58–59;
Madonna on the Pilaster,
69–70; meditation books,
14–15, *16;* organ, placement
of, 90–91, 93; Passion, 58,
68; Virgin Mary as statue, 63;
woodcuts, 14–15, *16,* 47, *88,*
100, 115, *117,* 118, *119,*
133, *137*
visualization, 30, 38, 44, 100–101
Vocem Mariae (Cima), 95, 102,
104, *106–107,* 259–268

Władysław, Prince, 105
Werrecore, Matthias, 118

CHRISTINE GETZ is a Professor of Musicology
and Dean's Scholar at the University of Iowa.

www.ingramcontent.com/pod-product-compliance
Lightning Source LLC
Chambersburg PA
CBHW060325100426
42812CB00003B/884